Exploring the Historic COAL BRANCH

A Guide to Jasper's Front Ranges

Daniel Kyba & Jane Ross

Disclaimer

There are inherent risks in hiking in wilderness and semi-wilderness areas. Although the authors have alerted readers to locations where particular caution is to be exercised, trail conditions may change owing to weather and other factors. Abandoned mines and other buildings or sites may be unsafe. Hikers use this book entirely at their own risk and the authors disclaim any liability for any injuries or other damage that may be sustained by anyone using any of the trails described in this book.

Front cover: Looking south from Cadomin Mountain.
Back cover: Trail riding along the Whitehorse Creek valley.

We acknowledge the financial support of the Government of Canada through the Book Publishing Industry Development Program (BPIDP) for our publishing activities.

Printed and bound in Canada by
AGMY Marquis Imprimeur Inc., Québec

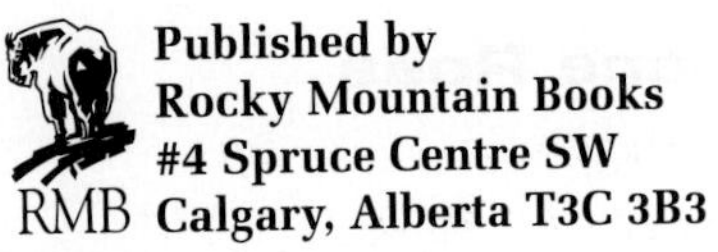

Published by
Rocky Mountain Books
#4 Spruce Centre SW
Calgary, Alberta T3C 3B3

National Library of Canada Cataloguing in Publication Data

Kyba, Daniel, 1951-
Exploring the historic Coal Branch

Includes bibliographical references and index.
ISBN 0-921102-83-6

1. Trails--Alberta--Coal Branch Region--Guidebooks. 2. Hiking--Alberta--Coal Branch Region--Guidebooks. 3. Cycling--Alberta--Coal Branch Region--Guidebooks. 4. Coal Branch Region (Alta.)--Guidebooks. I. Ross Jane, 1948- II. Title.
GV199.44.C22A4553 2001 796.51'097123'32 C2001-910625-4

Contents

Introduction

Welcome to the Coal Branch and reality. The Coal Branch is a multi-use area of Alberta where conflicting industrial, outdoor recreational and environmental interests interact. This book is an attempt to help people understand the issues involved while at the same time enjoying the natural beauty that is Alberta.

Visitors to the Coal Branch will quickly realize that it is not pristine wilderness. Man has been modifying the landscape for thousands of years. In the past, this ability to modify was limited by population and primitive technology allowing the environment time to repair many disturbances. Today the pace and scale of disturbance is such that nature cannot rebound on its own and people have to give nature a helping hand. Throughout the Coal Branch you will see some companies and individuals who help the environment and others who do not. Among the latter, the worst are those who pursue their narrow interests through misinformation. Such speciousness does two things: it discredits conscientious environmentalists and it distracts the public from addressing such issues in a sober minded and informed manner. In any public debate, especially where politicians and special interest groups are involved, truth must be served or the whole process becomes sterile.

Because the Coal Branch is an active area we deliberately stayed away from some places, especially Mountain Park where we assumed the Cheviot Project would go ahead. It was only at the last minute that we added several hikes in that area. Over the six years we worked on this book we had to change some trailheads, reroute some trails or remove them completely from this book. We even temporarily lost a lake. At the same time we saw the creation of a new park and the opening up of new areas for recreational purposes.

Readers attuned to Coal Branch history will notice new and different information. All history, especially oral-based history, is subject to error as dates become changed, names misspelled and stories muddled. References must always be cross-checked and facts independently confirmed. This checking process is usually drudgery but can sometimes lead to surprises. Our focus upon local history is an attempt to correct a limitation in our education. We were on holidays once in England and while touring a historical site, watched with envy a group of school children divide themselves into Anglo-Saxons and Normans to re-enact on that same battlefield the Battle of Hastings. When we went to school there was little of that type of connection between local geography and historical self identity. Much of this guidebook, through its historical sidebars, is an attempt to create that kind of connection.

Besides history, we have geological, biological and toponymical sidebars. As these sidebars very briefly address what can be complex topics, we recommend our bibliography at the back of this book if you wish to examine any issue at greater depth. As we wrote this book we made choices and compromises. There are topics that, for reasons of space, we have either ignored completely or reduced to the barest of mentions.

This guidebook introduces you to the Coal Branch by way of a driving tour that at leisure requires two days to complete. We have divided the Branch into three main regions: East Branch, West Branch and Head of the Branch. These areas share history and geography. We had originally planned to include the Cardinal River Road area as the fourth region, but decided instead that it was time to put this book to bed. For outdoor recreationalists, much of the Coal Branch is not a park. There are few signs along any trails and in some cases the maze of cutlines can be very confusing. Always carry a map, a compass and if on a bike, an odometer. A GPS is also very useful. We recommend, however, that GPS users develop their self-reliant compass skills first. Follow our trail directions carefully and remember that since you are in an active area, you may come upon roads, trails and cutlines that did not exist when we were there.

Carry out your garbage. Bury your poop. Do not unnecessarily disturb the plants and animals. Enjoy your experience and leave it the same so others can enjoy it, too. Thank you for buying our book.

~

Photo Credits

Archival photographs obtained from the Forest Technology School of the Department of Environmental Protection, the Glenbow Archives, the Provincial Archives of Alberta, the University of Alberta, the Edson Public Library and Luscar Sterco have been selected to enhance some of our sidebars. We also wish to thank: Alwynne Beaudoin, Robin Chambers, Norman Coulthard, Allison Dinwoody, Alfred Falk, John Farley, Charles Jacoby, Ed Jenkins, Corinne Marshall, Akemi Matsubuchi, Robert Scott, Amelia Spanach, Buster Stetsil and Felicia Taylor who have generously allowed use of their photographs. All other photographs in this book were taken by the authors.

Acknowledgments

The authors would like to gratefully acknowledge all those who have helped in some way in this endeavour: to Elaine Abbott, Robin Chambers, Natalie Clavett, Norman Coulthard, Allison Dinwoody, John Farley, Louis Hedberg, David Koshman, Marilyn Langevin, Bruce MacLock, Dennis McNaughton, Mickey Susnar and Felicia Taylor who joined us in our quest for trails old and new; to Ed and Mime Jenkins, Amelia, George and Linda Spanach and Diane Radmanovich for their hospitality; to Charles and Marg Jacoby for the hamburgers and booze after Jane's "rescue"; to Bruce MacLock and Elaine Abbott for sharing their cabin; to Arnold Aagason, Dick Corser, Bill Davies, William and Shirley Docherty, Ed Harrison, Edgar Jenkins, Glen Johnson, Nevis LeBranche, Dave and Ann Mahoney, Corinne Marshall, Mike Pavich, Randy Palivoda, Lillian and George Starling, Buster Stetsil, Garth Worthington and Peter Zezel for sharing with us their memories of their lives in the Coal Branch; to Allan Maydonik, Dane McCoy and Fred Munn of Luscar; to Art Warren of Inland Cement; to Julie Hrapko, botanist, and Ron Mussieux, curator of geology, Provincial Museum of Alberta, for help in their respective fields; and lastly, to Keith Nye who cheerfully looked after Smoky when we were on the trail.

A final special thanks to ABBA, Enya, Meatloaf, Mozart and Saffire for entertaining us during our highway trips. Your free copies of our guidebook are available for pickup at our home.

AREA MAP

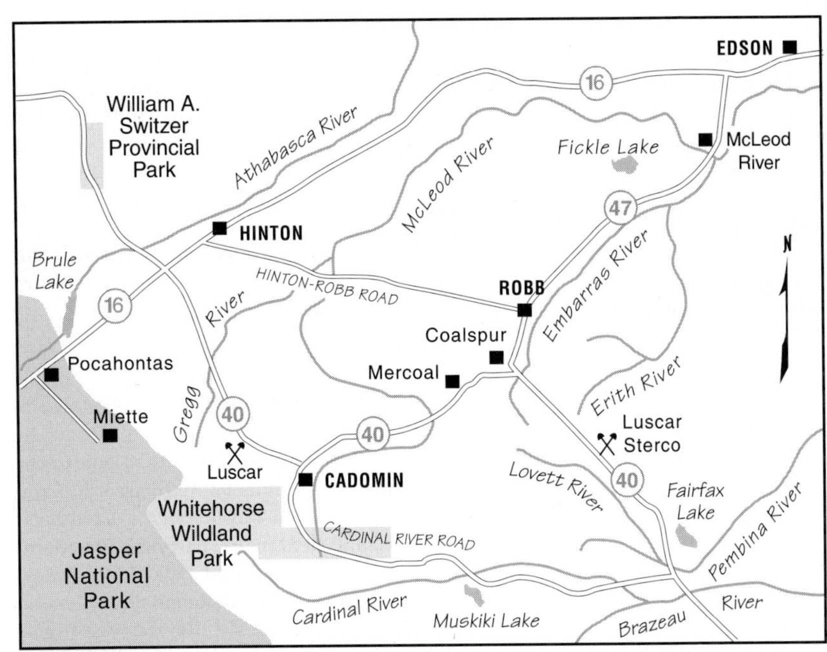

Dedicating the commemorative map, August 1, 1999.

WINDSHIELD TOUR

This purpose of this book is to introduce the visitor to the Coal Branch through descriptions of day and overnight trips, points of interest, and the area's history, flora and fauna. In order to familiarize you with the Coal Branch we have included a road trip that takes you south from Edson along Highway #47 to Coalspur with a side trip to Mercoal before continuing south along Highway #40. At the Cardinal River Road, you turn westward to climb over the Cardinal River Divide and drop down to Cadomin and the junction of Highway #40. Before continuing to Hinton, there is a side trip to Hell's Gate. The total distance is approximately 258 km. Given the numerous possibilities for stops and explorations, we suggest a trip of a minimum of two days. Beware, though, that other than the Bryan Hotel in Robb and the Cadomin Motel in Cadomin there is no other hotel accommodation in the Coal Branch. There are, though, a number of Recreation Areas and popular random campsites. Gas, food and camping supplies can be purchased in both Robb and Cadomin.

All distances are given in kilometres. Those in parentheses are from Hinton.

0.0 (257.8)	Junction of Highway #16 with Highway #47 Turn left onto paved Highway #47 to Robb and Coalspur.
3.1 (254.7)	Bickerdike Road The old locality and station of Bickerdike is 2.9 km west along the road. Bickerdike station was the head of the Grand Truck Pacific branch railway that opened the Coal Branch. See "The Sand Dunes" for further information. Continue south on Highway #47.
8.7 (249.1)	Lake Edson Sand Dunes stretch on both sides of the highway and once formed part of the southeastern shore of an ancient meltwater lake, Lake Edson. The sand dunes extend south for 16 km. See "The Sand Dunes" for further information.
14.8 (243.0)	Confluence of the McLeod and Embarras rivers The McLeod and its tributary, the Embarras, drain much of the Coal Branch. Just north of the confluence on the east side of the highway was Carl Svedberg's sawmill. This is also the site of an old community called McLeod River. Some buildings remain standing.
22.8 (235.0)	Fickle Lake Road The railway station of Erith, named after a village in Kent, England, was located here. On your right you can still find the station road. See the chapter on Fickle Lake.
30.8 (227.0)	Weald Group Recreation Area. See the chapter on Weald.

A reminder of the old community of McLeod River.

32.9 (224.9) Lambert Creek Recreation Area
For further information see the chapter on Lambert Creek.

38.2 (219.6) This is your first sight of the Rocky Mountains. The first range that you can see beyond the foothills is the Nikanassin Range. Beyond are the higher peaks of the Front Ranges.

41.0 (216.8) Prest Creek was named around 1911 for Benjamin J. Prest (1884-1967) who was the construction engineer for the Grand Trunk Pacific and Coal Branch railways.

49.6 (208.2) Coal Branch Cemetery
Despite the number of mining towns and camps there were, surprisingly, few cemeteries in the Coal Branch. Lovettville had a cemetery. So did Mercoal, Diss and Sterco. Another can be found at Mountain Park. This cemetery was established in the late 1990s and serves both current residents and those who left the Coal Branch but upon death wish to "return home."

52.5 (205.3) Robb
Present-day Robb is comprised of two historic mining camps, Bryan and Robb. The old settlement of Bryan forms the most populous part of present-day Robb. The Bryan name lives on in the Bryan Hotel, a popular watering spot. See the chapter on Robb for further information. Continue on Highway #47.

58.0 (199.8) Embarras River
On your left. You are now passing through the Robb Highlands. See Robb chapter.

59.2 (198.6)	Coalspur This is where the railway branches. Historically, the East Branch ran south to Lovett. Today it stops at the Luscar Sterco mine. The West Branch once ran up to Mountain Park but today goes to the Luscar mine with a spur to Inland Cement in Cadomin. Today, Coalspur is a summer village. See the chapter on Coalspur. Pavement ends just beyond the railway overpass.
61.2 (196.6)	Coalspur Recreation Area
61.5 (196.3)	Junction of Highways #47 and #40 Turn right for a side trip to the old mining town of Mercoal. Cross the bridge over the Embarras.
61.6 (196.2)	Spring Watch for a pipe on the right side of the road.
68.9 (188.9)	Mercoal You have been able to see old coal workings on your right for the past 500 m. These relate to the mine at Mercoal. In 1959, Mercoal was the last mine to close in the Coal Branch. Today, this unsigned hamlet is a summer village. See the chapter on Mercoal. Return to junction of Highways #40 and #47 near the Coalspur Recreation Area.
76.3 (181.5)	Junction Highways #47 and #40 Turn right and continue south on Highway #40. You drive for 15 km along a wide gravel road through lodgepole pine forest.
91.2 (166.6)	Shorty's Cabin Watch for a narrow roadway on your left leading into the forest. A 100 m walk brings you to a log cabin. It belonged to R. C. (Shorty) Armstrong who worked as a time keeper at the Sterco mine. Unseen just beyond the trees is the modern strip mine of Luscar Sterco.
93.4 (164.4)	Luscar Sterco Mine Since Luscar opened its surface mine at Coal Valley in 1977 the old mining towns of Sterco, Coal Valley, Foothills and Reco have completely disappeared. See Sterco-Coal Valley as well as Luscar Sterco Mine Tour.
94.0 (163.8)	Lovett River Recreation Area
96.3 (161.5)	Lovett River Snowmobile Staging Area
102.2 (155.6)	Silkstone and Lovett lakes turnoff These two lakes are accessed by vehicle and foot through the Luscar Sterco mine site. These reclaimed mining pits now attract large numbers of fishermen. See "Silkstone and Lovett lakes."

Shorty's cabin.

110.3 (147.5) Confluence of the Lovett and Pembina rivers
This is the original Pembina Forks. A popular random campsite can be found to the right where you can also find an old native sundance lodge and a large sawdust pile related to the W. G. Wagner Lumber Company.

115.2 (142.6) Fairfax Lake Recreation Area turnoff

120.0 (137.8) Pembina Forks Recreation Area

120.9 (136.9) Elk River Road. Keep to the right to remain on Highway #40.

127.5 (130.3) Cardinal River Road
Turn right onto the road. You are now heading west.

130.1 (127.7) Confluence of the Cardinal and Brazeau rivers
The Brazeau River drains into the North Saskatchewan River. A random campsite can be found on the right past the bridge.

134.2 (123.6) Thunder Lake
On your left, 100 m off the highway. Thunder Lake is the largest of a number of kettle lakes in the immediate vicinity. Kettle lakes are glacial features that were formed as the glaciers retreated. Ice blocks that had become detached from the main glacier were buried under glacial gravel deposits. As they melted, the overlying gravel collapsed into the depression. Surface and/or groundwater filled the depressions

to form kettle lakes. Associated with Thunder Lake is a complex of glacial eskers. These long, sinuous and gravelly mounds mark the location of drainage tunnels that had formed under the melting glacier. At Thunder Lake most of the eskers are found south of the lake.

144.1 (113.7) Smallboy Camp

Smallboy Camp dates to 1972 when Robert Smallboy (1898-1984) led a group of 160 Hobbema Cree here to live a traditional lifestyle to escape the corrupting influences of modern life. For several years previously, they had camped on the Kootenay Plains along the North Saskatchewan River. Smallboy Camp has no band status and cannot, therefore, file a land claim. Nevertheless, in 1996, in response to the Cheviot mine proposal, the camp claimed the Redcap Creek drainage, which covers approximately 40 per cent of the Cheviot mine project.

150.2 (107.6) Muskiki Lake

Access on your left. There is a boat launch but no other amenities including toilets. Muskiki Lake is one of the larger lakes in the Coal Branch boasting an area of nearly 35 ha. The depth of the lake ensures good overwinter protection for fish. In the late 1930s the Alberta government began managing the lake as a brook trout fishery, stocking it in 1938 and then again in 1975 and 1976. The original name Medicine Lick Lake refers to the calcium and magnesium in

Muskiki Lake.

the surrounding bog, which serve as a mineral lick to wild ungulates. By the mid-1920s the local name was shortened to Medicine Lake. Confusion with other "Medicine Lakes" led to the adoption of the Cree word for medicine, muskiki. In the mid-1920s, Medicine Lake Collieries prospected the area but the coal seams were extremely faulted and no development took place. In 1995 Muskiki Lake was designated a Natural Area.

154.1 (103.7) Grave Flats

Random campsite on your right. This natural meadow has been known as Grave Flats since 1908 when surveyor A. H. Hawkings camped near the grave site of Jacques Cardinal, a Metis whose traditional hunting ground included the surrounding region. The Cardinal River is named after him.

168.9 (88.9) Mile 12 Cabin

On your right approximately 200 m from the road. So-named because it was 12 miles from the Mountain Park forestry station, Mile 12 Cabin was first built in the 1910s by Harry King. During the 1920s outfitters used the cabin while wintering their horses here. The original cabin burned down and the present structure was erected in 1936. The cabin still sees occasional use by a local trapper.

171.3 (86.5) Redcap Creek

Redcap Creek is named after nearby Redcap Mountain, so named because of its reddish colour.

Mile 12 Cabin.

171.9 (85.9) Vista of the Cardinal River valley

180.8 (77) The Upper Cardinal Headwaters Access Trail
On your left. Also a random campsite. See Cardinal Divide chapter. From here the Cardinal River Road climbs sharply. The road is very rough. You climb out of the montane forest and into the alpine.

182.1 (75.7) The Cardinal River Divide
At the top of your steep climb you arrive at a parking area. Interpretive signs tell you that this watershed divides waters flowing into the North Saskatchewan drainage and eventually into Hudson's Bay from those flowing into the Athabasca River and hence the Arctic Ocean. See Cardinal Divide chapter. Continue down the other side of the Divide. The road is very rough. At the bottom of the Divide the road flattens and improves. You have entered the headwaters of the McLeod River.

187.1 (70.7) Mountain Park Recreation Area
On your right. Coal slack is everywhere making this a popular spot with OHVs. Coal was extracted from the seams at Mountain Park between 1911 and 1950 when the mine closed. Recently, the Cheviot mine project was to be headquartered at Mountain Park. See Mountain Park chapter. Continue past the Mountain Park cemetery and down the Cardinal River Road.

189.3 (68.5) McLeod River valley
You are now driving through the upper headwaters of the McLeod River as it drops approximately 200 m to the confluence with Whitehorse Creek. On your right watch for old railway trestles. Mountain Park was the western terminus of the branch line out of Bickerdike.

194.0 (63.8) Prospect Creek
A popular random campsite and trailhead. See the chapter on Prospect Creek. Just above Whitehorse Creek your road drops sharply. Straight ahead is Leyland Mountain.

196.5 (61.3) Whitehorse Creek Recreation Area
See chapter on Whitehorse Creek.

198.2 (59.6) Spring
On your left. If you are here during or shortly after a rainfall look near the base of the mountain. Water bubbles to the surface with such volume and force that it forms a small fountain. On the other hand, during dry periods the flow of water is reduced to a trickle creating barely a ripple on the surface of the small pond. Most springs in the Rockies are associated with a fault. Rainwater from the top of the mountain trickles down a fault line to where the fault re-emerges

somewhere beneath the surface of the pond. The greater the precipitation, the heavier the water flow and the more noticeable the presence of the spring becomes. Even during dry periods, though, water continues to be discharged from the spring, albeit in much reduced volumes. This flow probably represents water percolating up from a source deep beneath the ground.

198.9 (58.9) Inland Cement
On your right. The limestone of Cadomin Mountain supplies Inland Cement's plant in Edmonton. The quarry is now the terminus of the railway line that prior to 1950 ran up to Mountain Park. For further information see "Inland Cement Tour."

199.8 (58.0) Cadomin Cave parking lot
On your left. Cadomin Cave is a popular destination for spelunkers and hikers alike. See "Cadomin Cave" for further information.

201.0 (56.8) Commemorative map
On your left. The commemorative map was dedicated at the Coal Branch reunion 1 August 1999. Immediately to the left of the map is the Cadomin mine opening.

201.5 (56.3) Cadomin
Pavement announces your arrival at the hub of the west branch where you can find a motel, gas station, store and cafe. See Cadomin chapter. Continue north along the Cardinal River Road, crossing the railway tracks. Pavement ends. You now travel through Greasebone Flats as far as the junction with Highway #40.

204.7 (53.1) Junction with Highway #40.
The Cardinal River Road ends. Bear to the right and drive 2.7 km.

207.4 (50.4) Hell's Gate
On your right. You cannot see Hell's Gate from the road. Park at the intersection with a dirt road on your left. Drop down the hill to the McLeod River and look upstream for the "gate." Although not as treacherous or as spectacular as the Hell's Gate of Fraser River, B.C. fame, this section of the McLeod River can remind you of the former gorge during times of heavy water flow. The McLeod River has cut a channel down through the sandstones of the Brazeau Formation to a harder, more resistant sandstone conglomerate. Underlying this are the softer shales of the Wapiabi Formation. Hell's Gate, then, is the contact point between the Brazeau and Wapiabi formations. The softer shales of the Wapiabi Formation are found immediately downstream of Hell's Gate.

Hell's Gate.

The volume and velocity of water passing through Hell's Gate caught the attention of Dominion Land Surveyor A. L. McNaughton in 1912-1913, who suggested that Hell's Gate was "a suitable location for a small hydro electric plant...." The hydro plant, though, was never built.

210.1 (47.7) Return to junction of Highway #40 and the Cardinal River Road. Turn right, cross the bridge over Luscar Creek and climb a long hill. Luscar was named in 1921 by Alexander Mitchell who founded Luscar Collieries. Luscar is the name of the Mitchell family estate in Scotland. View of the Front Ranges on your left.

215.8 (42.0) Viewpoint overlooking Cardinal River Coals' Luscar open pit mine. On your left. See "Cardinal River Coals' Mine Tour."

218.3 (39.5) Cardinal River Coals' Luscar mine. On your left. You're back on pavement.

219.5 (38.3) Cardinal River Coals' former Gregg River mine. On your left. The Gregg River mine closed in the autumn of 2000 and the cleaning plant was dismantled. Nearby was the tiny mining community of Kaydee, which operated from 1932 to 1945.

220.0 (37.8) Cutblocks. The chequerboard pattern allows one block to mature while the adjacent block is harvested. Maturation of the lodgepole pine is about 100 years.

Gregg River falls.

221.1 (36.7)	Forest fire scar of 1988 on your right.
229.9 (27.9)	Highway turn-out. On your left. Park here and walk back along the highway for 500 m. The pretty Gregg River falls are on your right.
235.0 (22.8)	Gregg River See Gregg River chapter.
235.6 (22.2)	Gregg River Road See Gregg River chapter.
241.1 (16.7)	Teepee Creek A branch of Wigwam Creek. Teepee is a synonym for wigwam.
243.6 (14.2)	Wigwam Creek The mouth of Wigwam Creek is directly across from the natural meadow where Gregg Cabin now stands. This was a preferred camping spot and the creek was so named in 1927 for an Indian encampment that once could be found here.
257.8 (0.0)	Junction of Highway #40 and Highway #16. Turn left for Jasper, right for Hinton.

GUIDED DAY TOURS

The Coal Branch is not a park. It is a multi-use area where major industrial players—forestry, oil and gas and coal mining—are the engines of its economy. To learn how, why and what kind of imprint these industries have had on the landscape we recommend three day tours listed below. Each can be easily arranged either locally or through the Edson and Hinton Chambers of Commerce.

Luscar Sterco Mine Tour (Lovett Branch)

There is no better way to become acquainted with the Coal Branch than to take a mine tour. With the closure of the mines at Coal Valley, Sterco, Foothills and Lovett, mining along the Lovett Branch ceased for 20 years. Then, in 1976, Luscar Sterco received permission to strip mine three important seams: the Mynheer, the Silkstone and the Val d'Or. Over the past 30 years, the modern mine has obliterated the historic townsites with the exception of Lovett, which remains on private property within the mine's leasehold.

During the summer months, Luscar Sterco operates an all-day tour to its mine. The tours are very popular with old Coal Branchers and other visitors as well. So, as not to be disappointed, be sure to book your tour a day or two in advance. The mine requires registration by 3:30 p.m. the day prior to the tour.

Departing from Edson in a large company bus, your trip to the mine is made pleasant by games in which everyone can take part, and there are colouring pages for children. Once at the mine site you are greeted by a company spokesperson who acts as your tour guide for the mine portion of your day. As the mine is active, pits are being dug, mined and backfilled continuously. The pits that we visited, then, will not be the same as those that you might visit. You will, though, have a complete tour around active mine pits where you can see huge draglines at work, through the mine yard, and through reclamation areas where you learn that mining the coal is only half of the process. There will be, no doubt, several occasions when you disembark from the bus to walk around and stretch your legs. One stop will be at noon. Lunch—sandwiches, pop, and great desserts—is provided by Luscar Sterco. Who says there is no such thing as a free lunch?

We rate this tour as tops in anyone's Coal Branch agenda.

When	Every Wednesday during July and August.
Departure time	9:30 a.m.
Return	3:00 p.m.
Depart from	Edson Information Centre located in Centennial Park on Highway #16 westbound between 2nd and 4th avenues or Bryan Hotel in Robb.
Admission	Free
Register	Telephone 780-723-3339 and specify Edson or Robb pick-up point or visit the Edson Information Centre.

For visitors travelling through the West Branch there are two possible tours:

Cardinal River Coals Mine Tour (West Branch)

When Luscar opened its new Cardinal River Coals' mine in July 1970, a special issue of the local paper heralded the "Luscar comeback"; the historic underground mine at the town of Luscar had closed in 1956. The new modern open pit mine using truck and shovel to remove first the overburden and then the coal was headquartered at the old townsite. Surface mining slowly erased all vestiges and landmarks of the earlier period, replacing familiar creeks, springs and even mountains with contoured and re-seeded slopes. While many old Luscar families were saddened by the disappearance of their old haunts, the mine employed hundreds of miners. They, with their families, moved into Hinton diversifying the town's economy, giving it a major boost. The mine was expected to have a lifespan of 20 years; however, the richness of the seams enabled the mine's life to be extended. Meanwhile, Manalta Coals opened a similar mine in 1983 adjacent to the Cardinal River Coals' mine near the site of the historic Kaydee mine. Called the Gregg River mine, the Manalta operation likewise employed a substantial work force that contributed to Hinton's boom. Then, the inevitable happened. The coal ran out. In the autumn of 2000, Cardinal River Coals announced it was closing the Luscar mine at the end of the year. This announcement came hard on the heels of the closure of the nearby Gregg River mine, taken over by Luscar from Manalta Coals earlier in the year. The exhaustion of the mines was to have been replaced by Luscar's planned Cheviot mine located at Mountain Park. However, the Cheviot mine project is currently on hold, markets being too weak to make such a massive developmental outlay economically viable. It will take two years for Luscar to complete its reclamation at both mine sites. By 2003, the mine—and this tour—will be completely shut down.

Luscar has operated this tour for a number of years, its popularity evidenced by the number of people, some annual visitors, who sign up. Our trip, taken in the late 1990s, took us into working pits, to viewpoints and through reclamation areas. A complimentary lunch of sandwiches, fruit, pop and dessert made it a memorable experience. We highly recommend Coal Branch visitors take the tour while the opportunity to understand the scale and complexities of open pit mining still exists.

When	Every Thursday during July and August.
Departure time	10:00 a.m.
Return	2:30 p.m.
Depart from	Hinton Tourist Information Centre located on Highway #16.
Admission	Free
Register	Telephone 780-865-2777 or visit the Hinton Information Centre.

Inland Cement Tour (West Branch)

Visiting Cadomin or hiking in the area? You might want to consider arranging a conducted tour of Inland Cement's quarry located less than 3 km south of Cadomin. The quarry mines the rich limestone beds of Cadomin Mountain. These range in thickness from 150 mm to more than 200 mm. Of almost pure calcium carbonate, the limestone has few magnesium impurities making it ideal for the manufacture of cement.

The value of the limestone deposit was recognized as early as 1912 when the Mountain Park Coal Co. held a lease here. The company planned to erect kilns and produce lime but this project never materialized. It wasn't until the 1940s when Mike "Limestone Mike" Enrico started a small lime plant in the north quarry. In 1953 and again in 1954 Inland Cement was drawn to the site. After determining reserves of 22 million tons of high grade limestone at Cadomin Mountain, Inland built a cement plant in Edmonton in 1955. Operations at Cadomin Mountain began in the old north quarry in 1957. A south quarry was opened in the early 1960s but was abandoned by 1965. During those early years, the limestone was blasted and then transported by truck to the crusher located in a concrete building at the base of the mountain. The crushed stone then was transported to the railway by conveyor belt.

In 1965, to handle the limestone more safely, Inland moved the crusher underground and drove a 1.5 x 1.5 m raise upward from the crusher 230 m to the surface at an angle of 59°. In 1983 a new crushing system was brought on line with a 300 m, 3 x 3 m raise from the crusher, which is located 800 m inside the mountain. This is the only limestone quarry in the province that drops its quarried rock down a shaft. The crusher can handle 1200-1400 tonnes of crushed rock per hour, or up to 9000 tonnes in a 10-hour shift. From the crusher the rock is carried by conveyor belts to one of two underground storage bins blasted out from the inside of the mountain. Each bin holds 14,500 tonnes of crushed rock. From the crusher a series of conveyors moves the rock to the railway.

The quarry ships at least 110 trains each year of 80 cars, each car carrying 90 tonnes. This adds up to an annual production of approximately one million tonnes of crushed limestone. Most of the crushed limestone is shipped to Inland's cement plant in Edmonton, although a small amount is converted to ballast.

The profile of Cadomin Mountain as seen from the townsite of Cadomin has been altered by the quarry operation. Old time Coal Branchers credit the reduction in the ferocity of the Cadomin winds to the quarry, which has steadily chewed back the slope thus widening the gap between Cadomin and Leyland mountains.

Times	By appointment only. Telephone 780-692-3741.
Admission	Free
Note	The tour takes you to the crusher, the holding bins and around the quarry. Sturdy, waterproof footwear is recommended. Ear plugs may be considered when visiting the crusher.

HEAD OF THE BRANCH

The Coal Branch lies along the east slope of the Rocky Mountains between Highway #16 and the Brazeau River. Its western boundary is Jasper National Park. Its eastern boundary includes the Embarras River watershed. This roughly triangular piece of Alberta takes its name from the railway branch lines built here in 1912 and 1913 to service the coal mines being opened in the region. On a map, the Coal Branch railways appear as a wishbone. The stem runs southwest from Bickerdike to Coalspur. From Coalspur one leg runs southeast to Lovett while the other leg runs southwest to Cadomin and Mountain Park.

This area's modern history begins around 1900 when the concept of a second transcontinental railway began to be seriously considered. Discussions to merge the Canadian Northern (CNoR) and Grand Trunk railways began in 1902 and 1903. Negotiations fell through and both companies decided to build their own transcontinental railway lines. West of Edmonton this decision resulted in the CNoR and Grand Trunk's subsidiary, the Grand Trunk Pacific (GTP), running track, at times side by side, through the same corridor to the Yellowhead Pass and into British Columbia.

For their lines to be profitable, local traffic along their respective rights-of-way was essential. On the prairies this need was fulfilled by settlement of the homestead lands and the development of an agricultural economy based upon grain and cattle. West of Edmonton there was little land suitable for such prospects so both companies searched the area for minerals that could

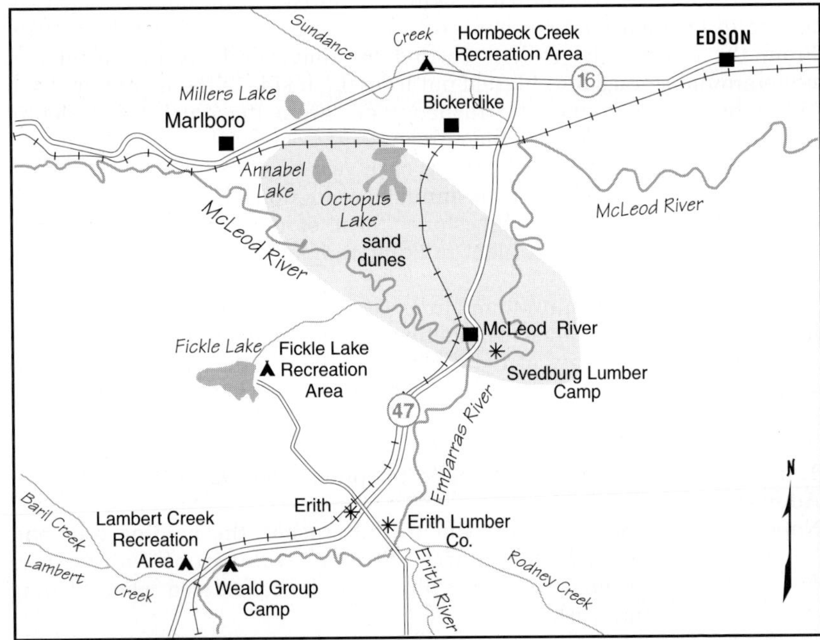

One of the numerous old wellhead sites found throughout the Coal Branch.

be exploited and shipped by their lines. As coal was already known to exist along the eastern slope of the Rocky Mountains, it was upon this resource that both railways focused their efforts.

Their search was further encouraged by hardball tactics on the part of their main competitor, the Canadian Pacific Railway (CPR). For all three railways, Crowsnest Pass was western Canada's primary source of steam coal. The mines were served by the CPR that, over time, came to regard the area as its own domain. Matters came to a head in 1906 when the CPR blocked the CNoR from purchasing Crowsnest coal by refusing the use of CPR cars to ship the coal or allowing CNoR cars on its line. What this meant for the CNoR and later the GTP was they had to bring in to western Canada, at great cost, steam coal from Pennsylvania to run their trains. What it also meant was that if these two new transcontinental railway lines were to become truly profitable, they had to secure their own western sources of steam coal.

These two companies sent their own exploration parties into the Coal Branch. For the CNoR there was Thomas Russell who, by 1906, staked coal finds at the headwaters of Mackenzie Creek and the mouth of the Cardinal River. Meanwhile, for the GTP, Raymond Brutinel began exploring and staking northwest from Lovett to Coalspur in 1907. By 1909, through the efforts of these two men and other players, almost all of the Cardinal River valley and its tributaries were being prospected and staked. The Cardinal River at that time was commonly known as the North Branch Brazeau and so its coal fields came to be known as the Brazeau coal lands.

The CNoR proposed to access the coal lands from Wolf Creek, immediately east of Edson. The company went so far as to survey and clear a railway right-of-way south to the confluence of the Brazeau and Cardinal rivers. That was as far as any development went. In 1909, the CNoR properties in the Brazeau

Coal Branchers

Robert Wesley Jones (1871-1947)
Occupation: civil engineer

R. W. Jones was an American who came to the Coal Branch via the Grand Trunk Pacific (GTP) Railway. Jones was a GTP divisional engineer whose responsibilities included not only choosing the actual routes of the railway's main and Coal Branch lines, but taking an inventory of the nearby available resources that could benefit the railway. He did his own reconnaissance work and, accompanied by his guide Pierre Belcourt, examined about 26,000 sq. km of the northern Rockies and foothills.

Reconnaissance work meant roughing it in the bush for several weeks at a time following not only the prescribed route of the railway but wandering 80 to 160 km off in either direction. The purpose was to select alternate routes that surveyors would later examine in greater detail prior to a final decision being made. Two factors had to be considered: the cost of building the railway across the terrain chosen versus the economic value of the country being traversed.

It was through this reconnaissance work that Jones, probably by 1907, became aware of the coal deposits at Mountain Park. In 1910 Jones and John Gregg staked their claims there and sought development capital. They found it in Britain and the Mountain Park Coal Company was formed in 1911. Jones' partnership with Gregg extended beyond Mountain Park. They staked the original coal leases at Luscar and briefly operated a prospect near Pocahontas.

By 1910 Jones had left the GTP and was a consulting engineer for the Alberta government and later a partner with Fairchild, Jones and Taylor, an engineering firm based in Edmonton. As the provincial railway engineer, Jones supervised the construction of all railway lines in the province that were being built under government guarantee. His railway work covered most of the Coal Branch. Besides the Bickerdike to Lovett line, he located the survey, in 1911, of the Coalspur to Mountain Park line and 10 years later did the same for the spur line to Luscar.

He was an original director with the Mountain Park Coal Company and remained on the company board until resigning in 1934. His resignation was a direct result of his involvement with Frank Seabolt and Harry King in a competing coal mine, Hinton Collieries Ltd. This last venture was a sad one. In 1938 an explosion in the pit killed five miners and injured several others.

Early photographs show Jones as a stocky, well-built man with a sporty handlebar moustache. He was a self-confessed baseball enthusiast and a very lucky man. Once, while doing survey work for the GTP, he was charged by a grizzly bear. With a single shot from his .22 calibre rifle at a reported 12 paces, Jones dropped the animal dead. It landed at his feet.

coal lands were amalgamated with the coal holdings of the German Development Company led by Martin Nordegg. The resulting holding company, called Brazeau Collieries, was a partnership wherein German Development would develop a coal mine while the CNoR would build a railway to that mine. They would eventually settle upon Nordegg as their mine site and their other holdings would eventually be released.

The CNoR right-of-way from Wolf Creek would be used as a pack and freighting trail for the development of a coal mine at Lovett by a GTP-affiliated syndicate. The GTP, through the efforts of Brutinel, would negotiate an approximately $12,460 per kilometre subsidy from the provincial government to build 93 km of rail line south from Bickerdike to Lovett. The elbow of this track would be at Coalspur to serve a mine being built by a group independent of either the CNoR or GTP. The Bickerdike-Coalspur section opened to traffic in October, 1912, and the section to Lovett opened three months later. The total subsidized cost of this GTP branch line was $1,140,000.

The 50 km of rail line between Coalspur and Mountain Park was not part of the original Alberta Coal Branch. One of Mountain Park's stakers in 1910 was R. W. Jones, who was a divisional engineer with the GTP. Since the GTP was already committed to its mine at Lovett, Jones turned to British capital to develop his claim that, in turn, chose to build and operate its own colliery railway. Construction of this new branch line began in January, 1912, and finished in July, 1913. Like its GTP counterpart, this branch line was also subsidized by the provincial government, this time at a total cost of $1,185,000.

The Coal Branch railways were constructed by an American firm, Phelan & Shirley. This company was a subcontractor to what at the time was North America's premier construction firm, Foley, Welch & Stewart. Across North America, starting around 1870, this company would build over 40,000 km of railway line at a total cost of over $1 billion. It was founded by a Canadian, John Foley, who immigrated to the United States to start a lumber business. Lumbering was a winter exercise and to keep his horse teams and men employed during the summer months, Foley soon got involved in railway contract work building grades and clearing rights-of-way. As the company grew it acquired as logistics expert and partner another Canadian, John W. Stewart.

Building a railway line, especially through wilderness, was more an exercise in logistics than muscle and equipment. Upon the completion of the railway survey, tote roads and cache camps were established along the proposed railway line. Camp buildings, warehouses, cookhouses, hospitals, stables, smithies and repair shops were erected. Foodstuffs, clothing, medicines and forage had to be calculated, procured, then hauled and distributed in winter over hundreds of kilometres of bush and dense forest. By the spring thaw all supplies, men, horses and equipment had to be in position for the beginning of construction. Stewart excelled at this type of project and materials management. During the First World War he led a handpicked Canadian construction battalion recruited from among the firm's employees. The Allied generals were astounded at the battalion's ability to lay track and move supplies to the front. By the end of the war Stewart reached the rank of major general and commanded all British engineering corps. By Stewart's worldwide standards, the construction of 143 km of Coal Branch railway was a minor challenge.

SVEDBURG RANDOM CAMPSITE

There is no recreation area with formal campgrounds at McLeod River. Rather, the area opposite the mouth of the Embarras River and on the east side of Highway #47 has long been used as a random campsite. You, then, have a choice of staying at the Weald Group Recreation Area 16 km south, at Lambert Creek Recreation Area 19 km south along Highway #47, at Edson 20 km north or random camping at McLeod River. If you choose the latter, remember that there are no amenities including washrooms or drinking water.

Confluence of the McLeod and Embarras rivers.

The Svedburg Mill Site

The open field along the McLeod River and opposite the mouth of the Embarras River was the mill site of the Svedburg Lumber Co. owned by Oscar Svedburg. In 1965 the mill was struck by a double disaster. Firstly, the company bridge over the Embarras River washed out during flood time then, secondly, about a week later the mill burned down with an estimated loss of $40,000. The fire was presumed to have started from a spark blown out of a fire pit by a strong wind that was blowing at the time. During the Second World War the mill reportedly employed German POWs.

1 THE SAND DUNES

MAP PAGE 25

The numerous OHV and dirt bike tracks you see in the sand dunes on both sides of the highway attest to the popularity of this area with these recreation seekers. While there are many trails to explore in the vicinity, most end in swamps that fill the low-lying areas between the dunes. We have chosen to present a looped trip that both leads you through the myriad of tracks in the sand dunes and gives you the opportunity to visit the old whistle stop of Bickerdike.

From the trailhead turn right onto the highway and go south for approximately 200 m to an intersection with a dirt road on your left. Turn onto this road. You will notice you are in a large sand dune that stretches on both sides of Highway #47. OHV tracks forge both straight ahead through the dune and to the north and to the south, paralleling Highway #47. Turn right onto the OHV track that heads south between two sets of hydro poles. At an intersection swing to the right along the OHV track that, within a short distance, brings you back to Highway #47. Cross the highway and continue

Day hiking, cycling

Rating full day

Distance 36.4 km

Level of Difficulty road and OHV track

Maximum Elevation 983 m

Elevation Gain 61 m

Map 83 F/7 Erith; 83 F/10 Bickerdike

Access

Park your vehicle at the sandy borrow pit located on the west side along Highway #47, 9 km south of Highway #16, or 53 km north of the intersection with Highway #40.

0.0 km	trailhead
0.0 km	Highway #47
0.2 km	intersection
0.3 km	intersection
1.0 km	intersection

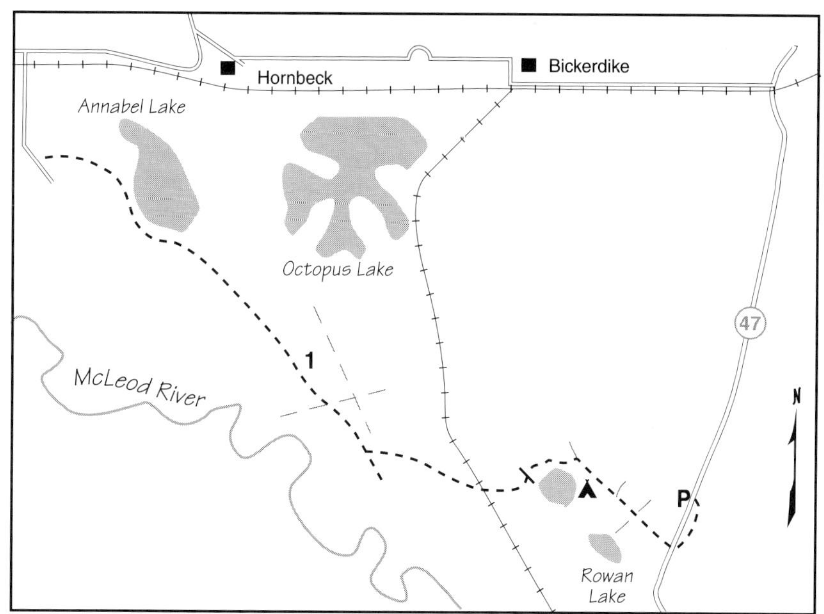

The view of one of the many lakes from the random campsite.

through the sand along an old roadway as it climbs steeply to the top of the dune and to a T-junction with a gravel road. Bear to the right crossing underneath another set of hydro lines. Within 300 m the gravel road dips down to bisect a wide clearing. Informal campsites dot the clearing indicating this is an alternate trailhead. Poking about you can find, hidden among a copse of poplar trees, a fenced-off old wellhead.

As you leave the clearing you climb along the ridge of a small dune. Below and to your left is a swamp that fills the low-lying ground. At the top of the dune your track intersects with a cutline. If you look left down the cut you can see the shimmer of water indicating one of many small lakes that dot the sand dune area. Ignore the cutline and continue along the OHV track as it now crosses

1.2 km	Highway #47
1.4 km	intersection
1.7 km	wellhead and random campsite
2.2 km	cutline
4.0 km	intersection
4.3 km	random campsite and viewpoint
4.9 km	intersection
5.2 km	begin braid
5.3 km	end braid
5.7 km	viewpoint
6.2 km	intersection
6.4 km	railway track
6.7 km	stream crossing
6.8 km	intersection
6.9 km	intersection
7.2 km	intersection
7.5 km	enter cutblock
8.2 km	leave cutblock
8.2 km	intersection
8.3 km	gate and intersection
8.5 km	intersection
9.0 km	enter cutblock
9.3 km	intersection
9.5 km	intersection
9.9 km	leave cutblock and gate
9.9 km	cutline and intersection
10.2 km	gate
10.4 km	McLeod River
10.5 km	meadow
11.1 km	intersection (corresponds with 9.9 km)
11.2 km	intersection
11.4 km	"upsy-daisy"
11.7 km	cutline
12.0 km	intersection
12.5 km	intersection
13.3 km	cutline and intersection
13.5 km	intersection
13.7 km	intersection
14.8 km	viewpoint Annabel Lake
15.6 km	gate
16.2 km	intersection
16.7 km	gate

from one dune to another. The boggy area at the bottom of the dip is mercifully short and you soon climb out onto an adjacent dune. It's a pleasant and pretty ride as you pass by saskatoon bushes, wild roses and stands of white poplar and jack pine that have colonized these ancient dunes. At an intersection bear to the left to keep on the main track. From here the dune you are on hugs the shore of a large lake on your left. At the top of a low rise there is an informal campsite and as pretty a lake view as you could wish for, making this is a perfect spot for a short stop. Loons and Canada geese can be seen on the lake, and the familiar tap-tap of woodpeckers rings through the woods.

Leaving the campsite continue along the top of the dune as far as another OHV track that joins from the left 500 m later. Turn left onto this track. As you travel up and down along the trail beware of deadfall that might present hazards. Along the crest of the dune you come to another viewpoint immediately on your left overlooking another lake. Here, if you are lucky you will see red-tail hawks that nest in the area. A short distance beyond the viewpoint your track forks. Take the right-hand track that leads down through the bush to the railway tracks. Cross the tracks bearing to the right to pick up the continuation of the OHV trail as it heads back into the forest. A stream crossing is made easier by some corduroy that has been laid over the wettest part of the trail. At a T-junction bear to the right and climb along what appears to be an old roadway. At the crest of the slope there is an intersection with another track on your left. Keep straight ahead, or to the right as far as a four-way intersection. Here, turn right. Within a short distance you enter a cutblock where your track swings lazily to the right. You cross the shoulder of a large sand dune and then back across an adjacent cutblock. At a fork in the trail go right along the soft, sandy old roadway. You dead end at a fence.

Close the gate behind you. Turn right onto the soft, sandy roadway as far as a fork where you will want to turn left. You cross an open field and enter into another cutblock. Separating two parts of the cutblock is a large dune, the lower shoulder of which you must cross. Once across the flat of the cutblock you come to a junction of tracks. Here

17.3 km	intersection
17.3 km	road
18.2 km	intersection
19.3 km	railroad track and intersection Highway #16A
22.6 km	Bickerdike Road
30.4 km	Highway #47
36.4 km	trailhead

Old roads and OHV tracks through the dunes make excellent bicycle roadways.

you can go either directly up the steep slope of the dune or you can go straight ahead along older track that swings up and then to the left where it intersects with the former track. Once again you are crossing a cutblock. Go as far as another fence and gate. Enter through the gate closing it behind you once on the other side. You are now leaving the cutblock and are back into the pleasant surroundings of the boreal forest.

Almost immediately you come to an intersection with an old cutline on the right and an equally old road to the left. To access the McLeod River turn left onto the road. The McLeod River is only 500 m down the roadway; you must cross a gate before arriving at the river's edge and the meadow that lies a little beyond. This makes a great alternate snack spot as the river is quite pretty. Return to the intersection bearing left onto the OHV track. You climb up a dune where, at the top, there is an intersection with another trail. If you wish to descend part way to the McLeod River and visit the romantically-named "Whiskey River Ranch," turn left. The "ranch" was, according to local people, never a ranch but an euphemism for a party shack. And the site certainly has the appearance of having seen a few parties in its day. Despite this, the view down to the McLeod is quite pleasing. Return to the intersection and bear left. Shortly you will come to an "upsy-daisy" where the trail waves across the dune you are riding on. Ignore first a cutline and then two trails, all of which join from the right, and continue through the mixed forest of poplar, aspen, spruce, jack pine and lodgepole pine. Along this stretch of the trail ants have been very industrious building some of the largest anthills we have ever seen!

Your track is once again riding the crest of a dune when you come to another cutline. Continue straight ahead on the main OHV track. Ignore intersections with two other minor trails. You can take an interesting break in your trip at a viewing spot overlooking Annabel Lake, one of the larger of the many lakes that dot the sand dunes. Trumpeter swans are known to nest in this area as well as several species of ducks. Then, passing an abandoned vehicle, continue to a gate. Past the gate there is an old road that bisects the track you are on. Continue straight ahead. The cool forest you have been travelling through now begins to open up and at a second gate with a cattleguard the forest gives way to the hay fields of a ranch on your right. Your excursion along the OHV track ends abruptly at an intersection. Bear to the right along a wide gravel road as it climbs slowly. Another gravel road joins on the left. Continue straight ahead past a number of small ranches.

You soon come to a railway track and an intersection with a paved road, the old Highway #16. Turn right onto the old highway. Only local traffic appears to use this road, thus making this a traffic-free ride as far as the intersection with the Bickerdike Road. Turn right onto the Bickerdike Road. This gravel road winds past acreages and small farms. On the final straightaway that leads to Highway #47 you cannot help but notice that the old Bickerdike railway station is now a private residence. The owners are obviously aware of the historic importance of their home as they have left in place the old station sign. A short distance later and you find yourself at Highway #47. Turn right and follow the highway for 6 km back to your trailhead.

The Sand Dunes of Lake Edson

Travelling south along Highway #47 from Edson you may be surprised by the large sand dunes that stretch on both sides of the highway near the Sand Dunes trailhead and extending southward almost all the way to Coalspur. What are sand dunes doing in the midst of the forested foothills?

When the continental ice sheets began to melt approximately 12,000 years ago large melt water lakes formed at the front margin of the glaciers. As the ice sheets retreated the water drained southward through melt channels from one lake to another carrying with it rock, sand and silt that settled on the lake bottoms. These lakes eventually drained leaving behind large areas of exposed lakebed. Northwesterly winds whipped the exposed sand into dunes that formed along the southeastern shore of the lakes. One such ancient glacial lake was Lake Edson located somewhere west of this dune field. Other dune fields can be found near Grande Prairie, Wainwright, Devon, Medicine Hat and in Wood Buffalo National Park.

A cross section profile of a sand dune shows a slope gently rising to a crest as the wind carries the sand particles forward. Once past the crest of the dune the wind velocity drops sharply causing the sand particles to be dumped at the base of the dune. Dunes "travel" as the wind continues to move sand up the wind-facing slope to the backslope. Most of Alberta's ancient sand dunes have been stabilized by jack pine, juniper, poplar, berry bushes and wild roses, all of which you can see along the Sand Dunes route. The depressions in between the dunes are occupied by muskegs.

Bickerdike

Previous names: Shirley, Mile 17

Bickerdike is probably named after Robert Bickerdike (1843-1928) who served as a Montreal Liberal M.P. from 1900 to 1917. Bickerdike was a crusader with two of his causes, the abolition of capital punishment and the outlawing of cigarettes, still under debate today. His opposition to capital punishment was based mainly upon his interpretation of the Bible while his anti-cigarette campaign was motivated by health concerns. The latter had its momentary successes. Bills outlawing cigarettes passed first reading in Parliament in 1903 and 1904 but never reached final approval. Bickerdike's connection to the Grand Trunk Pacific (GTP), which named the station after him in 1911, is unclear. The most likely possibility is through the insurance and underwriting business where he held numerous directorships.

Shirley is named after Robert D. Shirley, partner in Phelan & Shirley, railway contractors. Phelan & Shirley was an American firm that acted as a subcontractor to Foley, Welch & Stewart, the company that built the GTP and Coal Branch railway lines. Shirley was founded in 1910 when it was chosen as the point on the GTP main line from which the Coal Branch line would run to the Yellowhead and Pacific Pass mines.

Mile 17 is the distance count along the GTP main line from Wolf Creek.

The old Bickerdike railway station, now a private residence.

WEALD GROUP RECREATION AREA

Located so close to Edson and Highway #16, Weald Group Recreation Area has proven to be a popular spot for company picnics, family reunions, Boy Scout and Girl Guide weekend outings.

Located in the forested foothills, Weald Group Recreation Area is a great place to plan a few days' activities of, perhaps, fishing, field sports, day hiking, cycling or canoeing on the Embarras River. In the evening everyone can relax around the fireplace in the group shelter.

Location 38 km southwest of Edson along Highway #47
Facilities group shelter with fireplace, BBQ pit, pump, firewood, toilets
Note May be reserved only by organized groups for a maximum of two bookings a year.

Family reunions as well as school and club groups find Weald a convenient place to get together.

The Tackle Box

Embarras River
Fish Management Area: #4

Species rainbow trout to 1 lb., northern pike to 10 lb., bull trout to 5 lb.

Restrictions All bull trout (Dolly Varden) must be released.

Season 16 June to 31 August

2 OLD WEALD

MAP PAGE 33

Before the railways switched to diesel-powered engines in the 1950s, they relied on coal-fired steam engines. These old engines needed water, and plenty of it! To supply the much-needed water the railways built water storage towers every eight to 10 miles along the right-of-way. Adjacent to each of the water towers a small hamlet housing a few railway workers and possibly a post office and store sprang up. One such whistle-stop was Weald. This short walk takes you around the old Weald townsite and then down the tracks and into the bush to discover an illicit still that once belonged to that wiliest of bootleggers, Jack the Frog.

From your vehicle do not return to the Weald Group Camp access road. Instead, find the path that leads through the bush as far as its edge where you stumble upon some tin cans and a telltale depression in the ground. This marks one of the homes that once graced Weald. Cross the gravel Weald Group Camp access roadway. Two old well sites and a series of depressions mark another, larger home that once sheltered none other than Jack the Frog. Rejoin the access road, turn left toward Highway #47 and cross the highway.

Day hiking
Rating one hour
Distance 1.2 km
Level of Difficulty short walk with one stream crossing
Maximum Elevation 3243 m
Elevation Gain nil
Map 83 F/7 Erith

Access

Park your vehicle at the open area to the left of the gate leading into the Weald Group Camp. The camp is located along Highway #47, 31 km south of Highway #16, or 32 km north of the intersection with Highway #40.

0.0 km	trailhead
0.1 km	foundation
0.2 km	well sites and remains of Jack the Frog's house
0.2 km	old tote road
0.2 km	Highway #47

These concrete pillars are all that remain of the second water tower used by the railway.

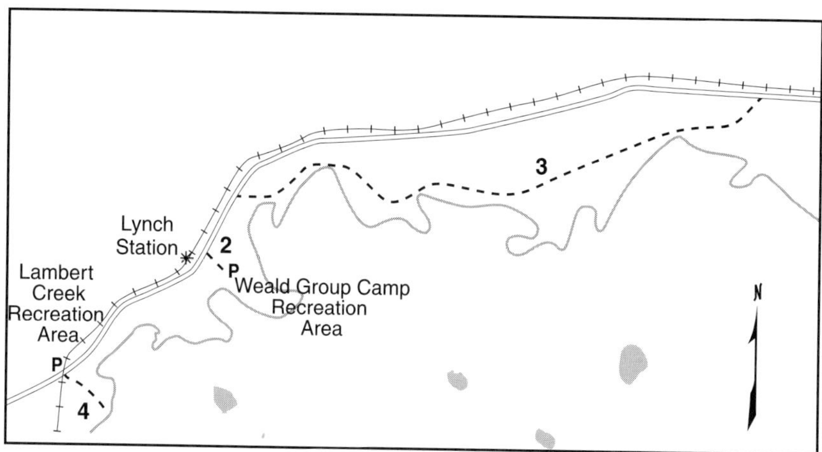

0.3 km	intersection
0.3 km	Lynch memorial
0.4 km	water tower foundation stones
0.6 km	yellow sign near siding end; black stump
0.7 km	cabin and Jack the Frog's still site
1.0 km	garden and building site
1.1 km	intersection
1.2 km	trailhead

Follow the old gravel road as far as the railway tracks ignoring an intersection with another old gravel roadway on your left. Directly across the tracks from you once stood a small railway station. Turn left to a new cairn erected in 1997 to Jim Lynch, a railway worker. Directly opposite was the railway speeder house where, when you cross the tracks, you can still see the outlines of the building's foundation. Next to the speeder house on the same side of the tracks was a bunkhouse, approximately 10 x 3 m in size, that housed the railway section men. It is, though, the concrete foundations of what had been the new water tower that catch your attention as they are the most dominant reminder of a time when Weald was a necessary link in the operation of the Coal Branch railway. Just beyond the water tower foundations, lying in a rubble heap, are the concrete remains of the first water tower.

Continue along the railway tracks for approximately 200 m to a yellow sign that marks the end of the railway siding. A black stump on the west side of the ditch indicates where you leave the tracks and turn westward into the bush. Within a few metres your pathway bisects a wide swath that had been at one time a logging road. Beyond this point your path broadens as it leads you directly to the site of Jack the Frog's still. There, in a clearing in the spruce forest, are the tumbled-down remains of his bootlegging operations. Although small, his was no fly-by-night operation. Examination of the remains of the log building reveal full dovetail corner joins, an indication of both his skill with an axe and his confidence in evading the scrutiny of the RCMP for he built this structure to last. Poking around the site you can see clear evidence of the day of reckoning when the law finally caught up to the Coal Branch's most noteworthy rumrunner.

Return the way you came as far as the concrete remains of the first water tower. Cut across the field on your way back to the highway. Another large concrete foundation, now almost obliterated, and the outlines of a garden where rhubarb still struggles against the invading grasses mark the home of the water tower maintenance man and his family. A short distance farther you come to the gravel roadway of the old Coal Branch highway. Close by there used to be the Weald post office, now no longer in evidence. Turn left and follow the old highway as far as the intersection with the access road. Turn right and follow it across Highway #47 and then to your vehicle.

You can still see the axe marks in the buckets and basins inflicted by the RCMP when they finally found and destroyed this still belonging to Jack the Frog.

Coal Branchers

John L'Heureux (ca. 1870-1956)
Occupation: entrepreneur

John L'Heureux is better known as "Jack the Frog," the Coal Branch's preeminent bootlegger. He was a Californian of French descent who arrived in the Coal Branch during the construction of the railway. With his wife Mamie, he opened a restaurant at Coalspur that soon developed a reputation for good food and generous hospitality. During this time he was already making moonshine and supplying the railway workers. Mamie began losing her eyesight so they closed the restaurant and moved to Weald where L'Heureux began making home-brew for a living during the Canadian prohibition. There is some conjecture that Mamie became blind because of drinking his alcohol.

The banning of the manufacture and sale of liquor began as a wartime measure and did not end in Alberta until 1923. Enforcing prohibition was difficult and the number of illicit stills proliferated. The Coal Branch, especially during its earlier days, had few recreational facilities. For the miners and railway workers, most of whom lived in communal bunkhouses, recreation often meant talking, smoking, gambling and occasionally prostitutes. Drinking facilitated these activities and even after the repeal of prohibition and the opening of beer parlours there was still a market for cheaper, poorer quality and sometimes lethal moonshine. The first reported Coal Branch death was alcohol related; in 1911, a railway worker was attacked by an alcoholic seizure and cut his jugular vein.

L'Heureux's moonshine had several quality standards. His private stock was distilled twice and was probably over 100 proof alcohol. It was clear white and burned cleanly in a spoon. His sales stock was less pure but still good enough to keep mantle lamps lit in miners' homes or power a speeder that had run out of gas. As he grew older he grew careless in the production of his moonshine and reportedly used improperly washed bleach bottles to store his product.

It was the railway men who acted as L'Heureux's distributors and guardians. They would buy the moonshine at Weald then resell it farther up the line along both branches. They would also warn L'Heureux whenever police were on the train by blowing their train whistle in a certain way as they approached Weald. Eventually though, in 1928, L'Heureux was caught by the police and spent several months in jail. Besides making moonshine, L'Heureux ran a stagecoach between Edson and Coalspur along the old tote road. With the opening of the Coal Branch highway during the 1940s, this business ended.

L'Heureux was a short, stocky man with half a nose that was the result of an operation to remove a cancer. He was generous to a fault and would give away sweets to children and bottles of his liquor to their parents. He was also notoriously absent minded. The bogs around Weald are said to contain gallons of his moonshine buried then forgotten.

John L'Heureux lies buried at the Glenwood cemetery in Edson.

3 WEALD LOOP

MAP PAGE 33

Staying at the Weald Group campground or nearby? The whole family can enjoy this easy walk or bike ride that skirts the pretty Embarras River as it slowly meanders its way north.

Follow the Weald Recreation Area access road back toward the highway. Turn right onto the highway and follow it for 800 m until you see a track leading off to the right. Follow this track as it first parallels the highway, then gently leads down through tall grasses to the Embarras River. What a pretty spot this is with the river slowly wending its way around a lazy bend. You then climb the riverbank to a T-junction. Bear to the right along an old four-wheel-drive track.

The track soon becomes a straightaway that continues for more than 3 km. Although lengthy flat stretches may conjure up images of boredom, this part of your jaunt is anything but boring. A profusion of flowers—orange western wood lilies, red and white clover, purple northern sweet vetches, red and orange Indian paintbrushes, and white and purple fleabanes—grow so thickly that

Day hiking, cycling

Rating half day

Distance 13.8 km

Level of Difficulty abandoned roadway

Maximum Elevation 988 m

Elevation Gain 30 m

Map 83 F/7 Erith

Access

Park your vehicle before the front gate to the Weald Group Camp Recreation Area along Highway #47. The Weald Recreation Area is located 31 km south of Highway #16, or 31 km north of the intersection with Highway #40.

0.0 km	trailhead
0.1 km	Highway #47
0.8 km	turnoff
1.3 km	intersection

Embarass River.

they threaten to obliterate the old road. Here and there, your road swings close to the river but most of the time you cannot see the Embarras. A cut across the road, a power line right-of-way and the sounds of highway traffic indicate you are approximately half way through your exploration. The old road now swings to the right, skirting an old borrow pit. Here, you are quite close to the Embarras River and you might want to scramble down to the river for a better view. If you are here in early August, watch for the telltale red fruit of wild strawberries that sprinkle the pit area. Look also for the delicate blue-eyed grasses that are also found here.

Soon past the borrow pit you come within sight of the highway. For the next 200 m your track follows a power line right-of-way. This is a difficult stretch, either wet and boggy if it has rained recently or deeply rutted if dry. In either case, you will probably have to push your bicycle through this section before coming to a fork in the road. Bear left; you quickly regain Highway #47. Turn left again and enjoy an easy ride back to the Weald Group Camp, ignoring all other turnoffs.

1.9 km	T-junction
3.0 km	cutline
5.3 km	cut across road
6.0 km	power line right-of-way
6.2 km	borrow pit
6.8 km	power line right-of-way and bog
7.0 km	intersection
7.1 km	Highway #47
8.0 km	intersection
11.8 km	intersection
11.8 km	intersection
12.3 km	intersection
13.0 km	intersection with Highway #47
13.8 km	trailhead

Lynch

Previous names: Weald, Mile 16

Lynch is named after Jim Lynch (1941-1996), a Canadian National Railway (CNR) track supervisor who died of a heart attack at this location. Lynch had worked for 17 years for the railway. In his memory, CNR renamed the Weald station in 1996 and a year later held a dedication ceremony at the cairn erected here in his honour.

The Grand Trunk Pacific named the station Weald in 1912. The word *weald* is Old English meaning "the woodland" or "forest." This is an appropriate descriptive name but it is unclear whether the station received its name solely from its meaning or after one of several locations in England including The Weald in Kent and villages in Oxfordshire and Essex.

Weald was never a large community. It probably held no more than two dozen people, most of whom worked for the railway as part of the water tower and track maintenance crews. Other local businesses included the post office, which closed in 1927, and a distillery, first shut down by the police in 1928. With the replacement of steam powered locomotives by diesel, CNR withdrew its permanent presence in the early 1960s and the village was abandoned. The Weald Group Camp preserves the original Coal Branch locality name.

Mile 16 is the distance count along the Coal Branch railway from Bickerdike.

LAMBERT CREEK RECREATION AREA

Confluence of Lambert Creek and Embarras River.

Although Lambert Creek Recreation Area boasts only a small number of campsites, this campground is popular with fishermen and with those who simply want a quiet weekend away.

Lambert Creek Recreation Area serves as a staging area for visitors wanting to explore the area around Weald, which has a group campground, and even the sand dunes some 20 km north.

Location Along Highway #47, 33 km south of Highway #16, or 29 km north of the intersection with Highway #40.
Facilities seven unserviced campsites, four day-use parking spots, cookhouse, pump, free firewood

The Tackle Box

Lambert Creek
Fish Management Area: #4

Species rainbow trout to 1 lb., arctic grayling to 2 lb. in upper reaches, northern pike to 8 lb. in lower reaches.

Restrictions Use of bait fish and the collection of bait fish are prohibited.
Best fishing in upstream beaver dams.

Season 16 June to 31 August

4 LAMBERT CREEK WALK

MAP PAGE 33

A pretty viewpoint overlooking the confluence of Lambert Creek and the Embarras River is the highlight of this easy walk.

Walk toward Highway #47 along the gravel road. Soon you will notice a track that leads off to the right leading down to Lambert Creek. This path created, no doubt, by the many fishermen who try their luck here, follows the creek under the highway bridge. Once on the other side of the highway, the fishermen's path peters out. So, angle over toward the railway bridge and pass under it. Here, your path once again follows along the banks of Lambert Creek. A beaver dam adds extra interest along the way.

Day hiking

Rating half day

Distance 1.7 km

Level of Difficulty short stroll with some bushwhacking

Maximum Elevation 990 m

Elevation Gain 10 m

Map 83 F/7 Erith

Access

Park your vehicle at the Lambert Creek Recreation Area parking lot located along Highway #47, 33 km south of Highway #16, or 29 km north of the intersection with Highway #40.

0.0 km	trailhead
0.1 km	intersection
0.2 km	highway bridge
0.4 km	railway bridge
0.5 km	beaver dam
0.6 km	roadway
0.7 km	intersection
0.9 km	random campsite
0.9 km	viewpoint
1.1 km	intersection
1.3 km	Highway #47
1.5 km	Lambert Creek Recreation Area turnoff
1.7 km	trailhead

A view of the Embarras River just below the confluence with Lambert Creek.

Lambert and Baril Creeks

Lambert and nearby Baril creeks recall early local timber operators.

Lambert Creek was recorded in 1911 by Dominion Land Surveyor R. V. Heathcott, who was surveying timber limits along the line of the Coal Branch railway. Each kilometre of railway required about 2100 railway ties that were supplied by tie camps located along the right-of-way. The tie camps were usually small affairs where no more than half a dozen men with broad axes would square logs taken from the surrounding forest into railway ties. On railway lines being built on an extremely tight budget, the logs would often be cut on the opposite two sides only: one side to receive the rail, the other to rest on the ground. The remaining two sides would remain uncut, retaining the original tree bark.

There was a tie camp at nearby Weald that may have been Lambert's operation. Exactly who Lambert was is unclear. In the 1920s there was a sawmill where there is now the recreation area. That sawmill was operated by Joseph Baril, after whom nearby Baril Creek is named. Baril would later move his operation to the mouth of the Erith River before selling out to Dick Corser and the Erith Tie Company in the early 1930s.

Baril built a dam on the upper reaches of the Erith River to regulate the stream's flow, then each spring would float his winter cut of logs downstream to his mill. Just past the mouth of the Erith there was a boom thrown across the Embarras River to catch the logs. One spring the dam burst and about 60,000 logs swept down the Erith, broke through the boom, and continued on to the McLeod River. The dam was never repaired as by now logging trucks began to be used to haul timber.

Just past the beaver dam, the path ends at a small set of rapids in the creek. An old, overgrown road to your left leads up the hill to a T-junction with another old road. Turn right and enjoy a pleasant walk above Lambert Creek through an open forest of poplar and spruce. The road ends at an informal campsite perched well above the Embarras River. The sound of rapids encourages you to walk beyond the campsite to a pretty viewpoint overlooking the Embarras River. Looking downstream to the set of rapids, you can see where Lambert Creek joins the river.

Return to the intersection with the road that led up from Lambert Creek. Do not go down the hill but continue straight ahead. The road you are on soon leads out to Highway #47. Turn left and walk down the highway to the Lambert Creek Recreation Area.

FICKLE LAKE RECREATION AREA

The close proximity of the Fickle Lake Recreation Area to Edson makes it a poplar day-use area for residents of that town, especially after working hours, as well as others who choose to camp at this quiet spot for several days at a time.

Located at the edge of a black spruce swamp, the Fish Lake Recreation Area dates to 1963 when oil patch exploration and drilling opened up the area. Even now you can find old wellheads and exploratory roads in the vicinity.

Location 31 km southwest of Edson along Highway #47 to the signed recreation area turnoff. It's another 10 km from the junction along a well-gravelled road to Fickle Lake.
Facilities 44 unserviced campsites, nine day-use sites, pump, free firewood, boat launch and floating dock, 30 parking spaces at boat launch
Note Boats are restricted to a speed limit of 12 kmp. No OHVs allowed.

The Tackle Box

Fickle Lake
Fish Management Area: #4

Long before the campground was built, Fickle Lake was well known for its wealth of northern pike, perch and whitefish. The lake supports sports fishing in both summer and winter. Lake levels are maintained by means of a weir located 1.5 km from the lake's outlet.

Species northern pike to 35 lb., yellow perch to 1 lb., whitefish to 6 lb., walleye to 5 lb.

Restrictions Walleye limit is zero in lake, tributaries and outlet stream. Use of bait fish and the collection of bait fish are allowed. Good ice fishing for whitefish and northern pike. All bull trout (Dolly Varden) must be released. Gas motors are allowed.

Season 16 June to 31 August

Members of surveyor R. V. Heathcott's crew in canoe with sail, Whitefish Lake (Fickle Lake), 1910. Courtesy Glenbow Archives, NA 945-40.

5 FICKLE LAKE WALK

Almost every campground has its own set of short trails for mom and dad to stroll along. The paths are great for young bikers, too! This easy, short ramble is particularly pleasant as it hugs the pretty lakeshore for much of the way.

Day hiking, cycling
Rating 30 minutes
Distance 0.9 km
Level of Difficulty easy stroll along lakeshore
Maximum Elevation 975 m
Elevation Gain 2 m
Map 83 F/7 Erith

Access

Park your vehicle at the Fickle Lake Recreation Area parking lot 9 km from the Fickle Lake turnoff along Highway #47. The turnoff is 23 km south of Highway #16.

0.0 km	trailhead
0.3 km	intersection
0.4 km	toilets
0.5 km	wood pile
0.9 km	trailhead

The Fickle Lake boat launch and dock are located adjacent to the Fickle Lake Recreation Area parking lot. Just to the right of the dock there are a couple of picnic tables and a fish cleaning station. The Fickle Lake walk begins here.

Go past the picnic tables along the gravelled path. For 300 m, the path winds in and out of poplar groves and alder bushes with the lake always to your immediate left. Reeds and lily pads grow close to the shore and if you're lucky you can spot Canada geese moving quietly among them. Prickly wild roses and purple fireweed add splashes of colour along the way. Here, you can find fishermen trying their luck from the shore or from fishing boats tied up to the shore trees.

The lakeshore path ends at the second landing. An indistinct path continues straight ahead but soon peters out in the tangle of long grass, trees

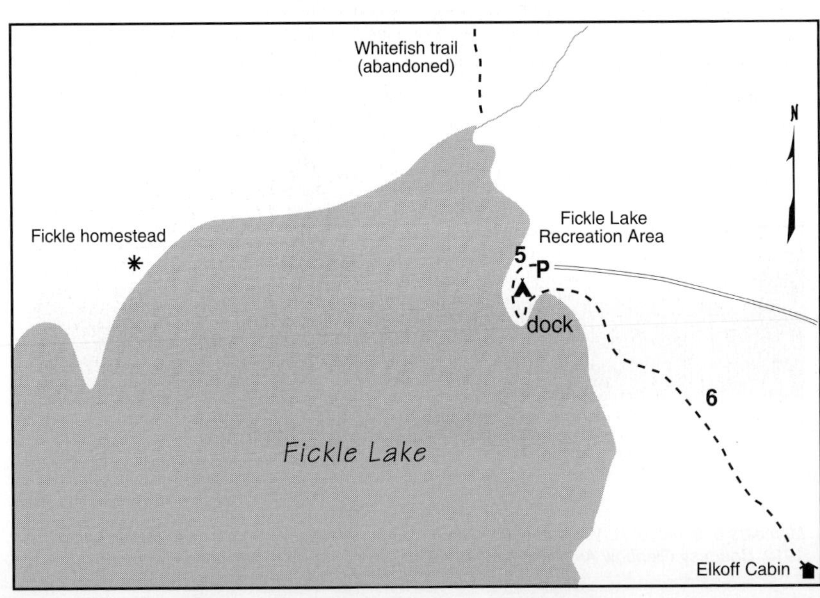

and bushes. Stay on the main trail that now swings to the right meandering behind a few campsites past a service node with a set of toilets and a woodpile. Watch for a squirrel's nest high in the spruce trees on your left. The white and black spruce trees have an understorey largely made up of Labrador tea that in late spring sports dainty white flowers.

The trail ends at a second service node next to campsite #9. To return to the parking lot walk straight ahead along the campground road past campsites 10 through 18. Continue past another service node to an intersection. Bearing left will take you to the main road where you will want to turn right and follow the road into the parking lot.

Fickle Lake

Previous name: Whitefish Lake
Cree name: Atihkamek Sakahikan

Fickle Lake is named after Charles R. Fickle (?-1944), a trapper who took out a homestead lease along the lake's northwest shore during the 1930s. This lease was cancelled in 1939.

Whitefish Lake is a translation of the original Cree name. Lake whitefish (*Coregonus clupeaformis*) were an important winter food source to aboriginals. Two prehistoric campsites dating back at least 6000 years have been found beside the lake and relate to the exploitation of this resource. With the coming of European settlement, Fickle Lake became the scene of a commercial whitefish fishery that lasted until the 1970s. Today the whitefish are the mainstay of the lake's winter recreational fishery, which has several times produced 5 lb. specimens. In 1989, a 32 lb. northern pike was pulled from the lake.

Fishing is still the reason why campers and day users come to this lake.

The name whitefish has been applied to dozens of lakes across Canada. This commonality created a problem in 1912 for Dominion Land Surveyor R. V. Heathcott when his original proposal that the lake be called "Whitefish Lake" was rejected by the Geographic Board on the grounds that this name was already in use elsewhere. "This lake has always been known as Whitefish and the only name that I can suggest is Attec-o-met [sic] which is the Cree name for whitefish," wrote Heathcott. This proposal was also rejected on the grounds that the Cree equivalent was in common official use.

6 TRAPLINE TRAIL

MAP PAGE 42

Staying at Fickle Lake? Looking for an easy walk that nevertheless can provide outdoor education for your children? The Trapline trail accommodates these criteria through the use of interpretive signs along the path as it meanders through the forest to the remains of the cabin of trapper Fred Elkoff.

Day hiking
Rating half day
Distance 2.6 km
Level of Difficulty easy stroll along groomed trail
Maximum Elevation 980 m
Elevation Gain 5 m
Map 83 F/7 Erith

Access

Park your vehicle at the Fickle Lake Recreation Area parking lot 9 km from the Fickle Lake turnoff along Highway #47. The turnoff is 23 km south of Highway #16.

0.0 km	trailhead
0.4 km	intersection
1.3 km	Elkoff cabin
2.6 km	trailhead

The parking lot at the Fickle Lake Recreation Area is the hub of most of the lakeside activity at this campground. The Trapline trail begins at the lake's edge to the left of the parking lot. The trailhead is signed.

One hundred metres after negotiating through the alders you break out close to the edge of the lake with its small sandy beach. In the spring and early summer Fickle Lake is the home to several breeding pairs of Canada geese. They seem to enjoy this small beach in particular so you may want to walk quietly so as not to disturb or agitate them. The adult geese are very protective of their young and will demonstrate aggressive behaviour toward anyone who they sense poses a threat to their goslings.

A sign at the end of the beach announces that the trail on which you are about to venture was used frequently by local trappers in the early 1900s.

Canada geese and ducks prefer the quieter bays of Fickle Lake.

The remains of Fred Elkoff's cabin.

Hence Alberta Environment's name for this trail. As your path swings into the forest and away from the lake watch for the dozen or more interpretive signs that have been erected by Alberta Environment on either side of the trail. Your first interpretive station is within 100 m of leaving the beach. This station illustrates the type of snare that Elkoff and other trappers used to trap fishers. A demonstration snare is located immediately behind the sign. Other demonstration snares with accompanying signage explain how trappers caught lynx, squirrels, snowshoe hares, coyotes, wolves, martens and even bears. How did trappers find their way through the sameness of the forest? What plants might they have used to stave off hunger? Answers to these and other questions are to be found in the interpretive signs.

About 400 m from the parking lot your path forks. Stay on the main path or the one on the left; the right fork leads to a swamp near the edge of the lake. You will know you are very close to Elkoff's cabin when you come upon the interpretive station explaining how trappers protected themselves from inquisitive bears that frequented the whereabouts of trappers' cabins. Around a corner you come to the fenced-off remains of Elkoff's 1940's cabin. A large interpretive sign tells you a little about Elkoff and explains what his cabin probably looked like. Look at the sketch of the cabin and then look at the collapsed remains. You can still see the good-sized logs with their lap-joint ends that were used in the walls, the flattened five gallon pails that protected the roof and the smaller trees that were used in the roof construction.

The path continues past the cabin for 20 m where it joins an old road. This is an old oil patch road that leads to a natural gas wellhead; today, the well has been sealed off and is no longer in use.

Return the way you came.

Coal Branchers

Frank "Black Frank" Knezevich (ca. 1880-1953)
Occupation: fur trapper

Black Frank.
Photo Corinne Marshall.

Frank Knezevich was the Coal Branch's most famous example of the oldest of local enterprises, fur trapping. Nicknamed "Black Frank" because of his black hair, he came from Eastern Europe and worked in the east branch mines before becoming a full-time fur trapper. He had a cabin beside the Pembina River directly across from the Pembina Forks Recreation Area. From there, his trapline ran in a loop along the Brazeau and Pembina rivers and took about 10 days to cover. Unlike most other trappers, Knezevich preferred to sell his furs directly to fur buyers in Montreal, where he would fly with his annual catch of pelts. One year, he reportedly cleared about $6,000 from his Montreal sales.

Trapping was originally the domain of local aboriginals and a Hudson's Bay Company fort near present-day Fort Assiniboine drew upon the fur trade resources of the upper Athabasca region including the Coal Branch between 1824-1877. An earlier fur trade fort built at the mouth of the McLeod River around 1800 probably did not last more than a few years. By the end of the 19th century prospectors entered the region and took up the trade as a means of earning the money needed to stake their summer explorations. This type of combined lifestyle, winter trapping-summer prospecting, continued into the 1920s and '30s. Fur trapping was also used to supplement the summer wages of Alberta forest rangers and game wardens. Ranger Charlie Hughes was given about 100 km of trap lines in the west branch covering an area north from Luscar to Mystery Lake and east toward the McLeod River. Hughes had the misfortune to do his trapping during the Depression when fur prices were depressed. One season's work brought him about $300.

A registered trap line would cover a geographic area several hundred metres wide and could be over 10 km long. The provincial government abandoned these long strips in favour of Registered Fur Management Areas (RFMA), irregularly shaped areas varying in size from about 200 to more than 450 sq. km depending upon the local geography and fur bearing capacity. In the Coal Branch today there are about 20 RFMAs with some earning the trapper up to $10,000 in a season depending upon animal populations and fur market prices.

Trapping was a lonely and physically demanding job, something that suited Black Frank who was an intensely private and fiercely independent man. One day in 1953, a forest ranger came to Black Frank's cabin bringing his mail. The ranger found only the dog tied in the kitchen and three horses penned nearby. Assuming that Knezevich was somewhere nearby, he left the mail in the kitchen and departed. A week later an Indian friend came to visit, noticed the mail lying untouched and immediately notified officials. A hastily organized search party found no trace of the man. The dog, presumably starving, had broken its leash and also disappeared.

Nearly 20 years later, in 1972, a hunter found the skeletal remains of a human body and a rusted rifle, with a live round of ammunition still in it, lying several feet away. A subsequent search of the site by RCMP turned up a cigarette lighter with the letter "K" on it. A pathologist declared the condition of the bones to be compatible with 15 to 20 years exposure. The skeleton was deemed to be Black Frank's and it was assumed he had suffered from a fatal heart attack. The loaded, rusted rifle found nearby was in a cocked position, still ready for firing.

ROBB

Of all the mining camps and towns that dotted the East Branch of the railway, only Robb has survived as a permanent townsite. As such, it is your only supply centre on the East Branch for camping supplies, food and petrol. It also boasts the only watering hole along the highway, the historic Bryan Hotel that we have designated the trailhead for your trips around Robb.

Present-day Robb is composed of three historic settlements, the mining camps of Bryan and Robb and a railway whistle stop at Mile 34. Little remains of the historic townsites; gone are the company log houses that in the 1930s rented for $10 a month, the school house, the cottage hospital, and the mine sites with their tipples, cookhouses and bunkhouses. A small historic church now a private home, a few log buildings, the hotel and the general store that had been the Jacoby store in Mercoal are the only reminders of the settlements' former days. Even the forestry station has closed. Yet Robb remains a vibrant community. Spurring this growth are the industries that form the new economy of the Coal Branch—oil and gas, strip mining at Luscar Sterco and the expansion of the logging and lumber industries. This has resulted in new housing that has pushed the town's borders northward beyond their historic boundaries and the survival of the riverside community of historic Robb and Mile 34.

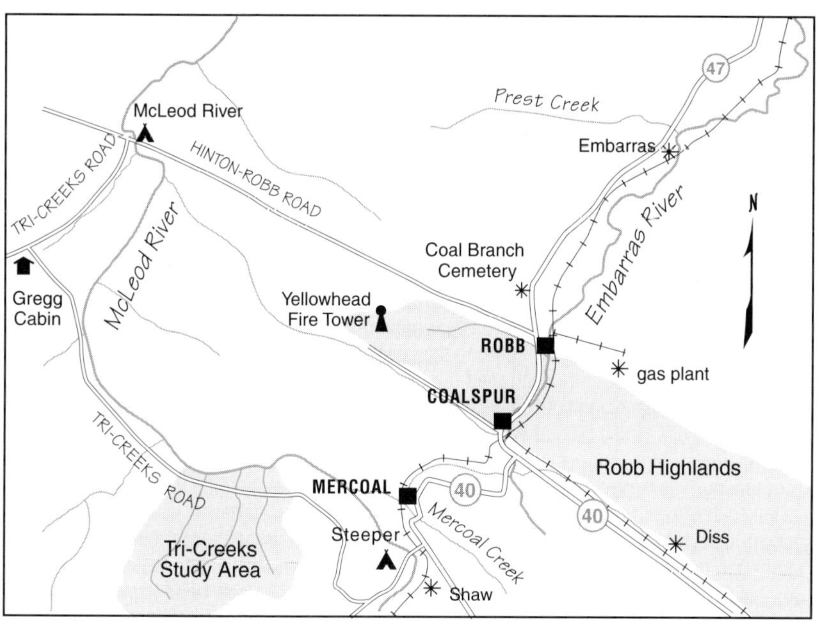

Lakeside

Mine No.: #775

Owners/Operators: 1918 Minehead Coal Co.; 1918-1920 Porter, Robb & Morino; 1920-1921 Balkan Coal Co.; 1921-1922 Alberta Standard Coal Co. Ltd.; 1922-1927 Balkan Coal Co. Ltd.; 1927-1950 Lakeside Coals Ltd.; 1950-1958 Minehead Coal and Oil Ltd.

Authorized Capital: $100,000 Balkan Coal Co. Ltd.; $660,000 Lakeside Coals Ltd.

Coal: sub-bituminous

Registered Trade Name: Minehead Coal

Market: domestic and steam

Mine Type: underground; strip pit

Total Extraction: 816,000 tonnes

Men Killed: 0

The first coal claims in the area were registered in 1910 by George Hugh Stewart and John A. MacDonald. Stewart was a Grand Trunk Pacific surveyor marking the route for the Coal Branch railway to Lovett. A syndicate including Alberta Lieutenant-Governor George Bulyea was unsuccessful in developing the site. Peter "Baldy" Robb began a prospect in 1918 and later that year formed a partnership with Dr. A. E. Porter and Eusebio "Joe" Morino. The three men sold the mine to Balkan Coal, a syndicate of 19 miners led by Alex Susnar, for $100,000.

This first Balkan coal company was taken over by Alberta Standard Coal owned by Richard J. McPeak, an Edmonton coal dealer. McPeak estimated he could mine the coal at $3.00 per ton per 200 tons per day, a point disputed by Balkan mine manager J. L. Parker who insisted the mine could not operate at less than $3.60 per ton. McPeak dismissed Parker and the company went bankrupt six months later. A reorganized Balkan coal company headed by George Bulaic took the mine over and operated it until 1927 when it was liquidated and its assets bought by Lakeside Coals, headed by Edwin A. McBain of Edmonton, owner of a mine at Wabamun.

Fire and water plagued Lakeside's operations. An underground fire, first begun in 1923, was never completely under control. It broke through the surface in 1943 and the company spent two years flooding the workings in a futile attempt to control it. They eventually gave up and abandoned the east slope to begin mining west where they encountered flooding from Bryan Creek. To stop the flooding they began to divert Bryan Creek.

In 1944 a spectacular fire destroyed the tipple, power plant and trestle. The fire started when chimney sparks ignited coal dust on top of the boiler house roof then spread over the roof when the fire hose was turned on it. Three rail cars on the trestle caught fire and began to roll toward the mine entrance. The first car derailed preventing the others from continuing. The trestle was blown up to prevent the flames spreading into the mine.

Lakeside never fully recovered from this disaster. They started a new underground seam, but stopped in 1946. Under new ownership from Saskatchewan, Lakeside began strip mining in 1949 over its underground workings. Caving suspended these operations by 1950. The Saskatchewan syndicate, called Minehead Coal since 1950, kept the leases, briefly attempted stripping again in 1955, then finally closed the mine three years later.

Bryan Mine

Mine No.: #1157

Owners/Operators: 1924-1938 Bryan Coal Co. Ltd.; 1938-1939 H. H. Croxton (Bryan Mine); 1939-1940 Bryan Power & Coal Co. Ltd.; 1941-1945 Thirty-Two Collieries Ltd.; 1945-1948 Bryan Hard Coal Co. Ltd.; 1949-1952 North Western Coal & Oil Ltd.; 1952-1954 Bryan Mountain Coal Co. Ltd.; 1963 King Coal (1963) Ltd.

Authorized Capital: $100,000 Bryan Coal Co. Ltd.; $100,000 Thirty-Two Collieries Ltd.; $500,000 North Western Coal & Oil Ltd.

Coal: sub-bituminous

Registered Trade Name: Bryan Mountain Hard Coal

Market: domestic

Mine Type: underground; strip pit

Total Extraction: 548 tonnes

Men Killed: 0

Bryan was an underground mine connected by a 4000 m-long spur line to the Coal Branch railway. It held a number of leases including one bought from an Idaho woman, Mrs. Edith A. Bick. The sale was on a royalty basis until the purchase price was paid. Bryan told Bick that since it would not be extracting coal from her property, there would be no payments for some time. Mrs. Bick asked the Mines Branch if this were true and heard a fascinating story.

Bryan Coal, the Mines Branch told her, had two years earlier assigned all its leases except hers to another company. Meanwhile all the coal being extracted was from her lease. Bryan Coal patched up its misunderstanding with Bick and continued operations until 1938. That year, a partnership including H. H. Croxton of Edmonton and Peter "Baldy" Robb bought the mine but were soon ordered to stop operating since they did not post a miner's wage bond. The partnership broke up and Robb, with Louis Stupar as president, formed Bryan Power & Coal. This new partnership lasted about a year before it too dissolved.

Archie Matheson, an insurance agent from Edmonton, organized Thirty Two Collieries, which reopened the mine in 1941. This company went bankrupt in 1944 and Matheson reorganized as Bryan Hard Coal. Like its predecessor, Bryan Hard Coal was an undercapitalized operation with its managers unable to solve the mine's continuing problems with water seepage and caving. The mine was ordered closed in 1948 through default in paying its miners their wages and it went bankrupt.

North Western Coal of Calgary abandoned the underground workings and began a strip pit. A year later, it started a new entry about 250 m west of the old mine and well away from the flooding and caving that stymied its previous operators. In 1952, North Western changed its name to Bryan Mountain Coal and continued both underground and strip operations. Lack of coal orders closed the mine in 1955 and it was abandoned in 1957. Some time afterward the tipple was destroyed by fire.

King Coal extracted coal from the strip pit for about a month in 1963.

7 ROBB TOWNSITE

Many visitors to the Coal Branch do not realize that present-day Robb incorporates three historic settlements, Bryan, Robb and Mile 34. This easy bicycle ride takes you on a pleasant journey through each of these settlements.

Cycling
Rating two hours
Distance 7.3 km
Level of Difficulty on and off road; 4 stream crossings
Maximum Elevation 1143 m
Elevation Gain 30 m
Map 83 F/2 Foothills

Access

Park your vehicle at the Bryan Hotel in Robb. The Robb turnoff is 53 km south of Highway #16 or 9 km north of the intersection with Highway #40.

0.0 km	trailhead
0.1 km	intersection
0.6 km	intersection
0.7 km	railroad crossing
1.1 km	intersection
1.3 km	bridge

Your trailhead, the Bryan Hotel, is named after the community that formed here in 1924 when the Bryan mine opened. Today, the old settlement of Bryan forms the most populous part of present-day Robb. We invite you to explore the old townsite of Bryan upon your return but for now, turn right onto Valley Road, a paved street that leads down toward the old Robb townsite. At the intersection with Bryan Road turn left to remain on Valley Road. Cross the railway tracks and go down the hill. At the bottom of the hill the road forks. Bear left onto Embarras Drive and follow it across a yellow bridge over the gurgling Embarras River. Ignore an OHV track that leads off to the left just past the bridge. Continuing along Embarras Drive

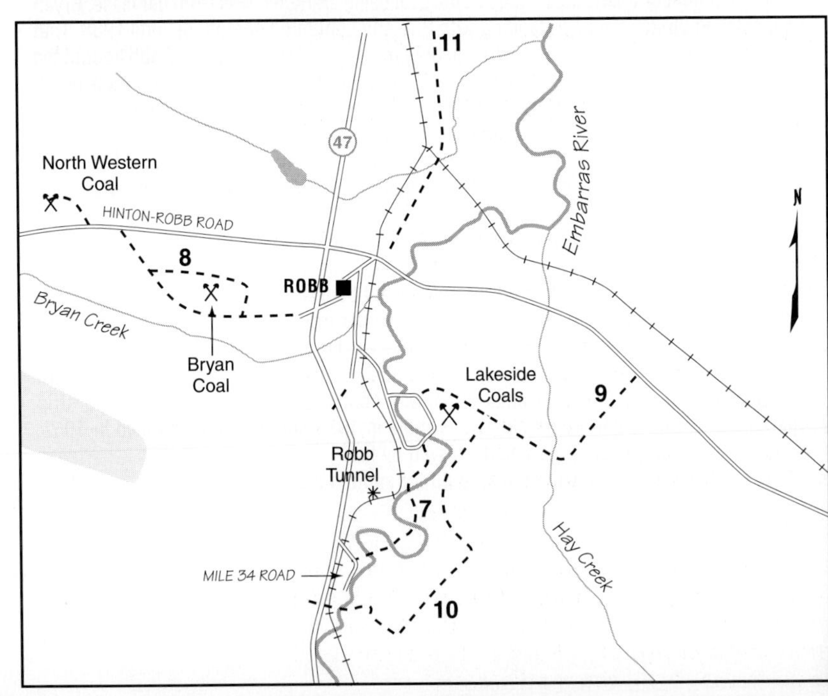

you are now entering the original coal mining townsite of Robb. Cross the river once again, this time via a blue bridge, and follow Embarras Drive as it swings to the right to the intersection with Balkan Drive. Here, in this quiet residential area, it's difficult to imagine the hustle and bustle that this coal mining town once exuded. Instead, today, there are sprawling lawns, luxuriant flowerbeds and large shade trees that line the entire length of Embarras Drive.

At the end of Embarras Drive a gravel pathway leads slowly upward through a pretty, cooling forest. Where the path leaves the forest, you climb more steeply along the river's embankment to the Robb railway tunnel built in 1912. You need to go around the tunnel to get to the other side of the hill, so turn left and follow the OHV track downhill and reenter the forest. In spring, accompanied by the sweet smell of wild roses, you wend your way through a pleasant forest of aspen, spruce and jack pine as far as the Embarras River. Cross the river, bearing slightly to the right to pick up the trail on the other side. Unless it is early summer after a heavy snowfall year you should have no trouble in crossing. It's a short ride to another river crossing where you must bear left about 30 m to find the continuation of your trail. Blast straight across the next two river crossings. You are now on the other side of the hill in yet another part of present-day Robb, the settlement of Mile 34.

Smaller than either old Robb or what used to be Bryan, Mile 34 is even quieter and possibly more idyllic than either of these two historic townsites. Ride as far as the intersection with the main road. Turn right and almost immediately cross the railway tracks. Climbing the hill out of the river valley you soon arrive at the intersection with Highway #47. Turn right onto the highway. A few hundred metres later there is a sand pit and OHV track on your right. Follow the OHV track through the sand pit and down along a pleasant old track to the end of Bryan Road. Within 100 m pick up an OHV track on your right. Cross Valley Road near where it crosses the railway tracks and continue along the track for a couple of hundred metres as it winds up and down along the railway right-of-way. You come out onto Valley Road. Turn left to the J&J General Store and pick up Valley Road as it leads downhill to the Bryan Hotel, your trailhead.

1.3 km	OHV track
1.6 km	bridge
1.7 km	intersection
2.0 km	OHV track
2.2 km	Robb tunnel
2.6 km	Embarras River
2.8 km	Embarras River
3.0 km	Embarras River
3.2 km	Embarras River
3.4 km	intersection
3.4 km	railroad crossing
3.5 km	intersection
3.7 km	Highway #47
4.0 km	sand pit and OHV track
4.7 km	Bryan Road
4.8 km	OHV track
5.1 km	Valley Road and railroad crossing
6.9 km	Valley Road
7.0 km	J&J General Store
7.2 km	intersection
7.3 km	trailhead

Coal Branchers

Peter Addison "Baldy" Robb (1887-1955)
Occupation: entrepreneur

P. A. "Baldy" Robb, ca. 1940. Courtesy Glenbow Archives, NA 4565-49.

Baldy Robb is the most beloved and mythologized among all the old Coal Branchers. He was a master storyteller with a wry sense of humour, a tireless community booster and an entrepreneur always on the lookout for the main chance. He was perhaps too quick to take advantage of an opportunity but with the passage of time, his skewed sense of business ethics that exasperated so many contemporaries became the source of the affection with which he is today held. Consulting engineer Len C. Stevens remembers, "Money didn't mean a thing to him, really. He was most careless in that respect, but if there was a devious way of doing anything, he'd find out what it was.... Altogether he was a good companion. He was good to talk to, he was likable, but when it came to doing business with him, he was a real Indian [sic]."

P. A. Robb was born in Scotland, immigrated to Canada with his parents when he was about four years old and settled in Manitoba. By the time he was about 20 years old he was following the Grand Trunk Pacific Railway westward, freighting in supplies to the railway camps along the right-of-way of the transcontinental and later the Coal Branch lines. By 1911 he was settled in Edson from where he continued his freighting business but would branch out into ranching, prospecting, running a stagecoach line along the Edson-Grande Prairie trail and politics.

Robb was probably first introduced to the Coal Branch in 1910 when he was Dominion Land Surveyor A. L. McNaughton's packer. McNaughton at the time was at Lovett where he surveyed the coal claims there that would form the basis of the Pacific Pass mine. Robb would begin prospecting on his own and in 1918 opened up a mine at what was then called Minehead. This mine was sold several years later and was renamed the Balkan mine. By this time Robb was deeply involved in politics and headed the Edson Conservative machine that controlled local federal civil service jobs and contracts. This political connection resulted in the renaming in 1923 of the Balkan post office as Robb.

Baldy Robb, over the years, would be involved in numerous ventures; some were successful such as his sawmill operation at Oke, near the site of the present-day Coal Branch cemetery; some were failures such as his attempts to reopen the Bryan mine; and others were breathtaking in their organized duplicity such as his outfitting business where every client was guaranteed a moose. How does such a guarantee work? Very simply. Robb would take his clients into the nearby bush and over several days lead them in circles. If the client shoots a moose, fine. If not, there would be a pre-shot moose, parcelled and readied for shipment, waiting at the train station. As to whether that client actually shot the moose was a minor point, as Len Stevens explains, "He [Robb] told me: 'when I guarantee a man, I am right behind him with my own rifle and I see that he gets that moose'...If he had to shoot it himself, the man had his moose. As far as he was concerned he [the client] was quite capable of lieing [sic] about it."

The origin of the nickname "Baldy" is obscure. Baldy Robb sported a fine head of hair, which, in a typical tall tale, he attributed to the liberal use of a very special oil.

8 BRYAN MINE

MAP PAGE 50

Tracing old roadways and railbeds and finding remains of buildings and sometimes artifacts all related to now-defunct coal mining operations is always an interesting way of spending an afternoon. This easy walk or cycle ride takes you through both the old underground Bryan mine site and the more recent open pit workings of the later mine.

From your vehicle, go up the gravel road to the left of the Bryan Hotel as far as the intersection with 49 Avenue. Turn left onto the paved street and follow it to Highway #47. Cross the highway and bear a little to the right to find the OHV track at the end of the highway guard rail. Descend the embankment to a T-junction of OHV tracks. Bear right. Shortly, there will be an intersection with another OHV track on your right that leads up a slope. Ignore it

Day hiking, cycling

Rating half day

Distance 11.2 km

Level of Difficulty OHV track

Maximum Elevation 1158 m

Elevation Gain 45 m

Map 83 F/2 Foothills; 83/F3 Cadomin

Access

Park your vehicle at the Bryan Hotel in Robb. The Robb turnoff is 53 km south of Highway #16 or 9 km north of the intersection with Highway #40.

0.0 km	trailhead
0.2 km	intersection
0.5 km	Highway #47
0.6 km	OHV track
0.7 km	intersection
0.9 km	intersection
1.9 km	intersection
2.3 km	intersection
3.0 km	intersection
3.1 km	intersection
3.3 km	Hinton-Robb Road
4.8 km	intersection
4.9 km	intersection
5.0 km	Bryan mine entry
5.7 km	Bryan mine end
6.6 km	Hinton-Robb Road
8.1 km	OHV track
8.4 km	intersection
8.7 km	intersection
8.9 km	railbed
9.0 km	intersection
9.1 km	intersection
9.1 km	pits
9.3 km	intersection
11.2 km	trailhead

The Bryan mine pit.

Derelicts at the Bryan mine site (below the cyclist.)

and continue straight ahead. At another intersection with a track on the right once again stay on the main track. Within 50 m the track forks. Keep to the left to remain closer to Bryan Creek. Almost immediately you will find coal slack to the left of the track, your first indication you are entering the old Bryan mine site. Pass through a large clearing where there are small piles of coal slack on your right. At another fork continue straight ahead ignoring the track to the right. Your OHV track now crosses a rather large spread of coal slack. Where it ends is yet another intersection with an old roadway leading off to the right. The area you have been travelling through is that of the first Bryan mine site. In order to visit the later workings of the Bryan mine, keep to the left at the intersection with the old roadway and climb to the Hinton-Robb road ignoring an intersection on your left along the way.

At the Hinton-Robb highway, which is a wide, good gravel road, turn left for 1.5 km to a junction with a road on your right. Exercise caution on this stretch of your trip; the Hinton-Robb highway is a busy logging haul road and can be very dusty. At the intersection turn right onto the secondary gravel road that leads to a construction camp. En route, there is an intersection with an old roadway. Swing left onto this roadway as it leads into the Bryan mine pit. If you wish you can follow the track through the pit to its end. Looking up from the floor of the pit you can see the coal seam that led the mine operators to exploit its easy accessibility.

Return to the Hinton-Robb highway and turn left. Turn onto the old roadway at the intersection that you took from the old mine site. Descend to the second intersection. Instead of bearing to the right to repeat the first part of your trip, turn left onto the old mine road. It's a bit rough as it goes up and down since the site is becoming quite overgrown with poplar and grasses that have colonized the coal slack. At an intersection with an OHV track keep to the left. An old mine railbed now appears on your immediate left. If you wish, take it rather than continuing along the paralleling roadway. Only by being up on the railbed can you find a couple of derelict cars and a small sawdust pile that are below you on your left. You next come to a crossroads of OHV tracks. Go straight ahead to another quick intersection and turn right. This brings you alongside several subsidence pits, now heavily overgrown but nevertheless presenting a nasty surprise for anyone bungling through the poplars and shrubbery. Subsidence pits are always related to old underground mines. Over the years, the wooden mine props that held up the roof of the tunnels collapse. Without their support, the roof caves in forming sometimes massive crater-like pits on the surface.

At the next intersection turn left onto the main OHV track that led you to the Bryan mine site. Follow it back to Highway #47 and onto 49 Avenue. Turn right onto the gravel road that leads down to the Bryan Hotel and your vehicle.

Bryan/Bryan Creek

Previous name: Mile 32

Bryan and Bryan Creek take their name from the Bryan Coal Company Ltd. that started the local mine in 1924. Bryan is company President James H. Bryan. His first Coal Branch mining operation was in 1921 at Reco where he had a contract with Blackstone Coal Ltd. to operate a simple strip pit. Using only a shovel fork and wheelbarrows, Bryan removed the 5 m of cover, stripped the coal and loaded it into rail cars. Prior to going into mining, Bryan was the vice-president and general manager of Lamson & Hubbard Canadian Company Ltd., wholesale fur dealers.

Bryan was a separate mining camp less than a mile from Robb. Over time Bryan was absorbed into Robb and is today regarded as that section of Robb above the Embarras River valley.

Mile 32 is the distance count along the Coal Branch railway from Bickerdike.

No. 43. Bryan mine tipple. Courtesy University of Alberta, 79-23-4189.

9 THE BURNING PIT

MAP PAGE 50

More than one coal mine was forced to cease operations owing to fire, for once coal catches fire it is very difficult to put out. Often the fire burned for years, slowly following the seam. On this tour up the seam of the Lakeside mine you witness the results of such an underground fire—heat-scorched earth, resultant luxuriant growth, massive subsidence and, lastly, the town's attempt to prevent fire from breaking out, this time above ground.

From the Bryan Hotel, turn right onto Valley Road, a paved street that leads down toward the old Robb townsite. At the intersection with Bryan Road turn left to remain on Valley Road. Cross the railway tracks and go down the hill. Valley Road ends at the bottom of the hill at the junction of Embarras and Balkan drives. Bear left onto Embarras Drive and follow it across a yellow bridge over the

Day hiking, cycling
Rating half day
Distance 7.1 km
Level of Difficulty OHV track
Maximum Elevation 1173 m
Elevation Gain 60 m
Map 83 F/2 Foothills

Access

Park your vehicle at the Bryan Hotel in Robb. The Robb turnoff is 53 km south of Highway #16 or 9 km north of the intersection with Highway #40.

0.0 km	trailhead
0.1 km	intersection
0.6 km	intersection
0.7 km	railroad crossing
1.1 km	intersection
1.3 km	bridge
1.3 km	intersection
1.5 km	intersection
1.6 km	braid
1.7 km	braid
2.4 km	burning pit
2.5 km	cutline and intersection
3.0 km	cutline
3.3 km	bridge
3.7 km	right-of-way and cutline
4.4 km	corduroy
4.5 km	intersection
4.6 km	road
6.2 km	Embarras River
6.5 km	intersection
6.6 km	railway crossing and intersection
7.0 km	intersection
7.1 km	trailhead

Even today you can feel the heat from the underground mine fire that continues to burn slowly.

gurgling Embarras River. Just past the bridge there is an OHV track that leads off to the left. It switches up the hill past several small piles of coal slack. At a fork keep to the right as you now climb fairly steeply along the coal slack-strewn roadway. At a second fork—really a braid—it's best to keep again to the right to climb through an open poplar forest. It's a pretty trail, surrounded by poplar bush and lined with alder. You are skirting the edge of the hillside that overlooks the old Robb townsite and it is not long before several opportunities present themselves to leave the trail to peer over the edge of the cliff to take in the view below. The townsite, nearly hidden among the trees from this vantage point, nevertheless is snuggled beside the river against a backdrop of green forested hills. Within a short distance you break out of the bush and enter a wide clearing. From this point you have your best view yet of old Robb and the surrounding hills.

The OHV track swings to the left climbing away from the edge of the hillside up through the clearing. Almost immediately you notice a number of small subsidences, a sure indication you are following along a worked seam of an underground coal mine. The first subsidence pit, although not large, is interesting because of the oxidized colour of the lip of the pit. The heat from the underground fire has been so intense that the soil has turned shades of yellow and orange. Fear that the heat might cause spontaneous combustion has led to the clearing of trees and bushes along the entire seam, hence the clearing. As you proceed up the slope the number and size of the subsidence pits increase to the point where some of the larger pits are almost crater-like. At a junction with a cutline, turn right and almost immediately, left, onto an OHV track that leads alongside large subsidence pits. Take a moment to examine the pits. The first time we were here we were stunned to find luxuriant ferns, some 1.5 m high, growing at the bottom of the pits while smaller versions covered the slopes adjacent to the pits. This type of growth is quite unusual for this part of Alberta. The next year we were equally surprised to find the pits barren of large ferns; more noticeable was the "rotten egg" smell of hydrogen sulphide emitting from the pits.

Within 50 m your OHV track ends at a T-junction, a cutline. Turn left and go steeply downhill. At the bottom there is a plank "bridge" that thoughtful souls have thrown across a small stream—Hay Creek. From here the track climbs steeply to a wide cutline. Following the OHV track you turn left to continue up the cutline. Once at the top of the hill you then descend just as steeply as you climbed. The base of the hill is quite boggy but again the track has been heavily corduroyed, making your passage dry if somewhat bumpy! At a four-way intersection continue straight ahead to the gravel road that you noticed from the top of the hill. Turn left onto the wide gravel road and follow it back to Robb. Remember that this is a major logging haul road so keep well to the right. After crossing the railway tracks, turn left at the store and gas station and follow the paved street around and down to the Bryan Hotel and your vehicle.

Lady Fern

Scientific Name ~ *Athyrium filix-femina*

The lady fern is a rather showy fern with large erect fronds. In moist, warm hollows it can grow up to 2 m in height. Its leaves are lacy with a general lance shape that ends in pointed tips. The spores are long and curved, almost kidney-shaped.

Habitat The lady fern is common throughout much of western North America. It can be found from as far north as Alaska, ranging southward through British Columbia, Alberta and Montana, to as far south as New Mexico and southern California. It prefers moist semi-shaded meadows, woods and stream banks.

Uses The young curled fronds known as fiddleheads can be boiled or baked and are considered a delicacy. Natives have been known to make tea from the roots to treat a variety of conditions and ailments while tea made from the stems was drunk to ease labour pains.

A combination of heat from the underground fire and a microclimate created by the subsidence have encouraged the growth of huge ferns at the bottom of the pits.

10 THE ROBB HIGHLANDS

MAP PAGE 50

This route takes cyclists through the pretty hills that encircle Robb offering plenty of opportunity for swift descents and steep climbs.

From the Bryan Hotel take the paved street, Valley Road, that leads down the hill. At the intersection with Bryan Road turn left, keeping on Valley Road. Cross the railway tracks and follow the road as it winds down the hill. The slope on your right was the location of the Lakehead mine tipple and trestle; if you stop to snoop around the top of the hill you can find a few clues—coal slack and some concrete pilings at the edge of the slope. At the bottom of the hill the road forks. Turn left onto Embarras Drive and cross the bridge. Look sharply as soon as you gain the other side of the river; the OHV track you want is on your left just a few metres beyond the bridge. Follow it as it winds up slope. It braids a total of four times and it doesn't matter which braid you take. However, at the third braid we

Pushing our way up the first pitch.

Cycling

Rating half day

Distance 9 km

Level of Difficulty OHV track; stream crossing; short bushwhack

Maximum Elevation 1204 m

Elevation Gain 91 m

Map 83 F/2 Foothills

Access

Park your vehicle at the Bryan Hotel in Robb. The Robb turnoff is 53 km south of Highway #16 or 9 km north of the intersection with Highway #40.

0.0 km	trailhead
0.1 km	intersection
0.6 km	intersection
0.7 km	railway crossing
1.1 km	intersection
1.3 km	bridge
1.3 km	intersection
1.5 km	intersection
1.6 km	braid
1.7 km	braid
2.4 km	burning pit
2.5 km	cutline and intersection
3.0 km	cutline
3.3 km	intersection
3.4 km	intersection (right connects with cutline at 2.5 km)
4.1 km	cutline (same as at 2.5 km)
4.2 km	viewpoint
4.6 km	stream crossing
4.6 km	sour gas line right-of-way

suggest you take the right fork because it leads up over top an exposed coal seam! It was this same seam that fed first the Minehead, then the Balkan and finally the Lakeside mines between the years 1918 and 1950. After the fourth braid the trail enters the cool forest and climbs slowly. The OHV track then enters a wide cut that follows the old coal seam, winding through a number of subsidence pits. As the trail leaves the wide swath ignore a junction with a trail on your left and continue to follow the trail as far as a T-junction.

Turn right; if you go left you are on the Burning Pit trail. The track leads gently downhill. If you're cycling remember that loose branches and low lying tree branches are natural hazards of the trail. Ignore an intersection with an old track on your left and continue along the main OHV track as far as a Y-junction. Bear left and continue downhill. At the bottom of the slope where the track curves to the left a secondary track joins on the right. Ignore it, bearing to the left on the main track. It's a pretty trail as the track meanders alongside the gurgling Embarras River and if you are here in midsummer you will be passing through a carpet of buttercups, daisies and northern sweetvetch. Your track then leads up, then down and then up a steep incline that takes you above the river that is still on your right.

At a T-junction with a cutline, swing right to descend the hill. Ahead, you can see an open field, but just when you think you are about to enter the clearing, your track swings left and climbs. On top

4.8 km	intersection
5.0 km	stream crossing
5.2 km	sour gas line right-of-way and cutline
5.6 km	intersection
5.7 km	intersection
6.0 km	right-of-way
6.1 km	right-of-way
6.2 km	Embarras River
6.5 km	Highway #47
7.1 km	Mile 34 Road
7.4 km	borrow pit
8.5 km	49 Avenue
9.0 km	trailhead

The bridge over the Embarras River as seen from Lakeside mine site.

Cycling through the pretty Robb highlands.

you realize you are actually travelling along an embankment that follows the Embarras. It's a pleasing view with old cutblocks ahead and to your left and to your far right nestled in the trees you can spot a few Robb houses. From here your track goes down a long slope where at the bottom there is a stream crossing. This may be wet owing to the OHVs but it is not impassable. Up the slope you go, crossing a gas pipeline right-of-way. Pretty views of the surrounding green hills begin to open up. At the top of the hill, after having passed through poplar bush, your track swings to the right. An intersection on your left leads to a random campsite or hunter's campsite. So continue along the main track that now descends steeply. You realize you are double backing when, at the bottom of the hill, you once again cross the same stream and proceed to climb a long, steep hill. And just like the last hill you climbed and then descended you once again come out onto the pipeline right-of-way. This time, though, your track swings left onto the right-of-way following it slowly to the top of the hill. On top, a delightful view unfolds of the hills that surround Robb and Coalspur. Follow the OHV track down the slope and to the right as the pipeline right-of-way swings to the right. On a bench above the highway and railway track the OHV track switches down the embankment all the way to the Embarras River. This you must cross; it's usually fairly shallow and should not present any problems. Once on the other side of the river the track turns right eventually wandering into private property at Mile 34 of old Robb. Rather than trespassing, we suggest you follow the pipeline right-of-way across the railway track, through a willow swamp that, thankfully, is only some 30 m wide and gain the slope up to Highway #47. Turn right and follow the highway back to the main Robb turnoff and the Bryan Hotel, both of which are well signed on the highway.

Robb

Previous names: Balkan, Minehead, Cement Tunnel, Mile 33

Robb is named after Peter Addison "Baldy" Robb (1887-1955), owner of the Minehead Coal Company that started the local mine in 1918. Minehead was the railway station and was probably named after a town in Somerset, England. Cement Tunnel refers to the railway tunnel built in 1912. Balkan is named after the Balkan Coal Company Ltd. that operated the local mine for six years. The word Balkan is an allusion to the Serbo-Croat origin of the company shareholders. The Balkan post office opened in 1922 and was renamed Robb in 1923. It remained open until 1992.

The exact origin of Robb is subject to some dispute. Baldy Robb himself is quoted as saying that the community was named "after some guy down east—a politician." Be this as it may, Robb, a prominent local Conservative, lobbied the postmaster general to have the post office named after himself. The train station, however, may have been named after William Doig Robb, CNR vice president and general manager in 1922. This Robb had a precedent: his two Grand Trunk Pacific predecessors had Edson and Hinton named after themselves. At the same time, anti-Communist feeling was intense, so having the Balkan station named after a cooperative (read Communist) mine may have been too much to bear for the CN executive.

Mile 33 is the distance count along the Coal Branch railway from Bickerdike.

Old Robb today.

11 EMBARRAS LANDING

MAP PAGE 64

This loop from Robb to the old sawmill site of Embarras Landing and back takes you through pleasant scenery along the Embarras River and along some sections of the first road ever built in this part of the Coal Branch.

From the Bryan Hotel turn left onto Valley Road and climb the hill swinging past the Robb store. Turn right onto the Erith Road and cross the railway tracks. Proceed to a crossroads. Turn left onto the gravel road, passing first the old Robb Forestry Station and then three intersections, the first being on your right and the next two on your left. It's generally a good road with a few soft spots if it has been raining recently. You realize you are on the

Cycling

Rating full day

Distance 30.9 km

Level of Difficulty highway; OHV track

Maximum Elevation 1135 m

Elevation Gain 91 m

Map 83 F/2 Foothills; 83/F7 Erith

Access

Park your vehicle at the Bryan Hotel in Robb. The Robb turnoff is 53 km south of Highway #16 or 9 km north of the intersection with Highway #40.

0.0 km	trailhead
0.1 km	intersection—Valley Road
0.5 km	railway crossing
0.5 km	intersection
0.8 km	Robb Ranger Station
0.9 km	intersection
1.3 km	intersection
1.3 km	railway crossing
1.9 km	intersection
3.4 km	gate
4.6 km	OHV track

On the flats of the Embarras River.

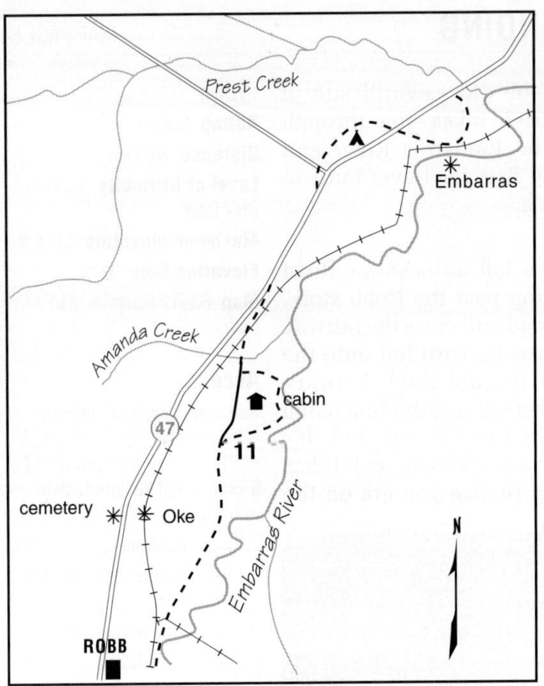

5.8 km	Embarras River meadow
6.2 km	cabin
6.5 km	begin braid
6.6 km	end braid
7.3 km	gate
7.3 km	intersection; begin braid
7.4 km	end braid; corral
7.4 km	intersection
7.5 km	road
7.7 km	Amanda Creek
8.2 km	gate
8.2 km	railway crossing
9.2 km	Highway #47
14.8 km	intersection
16.0 km	CN Embarras
16.1 km	foundation
16.4 km	intersection
17.7 km	Highway #47
19.4 km	intersection (corresponds with 14.8 km)
19.8 km	campsite
20.7 km	road
20.8 km	Highway #47
22.2 km	intersection (corresponds with 17.7 km)
26.6 km	Coal Branch cemetery
29.5 km	Robb turnoff
30.4 km	intersection
30.9 km	trailhead

old highway that runs underneath a hydro right-of-way, bypassing pasture land leased to the Robb Horse Association. At the top of a hill your progress is suddenly stayed by a barbed-wire fence across the road with a handmade sign "Horses At Large." Open the gate in the fence remembering to close it behind you. The old highway is once again running along a hydro right-of-way.

Swing right onto an OHV track that leads off to the right a short distance past the gate. You can continue straight ahead along the old highway if you wish but we think this diversion is prettier and more interesting. The track cuts down through a sand dune past stands of poplar and pine that offer cooling shade on a hot day. Your descent along this good, easy roadway is, at first, gentle then becomes steeper. The roadway then narrows to a mere track as it winds down the last pitch to the river flats of the Embarras. It's a pleasant scene with the sand hills on the opposite side of the river and the river snaking north en route to meet the McLeod at the settlement of McLeod River. Your track now swings to the left through tall grass still leading down but now gently through impressive stands of white poplar. Just past the haunting remains of a log cabin on your left you come out onto a broad meadow that is dotted with willows and more copses of white poplar. It's quite a pretty ride between the Embarras River and the sand hills on the opposite bank and the sand dune on your left. Ignore several OHV tracks that obviously lead to the river. At a Y-intersection bear left and climb up the sand dune to the top. Then descend easily through lodgepole pine forest to a T-junction at the bottom of the slope. To bear right is to return to the river, so turn left along the main track through a corral gate. Almost immediately you come to another T-junction where you want to keep once again to the left in order to return to the old highway.

Back at the old highway turn right and proceed to what appears at first to be the end of the road. It quickly becomes obvious that the railway track has bisected the old highway for you can easily see the continuation of the old highway on the side of the tracks. So drop down to your left and find the gate in the fence that allows you to cross the tracks. It can be a bit wet on the other side of the tracks for 5 m or so but as you climb back onto the old roadbed your track improves. This section of the old highway has not been travelled as frequently as the section you just completed but is still in good condition. Continue as far as Highway #47. Turn right onto the paved highway. Nearly 3 km later you come to a crossroads with a dirt track. Turn right onto what used to be the Tote Road. Once a main communication line between Edson and the coal mining communities of the East Branch, the old road now resembles a country lane. Framed by alders, the track leads down gently for a full kilometre where it ends at the railway tracks and a T-junction with an OHV track. Looking to your right you can see the Canadian National Railway's "Embarras" sign, so you know you are very close to the old sawmill site and community of Embarras Landing. To visit what remains of the landing turn left.

Within 100 m of the T-junction you come upon a foundation approximately 4.5 x 9 m of what was once a substantial building. Across the tracks an old barn that housed the sawmill's horses is still standing, now the last remaining vestige of this logging and milling enterprise. Your track joins a gravel road some 300 m later. If you turn right the road soon leads past a large informal campsite. Instead, turn left and follow the road back to Highway #47 passing an older cutblock on your left. Back at the highway turn left to begin your loop back to Robb. You can continue along the highway the entire way to Robb. We chose to trace the old Tote Road as much as possible. You can access the Tote Road 2 km up the highway at the same crossroads you took into Embarras Landing. Bear right onto the dirt track. It skirts a cutblock before dropping through poplar bush to an intersection with a good gravel road. Turn left. One hundred metres later you are back onto the highway. Turn right and proceed to the Robb cemetery, located on your right, with its coal cars at the entrance gate as a reminder of the history of the area. A brief stop here will acquaint you with some of the old Coal Branch names.

At the Robb turnoff sign bear left and follow the paved road back as far as the Robb store where you will want to turn right to continue around and down the hill to the Bryan Hotel.

Embarras River Landing

Previous names: Riviere d'Embarras (Lying-wood River), Windfall Creek, Mile 24

The Embarras River takes its name from the piles of driftwood that often clog its shallow, winding channel. It was probably named by local French-speaking Metis before being first recorded in 1859 by the Earl of Southesk. Embarras is French for barrier, which Southesk translated as lying-wood. Southesk was on a hunting expedition and chose to approach the Rocky Mountains via the Embarras. As he approached the gap through the Robb highlands, the trail became more difficult: "We crossed the Embarras no less than thirty-one times after dinner,—thirty-seven times in all during the day,—as we threaded the winding course of the river, going up its deep and narrow valley. The hills on each side were becoming steeper, higher, and more rugged, though still pine-covered to the top." From the vicinity of Coalspur, Southesk crossed back over to the McLeod and continued upstream toward present-day Cadomin.

In 1908 Dominion Land Surveyor R. V. Heathcott examined the area and translated the river's name as Windfall Creek. Mile 24 is the distance count along the Coal Branch railway from Bickerdike. The railway station was named Embarras around 1912 while Embarras Landing refers to the loading of timber onto railway cars.

Coal Branchers pronounce Embarras phonetically with the accent on either the first or second syllable.

Un embarras sur la Riviere d'Embarras.

COALSPUR

Unsigned on Highway #47, the summer village of Coalspur marks the end of paved road and the beginning of gravel for those travelling south. There are few, if any, remnants of the historic settlement remaining, most of the homes being of more recent construction. The majority of homes are prettily located alongside the Embarras River; a few are tucked beneath the Vitaly mine site on the other side of the highway. Other than the few owners relaxing in the sunshine or undertaking maintenance of their property, Coalspur is largely left to the swallows that have taken up residency underneath the highway bridge over the river.

Coalspur was never a large settlement, boasting at most 400 people. It was from here that the rail line branched, the Lovett Branch running south as far as Lovett and the West Branch veering toward the mountains to terminate at Mountain Park and Luscar. All trains stopped at Coalspur to take on water, passengers and freight. For Coal Branchers "going out" to Edson or perhaps Edmonton, the stop at Coalspur always meant a visit to Cam Matthews' hotel or the pool room to while away the time until the train was ready to pull out. From 1925 until after the Second World War, Coalspur was also the headquarters of the Brazeau Forest Reserve.

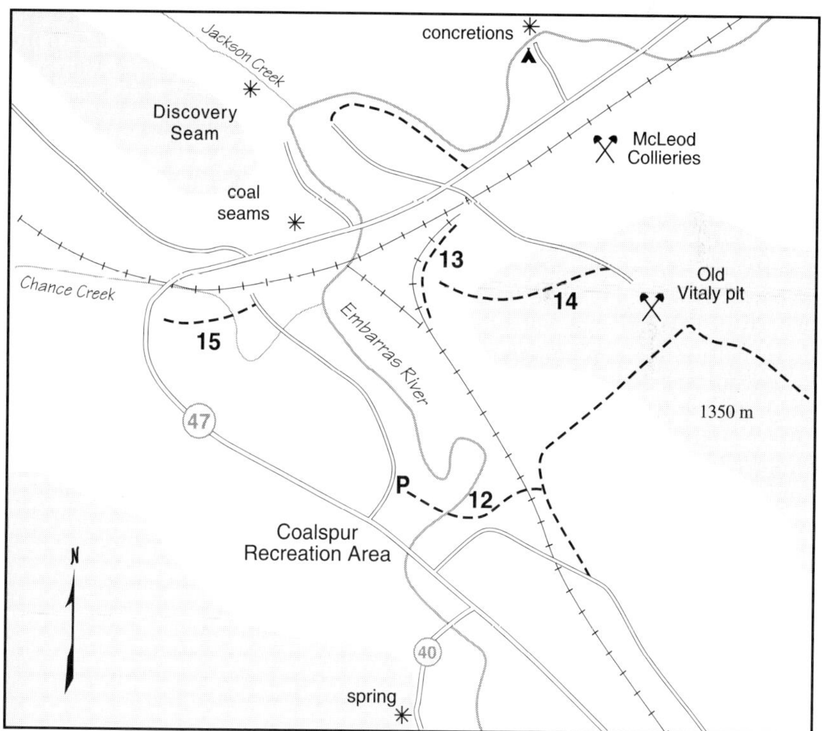

Coalspur today.

Coalspur, then, was a small but important centre. It claimed a one-room school with 32 pupils, some of whom came from as far away as Mercoal. There was Coglan's store where the miners' wives from the Yellowhead and Beacon mines could find barrels of pickles and heads of cheese, and the children could choose from different kinds of hard candy. Not large enough to support sport teams, Coalspur residents could enjoy a game of tennis on one of only three sets of courts found in the Coal Branch. Fishing and hunting were other activities that occupied spare hours during the summer months. In winter, residents hopped trains to cheer the curling or hockey teams at Sterco and Coal Valley. At least once a month, people from Robb and the Lovett Branch were welcome at Matthews' dance hall where music and liquid refreshments provided entertainment until well past midnight.

The current strip mining operation of Luscar Sterco plans to expand northward toward Coalspur. It is not expected that the hamlet will be directly impacted as the mining company will be stopping short of the Vitaly mine. The swallows will still be able to swoop and dive along the river as they have for the past 40-odd years, undisturbed by modern development.

Beacon Mines

Mine No.: #648

Owners/Operators: 1916-1921 Oliphant-Munson Collieries Ltd.; 1927-1928 Coalspur Collieries Ltd.; 1929-1930 Beacon Coal Co. Ltd.

Authorized Capital: $500,000 Oliphant-Munson Collieries Ltd.; $400,000 Beacon Coal Co. Ltd.

Coal: sub-bituminous

Registered Trade Name: Beacon Hard Coal

Market: domestic and steam

Mine Type: underground

Total Extraction: 109,000 tonnes

Men Killed: 2

Oliphant-Munson Collieries was a partnership between Captain William Oliphant and Robert H. Munson, an American lumberman and financier. Oral history relates that the partnership was formed in a New York poker game where Munson won from Oliphant shares in the mine. Broadly described, the relationship evolved into Munson providing much of the capital and Oliphant much of the management in the operation. They took over a lease formerly owned by Pacific Pass Coal Fields of Lovett and operated the mine until its closure in 1920. By then they were well underway in developing a strip mine at what came to be known as Sterco.

There were several reasons for the shift from underground to strip mining. In general, underground mines require less capital to start than strip mines but are more expensive to operate. Added to the issue of relative operating costs, the seam at Beacon started with an approximately 50° pitch, gradually increased to over 80° and got progressively dirtier as the entry was driven deeper.

Even by Coal Branch standards conditions at the mine camp were, at times, deplorable. The sanitation inspector reported filthy toilets, waste water from the kitchen running past the well, rusty kitchen utensils and bad food. In 1918, mine manager John Brownrigg and blacksmith Karl Krauze died owing to a fire and explosion. The fire had started in the mine office that was partitioned off to provide room for the daily supply of blasting powder to the miners. As the office burned, a number of detonator caps in the supply room exploded. Following the explosions and with the office burnt down, Brownrigg assumed the area was safe and organized a bucket brigade to try to save the nearby blacksmith shop that had also caught fire. As he was pouring water onto the building and with Krauze inside retrieving his bank book, what was left of the mine office exploded. Fifteen people were injured including William Oliphant Jr., son of the company president.

Following the accident Oliphant and Munson briefly attempted to reorganize the operation, but eventually chose to concentrate upon their Sterco property. Their decision to reincorporate as "The Mountain Coal Co." was blocked by the Mountain Park Coal Company on the grounds that their names would be too similar. The last two episodes were brief. Coalspur Collieries only prospected the site. Beacon Coal was a subsidiary of Sterling Collieries. Beacon's president was Robert H. Munson's son, Curtis. The arrangement was that Sterling agreed to sell a number of leases to Beacon in return for Beacon stock and a levy on all coal sold by it. Sterling "lost" on the deal since no mining work was ever done by Beacon.

Sterling shareholders did not receive a dividend in 1931.

Yellowhead

Mine No.: #220

Owners/Operators: 1910-1917 Yellowhead Pass Coal & Coke Co. Ltd.; 1917-1923 Yellowhead Coal Co.

Authorized Capital: $5,000,000 Yellowhead Pass Coal & Coke Co. Ltd.

Coal: sub-bituminous

Registered Trade Name: Yellowhead Coal

Market: domestic and steam

Mine Type: underground

Total Extraction: 315,000 tonnes

Men Killed: 6

The Yellowhead leases were first staked in 1907 and for a time were subject to a disputed claim by Pacific Pass Coal Fields of Lovett. Yellowhead Pass Coal & Coke took over the leases in 1910 and began development including the building of a 5 km spur line from Coalspur to its mine site. The first coal was shipped out via the Coal Branch railway in 1912.

The company president was Michael John O'Brien (1851-1940), a self-made millionaire who had made his fortune in the silver mines at Cobalt, Ontario, after an earlier career in lumber and railway contracting. As wealthy as he was, O'Brien could not match the business connections of his competitors at Lovett and never did arrange a long-term coal contract with the Grand Trunk Pacific Railway. The mine was never a paying proposition. Dirty seams and management conflicts bedevilled its operation. The lack of long-term coal contracts turned its production into an irregular series of rush orders broken by periods of idleness. The Grand Trunk Pacific's commitment to the Pacific Pass mine frustrated Managing Director George Henry Richardson: "As far as selling to the Grand Trunk goes, it is foolishness. They seem to take delight in

The Yellowhead Pass Coal & Coke Company, ca. 1912. Courtesy Provincial Archives of Alberta, Archives Collection A19,987.

keeping you closed down one week and over run with orders the next and are entirely unsatisfactory."

In 1915 a mine fire forced abandonment. O'Brien liquidated Yellowhead Pass but kept the leases. He then formed the Yellowhead Coal Company and renewed operations at the site. Fire broke out again in 1922 with three people killed owing to carbon monoxide poisoning. The entrance was blocked and the mine was closed pending resolution of its future. In March of the following year, camp residents were startled by a explosion that blew out the stopping and shot flames 10 m into the air from ventilation shafts along the outcrop. A cave-in inside the mine had sparked the explosion. A month later, there was still smoke coming out through holes along the ridge. The blown stopping was replaced. Facing an estimated $40,000 cost in opening a new seam beyond the fire, Yellowhead chose to abandon the mine.

The mine camp remained occupied for several years afterward. The rooming house and cafe were destroyed by fire in 1925. The Yellowhead Hotel was demolished in 1926.

McLeod Collieries

Mine No.: #339

Owners/Operators: 1912-1913 McLeod Collieries Ltd.

Authorized Capital: $100,000

Coal: bituminous

Market: domestic and steam

Mine Type: underground

Total Extraction: 5000 tonnes

Men Killed: 0

McLeod Collieries was an unsuccessful spin-off from Yellowhead Pass Coal & Coke Company Ltd. The mine was opened on leases abandoned by Yellowhead, while its principals originally were involved with that company. Two entries were driven near the base of the same hill later occupied by the Old Vitaly Pit. A short spur connected the tipple to the Coal Branch railway line at Coalspur. The operation, which was little more than a prospect, was not a success owing to faulting of the Mynheer seam and would eventually cost its owners about $40,000 before being closed.

Its owners included James A. Collins and John A. Hamilton, of Collins Brothers & Hamilton, an Edmonton based contracting firm specializing in reinforced concrete work. This company supervised the construction of the Wolf Creek and McLeod River bridges along the Grand Trunk Pacific Railway line. Collins and Charles H. Colgrove held leases along the McLeod River that in 1910 were assigned to Yellowhead Pass. The assignment process proved to be an awkward one and Colgrove was dismissed in 1911 from his position as mining engineer at Yellowhead. Colgrove would become the mining engineer at McLeod Collieries while Collins was company president. One of the directors was George B. Henwood, an Edmonton lawyer in whose name Leslie Jackson, in 1908, staked a coal claim along Chance Creek. Henwood would assign this claim to Yellowhead Pass two years later where it would become the core holding for that mining company.

Following the closing of McLeod Collieries, these men with one exception did not participate in further Coal Branch ventures. The exception was Colgrove who, in 1918, staked a small claim at Cadomin that was later taken over by the Cadomin Coal company.

Old Vitaly Pit

Mine No.: #1692

Owners/Operators: 1945-1953 King Coal & Lumber Co. Ltd.; 1951-1952 Long Coal Co.; 1960-1961 Blackstone Collieries Ltd.; 1961-1962 Coalspur Collieries Ltd.; 1962-1963 McLeod River Hard Coal Co. Ltd.; 1963 King Coal (1963) Ltd.; 1964 Earl Braun Ltd.; 1965 Coleman Collieries Ltd.; 1965 Mike Vitaly; 1968-1970 Foothill Coal Co.; 1970-1971 Coalspur Coal Co.

Authorized Capital: $20,000 King Coal & Lumber Co. Ltd.; $20,000 McLeod River Hard Coal Co. Ltd.; $1,210,000 Coleman Collieries Ltd.

Coal: sub-bituminous

Registered Trade Name: King Coal

Market: domestic

Mine Type: underground; strip pit

Total Extraction: 29,000 tonnes

Men Killed: 0

The tipple at the Old Vitaly mine site, 1966. Courtesy Provincial Archives of Alberta, Public Affairs Collection, PA3464/1.

The Old Vitaly pit is named after Mike Louis Vitaly (1893-?) who was involved with every company except King Coal & Lumber, McLeod River Hard Coal, King Coal (1963) and Coleman Collieries, that operated this mine. Vitaly was born in Italy and worked as a miner in Mountain Park and Lovett before becoming involved in over a dozen mining ventures in different parts of the Coal Branch and Alberta.

Faulted seams, undercapitalized companies and shrinking coal markets made this mine's history a series of investments based more, at times, upon good hope than good business sense. The one company with established markets and a sound capital base, Coleman Collieries, never went further than prospecting the site. Throughout most of its working life, the mine was underground. Stripping was conducted in 1949-1950 and again during the 1960s. Underground work ended in 1963.

King Coal, owned by Harold H. Croxton and family of Edmonton, began the mine, then leased it to Long Coal and its president, Mike Vitaly, several years later. King Coal abandoned the mine site after the tipple burned down in 1952. Blackstone Collieries rebuilt the tipple in 1960 and resumed operations. Its partnership, which included Vitaly, began to dissolve, impacting operations and attracting criticism from the district mines inspector, "A stalemate in the trouble between the partners has resulted in no further improvement [in conditions] being made, with Vitaly trying to produce enough coal to meet the payroll and other costs. Whole operation generally slipshod."

Extreme winter weather conditions at the mine site on the ridge top and seasonal markets added to its woes. Significant operations ceased with McLeod River Hard Coal when they struck a fault and ran out of coal. Successive operators did not find a suitable seam and the mine site became derelict by 1969.

COALSPUR RECREATION AREA

Strategically located near the junction of Highways #40 and #47, the Coalspur Recreation Area is a convenient staging area for explorations around the summer village of Coalspur, around Robb located 6 km to the north, or for trips out of the summer village of Mercoal to the west.

All three villages—Robb, Coalspur and Mercoal—were built on coal and there is plenty of opportunity to discover for yourself the haunting memories of the various underground coal mines that dotted the area. In addition, Coalspur acts as a jumping off place for trips along old logging roads or the old gravel highway built to connect the coal towns that sprinkled the map from Robb southward to the ghost town of Lovett.

Location 8 km south of Robb on Highway #40
Facilities 8 unserviced sites, cookhouse, pump, pit toilets

"No black? Put it back." Increased access to the Coal Branch as well as oil and gas exploration have seriously reduced fish stocks. The bull trout (which is actually a char and not a trout) live in cold mountain rivers and streams where food is scarce resulting in slow maturity. For this reason and owing to the severe shrinkage of its distribution range, now restricted to the foothills and mountain regions, the province has established a "catch and release" programme of Alberta's provincial fish.

12 TOTE ROAD LOOP

MAP PAGE 67

Staying at the Coalspur Recreation Area? This route offers the perfect morning constitutional or an evening stroll after supper, taking you along parts of the old Tote Road that once connected the old Lovett Branch coal mining towns.

From the cookhouse either drop down along the campground road to the ford across the Embarras River that you will then have to ford, or turn left on Highway #40 and walk up the highway crossing the bridge and then turning left at the first road. Both accesses bring you to an OHV track that leads away from the highway and toward the railway tracks. The Embarras River meanders along on your left as the track you are following leads you through the willows. Continue along the OHV track as it now climbs up to the railway tracks. It swings to the right to parallel the track. In late summer along this part of your route northern sweetvetch has grown into thick mats of intense blue mounds. Your track soon crosses the railway tracks. If, once on the other side of the tracks, you cannot readily see the continuation of the track, move forward about 20 m where you will have no difficulty in picking it up. Bear right. It's a pretty trail, covered from early to late summer in pink and white clover, daisies and buttercups. Shortly, your grassy track ends where the old dirt Tote Road joins, swinging you away from the tracks and into the cool forest of lodgepole pine and spruce. Labrador tea, mosses and kinnikinnick form a great part of the understorey beneath the trees. Although this part of your route follows only a short segment of the old Tote Road, it helps give you a glimpse of the type of roads that the Coal Branchers used until a highway was finally built in 1941. All too soon you emerge from the forest at a T-junction with a good gravel road. Turn right. The soft rolling outline of the Robb Highlands is directly ahead. Proceed downhill, crossing the railway tracks. At the bottom of the slope there is a junction with a track. If you wish to ford the river to return to the Coalspur Recreation Area, turn right. Otherwise, continue along the gravel road as far as the junction with Highway #47 where you will want to turn right to follow it back to the main entrance of the recreation area.

Day hiking
Duration half day
Distance 1.5 km
Level of Difficulty easy walk
Maximum Elevation 1193 m
Elevation Gain 15 m
Map 83 F/3 Cadomin

Access

Park your vehicle at the Coalspur Recreation Area on Highway #47, 61 km south of the Highway #16 junction or 500 m north of the Highway #40 junction.

0.0 km	trailhead
0.1 km	Embarras River
0.1 km	intersection
0.3 km	railway track
0.5 km	old Tote Road
0.7 km	intersection
0.8 km	railway crossing
1.2 km	intersection
1.3 km	Highway #47
1.5 km	trailhead

13 COALSPUR TOWNSITE

This trip takes you back in time to when Coalspur was an important railway junction point. Here the East and West branches split, the East Branch of the railway going south to Lovett, the West Branch heading west to Mountain Park. In addition, several mining companies exploited the rich Mynheer and Val d'Or coal seams. Today a few foundations, depressions and the modern summer village of Coalspur are the reminders of the importance of this town to the entire Coal Branch.

At the Coalspur Recreation Area there is an old gravel road behind the campsites. It leads you down into the Coalspur mine site. Because there is a "No Exit" sign on the road, there is almost no traffic making this route ideal for a family bike ride. A short jaunt through the pine forest brings you to the crest of a hill where you can look down on the railway tracks and Highway #47. Part way down the hill on your right is an old foundation probably not associated with the mine but with the community of Coalspur that sprang up around the mine workings. The road swings to the left and at the bottom of the hill cross the bridge over Chance Creek. The road ends shortly in a keyhole. Find an OHV track that leads toward the railway tracks. At the tracks, turn right. Within metres you come to a Y in the tracks. Follow the right arm of the Y across the railway

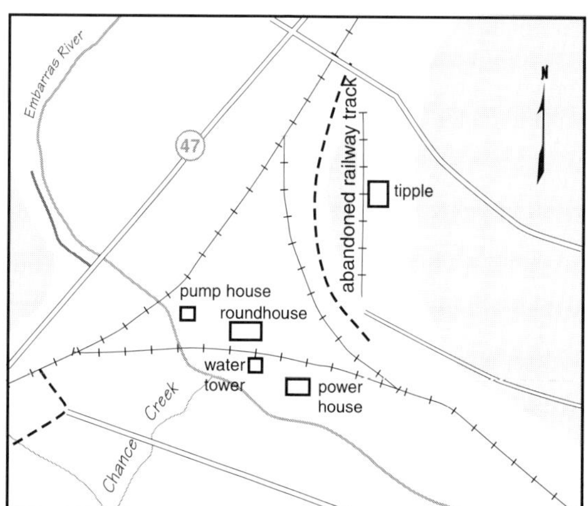

Day hiking, cycling

Rating half day

Distance 7.3 km

Level of Difficulty easy walk; some rough terrain

Maximum Elevation 1175 m

Elevation Gain 25 m

Map 83 F/3 Cadomin

Access

Park your vehicle at the Coalspur Recreation Area on Highway #47, 61 km south of the Highway #16 junction or 500 m north of the Highway #40 junction.

0.0 km	trailhead
0.8 km	foundation
1.1 km	bridge Chance Creek
1.1 km	key
1.3 km	trestle
1.5 km	foundations
1.6 km	railway fork
1.7 km	roadway
1.9 km	mine cars
2.1 km	slack pile & roadway
2.1 km	railway track
2.2 km	Highway #47
2.4 km	confluence Embarras River and Jackson Creek
2.8 km	Highway #47
2.8 km	McLeod Collieries
3.6 km	intersection
3.7 km	random campsites
3.8 km	Highway #47
5.1 km	Embarras River
5.2 km	coal seams
5.5 km	intersection
5.7 km	railway overpass
5.9 km	OHV track
6.1 km	Chance Creek
6.2 km	key
7.3 km	trailhead

The concrete foundations of the railway water tower.

bridge over the Embarras River. Poke around several concrete foundations you can find among the tall grass, on the left perhaps that of the railway repair shop and on the right those of a water tower. Cross the tracks, dip below and then up to a second set of tracks. Cross them and dip down to a field. As you cross the field toward an old mine roadway watch your footing as the tall grass conceals old railway ties and bits of metal.

Once on the road follow it past some old mine cars as far as an intersection with another dirt roadway. Turn left; to turn right takes you up a steep hill to the Old Vitaly mine. Cross the railway tracks and then the highway, dropping into the summer village of Coalspur. It's a pretty little hamlet tucked between the hills by the river. At the end of the road by the confluence of the river and Jackson Creek you can find an OHV track on your right. It swings lazily back toward the highway following the river on your left. At the highway turn left and go as far as an intersection with a dirt track on the left side of the highway. It leads down into a small random campsite by the river's edge. In the hillside on the opposite side of the river concretions protrude from the surrounding sandstone.

Return to the highway. Looking straight across and slightly up the hill you can see a small quantity of coal slack. This marks the location of McLeod Collieries, a small operation dating from the 1910s. Turn right at the highway and follow it past the summer village and across the bridge over the Embarras River. At the rock cut look up. There is no mistaking the coal seam or the signs of an old underground fire; you can still see steam rising from vents in the rocks and if you climb up the slope an acrid smell will greet you.

To return to Coalspur Recreation Area continue along the highway, crossing over the railway tracks and Chance Creek. Watch for an OHV track on the other side of the highway. It will lead you across Chance Creek to the old roadway that you took out of the recreation area.

Coalspur

Previous names: Lost Prairie, Mile 37, Mile 0

Coalspur is named after the 5 km-long spur line built along Chance Creek from the Coal Branch railway to the Yellowhead Pass Coal & Coke Company mine. The "coal spur" was first the locale's descriptive phrase that, by 1912, was condensed through common use into a locale name. The spur line was built in 1912 and was originally intended to be part of a longer branch line extending northwest along Felton Creek to the McLeod River where Yellowhead Pass held another coal lease. This property was never developed and the extended line was never built.

Lost Prairie was the name of the natural meadow along the Embarras River. This grassy area became the site of the headquarters camp for Phelan & Shirley, the railroad contractors who built both the East and West branches of the railway line. The camp soon turned into a permanent community that became the transportation hub and unofficial capital of the Coal Branch. The Brazeau Forest Reserve and the Alberta Provincial Police had their headquarters here. The local hotel was one of the first licensed hotels in the Coal Branch and was a popular watering hole for travellers as they waited for their train connection. Canadian National had its railway roundhouse and repair shops here. The Coalspur post office opened in 1914 and closed in 1967.

Mile 37 is the distance count along the Coal Branch railway from Bickerdike. With the building of the Mountain Park branch line in 1912, a second distance count from Coalspur to Mountain Park was established, hence Mile 0.

The Grand Trunk Pacific camp at Mile 37, ca. 1912. Courtesy Glenbow Archives, NA-915-27.

14 OLD VITALY PIT

MAP PAGE 67

Whether you're hiking or cycling, this short but steep loop from the Coalspur Recreation Area will invigorate you while introducing you to a small mining operation that never quite got off the ground.

From the campground turn right onto the wide, good gravel road that is Highway #47 and follow it north across the railway overpass. Pass an intersection with a gravel road on your left and continue across a bridge over the Embarras River. Approximately 500 m later, directly opposite the summer hamlet of Coalspur, there is a dirt track to your right that leads over two sets of railway tracks. On your right, at the base of the hill, there is a large pile of coal slack on your right. Make no mistake; it's a steep climb along the mine road first past another old road on your left and then a crossroads. Rounding a bend in a switchback in the road you break out of the forest and out onto the lower part of the Old Vitaly mine site.

The remains of an old wood loading chute on your right attracts you initially but the view of the Robb Highlands and the Front Ranges beyond vie

Day hiking

Rating half day

Distance 4.1 km

Level of Difficulty steep ascent and descent

Maximum Elevation 1325 m

Elevation Gain 147 m

Map 83 F/3 Cadomin; 83/F2 Foothills

Access

Park your vehicle at the Coalspur Recreation Area on Highway #47, 61 km south of the Highway #16 junction or 500 m north of the Highway #40 junction.

0.0 km	trailhead
1.1 km	bridge Chance Creek
1.1 km	key
1.3 km	trestle
1.6 km	railway fork
1.7 km	roadway

Today, Luscar Sterco is continuing to evaluate the coal seams at Coalspur.

Some small pits, slack piles and this remnant of the loading chute are the only physical reminders of the Old Vitaly pit mine.

for your attention. After exploring the lower site, continue along the mine road as it now switches to your left and climbs in a short but steep spurt to a T-junction. The road on your left leads downhill so bear to the right and climb much more slowly to the top of the mine site. This makes an excellent spot to stop and enjoy the nearly 360° panorama below you before you explore the old pit located directly below. A track leads to your right and down into the pit. In the pit, look up; you can easily see the impressive coal seam. It seems hard to believe that none of the companies involved in the Vitaly mine were able to make an economic go given the size of the seam.

Having explored the mine site, it's time to loop back to your trailhead. Continue along the old mine road that once again climbs through the forest, although not as steeply as before. In less than 1 km from the upper mine site a caterpillar track joins from your right. The track swings to your left while continuing to climb. Finally, where your track finally dips a little there is a cutline. This will lead you back toward the recreation area so turn right and head down the steep slope.

2.2 km	intersection and begin braid
2.4 km	Old Vitaly pit
2.5 km	end braid
2.6 km	viewpoint
3.1 km	cutline
3.7 km	railway track
3.8 km	OHV track
4.0 km	intersection
4.0 km	Embarras River
4.1 km	trailhead

Coal Seams

When you stand at the edge of the Old Vitaly pit you see a coal seam below you. Look west toward the railway overpass at the nearby roadside cut; there lies another seam. They belong to the Val d'Or seam and together with two other seams, the Silkstone and Mynheer, they were what created the East Coal Branch.

The Silkstone and Mynheer seams were first identified, named and mined at the Pacific Pass mine at Lovett. There, the Silkstone seam is about 5 m thick and about 35 m above the 4 m-thick Mynheer seam. The Silkstone, named after a British coal, was the first seam to be exploited at Lovett. It was heavily fractured, however, and the company turned its attention to the lower Mynheer seam.

The Mynheer at Lovett was reached via an underground mine, but at Sterco and Coal Valley something very different happened. Here, owing to folding, the Mynheer seam outcropped nearly vertically and thickened to an average width of about 75 m and depth of 50 m. This folding plus relatively little overburden allowed the two companies to operate very successful open pit mines. The fracturing mixed the coal with impurities, but after cleaning and because of the cheaper method of open pit mining, it was still a competitively priced steam coal. These were the only places the Mynheer could be worked in such a manner. An attempt at Reco failed as the seam was more fractured, thinner and covered with more overburden.

At Foothills it was again a different situation. It was an underground mine that worked the Val d'Or seam. This seam lay in line with the strata so there was less shattering and the coal could more easily be separated from any intervening clay layers. Other mines that operated in the Val d'Or seam included Bryan, Lakeside, Mercoal and Yellowhead. At Lakeside and Bryan the seams lay almost horizontal and resulted in coal blocks weighing as much as 300 kg being extracted. Special rollers were installed to crush the coal into more manageable sizes. One 600 kg monster was not crushed: it was taken from the Bryan mine and put on display at the National Museum in Ottawa.

The coal seam of Old Vitaly pit.

15 THE YELLOWHEAD PASS COAL & COKE COMPANY MAP PAGE 82

Old mine ruins are fascinating places to visit. During this trip you should be able to imagine this mine site at a time when a relatively small number of men made these hills reverberate with the sounds of sawing timbers, pounding railway spikes, dynamiting mine entries and "popping" billiard balls after a day's work. Even though the round trip is only a little more than 10 km, exploration of the site should occupy a full half day of your time.

From the campground turn right onto Highway #47 and follow it north across the railway overpass to an intersection with a gravel road on your left. This is the Yellowhead fire tower road. Turn onto this road and begin your long climb toward the fire tower. Pass an intersection with a gravel road on your left; it leads down to a block-off bridge across Chance Creek en route to a small cutblock. The

Cycling
Rating half day
Distance 12.5 km
Level of Difficulty steep descent; some bushwhacking
Maximum Elevation 1326 m
Elevation Gain 151 m
Map 83 F/3 Cadomin

Access

Park your vehicle at the Coalspur Recreation Area on Highway #47, 61 km south of Highway #16 junction or 500 m north of the Highway #40 junction.

0.0 km	trailhead
1.4 km	Yellowhead fire tower road
2.7 km	intersection
3.4 km	intersection
5.3 km	Yellowhead Pass mine site
5.6 km	cutline
6.1 km	subsidence pits
6.2 km	intersection
6.8 km	mine opening
6.9 km	tipple
7.0 km	"hotel"
7.1 km	road
7.2 km	right-of-way
12.5 km	trailhead

The concrete base is all that is left of the tipple that stretched across the valley.

next kilometre may be a bit rough especially if it has rained recently. Heavy vehicles that service and check on the sour gas wells in the area use this road regularly and they can leave deep ruts in the road surface. The first of these wells is accessed at an intersection with a road that leads off to the right. Keep to the left on the main road that improves once past this intersection. A series of long ascents followed by fun descents lead you from one hill to the next all the while climbing steadily. Approximately 2 km from the last intersection you approach a small valley that once was the scene of incredible activity, a small mining community of the Yellowhead Pass Coal & Coke Company.

Just before the bottom of the hill there is a gas line right-of-way on your right. If you wish to explore the old mine site we suggest you stop here to see all that is left of the entire mine site. Begin at the base of the right-of-way where, on the left, there is an old snow fence. Investigation reveals that it protects an old log building, now collapsed. Go up the right-of-way, following an OHV track that cuts through buttercups, white and red clover, colourful paintbrushes and dainty daisies that, in summer, fill the air with a sweet aroma. Cross a short, boggy stretch and gain the top of a low rise where you find an intersection with a cutline. To swing over to the old mine site turn left onto the cutline and climb steeply. Once on top you descend nearly as steeply. At the bottom the OHV track you have been following swings to the left, switching up a long hillside. At the top the track swings sharply to the left and crosses a "bridge" between several large subsidence pits, an indication you are directly above an old worked coal seam. Just past the subsidence pits your track forks. The well-used OHV track bears to the right. But you want to go straight ahead along an overgrown track that soon offers you a good vista on your left of the Front Ranges. From here the swath swings to the right climbing to the top of a slope. Ahead and below you

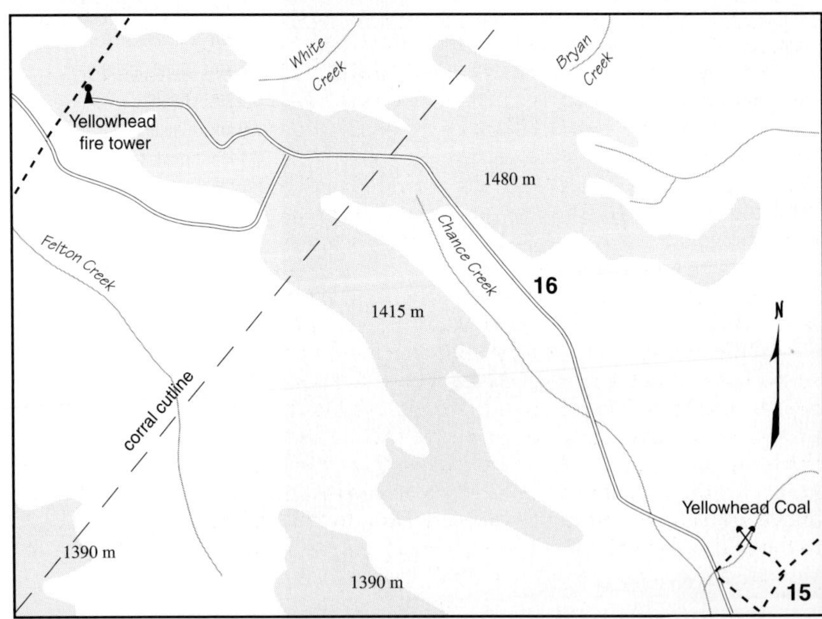

The site today as compared with that of 1912 on page 70.

can see the Yellowhead fire tower road as it snakes among the hills. Keep close to the trees on your right as you descend. It can be rather steep in places and the long grass and occasional deadfall can make your footing tricky. But it's a short descent. Suddenly you find yourself on a flat ledge overlooking the concrete remains of the Yellowhead Pass Coal & Coke Company's tipple.

The ledge you are on is actually an old railbed. If you turn left and follow it you soon pass what may have been the fan house. Located as it is near two mine entries, it was probably an extracting fan, one that sucked out foul air from the mine while fresh air was provided by means of a slope that was driven into the hill parallel to the main haulage. The railbed ends a couple hundred metres later at a collapsed mine entry. Return to the fan house and drop down the slope to the concrete remains of the tipple, crossing a small stream. After poking about the tipple turn left and walk down along what was the rail line. In summer the long grass threatens to camouflage the railbed but look for telltale coal slack and old rail ties. En route you pass an old tipple screen on your right that was used to sort the coal into different sizes. The size of the holes in this screen is fairly small suggesting it was used to sort "pea" coal. The old right-of-way leads gently down swinging a little to the left before passing a large concrete foundation on your right. The size of the foundation suggests this was once either the company hotel or boarding house for the unmarried miners. You are now in the middle of a wide field above the Yellowhead fire tower road. Drop to the road, turning left to return to the cutline where you left your bicycle. At the bottom of the hill to the left you can see wooden remains of a rail trestle.

Back at your bicycle return the way you came.

1907

It is getting crowded in the meadow along Prairie Creek where both the Brutinel and the Stanley parties are camped. Brutinel is Raymond Brutinel, a French emigre who has been hired by a Montreal-based syndicate of financiers closely connected to the Grand Trunk Pacific Railway. His job is to find mineral resources, including coal, along the line's projected corridor. He is well equipped with horses, provisions and the latest competitive intelligence his corporate clients can provide. The three Stanley brothers, in contrast, don't have such connections. They are freelancers operating on a shoestring and following a rumour. They heard there was coal along the Miette River and have gone there to look for it.

Brutinel is busy examining the nearby coal discoveries along Cold Creek where two of the claims are held by Prairie Creek's local residents, John Gregg and his trading post partner N. W. Jock. The Stanleys, meanwhile, are on their way back to Edmonton from the Miette River where they did not find any coal. Their trip is a bust. Then one evening, Brutinel's guide, William Paul, comes over to talk. William tells the Stanleys that his brother Patrick knows where there is coal and if the price is right they can lead them to it. They strike a deal and the Pauls abandon Brutinel. They lead F. Stanley to the southeast while J. N. and Oliver Stanley stay behind and wait. Brutinel in the meantime prepares to move out. He needs a guide, so he hires John Gregg and heads south to check out a series of coal claims at the head of Mackenzie Creek and the mouth of the Cardinal River. These claims are held by the Grand Trunk Pacific's competition—the Canadian Northern Railway.

Meanwhile, the Pauls show F. Stanley an exposed coal seam near the mouth of small creek. Stanley begins his prospecting and sends Patrick Paul back to Prairie Creek with coal samples. Patrick brings the two brothers back to the creek where, in July, they begin staking. Brutinel, in the meantime, via his roundabout route along the McLeod and Cardinal rivers, arrives from the south at the confluence of the Pembina and Lovett rivers. There on August 5, he stakes two claims and proceeds to further explore the area. On October 20, he stakes another claim, this one in the name of one of his employers, H. A. Lovett. With winter approaching, he and Gregg head for home moving northwest toward Coalspur.

When Brutinel reaches Coalspur he sees the Stanleys' stakes but is ignorant of a vital piece of information: the Stanleys neglect to pay their registration fee and their claims will be cancelled for nonpayment. But someone else knows. Leslie Jackson, who has been monitoring the land office in Edmonton, rushes in and on December 9, restakes the claims. The little creek soon becomes known as Jackson Creek where the original discovery seam near its mouth can still be seen today. For Brutinel, the missed opportunity at Coalspur does not matter. His stakings to the southeast are the beginnings of Lovett and the Pacific Pass mine where his interest in that venture will make him a millionaire. Jackson does not become a millionaire, but nonetheless makes some money after selling his claims that, in turn, lead to the creation of the Yellowhead Pass mine. As for the Stanleys, it was a hard luck trip to the end. They received nothing.

16 YELLOWHEAD FIRE TOWER

MAP PAGE 82

This rather lengthy bicycle trip leads you up, up, up to the Yellowhead fire tower where a visit with forestry personnel is always a pleasant experience. Instead of returning the way you came, loop back down a steep cutline for a thrill.

From the campground turn right onto the wide, good gravel road that is Highway #47 and follow it north across the railway overpass to an intersection with a gravel road on your left. Although unsigned, this is the Yellowhead fire tower road. Turn onto this gravel road to begin your long climb to the fire tower. Pass an intersection with a gravel road on the left; it leads down to a block-off bridge across Chance Creek en route to a cutblock. The Yellowhead fire tower road may be a bit rough for the first several kilometres especially if it has rained recently. The reason for this becomes clear at the next intersection with a road that leads off to

Cycling

Rating half day by bike

Distance 34.7 km

Level of Difficulty one steep descent

Maximum Elevation 1478 m

Elevation Gain 300 m

Map 83 F/3 Cadomin

Access

Park your vehicle at the Coalspur Recreation Area on Highway #47, 61 km south of the Highway #16 junction or 500 m north of the Highway #40 junction.

0.0 km	trailhead
1.4 km	Yellowhead fire tower road
2.7 km	intersection
3.4 km	intersection
5.3 km	Yellowhead Pass mine site
6.7 km	intersection
10.5 km	intersection
12.9 km	Yellowhead fire tower
12.9 km	cutline
13.2 km	begin braid
13.3 km	end braid
13.9 km	road
17.3 km	well site
20.7 km	cutline (corresponds with 13.9 km)
23.7 km	intersection
24.2 km	intersection
34.7 km	trailhead

Returning from the fire tower along a good gravel road.

the right. It was punched into the bush by oil patch companies whose heavy vehicles can churn the road into deep ruts. Keep to the left, or on the main road that improves once past this intersection. A series of long ascents followed by fun descents lead you from one hill to the next all the while climbing steadily. Approximately 2 km from the last intersection you dip into a small valley that once was the site of a bustling, if short-lived, coal mine, the Yellowhead Pass Coal & Coke Company.

The road now continues its climb, passing two intersections on the left en route to the fire tower. At both of these intersections stay on the main road. You are now only a couple of kilometres from the fire tower but if you are cycling you have a couple of long pulls to put behind you before coming out on top of the hill to arrive at the Yellowhead fire tower.

The site is fairly modest, a small residence for the seasonal staff who are here during the summer fire season and the fire tower itself. Depending on the time of day you arrive staff may be manning the tower. Unafraid of heights? Ask if you can climb the tower so you can admire the panoramic view of the 7500 sq. km that the forestry staff member oversees. You will probably be given the go-ahead and a pair of heavy gloves to protect your hands from the sharp edges of the steps. It's quite a view on top, a 360° sweep of forested foothills to the craggy peaks of the Front Ranges to the west. Back on terra firma you might ask to sign the guestbook; each fire tower and fire lookout has one. Even though the Yellowhead fire tower opened in 1956, the earliest guestbook dates to the beginning of the 1965 fire season.

To return, cyclists should locate the OHV track behind and to the right of the fire tower. Turn left onto the track for a steep but exhilarating 1 km ride to the bottom of the hill. En route you have glimpses of the Front Ranges and Mount Luscar, but you will probably be keeping your eyes glued to the ground in front of you watching for logs and loose rocks. At the bottom of the hill you come out onto a good gravel road. Turn right. Very little traffic uses this road so it is usually in excellent condition with pleasant views on your left of the surrounding rolling carpet of green forest. You wind up, down and around finally ending at a sour gas well with an old flame stack. Remember, do not go into the well site. Instead, stop outside the warning signs and take in the view before turning around for the last leg back to your trailhead. Go past the cutline that brought you out onto this road. Then ignore a road that joins on your right; it leads to another sour gas well. The next kilometre is all uphill, but then you come to a T-junction with the main Yellowhead fire tower road. Turn right for a great ride back all the way to pavement and Highway #47. Turn right and follow the highway across the bridge over the railway overpass and back to the Coalspur Recreation Area campground.

Alberta Forest Service

As early as 1882 and 1883 the federal government, recognizing the importance of the forests, established timber agents in Edmonton and Calgary respectively. After the formation of the province of Alberta in 1905 the federal government retained control over the province's natural resources including its forests. The Dominion Forestry Branch fought for and gradually won expenditures for qualified stable staff, lookouts, trails, cabins and tool caches. This growth was the result of the Forest Reserve and Parks Act that set aside 7,400,000 ha for the Rocky Mountains Forest Reserve. Ranger districts were set up in the reserve with each having a forest ranger who lived in and patrolled a district. Later, the reserve was divided into five administrative districts of which the Edson Forest is one.

On October 1, 1930, responsibility for all natural resources was transferred from Ottawa to the province of Alberta. The Alberta Forest Service (AFS) was then set up. In the late 1940s the joint federal and provincial Eastern Rockies Forest Conservation Board was established for the three forests, Crowsnest, Bow River and Clearwater. Aircraft patrol was reinstituted in 1950 and a FM radio/telephone system was installed at all fire towers and lookouts.

In response to a 1953 brief entitled "Forest Fire Protection in Alberta," the AFS was reorganized and expanded. One of the 22 recommendations in "The Fire Brief" was to build more fire towers and mountain lookouts. The Yellowhead fire tower was built in 1956.

The Yellowhead fire tower soars more than 24 m into the air.

17 BEACON MINES

MAP PAGE 92

This easy bike ride from the old railway whistle stop of Diss takes you along the Burma Road to one of the Coal Branch's earlier, smaller coal mines.

From your trailhead locate the old roadway that leads north. This is part of the Burma Road, built to link the communities of the Lovett Branch. Today, it is a rough 4 x 4 track but it is easily passable. Nevertheless, for those who worked on the road's construction, it must have been a miserable slog as muskegs and swamps plagued much of their route. This fact becomes clear where you cross a sour gas pipeline at the bottom of a hill. Swamps on either side of the roadbed necessitated the road builders to lay corduroy—logs laid side-by-side at right angles to the roadway—across the worst sections. Even now, decades after its construction, the corduroy is still doing its job of easing your passage over this perpetually wet area.

Shortly, the roadbed swings to the right, leaving the forest and paralleling the railway tracks for the next couple of kilometres. After a quick easy ride the roadbed turns to the right, away from the tracks, bringing you to the bottom of a steep pitch. The

Once, the Burma Road lived up—or down—to its name as a swampy, mosquito-infested route. Today, ditches have drained the worst of the swamps making this old road perfect for cyclists.

Cycling

Rating half day

Distance 12.2 km

Level of Difficulty old road; steep ascent and descent

Maximum Elevation 1417 m

Elevation Gain 150 m

Map 83/F2 Foothills

Access

Park your vehicle at the old locality of Diss. The turnoff is on Highway #40, 9 km south of the Coalspur Recreation Area or 8 km north of the Lovett River Recreation Area. From the highway, go 500 m, cross the railway track, then turn left onto a roadway and park in the immediate open area.

0.0 km	trailhead
0.6 km	cutline
1.4 km	intersection
1.6 km	sour gas line right-of-way
3.2 km	railway track
3.3 km	intersection
3.6 km	cutline
4.2 km	cutline
4.9 km	cutline
5.2 km	cutline
6.0 km	intersection
6.1 km	Mile 40 Creek
6.1 km	Beacon Mines
12.2 km	trailhead

Burma Road switches several times near the bottom of the hill and then climbs less sharply to the top of the ridge. The ridge is more than a kilometre long and we thoroughly enjoyed cycling this part of the trip. Four cutlines bisect the ridge; you cross the first cutline just after you gain the ridge top. The cutlines offer wonderful views to your left of layers of rolling foothills that stack up against the jagged outline of the Front Ranges. To your right you look out onto an undulating carpet of foothills' forest. At the end of the ridge there is an equally steep descent to the bottom to an intersection with another track. Keep right; the left-hand fork returns to the railway tracks. Following the track out of the forest you enter the old community of Beacon Mines.

Although Beacon Mines was never a large coal producer, there is enough physical evidence of its mining activity for you to warrant spending a little time exploring this old coal mine. Before following the road down the slope to Mile 40 Creek, you can find railway ties in the coal slack to the left of your roadway. At the creek you can find old trestle timbers half buried in the coal slack that was dumped along the creekbed. What captures your attention, though, is a large concrete pillar, tucked into the hillside slightly to your right. This is all that remains of the tipple. Nearby, adjacent to the railbed, you can find a series of concrete pads. From here turn right if you wish to follow what used to be a spur rail line; the old ties can still be seen occasionally, and always felt when cycling across them. The spur line continues a distance beyond the immediate mine site but ends in a willow swamp. Return the way you came.

Lost in Coalspur

For packer W. J. Hanlan, it was the job from hell. He was hired by Dominion Land Surveyor Albert H. Hawkins to pack in supplies while Hawkins surveyed the 13th baseline across the Coal Branch. For the next three months, in a continual rain that turned the countryside into one vast bog, Hanlan thrashed through the muskegs southeast of Edson cutting trail, moving supplies and watching his horses sicken and starve. Wrote Hawkins, "...three of our horses had died of hoof rot, which seemed to be caused by the constant travelling through mud, several others were afflicted and could take no loads, and to add to our troubles the feed was scanty and poor." Finally, on October 7, 1907, the survey reached Coalspur where the horses could recuperate in the natural meadow along the Embarras River.

There was, however, a problem. Hawkins the surveyor was lost. There was a supply cache waiting for him at Big Prairie along the McLeod River, but he thought the Embarras was the McLeod and sent Hanlan upstream looking for it. Hanlan spent eight days searching for the nonexistent cache, before returning to camp and telling Hawkins he had travelled "20 miles" and that they were on the Embarras River. Hawkins did not believe him. By now he was short of food and headed downstream to Big Eddy for provisions. As he travelled north he reached the confluence of the Embarras and McLeod rivers and saw that Hanlan was correct.

Resupplied, the survey continued west and Hanlan did not lose any more horses, though the animals remained stressed as Hawkins had not ordered any oats. By this time relations between the two men were permanently soured. Earlier, Hawkins had named Hanlan Creek after his packer. Now, near Coalspur, there are two other creek names: Lost and Dummy creeks. Whether the "lost dummy" refers to Hanlan or himself, Hawkins did not say. Regardless, they finished the season together, but in December Hawkins replaced Hanlan. Hawkins wrote that "he found a better man."

A sense of discovery is yours when you come across remnants of old abandoned mines such as this concrete pillar that once helped to support the tipple of the Beacon Mines.

Beacon Mines

Previous names: Oliphant Mines, Mile 40

Beacon Mines is named after the Beacon Hard Coal Mine, the name of the local mine, opened by Coalspur Collieries Ltd. in 1927, then taken over by the Beacon Coal Company Ltd. They abandoned it in 1930. Though the mine was closed, people continued to live at the camp for years afterward. The Beacon Mines post office opened in 1928 and did not close until 1948.

Oliphant Mines is named after Oliphant-Munson Collieries Ltd. They originally developed the property in 1916 and operated it until 1920. The Oliphant Mines post office was open from 1917 to 1919.

Oliphant is Captain William Oliphant (1850-1929). He was born in Scotland and spent his early years at sea. He settled in Canada in 1906 and became involved in mining ventures in the Coal Branch and Carbon, Alberta. He was described as a wiry old man who began each day with two fingers of Scotch—repeated liberally throughout the rest of the day. By 1922 he had sold out his interest in Sterling Collieries Ltd. and died seven years later in Victoria, B.C.

Munson is Robert Hallam Munson (1855-1943). He was born in New York state and entered the lumber business in Michigan and later via the Cowlitz Lumber Company in Washington state and British Columbia. By 1913 he began to invest in other enterprises and reportedly through a poker game won shares in Oliphant's Coal Branch venture. He died in New York City.

Mile 40 is the distance count along the East Coal Branch railway from Bickerdike.

18 THE BURMA ROAD

MAP PAGE 92

Sections of the original road that connected the mining communities of the Lovett Branch can still be found and traced almost as far as the southernmost mine at Lovett. It's an easy bike or OHV route that brings you to a viewpoint overlooking the modern workings of today's coal giant in this part of the country, Luscar Sterco's Coal Valley mine.

From the trailhead turn left onto the gravel road. It's a quick trip to the bottom of the hill where, to your left just before you cross the Erith River, you can find a random campsite. Once across the bridge you soon come to an intersection with the Burma Road on your right. Access onto this section of the road is a bit rough but once past the first 20 m it's a fairly good roadbed. Passing first a cutline and then a sour gas pipeline right-of-way, the Burma Road begins to climb, swinging to the left as it does so. At the top of a low rise the road passes a bog on its right and a series of seismic cutlines. One more cutline brings you to a Y-junction. Bear left to

Cycling

Rating full day

Distance 14 km

Level of Difficulty old road; steep ascents and descents

Maximum Elevation 1417 m

Elevation Gain 90 m

Map 83/F2 Foothills

Access

Park your vehicle at the old locality of Diss. The turnoff is on Highway #40, 9 km south of the Coalspur Recreation Area or 8 km north of the Lovett River Recreation Area. From the highway go 500 m, cross the railway track, then turn left onto a roadway and park in the immediate open area.

0.0 km trailhead

0.8 km campsite

The Sterco-Coal Valley mine at the end of the Burma Road.

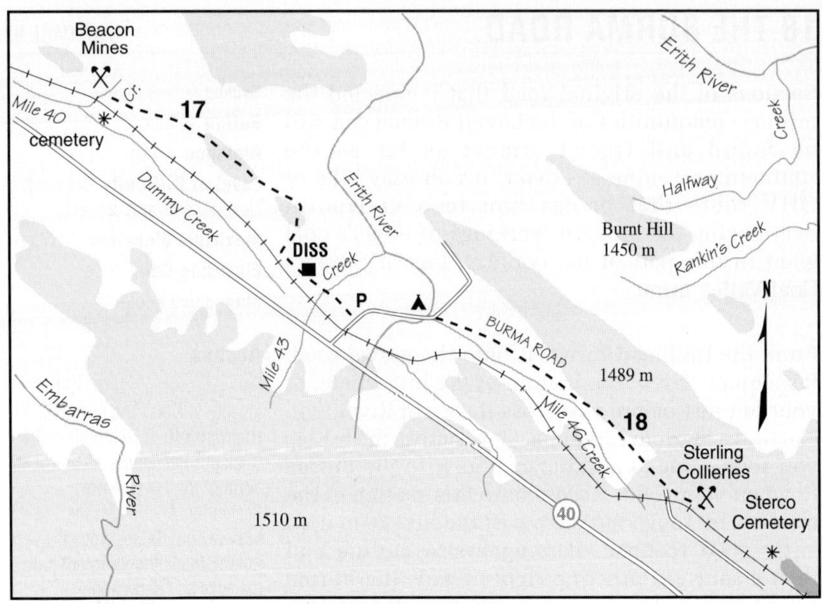

climb a short but fairly steep hill. Part way up the hill there is an intersection with a track on your left. Keep to the right; the top of the hill is straight ahead. On top, the Burma Road runs along the open ridge offering, on your right, a pleasant view of the low forested hills just beyond the railway tracks. But what catches your attention is the coal slack; it's everywhere. The Burma Road itself is made of it and piles of slack are spread over the next 500 m of ridge. An old test strip site, this section of the Burma Road appears to be destined for destruction, witnessed by the survey stakes planted by the Coal Valley mine. In case you thought you were still kilometres away from the active mine site, another 50 m along the old roadway brings you to an abrupt end to the old Burma Road. Straight ahead is one of the active pits and beyond that you can see a reclamation site. Although the last 500 m of the Burma Road may disappear, the Coal Valley mine will not be extending much farther north beyond this point; the seam that is being mined here, the Mynheer seam, is petering out making it economically unfeasible to work much past the current boundaries.

0.8 km	Erith River and Mile 46 Creek
1.0 km	intersection—Burma Road
1.7 km	cutline
2.1 km	sour gas line right-of-way
2.2 km	intersection
3.8 km	cutline
4.6 km	intersection
4.7 km	intersection
5.1 km	abandoned Sterco strip mine
5.4 km	cutline
5.6 km	Luscar-Sterco strip mine
10.2 km	return—corresponds with 1.0 km
10.8 km	intersection
11.6 km	sour gas well site and viewpoint
14.0 km	trailhead

Retrace your route back down along the Burma Road as far as the junction with the good, newer gravel road. To return the way you came bear to the left. We suggest, though, that to do so would be to miss a great viewpoint. Interested? Turn right at the intersection and climb sharply. At an intersection keep to the left, continuing to climb for another kilometre to the end of the road. Here there is a sour gas well site. Perched on the slope of the hill the site offers a wonderful panoramic sweep of the view to the west making your climb well worth the effort. This also makes a good place to rest and snack before a fun and fast ride all the way back to your trailhead at Diss, ignoring all intersections along the way.

Burma Road

Easy cycling on the Burma Road.

The Burma Road was opened in 1941, when the Mannix Company was hired to bulldoze it from Sterco to Coalspur. At the time Mannix had a stripping contract at Coal Valley so its equipment was readily available for the job. The three East Branch coal mining companies shared the cost of the fuel while $2,700 was raised by local subscription to pay for the operators' wages. The numerous swamps and muskeg holes along the route were corduroyed by local volunteer labour.

Up until then there were only two cars in the East Coal Branch and about 6 km of road between Foothills and Sterco. Both vehicles had been brought in by railway flat car. With the opening of the Burma Road, other vehicles were soon purchased and the isolation of the East Coal Branch mining communities began to end. Road conditions, especially after a rain, were terrible and travellers could expect to take up to several hours to cover the approximately 18 km to Coalspur from Sterco. Axes and tire chains were standard equipment in the motor vehicles daring to take on the Burma Road.

The original Burma Road was a Second World War project to link China to India with an access road over which war supplies could be sent. Coal Branchers quickly recognized the analogy of their own struggle to overcome their isolation with that of the Chinese and adopted the road's name. While road conditions along both Burma roads may have seemed similar at times, travellers to Coalspur at least never had to worry about Japanese air attacks.

In 1947 the Edson Seniors hockey team was forced to abandon their van on the Burma Road and walk 5 km to Sterco for a hockey game. Following the game, which ended about 10 p.m., they walked back to their van and managed the drive back to Edson where they arrived about 3:30 a.m. Gravelling and other improvements began on the road soon after it was built but it kept its original charm into the 1950s when it was incorporated into the Forestry Trunk Road system.

MERCOAL

Driving along Highway #40, it might be easy to miss the old townsite of Mercoal. This summer village is not even signed on the highway. Nevertheless, Mercoal does exist, a quiet summer village consisting of a number of cottages and homes strung along the old streets of the townsite. The stillness is broken by the occasional drone of a lawn mower. Much of the old town is left to the killdeers that swoop around Mercoal Creek where they have made their home and to the frogs that keep a noisy chorus until late into the evening.

Such an idyllic picture belies the industrial history of this town. In fact, you do not have to look far to realize Mercoal was built on coal. Coal slack is everywhere. The mine was one of the larger and more stable of the Coal Branch mines and supported a population of 1000 people in the early 1950s. By then the town claimed a 40-room hotel that had a beverage room and an 80-seat cafe. There was a grocery store or two, a drugstore that also housed the telephone exchange, a car dealership, a dry goods store, an eight-bed medical clinic under the care of a doctor and two nurses, two schools—one for grades one to three, the other for grades four to nine—a teacherage, a couple of churches, a Legion, a Bank of Nova Scotia, a community hall where movies, dances and concerts were held, a Roman Catholic church, curling and skating rinks and a baseball diamond. Unlike other mining camps, Mercoal's population was not segregated by class; its managers lived next

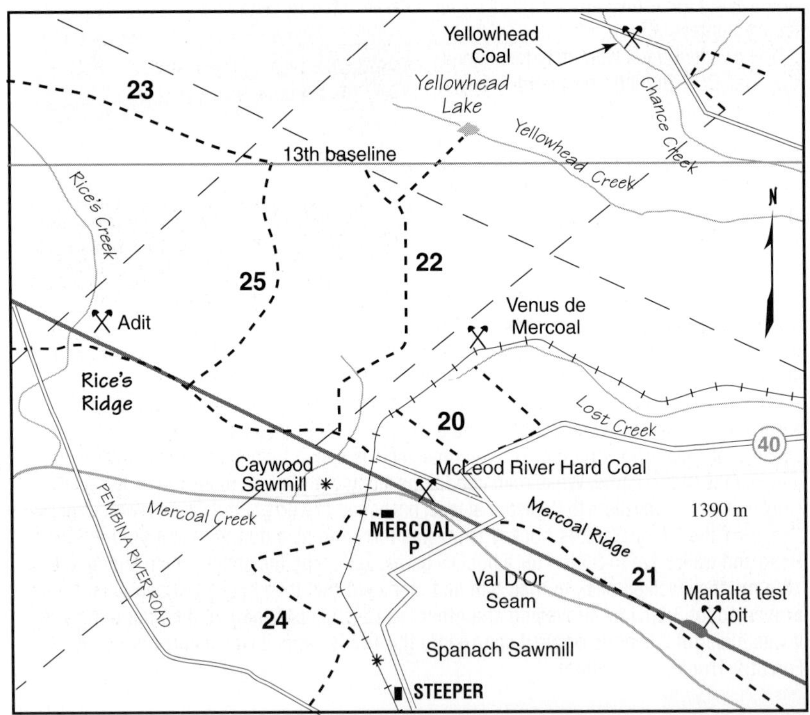

door to the timbermen and miners. On the other hand, Ukrainian workers who preferred to keep a few chickens, cows and horses lived on a hill northeast of town.

Like the other Coal Branch towns, Mercoal was a close-knit community, the members of which supported each other in times of sadness and jubilation. Support was badly needed when, in 1959, the mine closed, the last in the Coal Branch to do so. Most homes were demolished or removed to Edson or Hinton. The mine demolished its buildings and sealed the mine entrances. Only the odd home, a few foundations and a fire hydrant were proof that Mercoal once existed. Then in the 1970s, there was a brief flurry of activity and the government opened the empty lots for lease. A number of people, some from Mercoal, others not, built their summer homes here. Now a second generation of new Mercoal–ites come here each summer. But this tradition, too, is scheduled to draw to a close. The provincial government, in the late 1990s, decided not to renew the leases when the present ones expire in 2012. The present owners, like their predecessors, will have to demolish or otherwise remove their homes. This historic townsite will soon cease to exist.

Mercoal Hotel, n.d., had 13 rooms and a small beer parlour. It also served as a courthouse. Photo Amelia Spanach.

The Tackle Box

Mercoal Creek

Because of its deeply undercut banks, numerous pools and beaver dams, all of which allow fish populations to overwinter, Mercoal Creek is an excellent foothills trout stream.

Fish Management Area: #4

Species rainbow trout, eastern brook trout, whitefish, bull trout

Restrictions Use of bait fish and the collection of bait fish are allowed. All bull trout (Dolly Varden) must be released.

Season 16 June to 31 August

The remains of the mine tipple foundation.

The fire hydrant on the coal-slack bench overlooking Mercoal Creek is one of the few reminders that a substantial town and mine once occupied this area.

The Mercoal tipple, n.d.
Photo Charles Jacoby.

Mercoal

Mine No.: #846

Owners/Operators: 1920-1924 McLeod River Hard Coal Co. Ltd.; 1924-1928 Saunders Ridge Coal Co. Ltd.; 1928-1931 McLeod River Collieries Ltd.; 1932-1941 McLeod River Hard Coal Co. Ltd.; 1941-1952 McLeod River Hard Coal Co. (1941) Ltd.; 1952-1957 Canadian Collieries (Dunsmuir) Ltd.; 1957-1959 Canadian Collieries Resources Ltd.; 1963 Mercoal Collieries; 1963-1965 McLeod River Hard Coal Co.; 1965 Alberta Coal Ltd.

Authorized Capital: $20,000 McLeod River Hard Coal Co. Ltd. (Gurvich); $50,000 McLeod River Hard Coal Co. (1941) Ltd.

Coal: sub-bituminous

Registered Trade Name: McLeod River Hard Coal

Market: domestic

Mine Type: underground

Total Extraction: 4,757,000 tonnes

Men Killed: 11

Mercoal was started by Serbian miner Louis Stupar who, without the capital to develop his prospect, sold out within a year to N. Gurvich. The mine closed in 1924 owing to a strike, then was sold to Saunders Ridge Coal, mine owners at Saunders, near Nordegg. An American syndicate owned Saunders as well as another mine at Coleman in the Crowsnest Pass. In 1928 the name of their Mercoal operation was changed to McLeod River Collieries.

Conflict over certification between two rival unions, the United Mine Workers of America (UMWA) and the Mine Workers Union of Canada (MWUC), erupted at Mercoal in 1930. About 25 MWUC miners went on strike while their UMWA counterparts continued to work at the mine. The MWUC brought in protesters from neighbouring camps. The picketing developed into a number of fist fights and the company called for police to protect its UMWA workers. About 120 Alberta Provincial Police and special constables arrived in Mercoal, dispersed the outside picketers and ended the protest. The mine stayed UMWA.

The depressed coal market bankrupted McLeod River Collieries. It was taken over by McLeod River Hard Coal of Calgary. They operated the mine for 10 years before it too went bankrupt and was sold to McLeod River Hard Coal (1941), a subsidiary of Canadian Collieries (Dunsmuir) Ltd., a major B.C. mining company. Of all the companies that operated at Mercoal, this was the one that invested the most capital and extracted the most coal. The company, after several internal reorganizations and name changes, closed the mine in 1959. By this time it was the last major operator in the Coal Branch.

Fred and John Komperdo of Robb reopened the mine in 1963 as Mercoal Collieries and, with permission from Canadian Collieries, changed their name to McLeod River Hard Coal in alignment with their registered trade name. The Komperdos during this time also operated the Old Vitaly pit at Coalspur. Lack of coal markets forced the Komperdos to abandon Mercoal in 1965 and they sold their interests to Alberta Coal of Calgary.

Manalta Test Pit

Mine No.: #1799

Owners/Operators: 1965-1973 Alberta Coal Ltd.; 1973-1983 Manalta Coal Ltd.; 1983 Mercoal Minerals Ltd.

Coal: bituminous

Market: thermal

Mine Type: strip pit

Total Extraction: 18 tonnes

Men Killed: 0

The Manalta Test Pit belongs to a series of auger holes and trenches dug by Manalta Coal as it explored its coal lease in the area. The test pit was dug in 1974 and 18 tonnes of coal from the Val d'Or seam was taken out for washing and burn tests. The coal was designated a high volatile "C" bituminous coal suitable for the thermal coal export market. The explorations identified about 90 million tonnes of surface mineable coal. This followed 45 years of underground mining at Mercoal during which time about five million tonnes of coal was extracted from the Val d'Or seam.

Manalta formed Mercoal Minerals and proposed a $250 million (1981 dollars) 16-year project to produce about two million tonnes of thermal coal annually for the export market to Japan, the Pacific Rim and possibly Europe. Half of the coal would be reserved for Idemitsu Kosan Company Ltd. of Japan, the junior joint venture partner with whom Mercoal Minerals would operate the mine. Idemitsu was an energy company. Starting in the 1970s the price of oil rose steeply causing many energy companies to construct or convert to coal-fired rather than oil-fired power plants. Projections for Japanese thermal coal imports rose to over 50 million tonnes annually and Manalta was proposing two projects in the Coal Branch to tap that market. One was the Mercoal Project; the other was the McLeod River Project northwest of Mercoal.

The Mercoal and McLeod River projects would operate at the same time. The McLeod River mine, which proposed to straddle the McLeod River, was to be twice as large as the Mercoal operation and would have different joint venture participants. The projects reached the approval stage but they never went ahead. The levelling off, then drop in oil prices during the 1980s probably lowered the market projections for thermal coal causing both projects to be shelved.

Manalta is a contraction of Mannix and Alberta. Mannix Company of Calgary operated under contract during the 1940s and 1950s, stripping operations at Cadomin, Coal Valley, Kaydee, Luscar and Mountain Park. In 1953 several coal subsidiaries of Mannix were consolidated to form Alberta Coal. In 1965 they took over the lease held by the last underground operator at Mercoal, the McLeod River Hard Coal Company owned by the Komperdo brothers. The Komperdos had opened up a new entry in 1963 near the later location of the test pit.

While Manalta was unsuccessful in going ahead with its thermal coal projects, it did find success in the metallurgical market. Its Gregg River mine was a joint venture project with six Japanese steel companies and began operations in 1983.

19 MERCOAL TOWNSITE

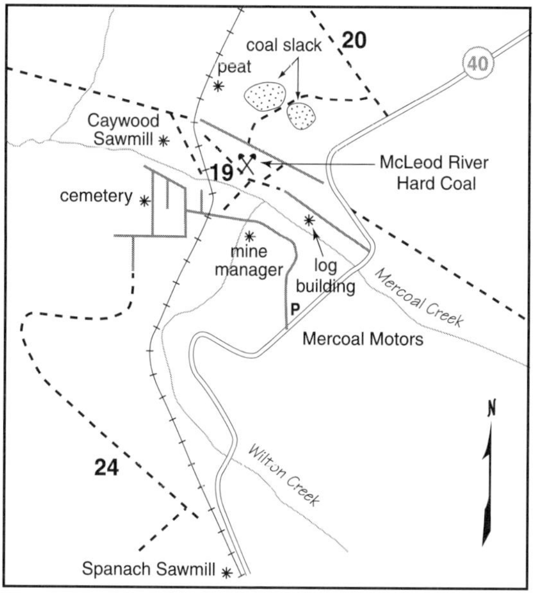

Day hiking, cycling

Rating half day

Distance 3.5 km

Level of Difficulty easy stroll

Maximum Elevation 1343 m

Elevation Gain 10 m

Map 83 F/3 Cadomin

Access

Park your vehicle at the former location of Mercoal Motors along Highway #40. The empty lot is on the north side of the highway, 50 km east of the west entrance into Mercoal. The west entrance is 7 km west of the intersection of Highways #40 and #47, or 22 km east of the intersection of Highway #40 and the Cardinal River Road.

0.0 km	trailhead
0.1 km	intersection
0.5 km	Wilton Creek
0.7 km	intersection, railway crossing, intersection
0.8 km	intersection
1.0 km	intersection
1.1 km	Mercoal cemetery
1.2 km	intersection
1.4 km	intersection
1.5 km	intersection, railway crossing, intersection

Unsigned on Highway #40 is the summer village of Mercoal, once a major coal mining town. It was also the last mine to close in the Coal Branch. This tour takes you past some of the historic landmarks of the old townsite.

Your trailhead is the former site of Mercoal Motors, a GM dealership established by local mill owner Bob Spanach. After his death, his widow, Amelia Spanach, changed the firm's name to Coal Branch Motors and continued to sell GM cars until the Mercoal mine closed in 1959. Today only the concrete foundation remains. From the site of the old car dealership find the coal-slack roadway that leads through copses of poplar trees as far as a T-junction with the west access road into Mercoal. Turn right onto this good gravel road and follow it as it winds its way past some of Mercoal's homes. Throughout this tour of the Mercoal townsite you go by a number of homes. For the most part these do not date to Mercoal's coal mining days. After the mine closed in 1959, the company demolished its buildings. With the exception of Spanach who continued to run a business out of Mercoal, private homeowners had to remove or demolish their property on orders from forestry, which feared that the abandoned buildings would be a potential fire hazard. For 15 years or so, the townsite remained largely empty, then the government decided to lease lots. Some leaseholders moved buildings in, others built on the spot. Mercoal has been a summer village since then. Recently, the leaseholders learned that their leases, which expire in 2012, will not be renewed.

On your left just prior to Wilton Creek there is an empty lot, once the site of the mine manager's home. Cross Wilton Creek and proceed up the road to the railway tracks ignoring an intersection with a track on your right. Cross the tracks and, ignoring an intersection on your right, continue to a T-junction with an old road. Turn right and follow the old street to the second intersection on your left. Situated close to this intersection was the schoolhouse and a teacherage. Turn left and walk along the roadway for 100 m where, on your right, you can find the Mercoal cemetery surrounded by a white fence.

After the closure of the mine and the removal of the homes from Mercoal the graveyard fell into disrepair. In 1975 Robb students cleaned up the area; this was repeated in 1992 by the Edson junior

1.7 km	Mercoal Creek
1.7 km	intersection
1.8 km	fire hydrant
1.8 km	foundation
2.0 km	intersection
2.0 km	railway track
2.2 km	peat fen
2.4 km	intersection
2.5 km	tipple foundations
2.5 km	intersection
2.6 km	intersection
2.7 km	intersection
2.9 km	original log building
3.2 km	Highway #40
3.3 km	Mercoal Creek
3.5 km	trailhead

Peat Fens

Many areas of the foothills and boreal forest regions of the province have poor drainage. Commonly called "muskegs," much of this poorly drained soil is actually peat lands. There are two kinds of peat lands, those comprised mainly of sphagnum moss and those comprised mainly of sedges. The peat you see along the railway tracks is of the latter composition. Peat hangs onto the water. Although many would refer to this peat land as a bog, the water you see rippling through the peat makes this area technically a fen. Unlike bogs whose moisture is fed only by precipitation, fens are fed by both surface water and precipitation and have, hence, more nutrients.

The Mercoal fen.

An unknown grave in the Mercoal cemetery.

forest wardens and the Edson Royal Canadian air cadets. Amongst the marked and unmarked graves are the resting places of three war veterans and three babies.

From the cemetery turn right and continue along the old road to an intersection where you want to turn left to loop back to the townsite. At the next intersection turn left again and within 100 m you have completed a loop. Close by were the Mercoal theatre and the Roman Catholic church and rectory. Turn right and walk to the railway tracks. The commercial hub of Mercoal was on your left on either side of the tracks. On the west side of the tracks were a dry good store, Bailey's clothing store, Conger's grocery store, another grocery store, the Mercoal cafe and a bank. At the end of the street the Spanach properties still remain on their original sites. On the other side of the tracks were a hotel, a pool hall, two stores and the mine office for McLeod River Hard Coal. Nothing remains of these buildings, some of which were quite substantial.

Once across the tracks turn left onto an OHV track that cuts across the coal-slack field. The track dips down to cross Mercoal Creek by means of a plank bridge. When you climb out of the creek you find yourself on top of a huge expanse of coal slack. Immediately, there is an intersection. Turn left onto a track and follow it past an old fire hydrant perched at the edge of the coal slack. You are now walking through the mine yard and close by you can find a concrete foundation. The OHV track swings slowly to the right to parallel the railway tracks on your left. At a T-junction with another OHV track bear left. This track will bring you down to the railway tracks. Do not cross the tracks but walk alongside them for 200 m. Here you will find a peat fen. Return to the road and climb up the roadway back to the townsite. On your right was the tipple where the coal was cleaned and sorted to size before being shipped to markets. Today only the foundation remains.

Almost immediately there is an intersection with an OHV track on your right. Turn onto the track and drop gently toward Mercoal Creek. Take an intersection with another OHV track on your left as far as a third intersection where you want to bear to the right. You are now on a roadway above Mercoal Creek that carries you past some homes. At the junction with Highway #40 turn right. Cross Mercoal Creek and within 200 m you have returned to the site of Mercoal Motors.

Coal Branchers

Louis Stupar (1892-1974)
Occupation: miner, prospector, mine owner, entrepreneur

Louis Stupar was born in Nis, Serbia, and immigrated to the United States where he found work as a coal miner in Great Falls, Montana. In 1912, with his wife Anna, he left Montana by horse and wagon and arrived in Lovett where he worked for six years at the Pacific Pass mine. His daughter Rose was born in Lovett shortly afterward and was the first non-native person born on the East Coal Branch.

Stupar was one of dozens of Coal Branch residents who as a sideline to their primary occupations prospected the area for coal. Either through luck or ability, he was more successful than most of them and eventually used his profits from his mining ventures to buy a farm and hotel at Edson. With Stephen Belkovich, in 1918, he staked what would become Foothills. Two years later he started Mercoal and in 1935, with Alex Susnar, took over the leases at Kaydee. In each case Stupar and his partner(s) would later sell their holdings to larger, highly capitalized syndicates that would more fully develop the properties. A 1939 attempt to operate the mine at Bryan in partnership with Peter "Baldy" Robb lasted less than a year.

Prospectors, such as Stupar, would look for coal outcrops along streams that cut the measures at an angle. They would do some preliminary work near the discovery seam to check whether the quality, extent and thickness of the coal seam warranted further exploration. To do this, they would trace the seam by finding other outcrops, observing the lay of the land and digging test holes. Tracing seams was, at times, an arcane art and experienced prospectors such as Stupar's partner, Alex Susnar, were reputed to have a sixth sense when it came to locating the line of coal.

Examining a prospect could take several seasons and was work a small entrepreneur such as Stupar could easily accomplish. Developing an underground mine was another matter. Yellowhead Pass managing director George Henry Richardson is instructive: it takes about three years to prove a mine and the initial costs, especially in an isolated location, are high. At Yellowhead, about $37,000 was spent in the first season (1909-1910) alone, freighting in supplies and equipment and constructing a mining camp before any work was done on the entries. Stupar learned his strategy of selling rather than developing the hard way after trying to develop his first mine at Foothills on a shoestring budget. His coal dealer disrupted his cash flow by delaying payment for the coal supplied. Meanwhile, his major creditor, the Grand Trunk Pacific Railway, upon whom he was totally dependent in shipping the coal, insisted he pay his bills. Unable to secure a line of credit, Stupar was forced to shut down operations and sell out to Winnipeg coal dealer A. E. Windatt. It is unclear whether Windatt was that same coal dealer who had delayed payment, but if so, it was a brutal leverage move on a small fish of an operator in an ocean of large sharks.

Physically, though, Stupar was no small fish. He was a well-built, imposing man with a bristling moustache and an unusual aversion: he would not have his picture taken, even by family members. This aversion probably dates from another time when he got caught in the situation of being in over his head. The conjecture is that he left Serbia in 1908, aged only 16, after becoming too involved in revolutionary politics.

20 VENUS DE MERCOAL

MAP PAGE 94

A voluptuous maid awaits you at trail's end!

From the old Mercoal Motors' site find the coal-slack roadway that leads through copses of poplar trees as far as a T-junction with the west access road into Mercoal. Turn right onto this good gravel road and follow it as it winds its way past some of the homes. Cross a small rivulet known as Wilton Creek and proceed up the road almost as far as the railway tracks. Do not cross the tracks but turn right onto an OHV track that cuts across the field. The track dips down to cross Mercoal Creek by means of a plank bridge. When you climb out of the creek you find yourself on top of a huge expanse of coal slack. Immediately there is an intersection. Keep to the right and follow the OHV track across the coal slack heading north. Ignore another intersection of tracks to continue to a T-junction with a good gravel road that is Mercoal's east access road. Turn right onto this road and follow it past a number of homes as far as Highway #40. At the highway turn left. Walk along the gravel highway for 200 m until you see an OHV track in the highway right-of-way on the left side of the road. Follow the OHV track for 1 km to a narrow cutline on your left. Turn onto the cutline as it leads into the pine and spruce forest. This cutline must be quite old for the cut itself is covered in long grasses, making for a soft underfooting. Your pleasant stroll ends abruptly, although you can see the continuation of the cut at the railway tracks below. Find a game trail that leads you down through the cut. At the bottom, hop across Lost Creek and climb up to the railway tracks. Cross the tracks and turn right. The Venus de Mercoal can be found a few hundred metres down the tracks.

We were somewhat surprised to find that the Venus is actually fairly small, having been carved into a sandstone rock adjacent to the railway tracks. Nevertheless, we found her quite charming, if somewhat worse for wear. Located several kilometres down the tracks from Mercoal, she begs a few questions. Who carved her? And why? No one seems to know for sure although it was suggested to us she was carved by the railway men of the "Blue Flea" and not by lovesick miners from

Day hiking
Rating half day
Distance 6.5 km
Level of Difficulty walk along cutlines and railway right-of-way
Maximum Elevation 1343 m
Elevation Gain 48 m
Map 83 F/3 Cadomin

Access

Park your vehicle at the former location of Mercoal Motors along Highway #40. The empty lot is on the north side of the highway, 50 m east of the west entrance into Mercoal. The west entrance is 7 km west of the intersection of Highways #40 and #47, or 22 km east of the intersection of Highway #40 and the Cardinal River Road.

0.0 km	trailhead
0.1 km	intersection
0.5 km	Wilton Creek
0.7 km	intersection
0.9 km	Mercoal Creek
0.9 km	intersection
1.1 km	intersection
1.2 km	intersection
1.5 km	Highway #40
1.7 km	OHV track along north side of highway

1.7 km	cutline
1.7 km	cutline
2.7 km	cutline
3.1 km	end cutline
3.2 km	Lost Creek
3.6 km	Venus de Mercoal
4.0 km	cutline
4.4 km	intersection
4.4 km	OHV tracks
4.9 km	cutline
4.9 km	intersection
5.0 km	coal slack
5.2 km	intersection
5.3 km	tipple foundations
5.3 km	intersection
6.5 km	trailhead

Venus de Mercoal today.

town. Perhaps the railway crews had plenty of time on their hands while in the Mercoal area and, once begun, stopped here regularly until she was finished. Interestingly, she may not have been their first attempt. On examining the rock we found another figure leaning against the rock face with its head buried in its arms. It and the Venus may have been carved by "BB" and "AP" in 1921, as the adjacent carving suggests.

To return to Mercoal walk back along the railway right-of-way past the cutline you descended to reach the tracks. Four hundred metres later you will see a trail on the left leading into the forest. Drop down, cross the little rivulet and climb the slope along the needle-strewn trail. When we were here on a hot long May weekend, patches of snow still lingered in the shadows. Almost immediately your trail is intersected by a cutline on your left. Ignore it, continuing straight ahead. Ignore as well the next intersection that will be on your right. The open forest of lodgepole pine provides welcome shade on a hot day. With its understorey of Labrador tea, the forest is a delight to walk through. In places you can still find evidence of corduroy laid over the softer, wetter spots along the trail. As you emerge from the forest you find yourself face to face with one of Mercoal's large piles of slack coal. Follow the path as it takes a 90° turn to the right around the base of the slack pile. It winds its way through two other slack piles where you can find bits left over from the town's mining days—a piece of cable here, old tires over there. At an intersection bear left. You are now back on Mercoal's east access road. Below you are the concrete remains of the tipple and the railway siding leading into the tipple site. At an intersection with an OHV track, bear right onto the track as it leads you down through the slack. Cross the plank bridge over Mercoal Creek. At the next intersection turn left onto the west access road and follow it back to the Mercoal Motors site.

Coal Branchers

Father Louis Etienne Culerier O. M. I. (1873-1946)
Occupation: Roman Catholic priest, missionary

Father Louis, as he was known, was the "Saint of the Coal Branch." He was born in Soulitre, France, and came to Canada in 1893 where he entered the Oblate novitiate and was ordained a Catholic priest in 1897. Between 1914 and 1927 he was missionary to a region served only by railroad and that stretched from Evansburg to Jasper. He wrote in his diary about his arrival in the Coal Branch, "The priest is thrown on the high road of the mission without money, without a portable chapel, without horses; he has no lodging, no church, and no means of building church or vestry: he must create everything."

The Coal Branch was at that time an isolated frontier region whose mining camps had not as yet settled into stable communities. The camps, populated mainly by single men, suffered from thievery, prostitution, alcoholism and religious indifference. Culerier, a tall, well-built and powerful man, often walked several hundred miles per month as he went from camp to camp, teaching catechisms, saying masses and performing his acts of kindness. During the 1918 influenza epidemic, he left Mountain Park one cold night and walked 33 miles along the railway track to bring a bottle of rum to a group of sick men at a sawmill; the rum, he believed, being the only sure remedy available for the flu. He described his pastoral work in a matter-of-fact way, "I stop to see families which are isolated, poor, badly housed, where the children need religious instruction. I say mass on a kitchen table, on a sewing machine, with no liturgical pomp. I meet families which are very good, very Christian and very poor, in the backwoods."

Culerier was one of several missionaries and volunteers who served the railway, mining and lumber camps west of Edmonton. These included the Salvation Army, Frontier College and various churches. The services offered to these isolated communities included reading camps, schools and religious instruction. Rev. G. S. Provis of the Anglican Western Canada Mission officiated at the first Coal Branch wedding in early 1913. The marriage took place near the end of steel, probably Lovett, between a Finn and a Swede with Provis communicating via an interpreter. The tiny congregation present improvised their inability to sing any hymns by playing a gramophone recording of "Has anyone seen my Kelly?"

In the 1917 provincial election, a Coal Branch Methodist missionary, Rev. W. H. Irwin, decided to attack the twin evils of alcoholism and machine politics by running for office. His charges against Peter "Baldy" Robb of political cronyism had some support amongst the Liberals (Robb was a Conservative) in the area. Irwin's assault against alcohol, however, alienated his political flock and he was forced to withdraw from the campaign.

Culerier stayed away from such political activism. With immense physical effort, persistence and endless goodwill he slowly developed a following and eventually built churches in Cadomin, Luscar, Mountain Park, Brule, Pocahontas and Jasper before leaving in 1927. The image he left among Coal Branchers was of the "good father" walking along the railroad track carrying a suitcase on his back and a sack on his chest; the two were attached by straps that ran across his shoulders. This improvised backpack contained a portable altar, religious effects and personal belongings. It weighed, according to Culerier, 34 kg.

21 MANALTA TEST PIT

MAP PAGE 94

This easy walk or bicycle ride takes you along Mercoal Ridge where two companies tried to mine the rich Val d'Or seam. One company tried to underground mine while, 10 years later, another company dug a test pit with an eye to surface mining.

Day hiking, cycling
Rating half day
Distance 14.6 km
Level of Difficulty old road
Maximum Elevation 1417 m
Elevation Gain 75 m
Map 83 F/3 Cadomin

A coal slack-strewn roadway behind the former site of Mercoal Motors winds through copses of poplar trees to a junction with the west access road into Mercoal. Turn right onto the access road. A brief stroll through the outskirts of the summer village brings you to Wilton Creek. Continue along the main road nearly as far as the railway tracks. Just before the railway crossing there is an OHV track that leads to the right. Follow it down the slope to a plank bridge over Mercoal Creek. Climbing out of the creek you arrive on top of a wide expanse of coal slack. Keep to the right at an intersection of OHV tracks and follow the main track as it heads north across the slack piles. At the next intersection of tracks continue straight ahead and up slope to a gravel roadway and house. Turn right onto this, Mercoal's east access road. Follow

Access

Park your vehicle at the former location of Mercoal Motors along Highway #40. The empty lot is on the north side of the highway, 50 m east of the west entrance into Mercoal. The west entrance is 7 km west of the intersection of Highways #40 and #47, or 22 km east of the intersection of Highway #40 and the Cardinal River Road.

0.0 km trailhead
0.1 km intersection
0.5 km Wilton Creek
0.7 km intersection

All that remains of the 1963 McLeod River Hard Coal Company's hoist house.

it as far as Highway #40. Cross the highway moving slightly to the right to an old roadway marked by a bright orange arrow nailed to a tree on the left.

It's always interesting and fun to poke about ruins and here, right at the intersection just behind the orange arrow, you can walk around the remnants of a log house. Scattered among the Labrador tea that makes up much of the forest understorey are the kind of items you might expect to find associated with a residence—an old coffee pot, pieces of a wood stove, a wash basin, tin cans. Who lived here? We don't know. Only these few artifacts tell us that someone once called this log shack home.

The coal slack-covered roadway takes you into the bush. Ignore a cutline on your left and continue as far as a T-junction. Turn left. Your road soon bisects a gas pipeline right-of-way. When crossing this clearing, you can catch a glimpse of the snowcaps of the Front Ranges on your right. Continue straight ahead. Within a few hundred metres you come to an intersection with a cutline on your left and a powerline right-of-way. The road now begins to lead downhill. To prevent vehicular traffic someone has thrown up a series of burms across the road; happily they do not present a serious obstacle to bicycles or OHVs. Almost immediately after crossing a small stream the roadway braids; it's best to keep to the right as you climb the hill. The braid ends at the top of the hill. Within a short distance you come to a major intersection of trails leading to both the left and the right. Turn onto the right fork. This takes you down slope to an old coal mine tipple.

Mine-run coal was sorted and cleaned in a building called a tipple. This tipple speaks to the underfunded capital of its former owners, for it was not a substantial building, being constructed only of heavy wooden timbers. Among the debris you can find screens that were used in the tipple to sort the coal according to size. Built on a steep hillside, this tipple relied on gravity to move the coal across the screens. Return uphill to the intersection. Turn right and continue along the main roadway to a cable hoist house where you can find the hoist still in place. It is located just to the one side of the top of the tipple. The hoist and the tipple both are associated with an ill-fated

0.9 km	Mercoal Creek
0.9 km	intersection
1.1 km	intersection
1.2 km	intersection
1.5 km	Highway #40
1.8 km	intersection
2.1 km	gas line right-of-way
2.5 km	power line right-of-way
3.3 km	stream crossing
3.3 km	begin braid
3.6 km	end braid
3.9 km	triple fork
4.0 km	tipple
4.1 km	triple fork
4.2 km	intersection
4.3 km	winch
4.4 km	intersection
4.5 km	intersection
4.6 km	Manalta test pit
4.7 km	cutline and intersection
4.9 km	cutline
5.3 km	fan house
5.6 km	cutline
6.5 km	cutline
6.9 km	Mercoal Creek
7.3 km	cutline
7.5 km	cutline; abandoned gas well site
14.6 km	trailhead

attempt in 1963 by Fred and John Komperdo of Robb who tried to resurrect coal mining in this area with an underground coal mine here on Mercoal Ridge. Two years and 8000 tons later, they were forced owing to lack of markets to sell their company, McLeod River Hard Coal, to Alberta Coal, a subsidiary of Mannix Company of Calgary.

Across the road and below you is evidence of a much more recent attempt to mine this part of Mercoal's Val d'Or seam. To see the test pit up close, backtrack to the intersection and turn right to go down slope. Turn right again at the next intersection. This track will take you along the east side of the Manalta test pit. The pit is approximately 100 m long and 35 m wide, about the size of a football field. Hoping to sell the bituminous coal for thermal markets in Japan, Manalta dug this test pit in 1974 and extracted 20,000 tonnes of coal. Although a deal had been signed with a Japanese company, the surface mine never went ahead and Manalta abandoned the test pit. The company made no attempt to reclaim the pit or reconfigure it to make it suitable for fish habitat. Over time the pit filled with surface and possibly groundwater.

At the end of the track you come to a T-junction with a cutline. Turn right to regain the road and turn left as the road leads uphill. Ignore a junction with an OHV track on your right and proceed for another 400 m. Keep a sharp eye to your right along the straightaway; you can almost miss a fan house that is tucked in amongst the small lodgepole pines and shrubbery. Today the fan house is incomplete, but when McLeod River Hard Coal built it in 1963, it would have been roofed and a large fan would have been inside its casing. The fan provided fresh air to the underground workings either by extracting foul air or pumping in fresh air.

Your road now descends a long hill. Five burms have been pushed across the road to block it to vehicular traffic and you have to clamber over two more burms on the upslope opposite. At the top of the hill there is a flat clearing to the left of the road. A cutline on the left joins the road at this point. Continue straight ahead on the roadway as it leads downhill to Mercoal Creek. As it descends, the old roadway degenerates to an OHV track. The creek area at the bottom of the slope is somewhat boggy but presents no real difficulty. The track swings to the right where it joins a cutline. Continue straight ahead and up to a clearing. To your right there is a broad field cut out of the forest. This was the site of a gas well, now long since abandoned. The view to the northwest offers fine views of the rolling hills beyond. After resting, return the way you came.

The Mannixes

In 1908, 27 year-old Frederick Stephen Mannix (1881-1951) won a bid to grade two miles (3.2 km) of Grant Trunk Pacific Railway right-of-way west of Stoney Plain. The project was a tiny one and one of a series of subcontracts let out under the auspices of Foley, Welch & Stewart, the American construction giant credited with building over 40,000 km of railway line in Canada and the United States.

Railway work was dominated by people such as the Foley brothers of Foley, Welch & Stewart or Sir Donald Mann, vice-president of the Canadian Northern Railway and a railway contractor in his own right. These powerful men and their companies would receive the contracts to clear and grade several hundred miles of railway right-of-way. They would then sublet all or some of their contracts to smaller firms who in turn might sublet it again and so on. The smallest subcontracts would be 100 foot (33 m) stretches called station work that were often awarded to nearby homesteaders seeking to build up their capital and who were at times equipped only with picks, shovels and wheelbarrows.

Mannix, with his mules and scrapers, had begun railway subcontracting in 1898. He was no station worker at the bottom of the subcontract scale, but he was leagues away from a Foley, Welch & Stewart, or even a Phelan & Shirley, the American subcontractor who built the Coal Branch railway. The railway construction boom ended by 1913 but Mannix's company continued to grow as it branched out into coal mining and heavy construction. In the Coal Branch Mannix had stripping contracts at Cadomin, Coal Valley, Kaydee, Luscar and Mountain Park. The stripping contract at Coal Valley led to another contract in 1941. That year Mannix bulldozers pushed through the Burma Road between Sterco and Coalspur. In the 1980s Mannix, through its Manalta coal company, was unsuccessful in developing two thermal coal projects near Mercoal. The Japanese metallurgical market proved to be a better investment. In a joint venture with six Japanese steel companies, Manalta opened the Gregg River mine in 1983. This surface coal mine operated for 17 years until 2000, when shortly after it had been sold to Luscar, it was closed owing to declining coal markets.

22 YELLOWHEAD LAKE

MAP PAGE 94

If you are here in the spring or summer, remember to bring a pair of binoculars with you. Yellowhead Lake is home to several breeding pairs of ducks and it's a delight to sit and watch them defend their part of the lake.

Find the coal-slack roadway behind the Mercoal Motors' site. Follow it as it winds its way through copses of poplar trees as far as the intersection with Mercoal's west access road. Turn right onto this good gravel road. It winds through part of the old town of Mercoal and crosses a tiny rivulet known as Wilton Creek. Turn right onto a coal-slack OHV track just before the railway crossing. The track crosses a field then dips down to Mercoal Creek, which you cross via a plank bridge. Upon climbing out of the creekbed you find yourself at an intersection of tracks in the slack. Turn left and follow the track as it skirts past an old fire hydrant and the concrete remains of Mercoal's coal tipple. The track you are following makes a 90° swing to the right to parallel the railway tracks on your left. At a T-junction with another track turn left and follow it down to the railway tracks. These railway tracks see at least four heavily-laden trains a day so exercise some caution before crossing them.

Ignore another track that joins on your left. Instead, continue following the main roadway as it leads westward toward the trees. The thick coal slack that makes up your roadway heads straight across a swampy area and crosses an unnamed creek by means of a rough plank bridge. Shortly afterward your road forks. Bear to the right on a well-used roadway. You have now left the swamp behind and have entered a pine forest. As you follow the main trail you either bisect cutlines or pass a number of intersections. The first cutline you bisect has a home-made sign, "Robb 6.37 m." After the "Robb intersection" there is a junction with an older track that joins your track on the left. Keep to the right. Your road now becomes a cutline. Unlike most cutlines, this one is a lovely roadway that leads gently up and then down through black spruce and pine forest. Continue past a junction with an old trail that leads off diagonally on your left. Pass three cutlines before arriving at a fourth.

Cycling
Rating half day
Distance 11.2 km
Level of Difficulty one steep descent
Maximum Elevation 1386 m
Elevation Gain 60 m
Map 83 F/3 Cadomin

Access

Park your vehicle at the former location of Mercoal Motors along Highway #40. The empty lot is on the north side of the highway, 50 m east of the west entrance into Mercoal. The west entrance is 7 km west of the intersection of Highways #40 and #47, or 22 km east of the intersection of Highway #40 and the Cardinal River Road.

0.0 km	trailhead
0.1 km	intersection
0.5 km	Wilton Creek
0.7 km	intersection
0.9 km	Mercoal Creek
0.9 km	intersection
1.2 km	intersection
1.3 km	railway crossing
1.4 km	intersection
1.5 km	bridge
1.6 km	fork
1.8 km	intersection—Robb turnoff

Here, bear to the right onto the cutline and leave the main OHV track. You remain on this cutline all the way to Yellowhead Lake. The Coal Branch is an active area with numerous cutlines, old roads and trails. It is easy to miss some of these when scooting by on either a bicycle or an OHV. You know you have missed the turnoff to Yellowhead Lake if you come to a 20 year-old cutblock and a narrowing of the main track.

Once onto the cutline, you climb lazily along a good track. En route to the lake you pass by four cutlines and cross the 13th baseline before coming to the top of a steep pitch. Here, there is another cutline on your left. Ignore it and begin your steep descent to Yellowhead Lake. Half way down the pitch you can see the glint of water through the trees at the bottom of the slope. Your track swings to left at the bottom of the hill and drops down to the lake's edge.

Yellowhead Lake is located in a tight valley surrounded by spruce and pine hills. It's a delightful spot, if not a quiet one! Breeding pairs of ducks call this lake home during the summer season and you can easily watch them across the lake. Where there are ducks, there are fish and fishermen have long come to this tiny lake to try their luck with brown trout that were stocked here in the 1930s, evidenced here and there by fishing line caught in the bushes and trees at the lake's edge. You cannot help but notice a number of dead trees half submerged in the water on the other side of the lake. This, no doubt, was caused by the dam built at the other end of the lake at the stream's outlet. This dam created Yellowhead Lake, thus making a fish stocking programme possible. If you want to take a look at the dam you will be disappointed to learn there is no trail around the lake. You can, though, get there by following a game trail that joins the roadway on the right. It leads you along the shoreline. Where the trail forks keep to the left, or as close to the lake as possible. The dam now needs a little repair and you might get a wet foot if you try to cross it!

Return the way you came.

2.2 km	intersection
2.4 km	cutline
2.6 km	intersection
2.9 km	cutline
4.0 km	intersection and cutline
4.1 km	cutline
4.3 km	cutline
4.4 km	cutline
4.7 km	cutline
4.9 km	13th baseline
5.1 km	cutline and top of slope
5.6 km	Yellowhead Lake
11.2 km	trailhead

Yellowhead Lake.

23 OLD WEST ROAD

MAP PAGE 94

This trip loops you along some of the old logging roads in the Mercoal area. These are excellent roadways, some offering terrific views of the Front Ranges.

Cycling

Rating full day

Distance 20.9 km

Level of Difficulty cutlines and logging roads

Maximum Elevation 1386 m

Elevation Gain 60 m

Map 83 F/3 Cadomin

Access

Park your vehicle at the former location of Mercoal Motors along Highway #40. The empty lot is on the north side of the highway, 50 m east of the west entrance into Mercoal. The west entrance is 7 km west of the intersection of Highways #40 and #47, or 22 km east of the intersection of Highway #40 and the Cardinal River Road.

0.0 km	trailhead
0.1 km	intersection
0.5 km	Wilton Creek
0.7 km	intersection
0.9 km	Mercoal Creek
0.9 km	intersection
1.2 km	intersection
1.3 km	railway crossing
1.3 km	intersection
1.5 km	bridge
1.6 km	fork
1.8 km	intersection—Robb turnoff
2.2 km	intersection
2.4 km	cutline
2.6 km	intersection
2.9 km	cutline
4.0 km	intersection and cutline
4.7 km	enter cutblock
5.0 km	cutline

From the old Mercoal Motors' site find the coal-slack roadway that leads through copses of poplar trees as far as a T-junction with the west access road into Mercoal. Turn right onto this good gravel road and follow it as it winds its way past some of Mercoal's homes. Cross Wilton Creek and proceed up the road almost as far as the railway tracks. Do not cross the tracks but turn right onto an OHV track that cuts across the field. The track dips down to cross Mercoal Creek by means of a plank bridge. When you climb out of the creek you find yourself on top of a huge expanse of coal slack. Immediately, there is an intersection. Turn left onto a track and follow it past an old fire hydrant perched at the edge of the coal slack on your left. The OHV track swings slowly to the right to parallel

Cycling through a cutblock en route to the Old West Road.

Try to avoid cycling through this pile! Feral stallions mark their territory by repeatedly depositing their 'buns' in the same spot.

the railway tracks on your left. At a T-junction with another OHV track bear again to the left. This track will bring you down to the railway tracks. Cross the tracks. Ignore another track that joins on your left. Instead, continue following the main roadway as it leads westward across a swampy area, a small unnamed creek and into the trees. Shortly afterward your road forks. Bear to the right on a well-used roadway. You have now left the swamp behind and have entered a pine forest. As you follow the main trail you either bisect cutlines or pass a number of intersections. The first cutline you bisect has a home-made sign, "Robb 6.37 m." After the "Robb intersection" there is a junction with an older track that joins your track on the left. Keep to the right. Your road now becomes a cutline. Unlike most cutlines, this one is a lovely roadway that leads gently up and then down through black spruce and pine forest. Continue past a junction with an old trail that leads off diagonally on your left. Pass four cutlines before entering a 20 year-old cutblock. In spring watch for clumps of dainty blue violets along the roadway. The roadway narrows as it winds through small lodgepole pine, but it soon straightens and widens. A few hundred metres into the cutblock you arrive at a cutline.

Bear left onto the cutline and proceed to a T-junction, the 13th baseline that follows a rough track at the edge of a recent cutblock. Swing left

5.5 km	intersection, 13th baseline and new cutblock
5.7 km	intersection
5.9 km	intersection
6.5 km	intersection
8.2 km	cutline
8.7 km	cutline
8.9 km	Pembina River Road
10.0 km	intersection
11.4 km	Old West Road
12.4 km	cutline
13.6 km	cutline
13.7 km	corral cutline
16.1 km	intersection and Pembina River Road
16.2 km	cutline
16.3 km	OHV track
16.7 km	Rice's Creek
17.4 km	intersection
17.6 km	cutline
18.7 km	stream crossing
19.1 km	cutline
19.2 km	cutline
19.3 km	fork
20.9 km	trailhead

onto the track and follow it as it curves to the right and up and over a low hill. One main advantage of cutblocks is the fact that they open up views. From the top of this rise you have a glorious vista of the Front Ranges marching along the horizon. Just past the top of the hill there is an intersection. If you turn left onto this track you go to Rice's Ridge. So instead, keep to the right as the track descends through the cutblock as far as a fork. Bear to the left to keep on the main track. At a T-junction bear to the left again to go down the slope through stands of young lodgepole pine and poplar. The good track and scenery make this a very pleasant trip. When we were here it had rained recently, the softer spots of the roadway capturing the tracks of a lone wolf. Ignore a series of old logging roads and cutlines that join quickly one after another, first on your right and then on your left. Straight ahead are the snowcaps of the Front Ranges. A couple hundred metres past the last cutline you arrive at the Pembina River Road. There is no mistaking this major haul route as it is a fairly wide, good gravel road. Unlike the lower section of the road, this part is of smooth gravel and without steep ditches and is not as active a haul route. Turn right onto the Pembina River Road and follow it for a full kilometre to an intersection with an old logging road that joins on your left. This pleasant roadway takes you 1.5 km through stands of poplar and pine to an intersection with the Old West Road that joins your road on the left.

The Old West Road stretches northwest from Mercoal down to the McCardell Creek area. If you keep to the right at the intersection you continue downhill along the logging road eventually ending in the swamp and confusion of rough and muddy tracks of McCardell Creek. So turn left onto the Old West Road to loop back to Mercoal. The Old West Road today remains an excellent roadway. It winds up and down bisecting two cutlines before crossing the corral cutline. From the corral cutline the Old West Road drops gently through pine, spruce and poplar forest for several kilometres to the Pembina River Road.

This lower section of the Pembina River Road is an active logging road and can be dangerous. The logging trucks tend to take the centre of the road and the steep ditches leave little manoeuvring room for anyone else. Fortunately, when you turn left onto the road you only have to travel less than 100 m to a cutline. Turn right onto the cutline. OHV tracks along the cutline swing to the right and down to Rice's Creek. This part of the track is often wet especially where it crosses the creek. Just past the creek the track climbs sharply up Rice's Ridge and then down the ridge to an intersection. Continue straight ahead; from here you can catch a glimpse of some of the rooftops of the houses in Mercoal. The OHV track swings to the right at the bottom of the slope, crosses a cutline and emerges from the forest to cross a meadow and a small creek. From there the track, now covered in old coal slack, winds up into the forest again, passing small piles of coal slack. Continue as far as an intersection. You have now looped back to the main track out of Mercoal. Swing to the right along the coal slack-strewn roadway, cross a plank bridge over a creek, cross the railway tracks and follow the track into Mercoal. Return to Mercoal Motors and your trailhead by swinging to the right at the top of the ridge, crossing Mercoal Creek. Climbing out of Mercoal Creek your OHV track parallels the railway tracks on your right as far as an intersection with Mercoal's west access road. Turn left and follow it back to your trailhead.

The Entrepreneurs

Until the late 1950s there were a number of small logging operations throughout the Coal Branch that took out timber leases to supply the many mines with props and the railway with ties. The lumber trade was divided seasonally. Winter saw the men fell trees and haul out the timbers to the various saw camps set up adjacent to their leases. Summer saw the men busy in camp cutting and planing lumber and cutting the timbers for mine props. A number of mines such as Mountain Park, Yellowhead and Lovett held their own timber rights and operated their own mills to supply the timber they needed. The Lovett sawmill, installed in 1910 before the arrival of the railway, was gasoline powered. As immediate local supplies of timber were depleted, the mining companies found it more convenient to purchase their timber rather than operate a lumber business on the side.

The search for adequate timber in the Coal Branch began around 1905 along the route of the proposed transcontinental Grand Trunk Pacific and Canadian Northern railways. The potential demand for railway ties soon expanded to mine timbers as coal leases began to appear south of the proposed railway lines. In 1908 John Gregg guided several individuals to the Cardinal River valley to investigate timber leases. By 1910 H. A. Calder of Edmonton held timber berths along the McLeod River between the Gregg River and Coalspur. Calder obtained these berths after winning in 1908 a contract to provide 300,000 railway ties for 160 km of Grand Trunk Pacific line west of the McLeod River. In 1912 the Department of the Interior established the Brazeau National Forest and the following year did a reconnaissance survey of the Coal Branch, mapping the region and evaluating its timber reserves. The survey noted that because fires had swept through the region, there were mature stands of timber only in small areas, and warned, "The demand for timber for the operation of the mines will be so large that it is doubtful if, in their present depleted condition, the forests can supply what will be required."

The survey's pessimism aside, there were enough timber berths available to support a series of entrepreneurs who supplied timbers to the local mines and ties to the railway. In the 1920s the largest operators were James M. Quigley and Duncan McPherson of the McPherson and Quigley Lumber Company, which worked along the McLeod River downstream from the current McLeod River Recreation Area. Its sawmill and camp were connected by a 17 km-long light rail spur line from Hargwen station on the Canadian National main line. At the same time Richard Caywood of the Burnt Mountain Lumber Company operated a small mill at Mercoal, P. A. "Baldy" Robb had a similar small mill near Robb while at the mouth of the Erith River, Joseph Baril had his sawmill. Meanwhile at Cadomin Richard Craig was becoming well established supplying mine timbers to the local mine.

McPherson and Quigley ceased operations in the 1930s while at Mercoal Caywood was replaced by Robert Spanach and the Spanach Lumber Company. Emil Johnson set up a sawmill and planer mill at Embarras where the E. B. Johnson & Son Lumber Company operated until about 1968 when son Darwin sold out to Dick Corser. Dick Corser's father, Art, bought out Baril around 1928 and continued operations as the Erith Lumber Company. The mill was connected to the railway at Erith station by 1.6 km of pole tow track along which ties were moved to the landing for rail shipment. Erith Lumber held timber berths along the East Branch between Erith and Lovett until 1992 when Dick Corser sold the family business to Sundance Forest Products.

Corser's sale to Sundance was part of a larger trend beginning in the 1950s when the provincial government began favouring larger operators in the allocation of timber berths at the expense of the local entrepreneurs. For similar reasons, both Dick Craig at Cadomin in 1956 and Amelia Spanach at Mercoal in 1959 gave way in favour of the larger timber lease holders such as North Western Pulp and Power in Hinton.

24 SPANACH MILL ROAD

MAP PAGE 94

This loop introduces you to the Spanachs of Mercoal and their story of fortune, misfortune and survival. You begin your trip at Mercoal Motors, formerly a GM dealership acquired and built by Bob Spanach. You also visit one of Spanach's mill sites, a planer mill at Steeper where Bob Spanach met his death.

Find the coal-slack roadway behind the old Mercoal Motors' site that leads through copses of poplar trees as far as a T-junction. This is the west access road into Mercoal. Turn right onto this good gravel road and follow it as it winds past some of Mercoal's homes. Cross Wilton Creek and proceed up the road almost as far as the railway tracks. Do not cross the tracks but turn right onto an OHV track that cuts across the field. The track dips down to cross Mercoal Creek by means of a plank bridge. When you climb out of the creek you find yourself on top of a huge expanse of coal slack. Immediately there is an intersection. Turn left onto an OHV track and follow it as it swings slowly to the right to parallel the railway tracks on your left. You climb a low rise to a T-junction. Here, bear left

Cycling
Rating half day
Distance 9.7 km
Level of Difficulty boggy area; one steep ascent
Maximum Elevation 1370 m
Elevation Gain 54 m
Map 83 F/3 Cadomin

Access

Park your vehicle at the former location of Mercoal Motors along Highway #40. The empty lot is on the north side of the highway, 50 m east of the west entrance into Mercoal. The west entrance is 7 km west of the intersection of Highways #40 and #47, or 22 km east of the intersection of Highway #40 and the Cardinal River Road.

0.0 km trailhead
0.1 km intersection
0.5 km Wilton Creek

The Spanach mill site today.

again. This track will bring you down to the railway tracks. Cross the tracks. Ignore another track that joins on your left. Instead, continue following the main roadway as it leads west across a swampy area, a small unnamed creek, and toward the trees. Shortly after reaching the trees your road forks. Keep to the left. Within a short distance you arrive at a cutline and intersection of OHV tracks. Bear left onto the cutline. The track is a little rough but manageable. You are now headed southwest through tall stands of lodgepole pine toward the McLeod River. When you arrive at Mercoal Creek the banks are too steep to negotiate so you must swing to the right to pick up the OHV ford across the creek. To get back onto the track and the cutline, once you have crossed the creek, bear left. The entire Mercoal Creek area is a little boggy but soon you are faced with a steep ascent as the cutline climbs a hill. Once on top, the cutline descends to an unnamed creek that it crosses. Another ascent, not as steep this time, and you are only a short distance from the Pembina River Road. At the road, turn left.

The Pembina River Road is a very active logging road and if you are here during the week you must exercise caution along this stretch. Also, the road is rough, with large stones. Fortunately, you only have to be on the Pembina River Road for approximately 200 m. Watch for an old road on your left leading off into the forest at your 11:00 o'clock. Once on this lovely roadway you veer away from the logging road and are surrounded by silence. Ignore an OHV track that leads off to your left and continue following the old roadway to an intersection of trails. Keep to the right, or straight ahead. Within metres you find yourself out of the forest and next to the railway tracks. Cross the tracks and turn right.

You have arrived at Steeper, once a railway whistle stop. Steeper was situated on this long field that is now bordered on the right by the railway tracks, on the left by Highway #40, and at the south end the highway bridge over the railway. Steeper was never much more than a railway siding. It was also the site of the Spanach planer mill where Bob Spanach died after his clothing caught in the machinery. To find what remains of the mill site walk through the field as it descends slightly.

0.7 km	intersection
0.9 km	Mercoal Creek
0.9 km	intersection
1.2 km	intersection
1.3 km	railway crossing
1.4 km	intersection
1.5 km	bridge
1.6 km	fork
1.8 km	intersection and cutline
2.2 km	Mercoal Creek
2.3 km	creek crossing
2.4 km	intersection and cutline
2.9 km	stream crossing
3.3 km	Pembina River Road
3.5 km	intersection
3.8 km	OHV track
5.2 km	intersection
5.2 km	intersection
5.8 km	Spanach mill site
6.4 km	intersection
7.5 km	OHV track
8.4 km	Mercoal
8.6 km	intersection
8.7 km	intersection
8.9 km	intersection
9.0 km	intersection; railway track; intersection
9.7 km	trailhead

Spanach's planer mill at Steeper operated by Vic Parenteau and Mike Marinkovich. Photo Amelia Spanach.

Several hundred metres later, above you and to your left you come to a large sawdust pile. This was only one of several mills and business enterprises undertaken and developed by Spanach until his untimely death.

To complete your loop back to Mercoal, retrace your steps to the railway tracks. Cross the tracks and return to the intersection of trails. Take the right-hand fork. The old roadway leads gently upward through an open forest, crests and then descends toward Mercoal. Ignore an OHV track on your left. For the most part it is an excellent route but occasionally, if it has been raining, you will have to navigate around a couple of large mudholes. You break out of the forest at the south end of Mercoal. A gravel street lies in front of you. Continue to the T-junction at the end, past several homes, and turn right. Continue past an OHV track that leads off to the left and follow the road as it makes a 90° turn to the left. At the next intersection, turn right. This will bring you to the railway tracks. From here continue straight ahead along the west access road all the way back to Mercoal Motors.

Coal Branchers

Amelia Spanach (b. 1926-)

Much of the history of the Coal Branch deals with the men—miners, mine managers, entrepreneurs—whose exploits built the Coal Branch. Few, though, were the women whose contributions warranted mention beyond that of a support role to their husbands. One woman who broke that mould was Amelia Spanach. At the young age of 23, with two small children, she was launched into the world of business and, for a person with minimal formal education, high finance. If there has ever been a female pioneer in a man's world, it was Amelia Spanach.

It all began on October 25, 1949. Her husband, Bob Spanach, was a well-known businessman in the lumber trade who supplied mine props for the Luscar, Mountain Park and Mercoal mines and ties for the railway. He also built and owned the Mercoal theatre, the GM dealership in Mercoal and a cafe/boarding house. From modest beginnings, his business had grown and by the 1940s he had 200 men in his employ. On that fateful day, he was driving to one of his logging camps when his vehicle became stuck. He returned to Steeper where he had a planing mill where he cut his railway ties. Starting up the machinery, he was fussing with some of the belts when his clothes became entangled. He died several hours later in an ambulance en route to Edmonton. The day of his funeral, the Mercoal mine closed in his honour.

Amelia suddenly found herself at the head of a substantial business. She and Bob had married in 1941, he 29 years of age, she 15.5 years. Until her husband's death, Amelia had been involved in the business in a modest capacity, meeting the train in Mercoal to pick up freight and spare parts for vehicles and equipment, and writing business correspondence on her husband's behalf. Bob's sudden death threw her into a turmoil. What was she to do? Much of her husband's business dealings resided in his head and he did not have a will. It would take six years for his estate to be settled, and meanwhile all his assets were frozen. She did not have the luxury of time to sort things out. The public trustee demanded she either sell his businesses or buy out her children's share of the estate. Selling was not a viable option; she was approached by a couple of prospective buyers for her husband's mine prop and railway tie contracts but the offers were too low. If she was to keep the businesses, she needed a loan.

Wedding picture of Amelia and Robert, 1941. Photo Amelia Spanach.

Bank after bank refused her. It seems hard to believe today, but in the 1950s—

and for decades afterward—banks took a patronizing view of women in business. Too, Amelia was only 23 years of age, and she had little direct knowledge of the day-to-day operations of a lumber business, to say nothing of Bob's other enterprises. In the end, it was Canadian Collieries, the mine at Mercoal, that advanced her the loan. It was not without a price, however; for years, the mine kept her contract at rock bottom prices. Getting a loan was only the first of many challenges she faced as a businesswoman. Within two weeks of her husband's funeral, Amelia lost the Mercoal theatre to fire. Then came the hassles over the GM dealership. General Motors sent a representative to Mercoal to explain to Amelia that she had to give up the dealership; she was a woman and GM flatly refused to deal with the fairer sex. Amelia didn't want to give up the dealership since Luscar, by then, had begun strip mining and the mine used the garage to service its vehicles and buy new vehicles. Her lawyer, who had urged her to keep the businesses that her husband had worked so hard to build, came to the rescue. Amelia "sold" the franchise to her husband's bookkeeper. General Motors was satisfied. But, in a separate contract, the bookkeeper acknowledged his figurehead role in Amelia's dealership.

For eight years she learned the ins and outs of the business, bidding on timber leases, establishing camps and hiring cat skinners and loggers, many of the latter being farmers from the Peace country who sought winter work in the mines or logging camps of the Coal Branch. A major contract was to supply the railway with ties. Then, in 1956, North West Pulp and Power Ltd. in Hinton obtained large timber leases. As her timber became depleted, Amelia faced a squeeze; North West had taken all remaining available land. When Amelia and the other small timber operators complained to the government, the minister for Lands and Forests declared if they couldn't make a living in the timber trade, they should raise sheep!

They say things happen in threes. In 1956 a devastating forest fire swept through the country, destroying her camps and one of her sawmills. With no insurance, Amelia was back at square one. Not all was lost, though. The mines preferred fire-killed timber for its props and of that she now had plenty. She purchased another sawmill and started over again. By now, though, only the mine at Mercoal remained. Diesel, not coal, fired the railway. Her dependency on the mines made her vulnerable to the whims of the marketplace. The mine had always placed its order for mine props for the following season in January and February of each year. Early in 1959, the mine told Amelia there would be no prop contract. Six months later, the mine closed.

But a glimmer of hope remained. Coal Valley was opening a strip mine and Amelia was promised the contract if she would upgrade her equipment. She did not hesitate. Purchasing a new fleet of bulldozers and other equipment, she moved her operations to Coal Valley. Three weeks later, the strip mine closed. The contract the mine had hoped for failed to materialize. As Amelia joked, "I've been in trouble ever since!"

Amelia and her family moved to Edmonton where she worked contracts, some for the city. Later, her son George took over and continues the family business as Spanach Construction Ltd.

25 RICE'S RIDGE

MAP PAGE 94

This trip takes you through a cool forest to a spectacular view of the mountains and the remains of a coal prospect dating from the 1930s before looping you back to Mercoal.

Cycling
Rating half day
Distance 12.3 km
Level of Difficulty cutlines and logging roads
Maximum Elevation 1386 m
Elevation Gain 60 m
Map 83 F/3 Cadomin

Access

Park your vehicle at the former location of Mercoal Motors along Highway #40. The empty lot is on the north side of the highway, 50 m east of the west entrance into Mercoal. The west entrance is 7 km west of the intersection of Highways #40 and #47, or 22 km east of the intersection of Highway #40 and the Cardinal River Road.

From the old Mercoal Motors' site find the coal-slack roadway that leads through copses of poplar trees as far as a T-junction with the west access road into Mercoal. Turn right onto this good gravel road and follow it as it winds its way past some of Mercoal's homes. Cross Wilton Creek and proceed up the road almost as far as the railway tracks. Do not cross the tracks but turn right onto an OHV track that cuts across the field. The track dips down to cross Mercoal Creek by means of a plank bridge. When you climb out of the creek you find yourself on top of a huge expanse of coal slack. Immediately there is an intersection. Turn left onto an OHV track and follow it past an old fire hydrant perched at the edge of the coal slack on your left. The track swings slowly to the right to parallel the railway tracks on your left. At a T-junction with another track bear again to the left. This track will bring you down to the railway tracks. Cross the

A view of the mountains opens when you enter a cutblock.

tracks. Ignore another track that joins on your left. Instead, continue following the main roadway as it leads westward across a swampy area, across a small unnamed creek and toward the trees. Shortly afterward your road forks. Bear to the right on a well-used roadway. You have now left the swamp behind and have entered a pine forest. As you follow the main trail you either bisect cutlines or pass a number of intersections. The first cutline you bisect has a home-made sign, "Robb 6.37 m." After the "Robb intersection" there is a junction with an older track that joins your track on the left. Keep to the right. Your road now becomes a cutline. Continue past a junction with an old trail that leads off diagonally on your left. Pass four cutlines before entering a 20 year-old cutblock. The roadway narrows as it winds through small lodgepole pine, but it soon straightens and widens. A few hundred metres into the cutblock you arrive at a cutline.

Bear left onto the cutline. You are now beginning the back side of the trip's loop. It's a short jaunt down the cut to its end and a T-junction on the 13th baseline. Here you find yourself at the edge of a much more recent cutblock. Cutblocks aren't particularly pretty, but they do open up the view and to your left you can catch a glimpse of the snowcap mountains to the west. Turn left and follow the rough track as it swings to the right and up over the brow of a low hill. What a glorious view awaits you at the top! The Front Ranges swing in a 90° arc, acting as a dramatic backdrop for the McLeod River valley below. If you look to your 2:00 o'clock you can see the Yellowhead fire tower overlooking this part of the McLeod River valley system. Just past the brow of the hill you arrive at an intersection of tracks. Make a sharp 90° turn to the left. From here you can see Rice's Ridge, a low, timbered ridge at the far end of the cutblock. The rough track takes you down along the eastern edge of the cutblock and toward the promise of even better views of the mountains. En route you pass two cutlines on your left before climbing Rice's Ridge. The top of the ridge was not logged and a stand of mature trees marks an intersection of tracks. Straight ahead the cutblock continues, opening a wonderful view of the mountains. To your left, looking down the track, you can see in the distance some of the rooftops of the houses of Mercoal. Before you complete your

0.0 km	trailhead
0.1 km	intersection
0.5 km	Wilton Creek
0.7 km	intersection
0.9 km	Mercoal Creek
0.9 km	intersection
1.2 km	intersection
1.3 km	railway crossing
1.3 km	intersection
1.5 km	bridge
1.6 km	fork
1.8 km	intersection—Robb turnoff
2.2 km	intersection
2.4 km	cutline
2.6 km	intersection
2.9 km	cutline
4.0 km	intersection and cutline
4.7 km	enter cutblock
5.0 km	cutline
5.5 km	intersection, 13th baseline and new cutblock
5.7 km	intersection
6.3 km	cutline
6.9 km	cutline
7.8 km	intersection and Rice's Ridge
7.8 km	subsidence pit
8.0 km	air shaft
8.2 km	discarded rails
8.3 km	adit
8.8 km	intersection
9.0 km	cutline
10.1 km	stream crossing
10.5 km	cutline
10.6 km	cutline
10.7 km	fork
11.0 km	fork
11.2 km	Caywood mill site
11.3 km	Mercoal Creek
11.6 km	intersection, railway crossing, intersection
12.3 km	trailhead

loop back to Mercoal, though, you will want to explore Rice's Ridge and the coal mining activity that has left visible reminders of former days.

Turn right onto a soft, old mine road as it leads up along the spine of Rice's Ridge through stands of lodgepole pine. Almost immediately on your left you can find subsidence pits where the roof of the coal mine tunnels below ground have collapsed. Beyond, peaking through the comb of pines, is the sweep of the mountains. Just past the top of the ridge where you once again enter the cutblock you come upon a very nasty air shaft on your right. Fortunately, thoughtful souls have marked the circumference of the shaft with metres of surveyor's tape to warn everyone passing by of the danger. The air shaft and subsidence you saw earlier are related to a coal mining prospect dating from the 1930s that tested the quality of coal under the ridge. It was a small prospect mine; nevertheless, fresh air was still needed for the miners and pit ponies who worked underground. They cut this shaft from the tunnel below straight up to the surface. How deep the shaft penetrates the rock is not known, but in any case do not attempt a closer look! If you want to see the mine entrance, or adit as they are sometimes called, continue along the track as it now leads down off the ridge and through the cutblock. At the bottom of the ridge the OHV track continues across a boggy stretch for several hundred metres before it ends at the Pembina River Road. Ignore it. Instead, once you reach the bottom of the ridge bear to the right where, amongst the spruce trees and willows, you can find the collapsed mine entry. If you have trouble identifying the entry look for something that looks like a small subsidence pit with cut mine timbers lying about. This unpretentious depression was the mine entry. Today it looks as though no man could walk into the mine using this entryway, so low and small it is. What you are looking at, though, is a collapsed entry that, no doubt, was much larger when it was built and in use.

To return your loop back to Mercoal, retrace your steps up and along the ridge as far as the intersection with the track that brought you to Rice's Ridge. Continue straight ahead as the rough track leads down off the end of the ridge. It winds through boggy patches before breaking out of the forest onto a wide meadow covered with dwarf birch. You know you are within striking distance of Mercoal when you see the coal slack on the track. Cross the meadow to Mercoal Creek, a small rivulet. Hop across and continue along the track as it reenters the forest. Within a short distance you cross a cutline. On your left and then on your right as well you can see piles of old coal slack, some of them covered by a thick layer of pine needles. Ignore another cutline. Within metres you come to a fork in the trail. You have now completed the loop. To return to Mercoal, bear to the right along the roadway as it crosses the unnamed creek. Go as far as an intersection on your right just before the railway tracks. Follow it down to a meadow and an old sawmill site belonging to the Caywoods of Mercoal. A large pile of sawdust and some telltale remains at the edge of Mercoal Creek are all that remain of this small mill.

Mercoal Creek is quite wide here but you can avoid getting your feet wet by walking to the left and up and over the culvert underneath the railway tracks. Climb the slope and follow the track across the railway tracks and back to Mercoal's west access road. Turn left and follow the access road back to your trailhead at the Mercoal Motors' site.

STEEPER

There is no recreation area with formal campgrounds at Steeper. But the popularity of the area is witnessed by the number of campers who with their tents, trailers and RVs occupy both sides of Highway #40 just west of the bridge over the McLeod River. There are no amenities such as toilets or pump water.

From here you can enjoy several trips that range from one hour strolls to kilometres of roadways old and new. Mercoal, with its myriad of old roads and trails, is just a short distance east on Highway #40.

Steeper random campsite.

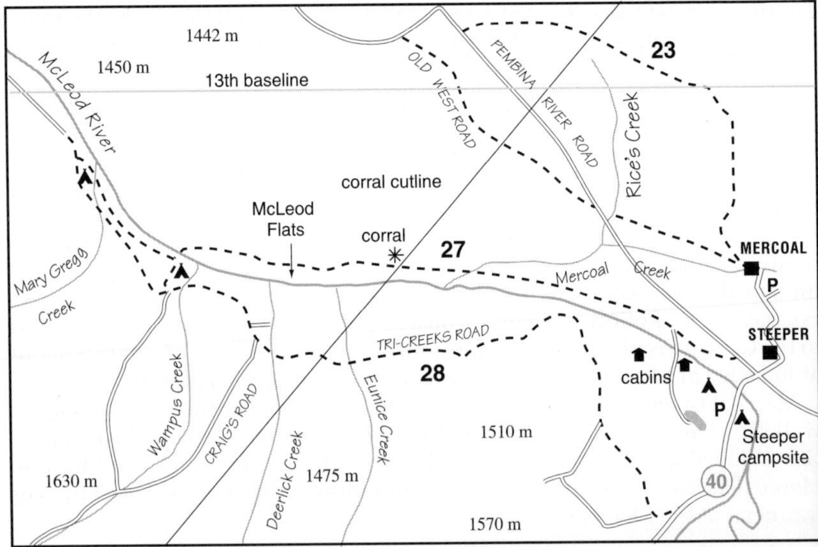

Athabasca Rainbow Trout

Scientific Name ~ *Oncorhynchus mykiss*

The Athabasca rainbow trout is the native Alberta rainbow found only in the headwaters and tributaries of the Athabasca, McLeod and Berland rivers. The introduction of rainbows from other drainages into the Athabasca basin has caused a "mixing" of the two types. Until today only the Tri-Creek area and several other streams retain the original Alberta form. The introduction of cutthroat trout has also resulted in hybridization, further threatening the native stock.

The subtle genetic divergence of the Athabasca from other rainbows probably began over 10,000 years ago when they were split from the Fraser River population during the last glaciation. Athabasca rainbows look like other rainbows except that they are smaller; often no more than 15 cm long. The size difference is owing to environmental rather than biological differences. Their uniqueness lies in their adaptation to local conditions that in some cases may be most severe.

In fact, individuals in the Eunice, Deerlick and Wampus creeks may be the slowest growing rainbow trout known in the world. Two year-old trout from Eunice Creek were found to be under 10 g in weight compared to over 100 g in two year-old specimens taken from a lake in Banff National Park. In upper Deerlick Creek the known spawning times are the latest in Alberta, beginning in late June and hatching as late as September. To test environmental differences, in 1984 and 1985 about 1500 endemic trout fry were released into the Steeper gravel pit. When caught in 1986, these fish were found to be about 2000 per cent larger than their one and two year-old Tri-Creek cousins.

Knowledge of these adaptations has been known for years, but little appreciated. A 1940's study of the McLeod River basin noted: "Rainbow trout are present in incredible numbers in every little creek and beaver dam, in the larger tributaries and in the main McLeod. The low temperature and poor food supply have converted these Rainbow into a dwarf race of absolutely no sporting value; though they mature and spawn, only a few long-lived specimens manage to achieve legal size—a noble 8 inches."

This lack of sporting value, according to the study, made the Athabasca rainbows an unwanted fish eating the food and occupying the space better reserved for arctic grayling and eastern brook trout. The study recommended restrictions on the legal length and even catch limits be removed for "McLeod Rainbows" in the hope of reducing their numbers. Eastern brook trout in the meantime would be introduced into several streams along the upper McLeod and a sports fishery established.

The advent of molecular biology has brought about a rethinking of the value of the Athabasca rainbows as well as a questioning as to what exactly is a rainbow trout. There is some evidence that rainbow, golden and even cutthroat trout are the same species. Be this as it may, the uniqueness of the native Athabasca rainbow trout has resulted in a call for their protection from other rainbow stocks and a restocking throughout their former range.

26 STEEPER CAMPSITE WALK

Day hiking, cycling
Rating one hour
Distance 3.9 km
Level of Difficulty easy stroll
Maximum Elevation 1325 m
Elevation Gain 10 m
Map 83 F/3 Cadomin

Access

Park your vehicle at the Steeper random campsite on the north side of Highway #40 by the bridge over the McLeod River. The campsite entrance is 11 km west of the intersection of Highways #40 and #47, or 18 km east of the intersection of Highway #40 and the Cardinal River Road.

0.0 km	trailhead
0.1 km	intersection
0.3 km	viewpoint first pond
0.6 km	intersection
0.9 km	second pond
1.0 km	base spit
1.2 km	end spit
1.5 km	second pond
1.7 km	intersection
1.8 km	viewpoint third pond
1.9 km	intersection
2.4 km	intersection
2.6 km	Highway #40
2.8 km	gravel pit entrance
2.9 km	intersection and fourth pond
3.3 km	intersection and base of first levee
3.4 km	end levee
3.6 km	second levee
3.7 km	end levee
3.8 km	intersection
3.9 km	trailhead

If you're staying at the Steeper random campsite and want to explore your immediate environs, this morning or evening walk is for you. Do bring your binoculars. Territorial and therefore very noisy lesser yellowlegs and Barrows goldeneye ducks watch you watching them.

There are a number of tracks in and around the Steeper campsite that you can easily explore on your own. We have chosen to tie them together in this short walk or bicycle ride. So, from the random campsite walk out to Highway #40. Turn right for 100 m to an intersection with a dirt track on your right. It takes you up a low rise to a crest overlooking the first and largest of four ponds. Ducks and sandpipers such as the lesser yellowlegs call these ponds home during the breeding season. Like all parents, they are very protective of their young; the ducks never let you get too close and will lead their clutch to the other side of the pond to disappear into the grass and sedges. It was the lesser yellowlegs that we could not ignore. Our approach sent them screaming into the air. As we dropped down to the edge of the first pond and then climbed up to the gravel flats they followed us.

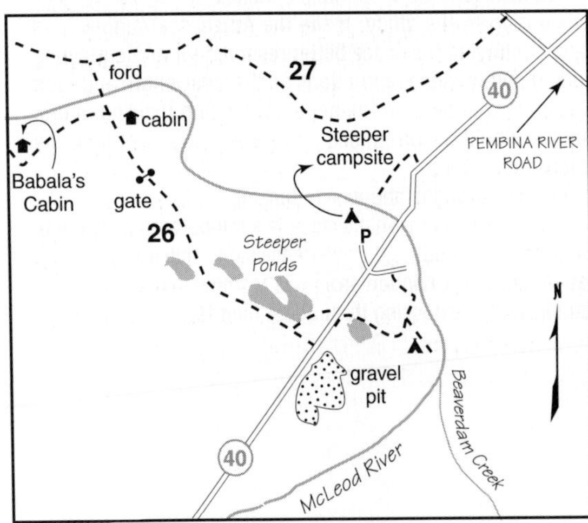

When you climb up to the gravel flat turn right and walk through the active gravel stockyard. If you think you could land an airplane on this hard, straight surface, you are right. Forestry developed and used this natural gravel deposit as an airfield for a short period in the early 1950s. Turn right onto another track on your right. It leads you past the lower end of the second pond and access to a spit of land that juts out into the first pond. We wandered along the spit to its end where we sat with our binoculars enjoying the display put on by the lesser yellowlegs. Return to the old airstrip, turn right and walk past the second pond to a track on your left that leads to the east side of the third pond.

Return to Highway #40, turn left and walk back toward the campsite for 200 m to a track on your right. It skirts the pond on its left and then drops down through the bush to an intersection. Turn right and climb up the levee. You will notice that there are two levees along this stretch of the river. Walk to the end of the levee, drop down through a dry pit and climb up the second levee. These levees have a very definite purpose. The heavy snowpack from the winter of 1950 was followed by a late spring. Then in June, summer arrived with a vengeance. Hot temperatures melted the snow turning the McLeod River into a raging torrent. As the floodwaters rose, they swept downstream taking out all bridges along the way. To prevent such a disaster again, the government built two levees here to keep the river in its channel.

To return to your trailhead follow the OHV track back to Highway #40. Steeper campsite is across the road.

Shore Birds

After Forestry closed the airstrip at Steeper, the site was quarried for its gravel in a truck and shovel operation similar to the process used in strip mining. The end result was a series of pits. Over time these pits have filled with both surface and groundwater to form a series of ponds. Certain shore birds such as killdeer and the lesser yellowlegs, and Barrows goldeneye ducks find these ponds perfect breeding and nesting sites. These birds prefer open areas with little cover. The killdeer with its distinctive black double breast band is a common shorebird found throughout Alberta and one that we saw at Robb, Mercoal and Steeper. Although it prefers open woodlands and fields, it moves to ponds and other muddy sites during the breeding season. To protect its young against us we watched the killdeer perform its trademark "broken-wing" ruse. The lesser yellowlegs, so-named because of its long, bright yellowlegs, also nests and raises its young close to water. One of the noisiest birds, the lesser yellowlegs is also fiercely protective of its young. Although we watched quietly from the OHV track above one of the ponds, we were repeatedly dive bombed by the parents in an attempt to drive us away. Once, a male accompanied us back across Highway #40 to sit in a tree shrieking "kip, kip" even as the sun set. They seem to be in a perpetual state of alarm for they continued shrieking during the night.

27 MCLEOD TRAIL

MAP PAGE 124

A delightful trip through park-like river flats is your reward for either braving a ford across the McLeod River or taking a longer access to Forestry's old McLeod Trail.

From Steeper's informal campsite, return to Highway #40 and turn right for 100 m to a gravel pit on your right. Turn right into the gravel pit. You will notice two sets of OHV tracks, one on the north side of a pond and another set of tracks on the south side of the pond. The tracks on the north side of the pond hug the treeline and end abruptly at the top of a low rise. Ignore this track. Cross over to the south side of the pond and pick up the OHV track that leads up over a rise and through some trees. The track dips down and swings to the left to cross a dry pit. The track climbs out of the pit and makes a sharp 90° turn to the right, skirting the south edge of the pit to its end. The track continues over a low rise where a small pond appears at your 11 o'clock on the left. Here, as well, there is a fork in your trail. Bear to the right. Follow the OHV track as it swings down through poplar trees and snakes its way between some older and smaller pits. This is a popular access to the McLeod Trail and the OHV tracks are deeply rutted, so if you are on bicycles you might want to exercise some caution. Once past the pits you come to an unusually-styled gate. Follow the OHV track as it crosses the meadow to several dilapidated outfitter shacks, a horse corral and another gate with a sign "Festus Creek: Mule Crossing." On the other side of the gate there is an intersection of tracks but, of course, you will want to continue down to the river. This is the ford across the McLeod River. Once across the river, follow the OHV track straight ahead to the intersection with the McLeod Trail, a distance of a couple of hundred metres. Continue straight ahead on the trail.

If the McLeod River is unfordable, a safer but slightly longer access to the McLeod Trail takes you across the river via the highway bridge just east of the Steeper campsite. Once you have crossed the bridge you wind up a steep hill. Ignore an OHV

Day hiking, cycling, horseback riding

Rating full day

Distance 16.6 km

Level of Difficulty river crossing

Maximum Elevation 1325 m

Elevation Gain 60 m

Map 83 F/3 Cadomin

Access

Park your vehicle at the Steeper random campsite on the north side of Highway #40 by the bridge over the McLeod River. The campsite entrance is 11 km west of the intersection of Highways #40 and #47, or 18 km east of the intersection of Highway #40 and the Cardinal River Road.

Note The preferred route to the McLeod Trail is via a ford across the McLeod River. OHVs and horses have little difficulty but hikers and cyclists must assess the situation before attempting to cross. In late spring and early summer or after a rainy spell the river will be high with a fast current, and it can be dangerous. A better time to attempt the ford is in late summer and autumn, unless it has been raining, when water levels are low. An alternate route to the McLeod Trail is also given.

0.0 km	trailhead
0.1 km	intersection
0.6 km	intersection
1.1 km	intersection
1.5 km	gate
2.5 km	gate; intersection and McLeod River ford
2.9 km	intersection
3.1 km	cutline
5.1 km	McLeod River braid crossing

Washing the mud from the gears.

track that joins on the left and continue as far as the Pembina River Road, which is signed. Turn left onto the road and climb past a hydro line right-of-way where you can see two sets of OHV tracks. If you are here during the work week, you must exercise caution. This is an active logging road. Combined with the fact that the Pembina River Road has rough gravel and steep ditches, this part of your trip is potentially dangerous. Fortunately, your trip up the Pembina River Road is short; a mere 400 m past the intersection with Highway #40 you come to an old forestry road, the McLeod Trail, that joins the Pembina River Road on the left. It leads northwest through tall stands of lodgepole pine. At first, the trail climbs slowly and then begins a long, gentle descent, winding through poplar and pine forest. When we were here it had rained heavily for several days previously and the mudholes created by the OHVs were deep, wide and numerous, all of which created some problems for us. In drier circumstances, we felt this part of the trail would be a good bicycle road. At the bottom of the hill the trail forks. Turning left takes you to the ford across the McLeod River. Instead, continue straight ahead.

From the intersection, the McLeod Trail braids over an upsy-daisy and passes a cutline on your

5.4 km	enter McLeod River braid
5.5 km	cutline
5.7 km	exit braid and enter McLeod Flats
7.0 km	Mercoal Creek
7.9 km	corral cutline
8.3 km	intersection
11.3 km	intersection
11.5 km	intersection
12.9 km	braid
13.0 km	intersection
13.3 km	McLeod River
16.6 km	trailhead

If McLeod River is unfordable:

0.0 km	trailhead
0.1 km	bridge
0.4 km	OHV track
0.8 km	Pembina River Road
0.9 km	OHV track
1.0 km	OHV track
1.2 km	McLeod Trail
3.9 km	intersection (corresponds with 2.9 km)

Gate crashing.

right. You soon enter a wide meadow dotted with willow, dwarf birch and the occasional copse of pine trees. For the next 10 km you travel along an excellent track through a delightful parkland marked by a series of pretty river flats and meadows. For much of the way you are accompanied by a low ridge on your right. For a while the trail runs alongside the river before crossing a dry, rocky braid of the McLeod. Climbing out of the braid, the trail winds through willows and stands of black spruce before forking. Horses follow the left fork; OHVs, cyclists and hikers dip down into the dry river braid and follow it to where the trail climbs out and onto another broad, pretty meadow. A kilometre or so later, the trail crosses Mercoal Creek at its confluence with the McLeod River. The creek is not very wide and its crossing presents no difficulties. Such a pretty trip is enhanced after you round a bend where, at your 11:00 o'clock, the Front Ranges come into view forming a dramatic backdrop to your parkland environment.

Almost a full kilometre after crossing Mercoal Creek the McLeod Trail bisects a cutline known locally as the "corral cutline." Now very dilapidated, the horse corral that once belonged to a local lumber mill owner, Amelia Spanach, can be found to your right. Ignore the cutline and continue straight ahead through the meadow. Keep on the main trail at an intersection where another trail joins from the left. The bluff that has been on your right most of your way now dips to the trail. Here, the trail narrows somewhat as it winds its way through stands of spruce trees before crossing another small meadow. It then enters an open forest of spruce and willow. This is an old growth forest evidenced by the presence of old man's beard hanging from the branches. At a fork keep to the right to remain on the main trail and cross a small stream. Bear left at the next fork. A kilometre later, the trail braids and then quickly forks. Bear to the right. You come out of the willows onto a rocky shoreline along the McLeod River where it takes a 90° turn to the northwest. At one time the McLeod Trail crossed the river here by way of a bridge to continue northward. But at a sandy beach beneath sandstone cliffs, you arrive at the end of your trail.

You may return the way you came or, as an option, ford the McLeod River from the beach to a random campsite opposite. From the campsite you can access the Tri-Creeks Road.

McLeod Flats

Previous names: Yellowhead Flats, Big Prairie

McLeod Flats is the local unofficial name for the approximately 10 km of river flats stretching upstream along the McLeod River from the 13th baseline near Antler Creek to Mercoal Creek. The flats takes their name from the nearby McLeod River.

The grassy flats have been used as a horse pasture by area residents including Jim Babala, an outfitter and Amelia Spanach, owner of a local lumber mill. Remnants of Spanach's corrals can still be seen beside what is locally called the corral cutline. The ranching potential of the area was first noted in 1907 by Dominion Land Surveyor A. H. Hawkins who wrote:

"...in the valley of the McLeod there are several very excellent hay meadows, one lying to the south of the [13th] base line being exceptionally well thought of. With the exception of one or two short breaks, this meadow, locally called the 'Big prairie,' extends up the river a distance of ten or twelve miles, and would make a most admirable cattle or horse ranch, as there is ample timber for shelter or buildings, and a large amount of excellent pasture, a considerable portion of which could be readily cut for hay, and in most favoured portions I have no doubt potatoes and oats could be successfully raised."

Hawkins at the time was following a horse trail up the McLeod, already then in existence. This trail would later be upgraded by Alberta Forestry and incorporated in their trail network as the McLeod Trail. Forestry called the area Yellowhead Flats. The present old road was built by Spanach as an access to their logging camps along Trapper Creek west of the McLeod River.

Taking a break along the McLeod Trail. Photo Norman Coulthard.

28 TRI-CREEKS ROAD

MAP PAGE 124

Although you can drive part of the way along this route, we suggest that because the Tri-Creeks Road is such an excellent cycling road, you will be glad you took the opportunity to enjoy its challenges. On a sunny day, though, this can be a hot trip so remember to take plenty of water.

From the random campsite at Steeper turn west on Highway #40 for 1.5 km to an intersection with a good gravel road on your right. Turn onto the road and climb a short but steep hill where at the top you catch your first glimpse of the Front Ranges on your left. It's a good gravel road that takes you to an intersection on your right. Turn right onto the signed McLeod Class III Road and follow this excellent cycling road as it dips downhill and then climbs and switches over a series of hills through a logging area. What we found interesting was the chequerboard-pattern the logging company has adopted in this area. On one side of the road there are mature or maturing stands of lodgepole pine while on the opposite side of the road there is an open cutblock that, when these are on your left, afford views to the west.

Day hiking, cycling, horseback riding

Rating full day

Distance 42.3 km

Level of Difficulty long ascents and descents along forestry road

Maximum Elevation 1415 m

Elevation Gain 180 m

Map 83 F/3 Cadomin

Access

Park your vehicle at the Steeper random campsite on the north side of Highway #40 by the bridge over the McLeod River. The campsite entrance is 11 km west of the intersection of Highways #40 and #47, or 18 km east of the intersection of Highway #40 and the Cardinal River Road.

0.0 km trailhead

1.5 km intersection

The Tri-Creeks Road winds past cutblocks in the forested foothills.

At the top of a hill you arrive at the junction with the Tri-Creeks Road. Turn right onto the road. You will continue along this roadway for nearly 9 km passing, at first, a cutline and OHV track and then dipping down and then climbing out of Eunice and then Deerlick creeks. Since the Tri-Creeks Road bears generally west then northwest, the view from the top of the hills gets prettier and prettier as you work your way up the road. Just past Deerlick Creek you pass, on your left, a rough track that is Craig's Road. Two kilometres later there is another intersection that you will ignore. It is at this point the Tri-Creeks Road enters an old burn area that is now partially camouflaged by a "doghair" forest of lodgepole pine. You continue to cycle through the old burn that crosses Wampus Creek as far as the intersection with Old Craig's Road. Turn right onto this unsigned old logging road. When we were here the intersection was muddy with deep ruts, but after 200 m the road improved to become a well-drained hard-packed road. As you wind down the hill you can hear through the doghair forest the murmur of the McLeod River. At the bottom of the hill there is an intersection on the right with another old roadway; this leads to a ford across the McLeod River. Within 100 m there is another access to a ford across the river. Ignore both of these and continue along the main track as it bends to the left to run alongside the river. It certainly is a pretty ride especially after splashing through a small no-name creek where a natural meadow opens the views ahead and across the river to interesting sandstone cliffs. Shortly afterward, you need to make a short detour where the McLeod River has cut into its banks carrying away a section of Old Craig's Road. So keep a sharp eye for a faint track on your left that leads through a meadow. If you miss it you will come to a ford across the McLeod River. Backtrack to the intersection in the meadow and follow the track into the lodgepole pine forest. Cross another small stream, pass a random campsite and go as far as the intersection with the continuation of Old Craig's Road. Turn onto the road as it continues to run alongside the river. You will soon arrive at a four-way intersection of tracks. Go straight ahead to the ford across Mary Gregg Creek.

The first time we were here the Mary Gregg was in full flood after a week of heavy rains. If you feel

2.3 km	intersection and McLeod Class III Road
4.8 km	intersection and Tri-Creeks Road
5.0 km	cutline and OHV track
11.5 km	Eunice Creek
13.1 km	Deerlick Creek
13.3 km	Craig's Road
15.4 km	intersection
15.9 km	Wampus Creek
16.5 km	intersection—Old Craig's Road
18.0 km	intersection and campsite
18.1 km	intersection
19.0 km	stream crossing
19.7 km	intersection
19.8 km	stream crossing
20.1 km	campsite
20.2 km	intersection (continuation of road from 19.7 km that has been washed away)
20.4 km	cutline
21.1 km	Mary Gregg Creek
21.1 km	stream crossing
21.2 km	intersection and random campsite
21.4 km	Tri-Creeks Road
21.7 km	intersection
22.1 km	Mary Gregg Creek bridge
22.3 km	cutline (same as one at 20.4 km)
25.1 km	intersection—Old Craig's Road (same as 16.5 km)
41.6 km	trailhead

If Mary Gregg is unfordable return to the cutline at 20.4 km.

20.6 km	intersection
20.9 km	Tri-Creeks Road
21.0 km	Mary Gregg Creek
21.4 km	intersection
21.7 km	intersection
21.9 km	intersection and random campsite
42.3 km	trailhead

A stream monitoring station.

nervous about crossing the creek, backtrack to the last intersection, a cutline, and bear right to follow it up through the forest, through a swampy but mercifully short meadow. At the far end of the meadow you turn off the cutline onto a track that will lead you back to the Tri-Creeks Road. If, at this point, you are tired, turn left onto the Tri-Creeks Road to return to your trailhead. Otherwise, swing right onto the road and cross the bridge over Mary Gregg Creek. Within 400 m you will see an intersection with a track on your right. Take it as far as another intersection where you will once again bear to the right. You are now swinging back to Mary Gregg Creek. Continue straight ahead to the confluence of the Mary Gregg and the McLeod River. A random campsite prettily located just above the confluence makes a fitting place to take a well-deserved rest and enjoy a snack before returning to the Tri-Creeks Road, swinging left onto it to enjoy the largely downhill ride to your trailhead.

An option on the return trip back to the trailhead is to drop back down to the McLeod River when you reach the intersection with Old Craig's Road. At the bottom of the hill there are several random campsites and fords across the river from where you can then access the McLeod Trail.

Wampus Creek

This creek was named in 1923 as the "home of the mythical wampus." The wampus, or common wampus cat (*Wampus wampus vulgaris*), lives in the American South where it has become embedded in the local folklore and is a popular high school mascot. Wampus cats are impossibly hideous "critters" with the head of a man, body of a wildcat and soul of a demon. Their preferred habitats are swamps and gloomy river bottoms. Despite their ugliness, wampus cats are incredibly vain creatures and will spend hours alone admiring their reflections in slimy pools of swamp water. Conversations among wampus cats are usually a brief "Ugly! Who are you calling ugly? You're ugly!" before a fight breaks out. Not surprisingly, courtship and mating are rare, short, brutish and traumatic affairs that do little to improve their ill humour. Wampus cats are ravenous creatures and will snarfle down anything though preferring such nutritious delicacies as live earthworms, mouldy fish, putrid squirrels and raw grizzly bears. Field naturalists repeatedly comment upon the cats' disgusting table manners.

A rare photo of a wampus cat lurking in the shadows of Wampus Creek.

The presence of wampus cats in the Cadomin area has sparked a debate among environmentalists. Some believe this is a rare and endangered sub-species (*Wampus wampus cadominensis*) that should be protected and accuse the provincial government of deliberately refusing to admit their existence so as to encourage unrestricted resource development in the area. Other environmentalists trace their presence to the arrival in 1913 of Bumpus Woody, Bright Rhodes and Howard Scott, all from Georgia, to work at Frank Seabolt's timber operation at Mountain Park. The wampus cats, they claim, were the Georgians' pets that later escaped into the surrounding forest. Therefore, say these environmentalists, wampus cats are an introduced species that should be eradicated and so restore the natural balance of earthworms, mouldy fish, putrid squirrels and grizzly bears.

The debate between these two groups continues with the subsequent growth in the local population of wampus cats and environmental consultants.

The Tri-Creeks Watershed Study

The Tri-Creeks Watershed Study was a 21 year-long (1965-1986) project to study the impact logging operations have on local fish stocks and to evaluate the effectiveness of provincial timber harvesting regulations in protecting those stocks. The study found that the logging did not have a negative environmental impact on the local fish habitat and population. Road construction, however, was found to be the main contributor of sediment in one of the streams.

The Tri-Creeks are the Wampus, Deerlick and Eunice creeks. For the first 10 years of the study these streams were studied to establish their preharvest conditions. During that time neither timber harvesting nor fishing was allowed in the watershed area. To separate the effects of road construction from timber harvesting, the Tri-Creeks road was built four years before logging operations began in the Wampus and Deerlick Creek basins. The Eunice Creek basin was untouched and acted as a control against which any effects identified in the Wampus and Deerlick basins could be compared.

North West Pulp and Power Co. (presently Weldwood Canada Ltd.) of Hinton harvested the Wampus (1979-1983) and Deerlick (1980-1984) creek basins under similar harvesting rules except that within the cutblocks along Wampus Creek there were streamside buffer strips of uncut timber while along Deerlick Creek there were no such buffer strips. All logging was done during the winter to minimize soil disturbance and scarification was completed within a year after the harvest. Since the study, the rules governing logging operations in Alberta have been tightened.

Tri-Creeks research area.

Rainbow trout are the most common fish species within the basin. Mountain whitefish use the streams as foraging areas in late spring and summer and spawn there in the fall. Bull trout predominate in the lower reaches of Eunice Creek. The Tri-Creeks are notable for being one of the few areas left where native Athabasca rainbow trout are still present. These trout may be the slowest growing individuals in the world. By age two, they will weigh less than 30 g owing to the cold water temperatures, short growing season and poor food supply. Rainbow transferred from Wampus Creek into less extreme habitats have shown higher growth rates.

The three streams remain closed to fishing and are checked annually for population estimates as part of a project to maintain a long-term database and to act as a reference against other provincial fish populations. One finding is that the fish in the Tri-Creeks basin have a 10-12 year population cycle. Whether this is because of outside environmental factors or the intrinsic nature of the fish is presently unknown. Unauthorized fishing in the Tri-Creeks basin is threatening to damage this ongoing historical record commonly seen as the best set of fish data in Alberta.

LOVETT BRANCH

The Lovett or East Branch is the original Coal Branch. Its railway was built and operated by a subsidiary of the Grand Trunk Pacific (GTP) that, at the time, was building its transcontinental line west to Prince Rupert. The railway, of course, needed secure supplies of steam coal to operate its western lines and GTP president, Charles Melville Hays (1856-1912), had a plan. In fact, he had two plans.

The first plan was to find and develop supplies of steam coal in western Canada. To that end a French emigre, Raymond Brutinel, was hired to explore the Canadian Rockies. More about him later. The other plan was to buy existing coal mines in the United States. In 1911, the GTP decided to purchase the options on 48 consolidated coal mining companies that together produced about 24 million tonnes of coal annually. The arrangement included a $10 million payment by the GTP to the holders of options on the properties. Though the papers were signed, the deal was never closed. An unlucky boat, the *Titanic*, would sink taking down Hays and the signed contracts in his possession at the time. Also sunk was the deal since, by then, the GTP board of directors had second thoughts about it.

The board's second thoughts were likely owing to Brutinel's success in tracing coal from Lovett northwest to Coalspur. Eventually about 16,200 ha would be staked and millions of dollars invested into the Lovett mine and

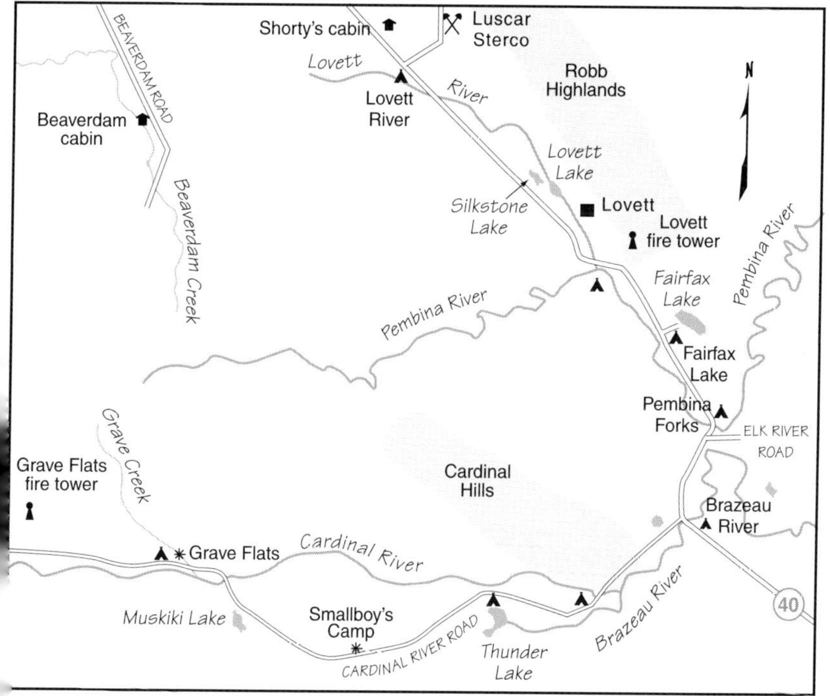

connecting railway. Lovett's investors formed Pacific Pass Coal Fields Ltd. Together they were a tight network of financiers and capitalists holding directorships on the GTP and hundreds of other companies. Decades before the phrase was invited, they were the Canadian establishment. Most of them were from Montreal.

Edward Black Greenshields led the group and served as Pacific Pass president until his ouster by H. A. Lovett. Greenshield's connections included directorships on the GTP, Bank of Montreal and Royal Trust Company. He was also a collector of Dutch landscape painting and in 1906 wrote the first book published in Canada regarding the visual arts.

Robert MacKay (1840-1916) was for a time regarded as one of the two dozen men in Canada who formed the basis of Canadian finance. Like Greenshields, he was a Bank of Montreal and Royal Trust Company director but included in his lengthy portfolio were seats on the board of the Canadian Pacific Railway, Bell Telephone and the Dominion Steel Corporation. He matched his capacity as a financial underwriter with politics. He was a Liberal senator.

William Molson MacPherson is, yes, of that Molson family. More important than beer to the Pacific Pass board was the fact that he was president of Molson's Bank. He served with Greenshields on the GTP board and held substantial timber interests in British Columbia near the future GTP right-of-way. As a bank president MacPherson shared the board table with John Theodore Ross and Vesey Boswell, president and vice president, respectively, of the Quebec Bank.

Nathaniel Curry (1851-1931) was another senator, this one a Conservative. He was a Bank of Nova Scotia director and with MacPherson served on the board of the Montreal Trust Company. Curry's jewel was the presidency of the Canadian Car & Foundry Company that, during the First World War, secured munitions contracts totalling more than $83 million. Curry would pay for his profit: his son died in Flanders.

James Naismith Greenshields was a top ranked corporate lawyer and at his peak regarded as second only to Zebulon Lash of the Canadian Northern Railway. He was also a significant financier and shared a seat with MacKay on the board of a pulp and paper company. Greenshields was a successful defence lawyer but was best known for a case he lost. In 1885 he served as chief counsel for Louis Riel. Riel ignored Greenshield's advice to plead insanity and was hanged.

Philippe Auguste Choquette (1854-1948) was a Quebec senator and served on the Pacific Pass board mainly as a political underwriter. He was a lawyer, a journalist and a hockey enthusiast. He was president of the Quebec Hockey Club whose team, the Quebec Bulldogs, were Stanley Cup champions from 1911 to 1913.

James Guthrie Scott was the most colourful member. He was a tireless promoter of a second transcontinental line and was instrumental in the formation and construction of the National Transcontinental Railway. This line, between Quebec and Winnipeg, was built by the Canadian government and in a cozy deal, leased to the GTP at no charge for the first seven years.

It was through the power and influence of these and other similar men that the Pacific Pass mine at Lovett was started and the Coal Branch railway built

The haunting Lovett townsite.

These men were buccaneers who rode the Laurier boom. At a time when a miner's take home pay might be about $40 per month, some of these individuals earned salaries upward of $25,000 per year as company presidents and paid no personal income or corporate sales tax. Through their interconnected networks they not only stood to profit directly as investors in the Lovett mine if it was a success, but were guaranteed preliminary profits as capital, insurance and materials were channelled to the project through the banks, trust companies, foundries, timber operations and other supporting businesses under their control. Their many capitalizations, such as those reported for the mining companies in this book, were often inflated. A "$5 million company" might have only one tenth that amount in real assets, the rest being common and often worthless stock. The purpose for this inflation or watering of share figures was to trap the unwary and disguise profits that might otherwise seem exorbitant.

Predatory instincts aside, some of them were magnificent philanthropists. MacKay was a Presbyterian and a stereotypical example of the stern Protestant work and religious ethic. He served as governor of three hospitals including the Notre Dame Hospital in Montreal, a Catholic operation. The MacKay family founded and funded the MacKay Institute for Protestant Deaf Mutes and the Blind. MacPherson was involved with the Boy Scouts and took an active part in the preservation of the Plains of Abraham as a historic site. Ross was national president of the SPCA while Curry donated liberally to various educational, religious and charitable institutions including Acadia University, which received about $100,000 of his largess.

Their wealth, connections and ability to hire the best professionals, such as mining engineer Fairfax Landstreet, did not serve them well in the end. Lovett was an unfortunate location for a mine and by 1920 they had all given up on that venture. Their influence with the GTP proved significant in the West Branch where R. W. Jones, unable to interest them in his Mountain Park coal claims, turned to offshore British capital instead with spectacular results.

Coal Branchers

Raymond Brutinel (1872-1964)
Occupation: geologist, entrepreneur, soldier

Raymond Brutinel is the forgotten man in Coal Branch history. This is remarkable, not only because of his amazing career, but also the fact that he is the man best able to claim the title of "father" of the Alberta Coal Branch.

He was born in Alet, France, and became an army officer. A devout Catholic, anti-clerical politics caused him to emigrate to Canada in 1905 and settle near St. Albert where he bought about 100 acres of land beside what is now the St. Albert Trail. A syndicate of Montreal financiers connected to the Grand Trunk Pacific hired Brutinel to explore and prospect the country along the projected route of the railway west from the Pembina River to Prince Rupert. What he was to look for was anything of potential value—agricultural land, timber, water powers, coal and other minerals. His patron in this enterprise was Montreal financier Edward Black Greenshields.

Brutinel's exploring parties, commonly labelled by contemporaries as "The Frenchmen," were made up in large part by former French army officers such as himself. Beginning in 1907 they staked the "coal valley" north from Lovett to Coalspur. Their findings encouraged the syndicate to form Pacific Pass Coal Fields Ltd., with Greenshields as president, and develop the mine at Lovett. Brutinel became one of the original directors and he negotiated with the provincial government the subsidy for the building of the Coal Branch railway to Lovett from Bickerdike. Joining Brutinel on the board was one of "The Frenchmen," Armand de Bernis, like himself a French emigre and military man and who had a horse ranch in central Alberta.

Aside from the Pacific Pass mine, Brutinel became involved in other ventures including the Edmonton Interurban Railway. This railway scheme, which never quite got off the ground, included two future Coal Branch players, Leon Bureau and Charles Barry, who would open a mine at Coal Valley on leases originally staked by Brutinel. His entrepreneurial successes made him a wealthy man and he moved to Montreal shortly before the First World War. At the outbreak of the war, Brutinel along with a number of other millionaires raised a motorized automobile machine-gun unit for service in France. These units eventually became the Canadian Machine Gun Corps with Brutinel, now major general, the commander. Military historians regard Brutinel as a pioneer in the field of mechanized warfare owing to the machine-gun tactics he pioneered at Vimy Ridge and that were later adopted by the French and British armies.

Brutinel moved back to France in 1920 after he retired from the army but maintained his ties with Canada. In 1940, as German panzers advanced toward Paris, he helped Georges Vanier, the future governor general, evacuate the Canadian embassy. In 1911 at Charles Fergie's request, Brutinel had joined the Canadian Institute of Mining and Metallurgy. He kept his membership and in 1961 joined its Fifty-Year Club.

Photographs of Brutinel are deceptive. They show a dapper individual with a pince-nez perched on the end of his nose above a tiny moustache. What the photographs do not show is that this delicate looking man was a prospector in the Canadian wilderness and a trench warfare survivor.

LOVETT RIVER RECREATION AREA

Lovett River Recreation Area is one of four recreation areas that are spread along Highway #40 from Coalspur in the north to Pembina Forks in the south. Well positioned between Coalspur and Fairfax Lake recreation areas, Lovett River campground entices visitors to linger in the area to discover for themselves the appeal of the Coal Branch.

Nestled along the pretty Lovett River opposite Luscar Sterco's mine, the Lovett River Recreation Area can serve as a jumping-off place to explore the entire Lovett Branch. For the fishermen in the family, the Lovett River boasts fine fishing, and Silkstone and Lovett lakes, both very popular with fishermen, are located nearby. If fishing isn't your thing, take a fascinating tour through the Sterco mine or explore some of the old trails in the immediate area.

Location 30 km south of Robb on Highway #40
Facilities 17 unserviced sites
Note pump, firewood, pit toilets

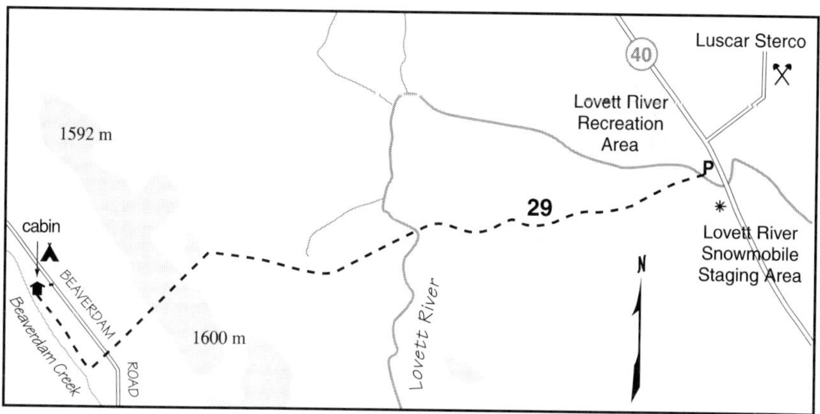

The Tackle Box

Lovett River
Fish Management Area: #4

Species rainbow trout to 454 g, bull trout to 1360 g, arctic grayling to 454 g

Restrictions Wall rainbow trout shorter than 17.5 cm must be released. Use of bait fish and the collection of bait fish are prohibited.

Season 16 June to 31 August

29 MILE 52 TRAIL

MAP PAGE 141

What an excellent way to spend an easy day cycling from the Lovett River campground! Following an old forestry road as it winds gently up and down through open pine and spruce forest eventually leads you to an old forestry cabin, helping to give you an appreciation for the life that the forestry personnel led.

From the Lovett River Recreation Area campground turn right onto Highway #40 for approximately 300 m where there is a rough 4 x 4 road that leads off to the right. Follow it as it goes over the rise and down across a stream. Once across the stream the old road becomes smoother and is generally in

Cycling
Rating full day
Distance 31.0 km
Level of Difficulty old road
Maximum Elevation 1539 m
Elevation Gain 137 m
Map 83/F2 Foothills

Access

Park your vehicle at the Lovett River Recreation Area. The recreation area lies along Highway #40, 18 km south of the intersection with Highways #47 and 33 km north of the intersection with the Cardinal River Road.

0.0 km	trailhead
0.1 km	intersection
0.2 km	stream
1.1 km	cutline
2.3 km	begin braid
2.4 km	end braid
3.1 km	begin braid
3.3 km	end braid
3.3 km	begin braid
3.4 km	cutline
3.5 km	end braid
4.1 km	begin braid
4.4 km	end braid
4.4 km	begin braid
4.6 km	cutline
4.7 km	end braid
5.1 km	cutline
6.4 km	intersection
6.5 km	stream crossing and intersection
6.7 km	cutline

Corduroy helps you cross some of the boggy sections of the forestry road.

excellent condition for the remainder of the trip. There are numerous cutlines and braids along this route that mark your progress. Your route, though, is never in doubt as the old road is clearly defined. The first cutline that crosses your roadway is followed a kilometre later by three quick braids. Another cutline crosses the road that then braids again within a short distance. You are climbing slowly but steadily. After one steeper pitch the roadway levels and then dips to descend a hill passing a cutline on your right. Keep to the left at two braids passing yet another cutline on the left. From here you can just barely see the Front Ranges through the cut. It's a most pleasant route as you pedal easily up and down the gentle rises. One more braid and two cutlines later you arrive at an intersection with a logging road on your left. At this point your road swings lazily to the right, levelling before descending to a tributary of the Lovett River. Here, there is a major fork in the road. The right fork stays on the bank above the river, but you want to take the left fork that goes down and crosses the stream. Half way up the embankment on the other side you arrive at a braid. Keep left, passing a cutline that bisects the road. It's now a long climb uphill followed by a quick descent. You next cross a small meadow grown in with willows, and an equally small creek.

The worst part of your trip comes shortly after leaving the meadow. Back in the forest again, you pass another cutline before arriving at a low, boggy stretch. Parts of this 200 m span have been corduroyed in an attempt to bridge the worst sections. Other attempts to make the road passable are evidenced by a series of pits that you can see on either side of the roadway. In order to try to build up the roadbed, the builders scooped out dirt from alongside the road thus creating the pits. They have filled with stagnant surface water, making, no doubt, a perfect mosquito nursery. We were here during a long, hot, dry spell so the mosquitoes were of no consequence, but in a rainy season we could imagine hurrying through this part of the trip. Soon, though, you are beyond the swamp and back along a good roadbed. Cross two small streams and ignore two cutlines. You have been climbing steadily and in some places the pitches have been steeper than others. Finally, you cross the divide that separates the McLeod and

6.9 km	begin braid
7.2 km	end braid
7.4 km	cutline
8.2 km	stream crossing
8.3 km	cutline
8.5 km	bog
9.2 km	stream crossing
10.1 km	stream crossing and cutline
10.2 km	cutline
10.6 km	McLeod and Embarras rivers divide
10.7 km	begin braid
10.8 km	end braid
10.9 km	stream crossing
11.7 km	Beaverdam Road and sour gas line right-of-way
11.8 km	intersection
12.5 km	Beaverdam trail
13.6 km	stream crossing
14.0 km	cutline
14.2 km	intersection
14.3 km	stream crossing
15.5 km	Beaverdam cabin
16.0 km	Beaverdam Road
19.3 km	intersection (corresponds to 11.7 km)
31.0 km	trailhead

Embarras rivers' watersheds. Appropriately, from here there is a good view of the Front Ranges and Cheviot Mountain. Now there is a fun, steep downhill run. It doesn't matter which braid you take going down the hill; in either case you soon come out onto a meadow that is dotted with willows and, in late summer, carpeted with asters. Back in the cooling forest once again you cross a small rivulet. Within a kilometre you break out suddenly from the woods to find yourself crossing a good gravel road that is the Beaverdam Road.

The old forestry road that you have been tracing crosses the Beaverdam Road and climbs the embankment steeply to re-enter the forest. An easier access to the continuation of the forestry road is to cross the Beaverdam Road veering a little to the left to a sour gas pipeline right-of-way. At the top of the embankment find the trail to the right that leads you back 100 m to the forestry road. Turn left onto the soft, needle-strewn roadway and follow it through open pine and spruce forest as it rolls over the low hills. At the bottom of a steep hill there is an intersection on your left with a much older road. Ignore this road. Continue along your roadway as it swings sharply to the right. You are now on a straightaway with a forested hillside on your right and a creek and moose pasture just beyond the trees on your left. A small creek crossing requires some caution as the home-made bridge is badly dilapidated. Cross a cutline, pass an intersection with another cutline on your left and cross a small rivulet. You are now gently descending with Beaverdam Creek still on your left. Beaverdam Creek lives up to its name; you can spy at least several beaver dams as you pass by. If you look carefully you can also locate the remains of a log cabin on the other side of the creek. Within 75 m your lovely forest trail ends in an open meadow dotted with willows. Straight in front of you is the Beaverdam cabin.

Unlike many old roads in the Coal Branch, this forestry road has not been cut up by OHVs thus making it perfect for bicycles.

Once the backwoods refuge of forestry rangers patrolling their region, this well-built log cabin is now privately owned as evidenced by the heavy padlock on the door and several outbuildings close by. We spent a few minutes examining the log-building skills of forestry personnel before continuing along the trail that now curves to the right through the willow swamp. In places the trail has been corduroyed indicating low, wet spots. These are minor annoyances and soon you find yourself back on the Beaverdam Road. Turn right onto the road. En route to your intersection with the old forestry road you climb two steep hills. At the bottom of the second hill you can easily see your intersection coming up on the left. Turn left onto the forestry road and return to your trailhead.

These half dovetail joins on the Beaverdam cabin attest to the skill that forestry personnel wielded with their axes.

Beaverdam cabin.

Mile 52 Trail

The Mile 52 Trail was a forestry trail that ran west from near Foothills to the Beaverdam cabin. Mile 52 was the point along the East Coal Branch railway where it connected to another trail that ran southeast to the Lovett Ranger Station. Its western connection was the Beaverdam-Grave Flats trail that ran north-south between Steeper and the Grave Flats cabin. The Beaverdam Road follows the northern section of this trail.

Most forestry trails were cut before 1920 and formed a network of routes along which forest rangers on horseback patrolled the Coal Branch in what was then called the Brazeau National Forest. Ranger cabins were spaced about 24 km apart, which was roughly a half day horse ride. The rangers traded their horses for pick-up trucks in the 1950s and, apart from usage as access routes in case of forest fire, trail maintenance and use declined. Many forestry trails, such as Mile 52, were upgraded into forestry roads.

Labrador Tea

Scientific name ~ *Ledum groenlandicum Oeder*
Other names ~ Hudson Bay tea, muskeg tea, marsh tea
Cree name ~ Mukeko-pukwa

Standing 40-80 cm high, Labrador tea is an evergreen shrub. Its long, narrow, dark green leaves curl at the edges. The upper surface of the leaves are leathery and are brown and fuzzy underneath. In late spring, the plant produces clusters of small white flowers with long stamens, giving the flowerhead a delicate, lacy appearance. When the fruit matures, in the form of a brown capsule, it pulls the stalk downward. Labrador tea was introduced into Great Britain at some point in the last century as an ornamental shrub.

Labrador tea in bloom.

Habitat Common Labrador tea often comprises much of the understorey of boggy areas or, in the case of the Lovett River Recreation Area, of moist coniferous forests. It has formed a symbiotic relationship with fungi present in the soil. The fungi penetrate the plant's roots carrying nitrogen and phosphorus compounds up into the plant. In return, the fungi receive carbohydrates, thus allowing both to flourish in the acidic and nutrient-poor soil.

Uses The leaves of Labrador tea contain narcotic substances and a toxic compound. Boiling the leaves releases these substances into the water. When drunk, the hot liquid produces an effect on our nervous system similar to the stimulant effect of black tea. The Cree also drank the "tea" to treat chest colds, fevers and other general complaints.

THE TOWNS OF THE LOVETT BRANCH

As you drive south of Coalspur along Highway #40 you pass through tall stands of lodgepole pine, largely unbroken by cutlines or other signs of human activity. To your left, though, you notice "No Trespassing" signs. These are posted by Luscar Sterco, who is strip mining the entire "coal valley" that at one time included the mining camps of Sterco, Coal Valley, Foothills, Reco and Lovett.

Sterco was the northernmost camp, located at Mile 47, followed by Coal Valley at Mile 48, Foothills at Mile 50, Reco at Mile 52 and Lovett, located at the end of the railway line, at Mile 57. The populace, with the exception of that at Coal Valley, was heterogeneous. Italians, Poles, Germans, Ukrainians, Serbians, English, Welsh, Scots, Irish, French and Belgians all lived and worked alongside each other in apparent harmony. Coal Valley was the exception. It was company policy to have a work force that was at least 75 per cent French. Each of these camps was a company town. Although there had been some consideration given to establishing one community to serve all the camps, the companies could not agree on the division of labour and profits that the one settlement would entail. In the end, each company built its own townsite immediately adjacent to its mine. This arrangement had certain benefits: the companies found it easier to control their work forces more directly and the miners did not have to travel miles to go to work. There was, though, a lack of town planning. This meant that often homes and businesses were built downwind of the tipple with the result that coal dust was everywhere. It was a housewife's worst nightmare. Not only did the coal dust seep under doors and windows, but it could cover sparkling white linens hung on the line with soot if the wind was from a certain direction.

Each camp was self-contained with its general store, hotel, boarding house, hospital, community hall, barber shop and pool hall. Sterco and Coal Valley

Foothills, ca. 1949. Two water towers, one at the top of the hill and the other at the bottom connected by a pipe, are central to the photograph. The train station is to the far right. Photo Ed Jenkins.

Sterco, 1952. Photo Ed Jenkins.

also boasted libraries and reading rooms. In addition, Coal Valley had a one-room school, a movie theatre, a skating rink, tennis courts and a Roman Catholic church. The church was, in fact, the only church along the Lovett Branch; all other denominations had to rely on itinerant preachers who worked a circuit out of Edson. Since they were company towns in which the company owned most if not all the buildings and businesses, entrepreneurs were few. Nevertheless, the miners could avoid the company store by patronizing peddlers who travelled up and down the rail lines selling everything from coats to spices.

A wagon road, built in the 1910s, connected the towns, making it possible to travel from one camp to another. This was critical to the social life of the Lovett Branch. Nearly every Saturday night the young blades from Foothills, a small camp of maybe 200 people in the 1930s, would walk to Coal Valley looking for some action, be it found at the bar, at a card game or at a dance. Locations of the weekly Saturday night dances were rotated through the towns, Sterco hosting one week, Coal Valley another. They were always well attended; the tickets were put in the pay envelopes! The women provided the food, the men provided the liquid refreshments. Sports were very popular. After a highway was punched through to Edson during the 1930s, that town was included in the hockey "league." There is a story of one hockey game between Sterco and Edson in 1947. It was winter, of course, and the Edson team had trouble on the Burma Road, bogging down in the snow. The entire team had to abandon their van and walk the rest of the way into Sterco. That was bad enough but after the game, which they won, they had to trudge back nearly 5 km to their van, dig it out and fight snow drifts all the way back to Coalspur where the road improved. They arrived back home in Edson at 3:30 a.m.

In 1952 Sterco mine shut down and the post office moved to Foothills. One after another the mines closed as markets withered away. The miners and hotel owners left. Only ghost towns remained. Then, in 1977, Luscar Sterco began its massive strip mining operation that, over the years, has obliterated all the towns of the Lovett Branch with the exception of Lovett itself. It remains the only true ghost town in the entire Coal Branch.

Brookdale

Mine No.: #833

Owners/Operators: 1919-1922 Brookdale Collieries Ltd.; 1922-1925 Superior Collieries Ltd.; 1925 A. Dino & Company; 1926 Vitaly, Dino & Company; 1926 Northern Alberta Coal Mines Ltd.; 1926-1932 Confederation Coal Company Ltd.; 1932 Commonwealth Coal Company Ltd.; 1934 Mount Cheviot Coal Company Ltd.

Authorized Capital: $20,000 Brookdale Collieries Ltd.; $30,000 Superior Collieries Ltd.; $30,000 Confederation Coal Company

Coal: sub-bituminous

Registered Trade Name: Superior Yellowhead

Market: domestic and steam

Mine Type: underground

Total Extraction: 67,000 tonnes

Men Killed: 0

This lease, formerly owned by Pacific Pass Coal Fields of Lovett, was first developed in 1919 by Brookdale Collieries to supply steam coal to the Edmonton, Dunvegan & British Columbia Railway. Otherwise known as the "Extremely Dangerous & Badly Constructed Railway," it ceased operations in 1920 and left Brookdale with its unpaid coal bill. Brookdale went bankrupt owing about $9000 in wages and $500 in Mine Owner's Tax. The money was never collected.

Superior Collieries, formed by the local miners, bought the mine in 1922. They were plagued by a lack of coal orders and went bankrupt in 1925 owing about $4000 in wages and $12,000 in other bills. The unpaid wages by Superior Collieries left some families destitute and receiving social assistance and advice from Alberta Provincial Police Constable T. Achees at Coalspur. "...[T]he people are frightfully short of food. From what I can gather there does not seem to be any prospects of these conditions getting better. These people are short of money and are continually asking me for assistance. I have advised the men to get out and look for work elsewhere. This advice they do not take kindly and seem to think the Gov't. should keep them. How to get these people out of this area I am at a loss to know."

A. Dino and Mike Vitaly briefly operated the mine before selling it to Northern Alberta Coal Mines, which was reorganized as Confederation Coal with Adam S. Matheson, an Edmonton lawyer, as president. Within a year the chief mine engineer quit, the miners were not being paid, and District Mine Inspector Thomas Horne was becoming irritated. Horne reported that there was neither a hospital nor first aid supplies at the camp and that the bunkhouse and cookhouse were unclean. In addition, injuries at the mine were not being reported to the Mines Branch. There was no reply from Confederation regarding these allegations and in 1929 the Workmen's Compensation Board issued an injunction to Confederation to stop operating.

In 1932 local miners formed Commonwealth Coal and agreed to buy the mine from Confederation for $12,000 to be paid from future coal sales. The Mines Branch warned the miners about the risks of giving up their right to pass wages through a partnership with Matheson: "We may state frankly that previous operations carried on by Mr. Matheson have been nothing but grief to this Dept. over delay and trouble in getting the men their wages. We are trying to get in touch with Mr. Matheson, but cannot, but look suspiciously on the construction of this partnership in view of past experiences at this mine."

The Commonwealth partnership dissolved that same year. The final sorry episode was brief. In 1934 Mount Cheviot Coal bought the site and stripped it of its equipment for use elsewhere. The company included J. Klassen who went on to help form K. D. Collieries, and Mike Vitaly.

Reco

Mine No.: #1014

Owners/Operators: 1919 Blackstone Coal Company Ltd.; 1919-1926 Blackstone Coal Ltd.; 1921 A. E. Oakley & Company #829; 1921-1922 Stupar, Oakley & Company #829; 1922 Sterling Collieries Ltd. #829; 1921 Johnstone Carscadden #829, #896; 1922-1924 Vitaly Company Ltd. #896; 1921 Bryan Coal Company #897; 1922 Ballarin & Sabotin #1014; 1924 J. Sabotin & Company #1014; 1925-1926 Reco Hard Coal Company Ltd.; 1926-1927 Elkhead Hard Coal Co.; 1928-1929 Melrose Coal Co.; 1930-1931 Val D'Or Collieries Ltd.

Authorized Capital: $500,000 Blackstone Coal Ltd.; $20,000 Reco Hard Coal Company Ltd.

Coal: sub-bituminous

Registered Trade Name: Reco Hard Coal

Market: domestic and steam

Mine Type: underground; strip pit

Total Extraction: 173,000 tonnes

Men Killed: 0

The story of these four leases, formerly owned by Pacific Pass Coal Fields of Lovett, is one of fractured seams, undercapitalization and bad management. Blackstone Coal tried initially to mine the coal but soon stepped away from direct operations to leasing its holdings. The lessees included Louis Stupar, founder of Mercoal and Foothills; Mike Vitaly, who would later be involved in over a dozen coal mining ventures in the Coal Branch and other parts of Alberta; and James H. Bryan, who would open up another mine under the same name, at Robb.

Mine No.'s 829, 896 and 897 were strip pits. No. 1014 was underground. In 1925, No. 1014 was combined with No. 896, and run by the Reco Hard Coal Company. Reco's parent company and only customer was the Reliance Coal Company Ltd., a Calgary wholesaler, the directors of Reco and Reliance being the same. The coal was sold by Reco to Reliance at a "low price," then re-sold by Reliance. By 1926 Reco went into liquidation leaving about $5000 in wages owed the miners and $500 owed the Workmen's Compensation Board. Since Reco was leasing the property from Blackstone, it had no assets. "In addition," wrote a government lawyer, "the directors from my examination of their affairs, appear to be personally without sufficient assets to justify suit against them for wages etc. and I would suggest that no good purpose would be served by commencing action against this Company...."

Reco's lawyers offered to pay half of the wages owing to the miners as a condition to resuming operations at the mine. The deal fell through. The companies following Reco did little more than prospect work, with the last owner, Val d'Or Collieries, transferring its operations to a mine at the head of Prospect Creek near Mountain Park.

Reco is a contraction of Reliance Coal. Coal Branchers continued living in the camp for years after the mine closed in 1927. The post office, which opened in 1925, was not closed until 1943.

Coal Valley

Mine No.: #1002

Owners/Operators: 1922-1951 Coal Valley Mining Company Ltd.; 1951-1955 Sterling-Coal Valley Mining Company Ltd.

Authorized Capital: $1,000,000 Coal Valley Mining Company Ltd.

Coal: sub-bituminous

Registered Trade Name: COVA Coal

Market: domestic and steam

Mine Type: strip pit

Total Extraction: 4,853,000 tonnes

Men Killed: 6

The Coal Valley Mining Company took over leases formerly owned by Pacific Pass Coal Fields of Lovett and discovered by Raymond Brutinel. Brutinel was an active member of the small Franco-Albertan business community in St. Albert where his activities caught the attention of two men, Leon Bureau and Charles Edouard Barry (1876-1940). Bureau had been sent originally to Canada in 1898 by the Geological Society of France to survey mineral deposits. He would later divide his time between St. Albert and France promoting various Canadian development schemes. Barry, a banker, was secretary of the Franco-Belgian Investment Company that acted as a conduit for European investment into western Canada. As a result, the Coal Valley Mining Company was formed by Belgian, French and Canadian capital with Bureau the first mine manager then afterward managing director. Barry was secretary and later became company president. Barry succeeded Louis Pratt, the company's first president and after whom the mining camp's original name, Prattville, had been named.

Following Charles Barry's death in 1940, his wife Annette Barry (1890-1968) became president. Madame Barry's great challenge came in 1944 when fire destroyed the mine tipple. Since this was wartime, the materials and equipment needed to rebuild the tipple and reopen the mine could only be obtained with the permission of the priorities board in Ottawa. To Barry's frustration, Ottawa was slow in giving that permission: "So I decided that I wasn't waiting any longer and I got on the phone and phoned the Department of Priorities in Washington…in a few days I got everything I wanted." The tipple was rebuilt and operations resumed within a year.

Sterling Collieries bought the Coal Valley Mining Company in 1947 and in 1951 amalgamated the two operations as the Sterling-Coal Valley Mining Company. The rebuilt Coal Valley tipple handled Sterco coal and next year absorbed the laid off miners from the abandoned Sterco operation. By 1955 Coal Valley no longer supplied steam coal to the Canadian National Railway and its last major customer, Abitibi Pulp & Paper Company at Iroquois Falls, Ontario, cancelled its coal order. The problem, according to Abitibi, was drought. There was no longer enough water in its reservoir to produce electricity so all its power needs were being drawn from the steam plant. To produce the extra BTUs a higher quality coal was needed, hence the cancellation of the Coal Valley contract.

Abitibi never renewed its coal order and the mine was abandoned later that year. Under the Mines Act, Sterling-Coal Valley was obliged to backfill its abandoned strip pits. The Alberta government granted the company an exemption to this requirement and the open pits at Sterco and Coal Valley remained. There were two reasons for the exemption:

1) During the spring water run-off would accumulate in the pits and prevent flash floods.
2) Filling the pits would require over 2,000,000 cubic yards of earth, making the cost prohibitive.

Luscar Sterco would backfill the old pits and reclaim the mine site over 20 years later.

Coal Valley tipple fire, October 29, 1944. Photo Buster Stetsil.

The Marion shovel and a dragline working in the pit. Photo Ed Jenkins.

Foothills

Mine No.: #771

Owners/Operators: 1918-1919 Central Alberta Hard Coal Ltd.; 1919-1951 The Foothills Collieries Ltd.; 1951-1957 Canadian Collieries (Dunsmuir) Ltd.; 1957-1961 Canadian Collieries Resources Ltd.

Authorized Capital: $20,000 Central Alberta Hard Coal Ltd.; $300,000 The Foothills Collieries Ltd.; $300,000 Canadian Collieries Resources Ltd.

Coal: sub-bituminous

Registered Trade Name: Foothills Hard Coal

Market: domestic and steam

Mine Type: underground; strip pit

Total Extraction: 2,560,000 tonnes

Men Killed: 16

Two Serbian miners, Louis Stupar and Stephen Belkovich, formed the Central Alberta Hard Coal Ltd. and took over two leases formerly owned by Pacific Pass Coal Fields of Lovett. Stupar and Belkovich had limited capital and by 1919 were in severe difficulty. They were owed about $5000 by their coal buyer and at the same time received no break from the Grand Trunk Pacific (GTP), which insisted they pay their shipping bills net 40 days.

They sold out to The Foothills Collieries Ltd., a Winnipeg syndicate headed by A. E. Windatt, a coal dealer whose company marketed not only Foothills coal, but also for a time Coal Valley coal. Like their predecessors, Foothills also had problems with the GTP. Vice President E. H. Bennest, a lawyer, complained bitterly in 1919 to the Alberta Mines Branch not only about his company's inability to get timely coal shipment weights from the railway but also the expectation that they were to pay what appeared to be a $25 per month bribe to the Edson Yard-Master before receiving such records. Bennest reminded the government department that it was upon these weight records that Foothills calculated and paid its Mine Owner's Tax:

"The service we get from the Grand Trunk in this respect is positively rotten and it is going to effect you to the extent of having to wait for our returns and remittances. If you can offer any suggestions as to how we might remedy this I would be pleased to hear from you."

The Mines Branch declined to get involved and wrote back telling Bennest that the company should estimate its coal shipment weights, make its tax payments accordingly, then make the appropriate adjustments after it received the railway records. Foothills began paying its Mine Owner's Tax promptly to the pleasure of the Mines Branch and presumably the Yard-Master.

In 1951 a B.C. mining company, Canadian Collieries (Dunsmuir) Ltd., bought the Foothills mine. By 1957, with the coal market shrinking rapidly, the company, now called Canadian Collieries Resources Ltd., began abandoning what was now a strip pit. It briefly reopened the pit in 1959 to supply coal for a heating unit at its Mercoal mine. In 1960 the mine was again closed and next year officially abandoned.

Sterco

Mine No.: #769

Owners/Operators: 1918 Rocky Hard Collieries Ltd.; 1918-1920 Oliphant-Munson Collieries Ltd.; 1920 Oliphant Collieries Ltd.; 1920-1921 Oliphant-Munson Collieries Ltd.; 1921-1926 Sterling Collieries Ltd.; 1926-1951 The Sterling Collieries Company Ltd.; 1951-1952 Sterling-Coal Valley Mining Company Ltd.

Authorized Capital: $3,000,000 Oliphant-Munson Collieries Ltd.; $1,000,000 The Sterling Collieries Company Ltd.

Coal: sub-bituminous

Registered Trade Name: Sterling Coal

Market: domestic and steam

Mine Type: strip pit

Total Extraction: 4,750,000 tonnes

Men Killed: 9

The coal seam was discovered accidentally in 1911 when it was exposed in a cutting made during the construction of the Coal Branch railway. Pacific Pass Coal Fields of Lovett held the lease for several years but never developed it, considering the coal to be "too fine." The mine was begun by Harry Ferris of Rocky Hard Collieries who ran a tiny strip operation. There was no plant to clean or sort the coal and the miners used wheelbarrows to remove the 3 m of overburden, then loaded the coal into boxcars. Ferris did not have the capital to develop his lease so he brought in Captain William Oliphant, partner at the Oliphant-Munson mine at Mile 40, for assistance. Oliphant, without informing his partner Robert H. Munson, began investing men and equipment in Ferris' operation. Munson eventually found out that Oliphant was using his resources to develop another property and successfully claimed his equity.

Rocky Hard Collieries amalgamated with Oliphant-Munson Collieries, with Ferris, for a time, being the mine manager. Oliphant-Munson introduced steam shovels, built a modern plant and in 1920 closed its original mine at Mile 40. In 1921 the company's name was changed to Sterling Collieries and by 1924 Oliphant was bought out.

In 1942 Sterling Collieries was the site of a social experiment: women were hired as rock pickers in the tipple. It was the Second World War, the men were overseas and there was a labour shortage in the coal mines where, under the provincial Mines Act, women were prohibited from working. The five women, Armstrong, Bochek, Curtin, Onions and Scott, worked in the tipple for several weeks before their presence caught the attention of the media and Mines Branch officials. The Mines Branch ordered that the women be discharged and replaced by men. Since there were no men to take their place, Sterling ceased coal production for several days and appealed to the federal government, which used the War Measures Act to override the provincial regulation and allow them to return to their jobs. Women worked in the tipple for the next three years until, with cessation of hostilities, they were replaced by returned servicemen. There were no complaints about the quality of work done by the "Sterco five."

By 1950 stripping at the Mile 47 Sterco pit ended and a new pit was opened at Mile 54. The coal from the new pit was trucked to the old plant at Sterco. Sterling Collieries bought the Coal Valley Mining Company in 1947 and in 1951 amalgamated the two operations as the Sterling-Coal Valley Mining Company. The Sterco plant was closed and the coal began to be shipped to the Coal Valley tipple. The coal from Mile 54 was of poor quality and often showed a rusty colouring. In 1952 operations ceased and the men were transferred to Coal Valley.

Camping at Fairfax Lake.

FAIRFAX LAKE RECREATION AREA

There are few prettier spots along the Lovett Branch than Fairfax Lake. Surrounded by pine and spruce forest, Fairfax Lake is a popular destination for families and fishermen alike. One of the most appealing aspects of Fairfax Lake is its campground. Built on the side of a hill, each site has a picture-perfect view of the lake. Good fishing and viewing of waterfowl such as loons, grebes and several species of ducks give campers and visitors plenty to do.

There has been a campground here ever since the mid-1960s when Alberta Forest Service developed a rustic campground close to where the dock is now located. In 1985 the campground was expanded and the entire recreation area upgraded to its present configuration.

Location 50 km south of Robb along Highway #40
Facilities 39 lakeside unserviced sites, 5 day-use parking spots, vault toilets, pump, boat launch
Note maximum boat speed is limited to 12 km/hr.

The Tackle Box

Fairfax Lake
Fish Management Area: #4

Species rainbow trout to 900 g, stocked annually, eastern brook trout to 1800 g

Restrictions Wall rainbow trout shorter than 17.5 cm must be released. Use of bait fish and the collection of bait fish are prohibited.

Season 16 June to 31 August

Achoo! Pollen Analysis at Fairfax Lake

During the 1980s, researchers with the University of Alberta conducted palynological research at a number of sites along the Eastern Slopes, including Fairfax Lake. They drew core samples from the lake bottom to study the pollen trapped in the mud. By studying the ancient pollen, the researchers learned what plants grew in the area, and therefore, what the climate was like thousands of years ago.

The record showed that prior to 11,000 years ago the area around Fairfax Lake was treeless tundra. The dominant plants were willow, sage, grass and sedge. The climate at that time would have been dominated by a near permanent high pressure ridge over the continental glacier to the north. The clockwise flow of air around this high pressure ridge, combined with the compression and resulting warming of air dropping off the ice sheet, would have produced strong, relatively mild, dry southeasterly winds. The climate, therefore, at Fairfax Lake was dryer and less seasonable than it is today.

Coring. Photo Alwynne Beaudoin.

As the continental ice-sheet receded, the weather pattern and vegetation changed. Spruce began to appear at Fairfax 9000 years ago followed by pine about 2000 years later. This reflects the slow disintegration of the ice-sheet and breakdown of the glacial high pressure ridge. During this time, the dominant winds shifted from the southeast to the west resulting in the more extreme seasonal temperatures we experience today. Since about 7500 years ago there has been no significant change to the vegetation and climate at Fairfax Lake.

30 FAIRFAX LAKE WALK

NO MAP

Day hiking

Rating one-half hour

Distance 0.6 km

Level of Difficulty easy stroll along groomed trail

Maximum Elevation 1322 m

Elevation Gain nil

Map 83/C15 Cardinal River

Access

Park your vehicle by the dock at the Fairfax Lake Recreation Area. The recreation area dock is 600 m from the Highway #40 turnoff, 39 km southeast of the intersection of Highways #40 and #47.

0.0 km	trailhead
0.1 km	fishing spot
0.2 km	groomed trail end
0.4 km	trailhead
0.5 km	groomed trail end
0.6 km	trailhead

On a warm summer's evening after a day of swimming and fishing, there can be nothing better than a stroll along the lake's edge to watch the loons dive for their supper or a merganser duck leading her clutch out of harm's way.

From the dock turn right and walk to the east end of the parking area where you cannot miss the wide, wood-chip path leading into the open forest with an understorey of lungwort, wild roses, Labrador tea and dogwood. The Department of Environmental Protection has teamed with Watchable Wildlife to erect a number of interpretive signs on this path and the one on the other side of the parking lot. The first of these is about the kingfisher, a bird that lives up to its name along these shores. You will find the sign at a popular fishing spot shortly beyond the trailhead. The belted kingfisher, though, is not the only creature that fishes the lake. For people living and working in the coal mines along the Lovett Branch, hunting and fishing were both recreational pursuits and a cheap way of stocking the larder. Most lakes in the

Fairfax Lake remains a popular campground with fishermen.

Coal Branch do not have suitable spawning habitat and must be stocked each year. Not so Fairfax Lake. With its healthy fish population the lake was a favourite destination of the families who came here in the summer months by horseback to camp along the lakeshore. When the first campground was built here in 1964 by Alberta Fish and Wildlife, the department realized increased accessibility would cause fish populations to plummet. So the decision was made to stock the lake with eastern brook trout and rainbow trout. Monitoring over the next several years showed that the brook trout reproduced well, making further stocking unnecessary. However, since it was also discovered that rainbow trout did not reproduce well here, there is an annual stocking of rainbows. Trout in Fairfax Lake reach a maximum size of 1360 g, or 3 lb.

Another 100 m brought us to a picnic table at the end of the groomed trail. However, the trail, now ungroomed, continues to wander along the edge of the lake for another 100 m or so. En route, we read a second interpretive sign, this one about the black bear. Finally, the trail peters out to a game trail. It was such a pleasant walk that we hope there are plans to extend the groomed trail in the next few years.

Returning to the parking lot, cross over to pick up a narrower but similarly groomed trail on the other side. It, too, skirts the lake's edge passing a picnic table and an osprey interpretive sign. It ends 25 m beyond, below the campground, at an interpretive sign for the bald eagle. A number of social paths lead up the embankment to the campsites.

Fairfax Lake

Previous name: Lohoar Lake

Fairfax Lake is probably named after Fairfax Stuart Landstreet (1861-1939), a New York mining engineer and venture capitalist who, in 1908 and 1909, evaluated what eventually became the Pacific Pass coal leases at Lovett. It is unclear whether Landstreet was under contract to the coal syndicate that owned the leases or whether he was investigating possible investment in the prospect. During his 1909 visit, he was accompanied by his 13 year-old son, Fairfax Jr. Fairfax may also allude to the Fairfax District in West Virginia, at that time a major centre for U.S. coke production and where Landstreet held a significant business interest. In 1918 he became vice-president of Consolidated Coal Company, the second largest coal company in the U.S. Consolidated Coal underwent several transformations over the years and in 1968 its subsidiary, Consol of Canada Inc., entered into a joint venture with Luscar Ltd. The new company was named Cardinal River Coals Ltd.

Lohoar Lake, the local unofficial name, recalls the accidental drowning of James Lohoar (ca. 1873-1917) in the lake. Lohoar was in a boat with two boys when it capsized. He managed to get the boys onto the upturned boat, but drowned when he tried to swim to shore and get help. The boys were eventually rescued. Lohoar was a miner and timber man at the nearby Pacific Pass mine. He lies buried at the Lovett cemetery.

PEMBINA FORKS RANDOM CAMPSITE

There is no recreation area with formal campgrounds at Pembina Forks. Rather, the area on the west side of the highway and immediately adjacent to the Pembina River has long been used as a random campsite. You, then, have a choice of staying at the Fairfax Lake Recreation Area 5.4 km south, at the official Pembina Forks Recreation Area 9.7 km farther south, at Lovett River Recreation Area 16.3 km north all along Highway #40, or random camping at Pembina Forks. If you choose the latter, remember that there are no amenities including washrooms or drinking water.

Pembina River / Pembina Forks

Previous names: Summer Berry River, Elder Berry River, Mile 4
Cree name: Nipiniminan Sipiy (Summer Berry River)

In 1816 fur trader Ross Cox was heading down the Athabasca River from Jasper. "At eleven a.m. we passed a small river from the eastward, called the Pembina, from a profusion of berries of that name which grow on its banks." The berries referred to were high-bush cranberries (*Viburnum sp.*). This was a popular fruit among voyageurs who coined the word pembina and applied it to several rivers and streams in western Canada. Summer berry is a literal translation of the Cree "nipiniminan," which is their word for high-bush cranberry. The river was known to fur traders as early as 1796 who mistranslated nipiniminan as elder berry. In 1809 Peter Fidler, on a map of the region, called the Pembina the Summer Berry River.

The confluence of the Pembina and Lovett rivers is the original Pembina Forks. This name came about before the 1920s when the Lovett River was still called the Little Pembina River, hence the forks being where the two Pembinas met. This name would be transferred south to the Pembina Forks Recreation Area. Mile 4 is the distance count along the forestry trail from the Lovett Ranger Station to the forks and the forestry cabin located there. From here the trail forked with one branch heading southwest to Grave Flats and the other south to the Brazeau River.

An old sundance lodge at Pembina Forks.

Lovett

Mine No.: #233

Owners/Operators: 1910-1913 Pacific Pass Coal Fields Ltd.; 1913-1916 Canadian Coal & Coke Co. Ltd.; 1916-1920 North American Collieries

Authorized Capital: $5,000,000 Pacific Pass Coal Fields Ltd.

Coal: sub-bituminous

Registered Trade Name: Imperial Coal (Cdn. Coal & Coke), Western Crown Coal (North American Col.)

Market: domestic & steam

Mine Type: underground

Total Extraction: 519,000 tonnes

Men Killed: 5

This was the mine that started the Alberta Coal Branch. Bad seams and fire made it a failure.

Raymond Brutinel had been hired by a group of Montreal financiers with close ties to the Grand Trunk Pacific Railway to search for coal. Starting in 1907 he staked about 16,200 ha of the "coal valley" from Lovett northwest to Coalspur. The next year the syndicate brought in an American mining engineer, Fairfax Stuart Landstreet, to evaluate the property and in 1909 formed Pacific Pass Coal Fields.

This group was a who's who of Canadian business with an intertwined network of directorships linking banks, trust companies, foundries, timber companies and railroads. Its president was Grand Trunk Pacific and Bank of Montreal director Edward Black Greenshields. They formed an umbrella company, North American Collieries, which would included Pacific Pass, and mines at Lethbridge, Drumheller and Evansburg. Their corporate lawyer was H. A. Lovett.

Mine development began in 1910. Upon the arrival of the Coal Branch railway in December 1912, there was present a fully equipped mining camp with homes, hospital, colliery office and tipple. Yellowhead Pass managing director, George Henry Richardson, benchmarked this highly capitalized operation in 1915 and doubted its continued success, "Their big trouble has been that the coal they have been mining has been very soft and will not stand preparation for the Domestic market, the percentage of finer coal being so great that it gives them an average selling price below what it cost to mine the coal.... Their only chance of making good is to have a maximum output at a minimum cost and to market as much mine run coal as possible. Even with this it is doubtful that they can keep the mine running as their overhead expense is very high. This due to foolish expenditures in machinery as many thousand dollars worth is lying useless around the mine. They have also a highly paid selling organization, extensive leases, two power plants, many offices, and the interest on money foolishly spent."

Richardson noted the Grand Trunk Pacific was buying much of their coal "mostly because the branch line would be a total loss otherwise."

The company went through two restructurings but could not turn itself around. A fractured seam forced abandonment of one section. Underground fires in 1915 and 1916 forced the abandonment of others. Unable to find a suitable new prospect, the directors cut their losses by closing the mine and letting go of their leases. Ironically, those leases formed the basis of three very successful mining ventures: Coal Valley, Foothills and Sterco.

British Collieries

Mine No.: #365

Owners/Operators: 1911-1916 British Collieries (Brazeau) Ltd.

Authorized Capital: $5,000,000

Coal: bituminous

Mine Type: underground

Total Extraction: 0 tonnes

Men Killed: 0

Despite being assigned a mine number, British Collieries was never a mine. It was a prospect that ceased operations in 1913, probably because of the recession of that year. Work had proceeded as far as building a mining camp and surveying the right-of-way for 56 km of railway to that camp from Lovett.

The "Laurier Boom" began in 1910 and was a period of staggering economic expansion for Canada during which time both the country's population and gross national product would nearly double. Business enterprises were started, in Grand Trunk Pacific President C. M. Hays' dry words, "trusting somewhat the future." The frenzied trusting resulted in the subscription to numerous ventures that in more rational times would never have merited serious consideration. It is not clear whether British Collieries was such an irrational venture, but be that as it may, with the advent of the Balkan Wars in 1913, capital markets dried up, the boom ended and British Collieries shut down. Though its Winnipeg office remained open until 1922, there was never a serious effort to reopen the mining camp.

The first leases were issued in 1909 and were eventually assigned to Edward Brown, a Winnipeg financier. Brown headed a Canadian-American syndicate whose $5,000,000 capitalization would be matched only by the Pacific Pass operation at Lovett. Brown was an impressive player at a time when politics underwrote major business ventures. He was the Manitoba provincial Liberal leader and between 1915 and 1922 served as treasurer in the T. C. Norris government. Norris and Brown came to power with the help of another man who was part of the British Collieries syndicate: Sir Douglas Colin Cameron (1854-1921). Cameron, a lumber baron and between 1911 and 1916 lieutenant-governor of Manitoba, is well known to constitutional historians as he was one of the few lieutenant-governors to play an active role in the downfall of a government. In 1915 he forced the calling of a Royal Commission to investigate allegations of the illegal misappropriation of funds granted for the construction of the Manitoba legislative building and so caused the downfall of Conservative Sir Rodmond Roblin's government. Cameron, of course, was a federal Liberal appointee.

The presence of the empty mining camp in an extremely isolated location along Chimney Creek fascinated Coal Branchers who, not aware of the mine's true origins, created their own oral history about it. They called the camp Germantown and speculated that it was started with German capital with even Kaiser Wilhelm involved. With the advent of the First World War, the miners were called back to Germany to fight and the mine ceased operations. This story is probably a faint echo of a discontinued mining operation, started by German capital, which occurred in 1910 southeast of British Collieries along the Blackstone River. There, Martin Nordegg and the German Development Company proposed to start a mine. That venture ended when Nordegg and Mackenzie & Mann pooled their resources to form Brazeau Collieries and started a mine at Nordegg.

31 SILKSTONE AND LOVETT LAKES

MAP PAGE 163

Silkstone and Lovett lakes are Luscar Sterco's showpieces of reclamation, evidence of what is achievable at a foothills' mine. While visitors can learn to appreciate the scientific planning and knowledge that went into the reclamation, most people are drawn to these lakes because of the fishing. Stocked in 1992 and again in 1995 by the Fish and Wildlife branch of the Department of Environmental Protection, the 18 m-deep lakes now have self-sustaining populations of rainbow trout. So bring your fishing rod!

The information board at the trailhead has a route map that shows your way down to two old mining pits, now reclaimed and renamed Silkstone and Lovett lakes. It's a straightforward walk or bike ride (no motorized vehicles are allowed past the barricade), but the route map is, nevertheless, a good idea since you have to pass by two active mine pits and cross a busy haul road. After an initial steep descent your roadway winds up and then down through a mining area that will be reactivated in the near future. It is a hostile, moonscape-like environment in which you find

Got one!

Day hiking, cycling
Rating half day
Distance 5.8 km
Level of Difficulty walk through active mine area
Maximum Elevation 1356 m
Elevation Gain 30 m
Map 83/F2 Foothills

Access

Park your vehicle at the trailhead parking area 1 km east of Highway #40. The turnoff is 26 km south of the intersection with Highway #47 or 25 km north of the intersection with the Cardinal River Road.

0.0 km	trailhead
1.1 km	mine road
1.5 km	intersection
1.7 km	Silkstone Lake
1.9 km	intersection (corresponds with 1.5 km)
2.5 km	outlet channel crossing
2.6 km	Lovett River bridge
2.7 km	old highway #40
3.0 km	intersection
3.1 km	Lovett Lake picnic area
5.8 km	trailhead

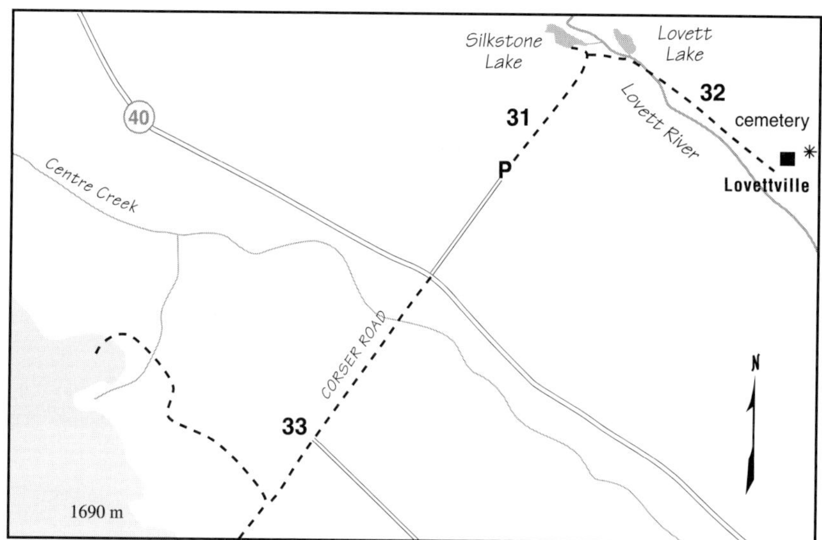

yourself. Rock and gravel overburden have been thrown up during the creation of pit 20, on your left, and pit 21 on your right. The pits have filled with water but are desolate and forlorn in appearance. A little vegetation struggles along the top of the overburden but as you wend your way down past the pits toward the haul road the bleakness of your surroundings intensifies. Stop at the haul road; 154-tonne trucks have the right-of-way!

Once across the haul road the scenery changes dramatically. Gone are the barren heaps of rock and gravel. You are now descending gently through a large reclamation area that boasts of extensive stands of lodgepole pine and white spruce. In the distance you can spy another haul road. The scene this time is very different from what you just experienced. Reclamation has been extended right up to the edge of this other haul road that is nearly camouflaged by the newly-contoured slopes on the other side of the lakes. At a signpost you have a choice of going to either Silkstone Lake via the left fork or to Lovett Lake via the right-hand fork.

We chose to visit the upper lake, Silkstone, first. A short walk drops you to one end of the lake where, if you are lucky, you can spot muskrat along the lake's edge or geese nesting on one of the floating platforms in the lake. On a hot day the placid waters look inviting. Swimming, however, is not allowed. In planning the reclamation of these two mine-cuts, the pit walls were resloped to provide optimum fish habitat, but the drop at the edge of both lakes is, nevertheless, very steep. Meanwhile, fishermen have created a rough path that stretches along one side of the lake that you can follow if you wish.

Returning to the intersection of the two trails, bear left along the rough roadway leading down to Lovett Lake. Cross Silkstone Lake outlet where it discharges into the Lovett River below and pick up the pathway that wends its way down the slope to a bridge over the Lovett River. Mining did not disturb this section of the Lovett River; rather, it has been left in its natural

Strip pit. Courtesy Luscar Sterco.

The pit has been contoured and the shoreline defined. Courtesy Luscar Sterco.

In 2000 grasses and lodgepole pine trees grow along the shoreline. Courtesy Luscar Sterco.

state. After climbing out of the river crossing you arrive at a T-junction with a good gravel road, the old highway #40 that runs through part of the mine site. Although you cannot see it owing to the reclamation work along its shoreline, Lovett Lake is directly in front of you. A visit to the picnic shelter at the end of the lake is but a short walk to your right. Exercise some care. The old highway is not used as a haul road but mine vehicles do scoot up and down it and tour buses visiting the mine use the old highway as access to the picnic area.

Return the way you came, remembering to bear left at the trail intersection to return to your vehicle.

The Reclamation of Pits 31E and 42

In walking from the trailhead down to the lakes you are struck by the sharp contrast between the active mine areas and the 64 ha of reclaimed land around the old mine pit 31E, now called Silkstone Lake, and pit 42, now Lovett Lake. All mine lands must be returned to a level of productivity at least equal to or better than what was there prior to disturbance. The Coal Valley mine, operated by Luscar Sterco Ltd., has planned forestry, wildlife habitat and recreation as the final land uses for the mine site.

Coal Valley uses two methods to extract the coal, truck and shovel in the open pits and dragline in areas where the coal seams are less deformed. Reclamation of strip-mined lands is a well-developed science on the plains. However, mine-cut lake development as a viable alternative to backfilling and contouring mine-cuts, or pits, had not been tried in the foothills when the Coal Valley mine commenced operations in 1978. Therefore, studies of natural lakes in the area and of pre-1950s abandoned pits were undertaken to give the environmental planners at the mine the information they needed to construct two mine-cut lakes designed for a self-sustaining fishery as a recreational end use. The two mine-cuts identified for this experiment were pits 42 and 31E.

Mining of the Mynheer seam in pit 42 began in 1981 and was completed in October 1984, when mining in pit 31E of the Silkstone seam commenced; the dragline left pit 31E in August 1985. In both cases, lake development beginning with the resloping of the pits commenced even before the dragline pulled out. Once the pits had been reconfigured to maximize potential fish habitat, they were allowed to fill with groundwater. Meanwhile, construction of the outflow from Silkstone Lake to the Lovett River had begun and was completed in September 1986. Unlike Silkstone Lake, Lovett Lake has no outflow channel. Instead, a series of springs flows into the river. Reclamation of the surrounding area proceeded apace. The overburden was levelled and contoured by December 1985. Six months later the entire area was covered with 30 cm of topsoil allowing seeding with a special blend of grasses and legumes. Aquatic plants were transplanted from nearby lakes allowing Silkstone and Lovett lakes to reach a productive state much sooner than would normally have been the case. Once the ground cover was well established, the area was planted mainly in lodgepole pine and white spruce, although some aspen, green alder, dwarf birch and willow were also planted in order both to mirror the natural vegetation cover and to satisfy future forestry needs. Reforestation was completed in 1991. Today, it is not unusual to see elk, white tail and mule deer browsing on the slope sides.

So successful has been the reclamation of these 64 ha that Luscar Sterco is planning potentially seven more mine-cut lake developments that would boost the recreational attractions of the area as well as proving to be a boon to fish and wildlife of the region.

32 LOVETT TOWNSITE

An evocative visit to a ghost town complete with a number of extant buildings and a small cemetery are yours to experience on this short trip.

After an initial steep descent from your trailhead, the roadway winds up and then down through a mining area with pit 20 on your left and pit 21 on your right. Cross the mine haul road. You are now in a large reclamation area of lodgepole pine and white spruce. In the distance you can spy another haul road. At a signpost bear to the right for Lovett Lake. Cross Silkstone Lake outlet where it discharges into the Lovett River below and pick up the pathway that wends its way down the slope to a bridge over the Lovett River. After climbing out of the river crossing you arrive at a T-junction with a good gravel road, old highway #40 that runs through part of the mine site. The old highway is not used as a haul road but mine vehicles do scoot up and down it and tour buses visiting the mine use it as well, so exercise some caution after you turn right onto the old highway. From here, it's a straightforward jaunt along the road wending past

Day hiking, cycling

Rating half day

Distance 6.6 km

Level of Difficulty walk through active mine area

Maximum Elevation 1361 m

Elevation Gain 35 m

Map 83/F2 Foothills

Access

Park your vehicle at the Silkstone and Lovett lakes trailhead parking area 1 km east of Highway #40. The turnoff is 26 km south of the intersection with Highway #47 or 25 km north of the intersection with the Cardinal River Road.

Note Because Lovett townsite is located within the boundaries of the Luscar Sterco mine, access is controlled through the mine office. Contact the Human Relations office at 794-8100. The senior pit foreman determines accessibility.

0.0 km	trailhead
1.1 km	mine road
1.5 km	intersection
2.1 km	outlet channel crossing
2.2 km	Lovett River bridge
2.3 km	old highway #40
2.6 km	intersection
3.2 km	intersection
3.3 km	Lovett townsite
6.6 km	trailhead

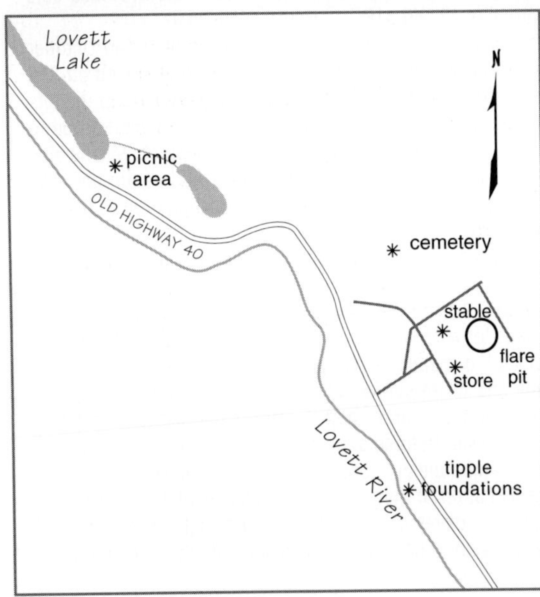

Lovett from hillside above townsite.

the new mine site and through the shallow Lovett River valley. On your right are the rail line and Lovett River; on your left a hillside that has remained untouched by Luscar Sterco. One kilometre after turning onto the old highway you arrive at the ghost town of Lovett.

A track on your left leads you up the slope to the old ghost town. The store with its name just barely visible above the door is the largest building on site, but in addition you will find a number of log and frame buildings, foundations and depressions of structures no longer standing. A grave marker dedicated to Nick Shurvin, the "mayor" of Lovett, is located nearby. Almost all early mining towns were built immediately next to the mine workings. An old mine adit can be located just down the slope past the stable. The cemetery can be found amongst the trees past the stable and up the slope.

The modern mine can be found just over the brow of the hill. Take an old roadway that leads up hill from the stable. Poking around in the trees you can find an old flare pit and beyond here you arrive at the new workings. To your right you can see an exposed coal seam in the creekbed. Returning toward the townsite, you have a bird's-eye view of Lovett, the Lovett River and the workings of the Alberta Canadian Collieries Ltd. across the river.

Lovett/River

Previous names: Lovettville, Fergie, Mile 57, Little Pembina River

Lovett and Lovett River are named after Henry Almon Lovett (1866-1944), a corporation lawyer who was president of Canadian Coal & Coke Company Ltd. (Pacific Pass Colliery), owner of the local mine. The first coal claims in the area were staked in 1907, one of them being in Lovett's name. At that time he was a lawyer for the Montreal based syndicate that first explored, then beginning in 1910, developed the coal deposits. Corporation lawyers, otherwise known as entrepreneurs-at-law, were prominent at the turn of the 20th century as businesses became intricately involved with government in defining the limits of their activity. Lovett was a top-ranked lawyer with the Grand Trunk Pacific Railway and was one among a rarified group including future Prime Minister R. B. Bennett, who worked for the Canadian Pacific Railway and the best of them all: Zebulon Aiton Lash of the Canadian Northern Railway.

Fergie was named in 1912 after Charles Fergie (1857-1924), the consulting mining engineer at the mine, then owned by Pacific Pass Coal Fields Ltd. Fergie was born in Lancashire, England, and came to Canada in 1887. He was an original member of the Canadian Mining Institute and its president for two years. Mounting financial losses led to the reorganization of Pacific Pass as Canadian Coal & Coke and Fergie was removed during the management shake-up. Lovett, now president, in a Stalinesque move, renamed the mining camp after himself.

Lovett was the station name, while Lovettville was the post office name. The post office opened in 1914, had its name changed from Fergie to Lovettville in 1915 and closed in 1935. Residents preferred to call their community Lovett.

Mile 57 is the distance count along the East Coal Branch railway from Bickerdike.

The Lovett River is a tributary of the Pembina River, hence its original name the Little Pembina River. Despite the name change in 1927, the latter name remained in popular local use into the 1930s.

Lovett townsite, ca. 1912. Courtesy Provincial Archives of Alberta, Archives Collection A20012.

33 CORSER ROAD

MAP PAGE 163

This trip may appear to be of short duration, but the steep ascents and descents make it a challenge for cyclists. Your reward? A view of the foothills and the Sterco mine from high on a hillside, plus an exhilarating return ride to your vehicle.

From the Silkstone and Lovett lakes trailhead, return downhill to Highway #40. Straight ahead, serving as a dramatic backdrop to the scene in front of you, are the peaks of the Front Ranges. Your destination is beyond the clearing that you can see high up in the rolling forested hills before you. Cross the highway to begin your trek up Corser Road.

Cycling

Rating half day

Distance 18.6 km

Level of Difficulty wellhead road; steep ascents and descents

Maximum Elevation 1570 m

Elevation Gain 61 m

Map 83/F2 Foothills; 83 C/15 Cardinal River

Access

Park your vehicle at the Silkstone and Lovett lakes trailhead parking area 1 km east of Highway #40. The turnoff is 26 km south of the intersection with Highway #47 or 25 km north of the intersection with the Cardinal River Road.

0.0 km	trailhead
1.0 km	Highway #40
1.4 km	Centre Creek
3.0 km	intersection
3.6 km	stream
5.2 km	intersection
7.2 km	intersection
8.6 km	stream
9.3 km	abandoned wellhead clearing
18.6 km	trailhead

Approaching the pitch up Corser Road.

Corser Road is a good gravel road that undulates past boggy moose pasture, crosses Centre Creek and continues straight ahead past an intersection with West Road. You climb slowly in gentle steps as far as a small stream crossing. Beyond this point Corser Road begins its no-nonsense climb, winding up and around the hills. After making a sharp 90° turn to the right, the road passes through a clearing. So far, Corser Road has proven to be a rather pretty ride. Your route becomes even prettier once past the stream crossing as the road winds around, then down and then up, burrowing ever deeper into the hills. At a Y-junction keep to the right along the better-used roadway. You are climbing sharply now as you enter one of the small cutblocks that you saw from the trailhead. A couple of kilometres later you skirt another cutblock, this one approximately 15 years old so the lodgepole pine are well established but not so tall as to block vistas looking toward the Luscar Sterco mine. Bear right again at another Y-junction. The roadway narrows and has seen much less traffic than the rest of Corser Road, witnessed by the grass growing down the middle. The infrequent traffic has resulted in a road that is in excellent condition for cycling. The road snakes down and around to the left crossing a bridge over a small creek. It then churns its way steeply over loose rocks, looping to the left as it climbs to your final destination, an old wellhead site.

The wellhead has long since been dismantled but the site remains clear of trees so that you can enjoy a great view of the foothills to the east while catching your breath after a strenuous ascent.

Your exhilarating descent ends at Highway #40. Once across the highway you must climb to the trailhead and your vehicle.

Sour Gas

Liberally scattered throughout the Coal Branch are numerous natural gas well sites. Some, like the one at the top of Corser Road, have been dismantled; others are still in production; and even others are continuing to come on stream. An aerial view of the Coal Branch would show a network of roads punched through the forest to terminate at such a site. Needless to say, the oil and gas industries are major players in the economy of today's Coal Branch.

The commercial presence of natural gas in the Coal Branch was first recorded in 1915 when a natural seep was discovered about 2 km north of the Yellowhead Pass mine near Coalspur. Managing director George Henry Richardson recommended the gas be used to run the power plant at the mine site, but the idea was never implemented. In the 1920s the Coalspur area was explored by Imperial Oil, which drilled several wells. By 1931 the Lovett area was also being explored, this time by a consortium including Hudson's Bay Oil and Gas. It would not be until the 1950s, however, that petroleum and natural gas exploration would become a major concern in the Coal Branch.

The two biggest gas fields are the Hanlan and Edson fields that together hold an estimated 70 billion m^3 or about four per cent of provincial reserves. Recent new gas reserves include the 1997 announcement by Talisman Energy Inc. of Calgary of a new gas field near Lovett.

Natural gas is a mixture of hydrocarbons, mostly methane. Created under conditions of extreme heat through the decomposition of organic matter in sedimentary rock, much of Alberta's natural gas contains hydrogen sulphide (H_2S), which sours the sweet gas and must be removed before the gas can be marketed. The Hanlan field east of Robb, plus several smaller fields including the Lambert field, have sour gas. These fields are part of "sour gas alley," which stretches in an 80 km-wide band from Fox Creek south to Pincher Creek. An important by-product of our natural gas production, then, is sulphur; in fact, Alberta produces about 45 per cent of the world's sulphur. It is largely used to make fertilizers.

Controversy swirls around sour gas. Why? Hydrogen sulphide is a deadly and corrosive acidic gas. In certain concentrations it irritates eyes and causes headaches and nausea. Residents of "sour gas alley" living close to either a sour gas plant or a flare stack have long complained of birth defects in cattle and humans, and there is a growing body of data that points to hydrogen sulphide as the culprit in brain damage, balance problems and short-term memory loss. In greater concentrations, hydrogen sulphide paralyses sense of smell. At 500 parts per million, H_2S can knock a man unconscious. If not rescued within four to six minutes, he will die. This is why sour gas well sites are posted with the warning "Do not enter."

There are a number of ways H_2S can be released into the atmosphere. Some of it, determined to be unmarketable owing to its low amount, is flared where it is largely converted into sulphur dioxide (SO_2); SO_2 is the villain in acid rain. Flaring, however, does not convert all the H_2S into SO_2; inevitably anywhere between 20 and 40 per cent of the gas spewed from flare stacks is raw sour gas. Even marketable quantities of sour gas, which are pipelined to gas processing plants where the sulphur is extracted, are not 100 per cent safe; leaks can occur at well sites or from the pipeline itself and sadly, gas blow-outs are not uncommon in Alberta.

In response to decades of complaints, industry, government and environmental groups have conducted study after study, all with inconclusive results. Conflicting evidence and a self-regulating industry will mean that the controversy will continue.

Sour gas well site.

34 LOVETT FIRE TOWER

Fire towers are natural destinations for those who enjoy modest elevation gain and great views. In addition, this trip underlines the importance of primary resource industries—forestry, coal mining and natural gas—to the economy of the Coal Branch and to the province.

Day hiking, cycling

Rating half day

Distance 13.8 km

Level of Difficulty one steep pitch

Maximum Elevation 1509 m

Elevation Gain 176 m

Map 83 C/15 Cardinal River; 83/F2 Foothills

Access

Park your vehicle at the Pembina Forks. The forks lie along Highway #40, 34 km south of the intersection with Highway #47 and 17 km north of the intersection with the Cardinal River Road.

0.0 km	trailhead
0.1 km	intersection
0.5 km	intersection
0.8 km	intersection
1.5 km	intersection
2.0 km	wellhead
2.2 km	sour gas line right-of-way
4.9 km	intersection
5.7 km	intersection
6.3 km	intersection
6.8 km	intersection
6.9 km	Lovett fire tower
13.8 km	trailhead

You are now on the old Coal Branch highway. Within 20 m there is a crossroads with an OHV track. Ignore it continuing along the old highway. On your left there are signs to warn you against trespassing onto Luscar Sterco mine property, which extends northward from here past the main entrance into the Coal Valley mine site. Ahead, you can see some of the workings of this strip mining operation. The Lovett River, meanwhile, winds its way slowly alongside the road on your left.

Forestry, coal mining and natural gas exploration—mainstay industries of the Coal Branch—come together in this one scene.

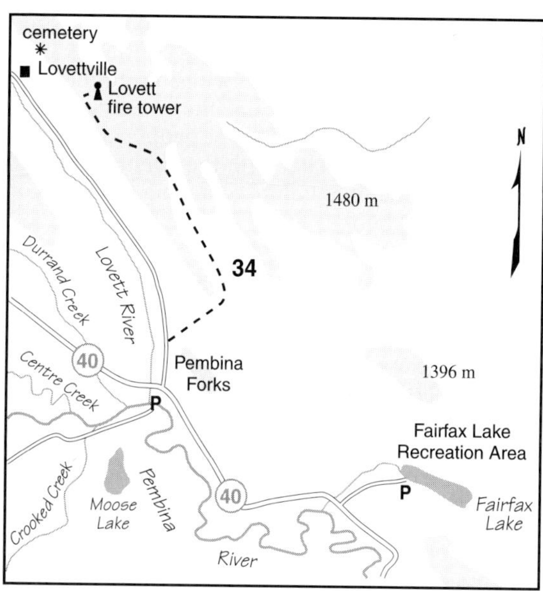

The old highway you have been following ends abruptly at an intersection with a barricade. To proceed farther along the old highway is to trespass onto active mining property thereby incurring the concern of mine officials who are liable for your safety. Follow the new gravel road as it swings sharply to the right. Ignore a gravel road that joins on your left a few metres beyond the previous intersection. That gravel road leads down to the continuation of the old highway but do not tempt fate or the good humour of the mine's senior pit foreman. Instead, continue along the mine bypass roadway, through a crossroads and past a wellhead site. With a pipeline right-of-way on your left you enter an old small cutblock on your right. Soon, though, you are back into tall stands of lodgepole pine. The road dips down and then up, climbing slowly as it swings to the left toward the Lovett fire tower. You can catch glimpses of the fire tower now and again through the trees.

The alternating red and white sides of the fire tower cupola are suddenly directly ahead and above you where your road ends at a T-junction. Turn left climbing past a well site and access road on your left. Within 500 m you come to an intersection with the old Coal Branch highway that joins your road on the left. As before, this road is closed as it leads directly into the Luscar Sterco mine site. Bearing right, you break out almost immediately onto a sweeping vista. To your left are the reclaimed areas of the old worked-out seams, now gentle green hills that roll northward toward the active mining pits. A truck and shovel method of removal was being used when we were here and we could easily hear and see the mine trucks as they roared up and down the haulage road. In the distance farther to the right you can see the tipple for the entire Coal Valley mine. Your road deteriorates somewhat as it dips down a small slope.

At a T-junction bear to the right along a rough 4 x 4 track that climbs stiffly up a cutline. It passes through a small cutblock that allows for a wide panoramic view. The Lovett fire tower, a physical presence guarding the rolling forested foothills of the Lovett Branch, is in front of you; reforestation of the cutblock through which you are climbing reminds you of the importance of logging to the area; and, if you turn around, you can see below oil and gas well sites adjacent to the Luscar Sterco coal mine.

Climbing the cutline road you come to an intersection with a road that takes a 90° turn to the right. The cutline continues straight ahead but you want to keep on the 4 x 4 track that swings up to the fire tower past a gate. A small residence, a power plant and the fire tower itself make up the Lovett fire tower site. Visits with the tower people are usually pleasant affairs, for their life can be lonely. A chat with the person on duty will also reveal the nature of their seasonal job. Before returning the way you came remember to ask to sign the guest book.

Fire Detection

Fire towers and mountain lookouts across the province form the first line of defence against forest fires. The work carried out at the towers and lookouts is known as "fixed" detection; this remains the backbone of the detection system of the Alberta Forest Service (AFS). For areas not covered by towers and lookouts, fire detection relies on regular aircraft patrols. Of the 135 towers and lookouts in the province, 110 are fire towers such as the Lovett fire tower. Each has a working radius of approximately 40 km with some "slopover" into another lookout's area. This "slopover" is useful in pinpointing a fire more accurately.

The Lovett fire tower.

Some fire towers, such as the Lovett tower, are easily accessible; others are more remote. In either case, it takes a special kind of person to be at a fire tower. Needless to say, a critical criterion for the job is sharp eyesight! But equally important is the ability to live alone. Usually at the end of a season, the fire tower people are quite happy to leave, some uncertain whether they want to return. But just as commonly, when the AFS sends out letters of application in midwinter for the next season, they are ready to return for another season among the clouds.

WEST BRANCH

The presence of steam coal in the Mountain Park area was known as early as 1906 but was not developed by either of the two major players in the Coal Branch at that time, the Canadian Northern (CNoR) and Grand Trunk Pacific (GTP) railways. The CNoR held coal claims at the head of Mackenzie Creek but chose not to develop them owing to the surrounding terrain and an arrangement with Martin Nordegg with whom it found a better prospect at what became Nordegg. Meanwhile the GTP, through Raymond Brutinel's efforts, had decided to support the development of the Pacific Pass mine at Lovett on the East Branch.

So it came to be that, in 1910, John Gregg and R. W. Jones, after staking their Mountain Park claims immediately to the west of the CNoR lands, eventually turned to Great Britain for the capital and political muscle to access, develop and hold their leases. That the money to develop was found in Britain was no surprise. The 1900-1913 Laurier boom was a period of staggering expansion for Canada wherein foreign money and people poured into Canada. The country's population grew by over 40 per cent and was projected to reach 145 million by 2000. The Gross National Product more than doubled between 1900 and 1910 and was projected to double again by 1920.

It was these numbers that caused Prime Minister Sir Wilfred Laurier to predict that the 20th century would belong to Canada. This was not an unreasonable claim

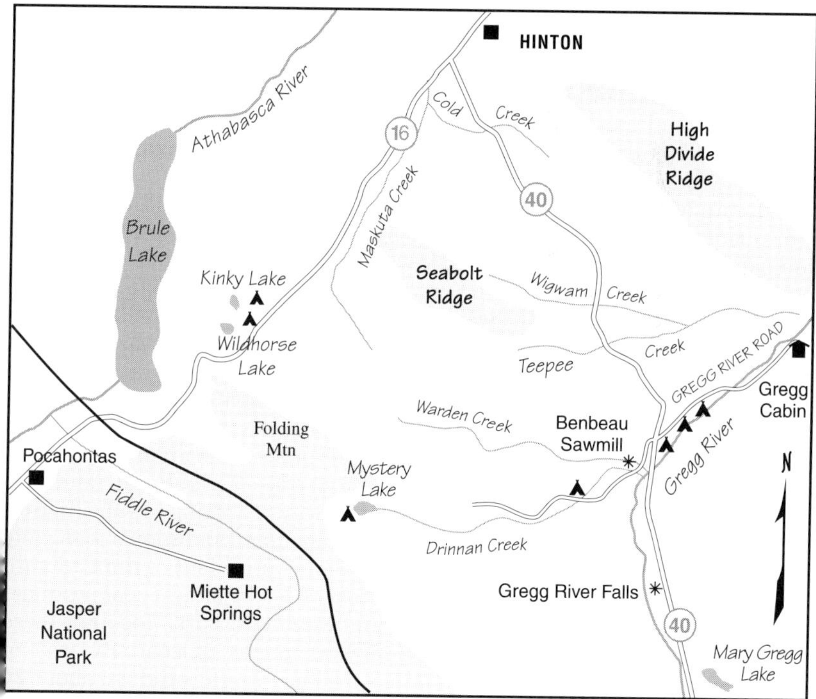

since at the time Canada's rate of growth was outstripping that of the United States. All this would come to an end during the 1913 depression but, in the meantime, the country grew and grew with no end in sight to the opportunities to invest and profit. Much of the foreign venture capital that fuelled this growth came from Britain. In 1906 about $68 million of British capital was invested in Canada; by 1913 the annual figure had soared to $376 million. By way of comparison in 1913, the United States invested $135 million in Canada.

In the West Branch the British money came two ways, by direct investment by British individuals as was the case at Mountain Park and, later, Luscar and indirectly by way of a development company as was the case at Cadomin. The Mountain Park and Luscar stories basically belong to one family, the Mitchells of Scotland. That family's association with coal began in 1835 with the formation of the Alloa Colliery Company, Alloa being the name of a town near their mine in Clackmannanshire. This company would go through several reorganizations before becoming in 1898 the Alloa Coal Company Ltd. with Alexander Mitchell Jr. as president.

Mitchell was the proverbial aristocrat born with the silver spoon in his mouth. It would be his son Harold who would receive the knighthood but photographs of Alexander show a handsome, well-bred man looking over a world that was his oyster. Be this as it may he was not lazy. He believed in hard work, duty and discipline with time off for fox hunting, travel and cartography. He was a soldier during the First World War and commanded a unit at Gallipoli. After the war he would show his mettle on the corporate battlefields reorganizing what up till then was a struggling Mountain Park Coal Company.

One of Alloa's employees was a man from Linlithgowshire on the other side of the Firth of Forth, Robert Drinnan. Drinnan had already immigrated to Canada when Mitchell, in 1911, invested in the Mountain Park venture. Their paths would not cross until about 1920 when Mitchell was reorganizing the Mountain Park Coal Company and enticed Alloa-trained Drinnan away from Cadomin where he was general manager.

Cadomin, which opened in 1917, was a Canadian Dominion Development Ltd. operation, Canadian Dominion being a Liverpool-based development company formed to channel British investment into any number of ventures. Development companies rode the wave of prewar British investment abroad as Victorians nowhere near as wealthy or powerful as the Mitchells sought to invest their savings almost anywhere there was a better return than at home. Land settlement schemes, mines, pulp and paper companies, railways both steam and electrical were the more popular projects floated. Some were little more than "humbugs" preying upon the small investor. Many, however, proved to be long lasting and profitable enterprises. Canadian Dominion's investment portfolio included townsite properties, agricultural land and mines including Cadomin, all tied together by way of a string of subsidiaries.

A Canadian, Frederick L. Hammond, was Canadian Dominion's managing director at its Winnipeg office and would become president of the Cadomin Coal Company. Hammond's mine would prove to be the largest coal producer in the Coal Branch followed by Luscar and Mountain Park. Together these three mines would produce over 24 million tonnes of coal. By way of contrast, all the other Coal Branch mines together would produce about 20 million tonnes of coal.

The West Branch proved to be the largest and presumably most profitable sector of the Coal Branch. It was here that the first claims were staked, yet owing to circumstances within the CNoR and GTP, its development followed that of the east and head of the branch. In terms of early Coal Branch development history, it was the Cinderella stepchild and proof positive of how often intangibles such as luck and timing can affect the best planned of long-term schemes.

Coal Branchers

Frederick L. Hammond (1874-1941)
Occupation: developer, mine owner, publisher

Frederick Hammond was the developer and owner of the Cadomin mine. Hammond was born in Port Dover, Ontario, and graduated in political economy from Harvard University. He joined the Winnipeg office of Canadian Dominion Development Ltd. and became its managing director. Canadian Dominion was one of a network of Anglo-Canadian affiliated companies based in Liverpool, England, formed to attract British venture capital into western Canada. This group of development companies was started in 1910 by Edward Baillie and would become involved in a diverse range of projects including orchard development in the Kootenay region of British Columbia, townsite property in Port Arthur (now Thunder Bay), Ontario, mining in Nelson, B.C., and of course, the Cadomin mine.

The coal seam at Cadomin was first discovered during the survey of the railway between Coalspur and Mountain Park and was brought to Hammond's attention, possibly through his brother-in-law Thomas McNabb Burnett, who staked in 1911 what later became known as the east mine. Hammond hired James A. H. Church, a mining engineer, who examined the area and that same year staked the west side of the McLeod River. The property remained undeveloped until 1917 when the Cadomin Coal Company Ltd. was formed and there were further stakings in the names of Baillie and Canadian Dominion sales manager Percy G. Ebbutt. Hammond became president of Cadomin Coal. On the board was his brother-in-law Burnett, while Baillie was corporate secretary.

Hammond built a residence in Cadomin and during his visits to the community participated in its social development. He was remembered by some Coal Branchers as a slightly built man with a strikingly beautiful wife and three daughters. In 1924 Hammond presented to Father Louis Culerier $1000 and a site for a Roman Catholic chapel.

In 1930, Hammond retired and began to indulge in his literary interests. He purchased two British publications, *The Fortnightly* and *The English Review of London,* and hired a young man from Brule named Lovat Dickson as his editor. Dickson was studying English literature at the University of Alberta and before being sent to London, had been editor of the *Blue Diamond Weekly* in Brule. Thanks to Hammond's patronage, Dickson would rise in London society to become an internationally known publisher and literary critic. In his multi-volume autobiography, he paints a vicious picture of Hammond, describing an indecisive, reclusive, bored man living out an idle life along the Mediterranean coast of France. "We used to talk until the early hours of every morning because he suffered from insomnia and made me suffer too. We talked of everything, but mostly of literature. He fancied himself a great reader, but although he bought a lot of books he was hardly ever to be seen reading one." Dickson resented Hammond's editorial interventions in the two magazines and grew to detest the man. Their final meeting was on a moving train from which Dickson jumped and ran away.

Hammond returned to Canada in 1937, resumed his position as president of Cadomin Coal and remained active in its management until his death in Edmonton.

MCLEOD RIVER RECREATION AREA

Originally built in the early 1960s the McLeod River Recreation Area was upgraded to 22 campsites in 1981. The close proximity of the recreation area to both Hinton and Robb makes it a popular spot with residents of those towns as well as others who choose to camp for several days at a time at this quiet campground.

The recreation area offers a variety of activities that the whole family can enjoy. Fishing is particularly good. If bird watching takes your fancy, use any of the trails in the area to look for great grey owls, grey jays, pine siskins, spruce grouse, woodpeckers, Canada geese and a variety of ducks. You can even follow in the footsteps of others before you and try your hand at panning for gold!

Location Twenty-four kilometres southeast of Hinton along Weldwood's Robb/Hinton Road or 19 km west of Robb along the same road.

Facilities 22 unserviced campsites, pit toilets, water pump

Note no horses

A well-groomed path behind the campsites leads you along the river's edge.

The Tackle Box

McLeod River
Fish Management Area: #4

Species northern pike to 10 lb., walleye to 8 lb., bull trout to 5 lb., rainbow trout to 10 lb., whitefish to 2 lb.

Competition Winner Rocky Mountain whitefish, 2.819 lb., 1990

Restrictions Walleye limit is 3 longer than 43 cm. All bull trout (Dolly Varden) must be released. All rainbow trout shorter than 17.5 cm in length must be released. Use of bait fish and the collection of bait fish prohibited 1 April to 16 August.

Season 1 April to 31 October

35 MCLEOD RIVER CAMPGROUND LOOP

NO MAP

Looking for a short and easy walk or bike ride that everyone in the family can enjoy while staying at the McLeod River Recreation Area? This loop takes in both the recreation area and adjacent areas for an interesting one hour of activity.

If you're camping here you can pick up this easy loop by walking to the river's edge where Alberta Environment has built a good gravel path. The path parallels the McLeod River all the way from the old bridge site located farther down the road from the campground to the new bridge over the McLeod. Turn left onto the trail and follow it as far as the new bridge where it ends. It's a pretty and easy stroll or bike ride, with the river on one side and the well-treed campsites on the other. An informal path underneath the bridge connects Alberta Environment's campground with random campsites across the road. Once on the other side of the road scramble up the embankment to the trails that crisscross the area. Turn right and follow the main track past a viewpoint looking across to the confluence of the Gregg and McLeod rivers.

Walking, cycling
Rating one hour
Distance 3.8 km
Level of Difficulty easy stroll or bike ride; scramble below bridge
Maximum Elevation 1157 m
Elevation Gain 10 m
Map 83/F6 Pedley

Access

The McLeod River Recreation Area is 19.3 km from Robb or 24 km from Hinton along the Hinton-Robb Road. There is no real trailhead. You can pick up the trail anywhere between the campsites and the McLeod River. Distances are marked from the McLeod River bridge.

0.0 km McLeod River bridge
0.9 km random campsite

At the confluence of the Gregg and the McLeod rivers.

Along the McLeod River.

Continue along the main track to the far end of the area. Find an OHV track and follow it as it meanders through the bush, now away from the McLeod River. Within a short distance you find yourself at a random campsite complete with a large fire pit. The OHV track now swings sharply to the left. Follow it back to the Robb Road and turn left. Swing right into the McLeod River Recreation Area and take the road all the way down to the river, ignoring the campground road on the left. A guardrail prevents vehicles from going farther. Even though the topographical maps show a bridge across the river, no bridge has spanned the river at this location for many a year. It's a pretty and somewhat dramatic setting. Across the river you can easily see the cookhouse for the group campground. On this side of the river on your right, high cliffs loom over a bend in the river inviting further exploration. OHV tracks lead down to the base of the cliffs and to several random campsites. Returning to the old bridge site drop below the guardrail and find Alberta Environment's campground trail and follow it back to your campsite.

1.1 km	Hinton-Robb Road
1.1 km	White Creek Road
1.2 km	McLeod River Recreation Area road
1.6 km	front entrance campsites
1.9 km	campsite #19—lightning strike tree
2.1 km	back entrance campsites
2.4 km	barrier—former bridge site
3.8 km	McLeod River bridge

Not the 'Gold' Branch

The first interest in the mineral resources of the Alberta Coal Branch was focused not upon its coal, but its gold. The story begins in the mid 1800s when placer deposits of gold were found in the gravel bars of the North Saskatchewan near Edmonton. By 1862 there were over 300 gold miners in the Edmonton area. Over time prospectors began testing other streams and rivers for gold traces and found them in the Athabasca and McLeod rivers.

The gold they found were not gold nuggets, but gold flour, that is, tiny flakes of gold no more than 0.1 to 0.5 mm in diameter and only a few hundredths of a millimetre thick. Because these flakes were so tiny, they suspended in flowing water and settled only where water velocity decreased dramatically such as on the inside of a meander or in a mid-channel sandbar.

With the gold being found in the sandbars, speculation naturally arose as to the source—the mother lode. Prospectors began travelling farther and farther upstream looking for the source of gold. Records of their trips are scanty, but in 1886 we know there were two parties in the Coal Branch along the McLeod River.

One party, made up by George Philledeau, Adolph Mangot and John Morris, entered the Coal Branch via the Brazeau and Cardinal rivers, crossed the Cardinal Divide to the Pembina, then from the Pembina crossed over to the McLeod, which they then followed downstream to the Jasper Trail near present-day Edson. They found traces of gold along the Brazeau, nothing in the Pembina and enough gold in the McLeod to warrant a second trip. The second 1886 party, made up by N. P. Nelsen and George Burke, followed the McLeod upstream to the Gregg River. From here their directions are vague, but it appears they followed the Gregg River to Drinnan Creek then went up the Drinnan to Mystery Lake. They found traces of gold but not in large enough quantities to justify any placer diggings.

In 1898, James McEvoy of the Geological Survey of Canada followed the McLeod River north from the mouth of Beaverdam Creek. He noticed coal along the river. He also spotted gold: "Some prospecting has been done on the McLeod, in which a certain quantity of gold was obtained. It is found chiefly in a small seam in the river gravels, principally composed of dark material derived from the shales." In 1909 there was the Embarras gold rush. That year gold claims along the Embarras River were staked by H. T. James, Ben Farnier and Jim Hopkins. They tried to keep the location of their strike a secret, but word got out and on their return trip to the Embarras, the three men were followed by several other parties of would-be gold seekers. As was the case along the McLeod, there was not enough gold in the Embarras to justify any mining operations and the gold rush fizzled out almost immediately after it began.

The amounts of gold found upstream along the McLeod was minute, but downstream from Edson there were enough accumulated gold deposits in the gravel bars to justify during the early 1930s the McLeod River Gold Dredging Company. Gold prices during the Great Depression were high, but as the Depression eased, prices dropped as did accordingly the operations of the Gold Dredging Company.

The source of the gold was for a long time subject to speculation among geologists. The Athabasca River mother lode was finally found in 1987 in quartzite deposits in Jasper National Park. As for the source of the McLeod River gold, so far no one knows.

The importance of the early gold seekers to future Coal Branch development is indirect. They never found the gold in the quantities they sought, but as they explored the country it is inconceivable they did not recognize the presence of coal in the area. They would have given it little mention because at the time it held no economic value. With the announcement that a transcontinental railway would be built through the northern Rockies, coal suddenly became valuable. And, thanks to the gold seekers, there was a basic body of knowledge of the Coal Branch that would help direct the coal seekers to their claims.

36 MCLEOD CLASS III ROAD

A rather lengthy bicycle ride takes you up into the hills through a series of cutblocks for excellent views of the McLeod River valley. If you are here in late summer, remember to keep a sharp eye for bears. The Coal Branch is justifiably proud of its huckleberries, which grow in profusion. Bring a pail. If you are lucky you can pick enough for a pie.

Cycling
Rating full day
Distance 34.6 km
Level of Difficulty bike ride on forestry road
Maximum Elevation 1507 m
Elevation Gain 360 m
Map 83/F6 Pedley

Although it's a mere 700 m from the bridge over the McLeod River to the intersection with Tri-Creeks Road, you must climb steeply out of the river valley. At the intersection, bear left and follow the Tri-Creeks Road as it gently rises and falls for approximately 4 km as far as the intersection on your right with the signed McLeod Class III Road. En route, you pass a random campsite on your left. When we were here, vehicular traffic on the Tri-Creeks Road was light making this a pleasant bicycle ride.

The McLeod Class III Road is narrower than the Tri-Creeks Road but is nevertheless a good gravel road for cycling. You climb steadily along the road, turning right at the first intersection to keep on the McLeod Class III Road. This is hilly logging country with alternating cutblocks and as you climb, vistas to the south and west open up. Ignore five intersections with logging access roads on your right. The next intersection is a definite fork. Keep to the left. A gentle climb carries you past an intersection with a logging access road. Five hundred metres later the Bighorn Trail crosses the road. We were here a year before Weldwood was planning to upgrade the access and route to the Bighorn Trail along the High Divide Ridge. So when you take this trip the signage for the Bighorn Trail may be different from what we saw. The trail, as we saw it, appeared well marked by a series of small hiking signs that lead the hiker along a well-defined path that skirted the edges of the cutblocks as it climbed toward the High Divide Ridge.

Past the signage for the Bighorn Trail you ignore first one, two and then a third intersection with logging roads, travelling for a short period beside Teepee Creek. You continue to climb slowly. Now you have Wigwam Creek and a black spruce forest below you on your left. Watch for the next

Access

Park your vehicle at the McLeod River Recreation Area along the Robb Road, 24 km east of Hinton or 19 km west of Robb. Distances are marked from the McLeod River bridge.

0.0 km	McLeod River bridge
0.7 km	Tri-Creeks Road
2.8 km	random campsite
4.6 km	McLeod Class III Road
5.4 km	intersection
6.1 km	intersection
6.5 km	intersection
7.9 km	intersection
8.1 km	intersection
8.8 km	intersection
10.0 km	intersection
10.5 km	Bighorn Trail
12.0 km	intersection
12.2 km	intersection
13.3 km	intersection
16.9 km	intersection
19.0 km	intersection and random campsite
20.3 km	intersection
23.1 km	Bighorn Trail
23.4 km	intersection
25.8 km	intersection [corresponds to 8.8 km]
34.6 km	trailhead

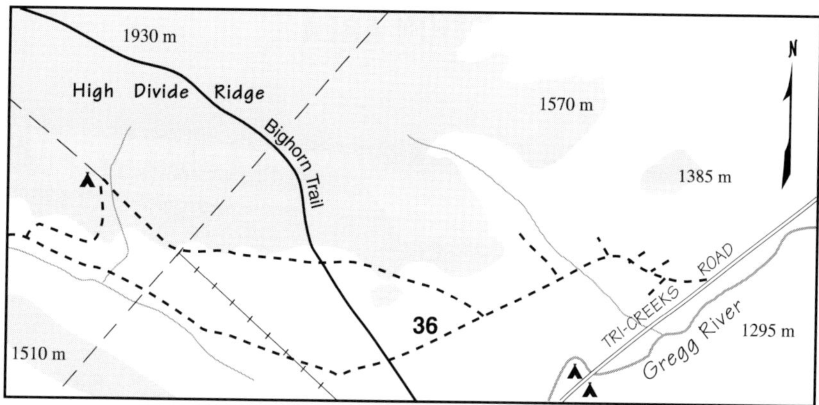

intersection with a logging road on your right. You want to bear right onto this rougher and, if it has been raining, softer roadway. This is a slightly narrower logging road that leads uphill sharply along the edge of a cutblock. When you finally arrive at an intersection at the top of the pitch turn right; a random campsite is off to the side of the road. You are now paralleling the McLeod Class III Road below. Ignore an intersection with another logging road, pass the signs for the Bighorn Trail and continue downhill to an intersection with the McLeod Class III Road. You are now back on familiar territory as you turn left. If it was a puff and a push to climb up the road from the Tri-Creeks Road, you now can savour a fun ride all the way back down the hill. At the Tri-Creeks Road turn right. The 8 km bicycle ride along what is relatively flat terrain brings you back to the recreation area.

Bighorn Trail

The Bighorn Trail was the original trunk route along the east front of the Rocky Mountains. It ran south from Hinton to the mouth of the Bighorn River where it connected with the Morley Trail, which continued south toward Morley. A forestry trail, it was completed in 1916, although its corridor was a well-used Indian route for centuries before.

Its first recorded use was in 1800 when North West Company fur trader Duncan McGillivray followed it from near Nordegg to the Brazeau River. Until the construction of the Grand Trunk Pacific and Canadian Northern railways between Edmonton and Jasper, the preferred access route into the Coal Branch was from the south via the Bighorn. Geologist D. B. Dowling, who arrived by this route in 1909, explains, "These trails are well travelled, and are on hard ground, so that they are preferable to the present approach from the east, which, in places, is through soft muskeg for considerable distances."

As a forestry trail in the 1920s and 1930s, the Bighorn left Hinton and followed the High Divide Ridge to Gregg Cabin, then onto Grave Flats and the Brazeau River.

The stretch between Gregg Cabin and Grave Flats is now road. South from Grave Flats to the Brazeau the route has been cut up by forestry and wellhead roads and is now a popular OHV track. Only north of Gregg Cabin along the High Divide Ridge does the trail remain in near pristine condition. Here, Weyhauser is preserving the Bighorn Trail for historical and recreational purposes.

GREGG CABIN RECREATION AREA

The new log cookhouse.

The West Branch of the Coal Branch has very few recreation areas. In fact, the Gregg Cabin Recreation Area is the only one north of Cadomin, and as we go to print it is only a day-use facility. There are, though, plans to upgrade the recreation area to an overnight campground. Until now, vacationers have had to random camp nearby and no doubt will welcome the upgrading.

Weldwood and Foothills Model Forest have had a presence in the immediate vicinity of the historic Gregg Forestry Cabin for a number of years, ever since they designed and built a number of groomed trails throughout the area. To inform the public about the need for forest management, the partners developed an interpretation programme that, in the last several years, has fallen into disuse. However, as part of the recreation area's upgrade, the interpretation programme is being revived and upgraded.

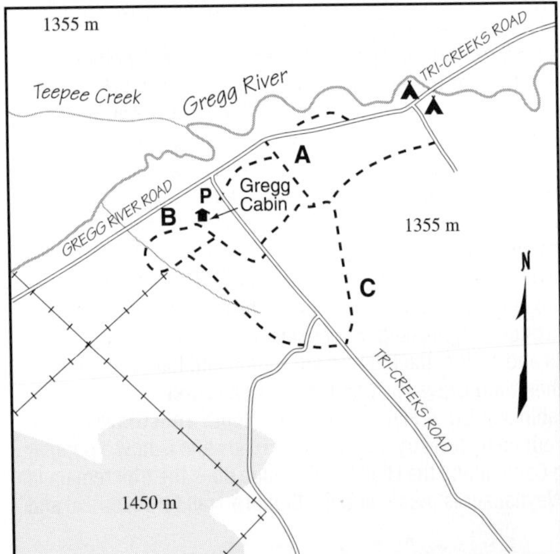

Location 8.5 km east of the Highway #47 along the Gregg River Road or 10 km west of the Tri-Creeks and Robb Road junction

Facilities day use only, cookhouse, pit toilets

Note No water pump at time of printing

Authority Alberta Environmental Protection, Weldwood

FORESTRY MANAGEMENT TRAILS

Park your vehicle at the Gregg Cabin Recreation Area on the Gregg River Road, 8.5 km east of the Highway #47 junction or 10 km west of the Tri-Creeks and Robb Road junction. The trailhead is the large sign 100 m south of the recreation area cookhouse.

A number of years ago Weldwood, recognizing the popularity of the area surrounding the historic Gregg Cabin, constructed a number of groomed trails in the immediate vicinity. An interpretive programme, aimed to educate the public about forest management, was put in place. Now, a revival of this programme has been planned as part of Weldwood's upgrading of the recreation area. However, as we go to print, this plan has not yet been implemented. So, using existing trails, we have identified three loops for visitors staying at the Gregg Cabin Recreation Area.

Short Loop-route A

Day hiking, cycling

Rating one hour

Distance 2.8 km

Level of Difficulty easy stroll or bike ride

Maximum Elevation 1265 m

Elevation Gain 25 m

Map 83/F3 Cadomin

0.0 km	trailhead
0.0 km	intersection
0.0 km	intersection
1.0 km	intersection
1.0 km	Tri-Creeks Road
1.2 km	intersection
1.8 km	intersection
2.0 km	intersection
2.5 km	100 millionth tree
2.5 km	50 millionth tree
2.6 km	Tri-Creeks Road
2.7 km	intersection
2.8 km	Gregg Cabin Recreation Area

Beginning at the signpost just south of the Gregg Cabin there is an intersection of several trails within metres of each other leading you to a choice of routes. To take the Short Loop go straight ahead at the first intersection, but bear left at the next quick intersection. A 100 m swing through the cool forest brings you to the Tri-Creeks Road where you want to turn left and go downhill to an intersection with another groomed trail on your right. The trail undulates gently for one half kilometre to the next intersection. Turn left to begin your swing back to the recreation area; otherwise you are on the Long Loop. A short walk or ride brings you to another intersection. Turn left again. The trail soon joins a gravelled path that leads past a scarified plot on your right. Take a quick detour into the plot to read Weldwood's' plaque announcing that the small tree in front of you is the company's 100 millionth tree planted. Back on the gravel path, on your left, there is another short fork. On June 8, 1991, Weldwood planted its 50 millionth tree in this plot. Return to the gravel path, then turn left. The Gregg Cabin Recreation Area is directly across the Tri-Creeks Road. As you walk along the roadway into the recreation area the roadway forks. If you bear to the left you will return to the trailhead. Swinging to the right will take you directly back to the recreation area and your vehicle.

The Gregg Cabin used by forestry rangers. An interpretive sign for the cabin is located just southwest of the cabin.

Along one of the Forest Management trails.

Day hiking, cycling
Rating one hour
Distance 1.4 km
Level of Difficulty easy stroll or bike ride; one stream crossing
Maximum Elevation 1255 m
Elevation Gain 15 m
Map 83/F3 Cadomin

0.0 km	trailhead
0.0 km	intersection
0.0 km	intersection
0.1 km	intersection
0.6 km	intersection
0.7 km	stream crossing
0.8 km	intersection
1.4 km	Gregg Cabin Recreation Area

West Loop-route B

By the signpost at the edge of the forest there is an intersection of several trails. Go straight ahead at the first intersection but bear right at the next junction. You are now walking or cycling along a well-groomed trail as it passes through a forest of lodgepole pine. Within a short distance you arrive at a fork where you will want to bear left; if you turn right you will return to the Gregg Cabin. A pleasant trip brings you to yet another fork. This time keep to the right to begin your loop back to the recreation area. Cross a small stream. Almost immediately there is another fork. Bear to the right. A pleasant walk or cycle through a meadow returns you to the Gregg Cabin and your vehicle.

Long Loop–route C

Day hiking, cycling

Rating half day

Distance 8.4 km

Level of Difficulty easy stroll or bike ride

Maximum Elevation 1325 m

Elevation Gain 85 m

Map 83/F3 Cadomin; 83/F6 Pedley

0.0 km	trailhead
0.0 km	intersection
0.0 km	intersection
0.1 km	intersection
0.6 km	intersection
1.3 km	begin braid
1.6 km	end braid and intersection
1.8 km	intersection
2.3 km	road crossing
2.8 km	Tri-Creeks Road
3.3 km	intersection
4.2 km	intersection
4.9 km	intersection
5.7 km	road
6.1 km	intersection
6.1 km	Tri-Creeks Road
7.0 km	intersection
7.4 km	Tri-Creeks Road
7.6 km	cutline
8.2 km	Gregg River Road
8.4 km	Gregg Cabin Recreation Area

By the signpost at the edge of the forest there is an intersection of several trails. Go straight ahead at the first intersection but bear right at the next junction. You are now walking or cycling along a well-groomed trail as it passes through a forest of lodgepole pine. Within a short distance you arrive at a fork where you will want to bear left; if you turn right you will return to the Gregg Cabin. A pleasant trip brings you to yet another fork. Keep to the left once again otherwise you will be on the West Loop trail. Now, you begin a longer section of the trail that leads gently uphill. At a braid in the trail keep to the right. When you reach the end of the braid there is an intersection where you want to bear left. Keep left at another intersection 200 m farther down the flat trail. An easy downhill trip through the open forest ends at a gravel logging road. Cross the road and pick up the continuation of the trail that leads you back into the open forest. Shortly, you arrive at the Tri-Creeks Road. Cross the road and find the "Wilderness Trail" sign. Follow the forest trail downhill to a T-junction. Bear to the left. An excellent downhill trail brings you to another intersection. Keep to the left again. At the next intersection, bear to the right this time; otherwise you will be on the Short Loop. A longer trip that continues downhill ends at a logging road. Turn left onto the road remembering to watch for logging trucks that still use this road. Continue along the logging road to its junction with the Tri-Creeks Road. Turn left. The Tri-Creeks Road is a good, wide gravel road that continues to a junction with the Gregg River Road. En route, if you wish, watch for an intersection with a pleasant trail on your right. Although not a long swing, it does take you off the road, which can be dusty if there is traffic. Soon you are back on the Tri-Creeks Road. Go straight ahead at the junction with the Gregg River Road. Soon there will be the sign for the Gregg Cabin Recreation Area on your left.

Coal Branchers

John Gregg Jr. (ca. 1874-1945)
Occupation: fur trader, guide/packer, prospector

John Gregg's Coal Branch career spanned the history of the area. He began as a fur trader before there was any significant outside economic interest in the area; became a guide when that interest began and ended as a prospector and successful investor as that interest materialized in the form of coal mines.

Gregg was an American, born in Montana about 1874. He arrived at Prairie Creek, near Hinton, around 1894 where he became a partner with N. H. "One-eyed" Jock, a local fur trader and trapper. Gregg's guiding business put him in early contact with prospectors in the Coal Branch. In 1907 he took Raymond Brutinel's party to the Lovett River where they prospected and staked what eventually became the Pacific Pass mine at Lovett. Next year, Gregg was back in the area, guiding another party to the Brazeau coal lands along the Cardinal River. By this time Gregg was doing his own prospecting and together with Jock, around 1907, staked several claims along Cold Creek near Hinton.

In 1904 Gregg married Mary Cardinal who is credited with leading him to the Mountain Park coal area that he staked in 1910 with R. W. Jones. This staking, together with Luscar in 1918, also with Jones, put Gregg into that small minority of prospectors in the Coal Branch whose investigations and stakings actually led to some form of financial security. The story, popularized by Alberta historian James MacGregor, where Mary Cardinal directs John Gregg to the Mountain Park coal, is likely not true. Gregg was already guiding other prospectors in the region. By 1906 the Mountain Park area was being prospected by Thomas Russell and in 1910 these claims were evaluated by American mining engineer Charles Hower. Meanwhile, there were stakings southeast of Mountain Park toward Grave Flats and at British Collieries. R. W. Jones was already aware of the Russell claim and by 1908 had collected and analyzed coal samples from the region. Gregg was probably aware of these activities through his guiding and packing business, before making his first claim there in 1909. Gregg had bear problems at Mountain Park that year. A grizzly tore into his food and left him with no supplies. Luckily, next day, he shot two caribou and when he later returned to Prairie Creek, he not only had coal samples to show Jones, but also caribou meat to share.

Luscar chairman, Sir Harold P. Mitchell, met Gregg in 1921 and described him as a "quiet, thin, hard-bitten man, who had, with difficulty, settled down to an everyday life." By now Gregg was a widower. Mary Cardinal passed away in 1915. His two lively stepdaughters from Mary's first marriage, Lucy and Gladys, had died earlier. Alone, Gregg moved to Florida where he died in 1945.

WARDEN FLATS RANDOM CAMPSITE

There is no recreation area with formal campgrounds at Warden Flats. Rather, the area on the former site of the sawmill, immediately adjacent to the Gregg River and east along the Gregg River Road up to the first bridge, has long been used as random campsites. You, then, have a choice of staying at the Watson Creek Recreation Area 29 km south on Highway #40 or at Hinton 23 km to the north. If you choose to random camp, remember that there are no amenities including washrooms or drinking water.

Warden Flats / Creek

Previous names: Grizzly Flats, Drinnan Flats

The Warden Flats takes its name from nearby Warden Creek. It's named after an old trail that followed the creek to the flats and originated at Prairie Creek. This trail was used by Jasper Park rangers and presumably the warden during the early 1920s when the park's north-south boundary ran along the east side of Range 25. Parks built a cabin called Boundary Cabin beside Drinnan Creek but abandoned it in the late 1920s when the park boundary was shifted west to its present location. The reason for the shift was the presence of marketable timber along Drinnan Creek and its tributaries. This timber would later be exploited by a sawmill at the site otherwise known as Camp 33 or the Benbow mill.

The trail and a telephone line strung along it fell into misuse and it would not be reopened until 1945 when Alberta Forestry removed the line and cleared the overgrowth. The original trail predates the national park's presence. Its first recorded mention was in 1910 by Dominion Land Surveyor Hugh McGrandle who stated that it left John Gregg's homestead at Prairie Creek and ran "in a southeasterly direction until the west fork [Gregg River] of the McLeod River is reached."

The Flats were a crossroads. From here one could travel northwest along the Warden Creek trail to the Jasper Park entrance; due west along the Mystery Lake trail to Mystery Lake and Miette Hot Springs; northwest along the Bighorn Trail to Gregg Cabin and Hinton; and south along the Bighorn Trail to Luscar and Cadomin. The Flats became a popular summer camping area for Luscar residents, a number of whom set up permanent tents. From here they would either fish the nearby streams, visit the Miette Hot Springs or go sheep and grizzly bear hunting to the west on the heights around Mystery Lake.

Grizzly Flats takes its name from Grizzly Creek, the local unofficial name for nearby Drinnan Creek. This name was used well into the 1940s. Drinnan Flats is a later unofficial name taken from the same stream.

The Tackle Box

Warden Flats Fish Management Area: #4

Species Gregg River: rainbow trout, brook trout and arctic grayling to 1 lb., bull trout and rocky mountain whitefish to 2 lbs. Drinnan Creek: rainbow trout, bull trout and rocky mountain whitefish to 1 lb. Warden Creek: small rainbow trout and bull trout.

Restrictions use of bait fish and the collection of bait fish are prohibited. All bull trout (Dolly Varden) must be released. Gregg River restricted to downstream from Berry's Creek.

Season 1 April to 31 October

37 GREGG RIVER LOOP

Day hiking, cycling
Rating half day
Distance 8.7 km
Level of Difficulty old roadways with two stream crossings
Maximum Elevation 1387 m
Elevation Gain 60 m
Map 83 F/3 Cadomin; 83 F/4 Miette

The fairly flat terrain and good gravel roads make this short jaunt excellent for cycling. A visit to an abandoned sawmill and a fun crossing of the Gregg River add zest to this family outing.

From the campsite return to your access road off Highway #40. Turn left and follow the road to the bridge across Warden Creek; this is a new bridge built in 1996. The campsite that you just left acts as an informal staging area for hikers, cyclists and equestrians heading west for the high country of the Front Ranges. The road, which is well-maintained, sees regular use by these user groups.

Once across the creek your road climbs slightly to a broad, flat meadow. The blue outline of the Front Ranges lies in the distance. What dominates your immediate attention, though, is an old, rusty incinerator. This is the only artifact remaining of Jack Benbeau's sawmill at what was called Camp 33. An intersection with a four-wheel-drive track on your right gives you easy access to the site.

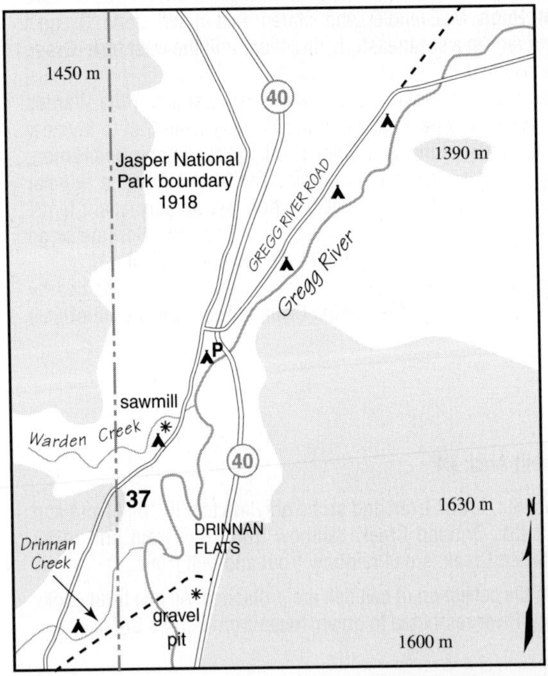

Access

Park your vehicle at an informal campsite near the Gregg River bridge on the west side of Highway #40. The campsite turnoff is 23 km south of Highway #16, or 25 km north of the intersection with the Cardinal River Road. The campsite lies 300 m down the road beside the Gregg River.

0.0 km	trailhead
0.3 km	intersection
0.4 km	Warden Creek
0.6 km	mill site and intersection
0.9 km	intersection
1.1 km	intersection
4.1 km	Drinnan Creek bridge
4.4 km	intersection
5.2 km	gravel wash
5.5 km	Gregg River
5.8 km	intersection
6.1 km	gravel pit
6.3 km	Highway #40
7.3 km	intersection
8.0 km	intersection
8.3 km	Gregg River bridge
8.4 km	intersection
8.7 km	trailhead

The Benbeau sawmill was one of many such industrial sites that could be found at any time throughout the Coal Branch.

Poking around the old sawmill reveals a large sawdust pile and numerous dangerously sharp pieces of broken metal and glass. Be careful.

Continue west along the road ignoring an intersection with an old grassy roadway that joins on your left where the road makes a 90° turn to the north. A short distance beyond here you come to yet another intersection. Turn left onto this good gravel road and begin almost immediately to climb a long hill. At the apex of the hill the Front Ranges come into view again. Then, if you are cycling, it is an exhilarating ride downhill to Drinnan Creek. Cross the one-lane bridge and climb a low rise. Look sharply for an intersection joining from behind on your left. Turn left onto this road. You are now on the backside of the loop heading in a generally southeasterly direction toward Highway #40. This road is used less frequently than the other road but is, nevertheless, in good condition. It is a flat run down the road through a gravel wash as far as the Gregg River. No bridge crosses the Gregg at this point but the river is shallow, if wide, with a stony bottom so crossing should not be a problem.

Once across continue along the road; it dips to cross a ditch but otherwise offers a flat run. You will have to climb a short hill to gain the gravel pit above. The view from the gravel pit looking west up Drinnan Creek valley is quite pretty. Turning your back on the mountains follow the road out of the gravel pit back to Highway #40. Turning left onto the highway you will have an easy ride downhill to the Gregg River bridge. En route you will pass a Weldwood reforestation area. These lodgepole pine were planted by Weldwood between 1970 and 1979. The next harvest will not be until 2069, about 100 years! Once across the Gregg River bridge the intersection leading to your trailhead is a short distance beyond. There will be no problem in locating the campsite and your vehicle 200 m up the road.

Stone hopping across the Gregg River.

Drinnan Creek/Mount Drinnan

Previous names: Grizzly Creek, West Branch of the West Fork McLeod River

Drinnan Creek and Mountain are named after Robert G. Drinnan (1874-1940), a Scottish mining engineer. He worked for the Alloa Coal Company, owned by the Mitchell family before immigrating to Canada where he worked at Crowsnest Pass before coming to Cadomin in 1918 to become general manager of the newly opened mine.

Two years later, Alexander Mitchell was seeking a solution to Mountain Park's management problems and renewed his acquaintance with Drinnan. In 1921 he lured Drinnan to Mountain Park with the offer of company shares and a seat on the board of directors. Drinnan's arrival coincided with the development of Luscar. Since the Mountain Park and Luscar mines were run by separate companies but shared the same directors, Drinnan became general manager of mining operations for both mines. He held that position until 1938 when he resigned owing to ill health.

In 1925, Alberta geologist Ralph L. Rutherford recommended this stream be named after Drinnan "...who did considerable early prospecting in the Kootenay rocks in the area drained by this creek." Drinnan had operated a prospect on the northeast side of Folding Mountain in 1910 and 1911 and had traced the seam southeast to Drinnan Creek and beyond. His partner in this exploration was geologist James McEvoy who had traversed the Coal Branch 12 years before.

The local unofficial name for the stream was Grizzly Creek. Grizzly Creek was so-named because it led hunters into grizzly bear country to the west. The pass between Mystery Lake and the Fiddle River is a significant grizzly corridor. Local use of the name Grizzly Creek continued into the 1940s.

In 1911 Dominion Land Surveyor John Francis called Drinnan Creek the West Branch of the West Fork McLeod River. By West Fork McLeod River, Francis meant the Gregg River.

38 MYSTERY LAKE TRAIL

2 MAPS

Although this trip is only 21 km in length, we recommend you take two days to cross over to Miette. Mystery Lake is a pretty stopping place to spend the night and possibly explore the ridges that surround the lake before continuing your way to the Aquacentre for a soothing soak.

From the random campsite adjacent to Drinnan Creek walk up the road passing first a trapper's cabin and then a short distance later a random campsite, both on your right. Your walk through lodgepole pine forest is interrupted at a Y-junction in the track. Bear left. The road winds slowly along a ridge with a valley below on your left. You walk by an old barbed wire and log fence before you come to an intersection with an OHV track. Bear left onto the OHV track as it winds down the ridge bisecting a horse trail en route to Drinnan Creek. Cross Drinnan Creek and walk up the rocky gravel wash to a T-junction with an old roadway or OHV track. Turn right onto the track. Bearing left will take you back to the trailhead. Within a short distance your track leaves the spruce and pine forest to enter the first of five natural meadows, this one bisected by a cutline. The track ducks back into the forest bringing you to Drinnan Creek. A short but pretty walk alongside the creek ends with a creek crossing. There is yet another creek crossing within 500 m that once again puts Drinnan

Backpacking, horseback riding

Rating two days

Distance 21.5 km

Level of Difficulty steady walk; river crossing; bushwhack, steep pitch

Maximum Elevation 1510 m

Elevation Gain 185 m

Map 83 F/4 Miette

Access

Park your vehicle at an informal campsite beside Drinnan Creek 8.1 km up the Mystery Lake road. The turnoff to the Mystery Lake road is on the west side of Highway #40, 21 km south of Highway #16, or 27 km north of the intersection with the Cardinal River Road. The campsite is 50 m past the Drinnan Creek bridge.

Note this hike requires two vehicles.

0.0 km	Mystery Lake road
0.9 km	random campsite
1.3 km	Warden Creek bridge
1.4 km	mill site and intersection
1.8 km	intersection

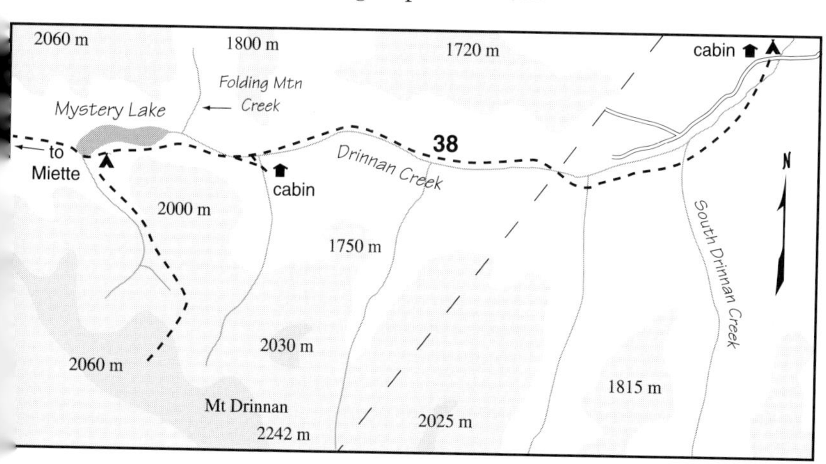

Creek on your right. Within 50 m of this last stream crossing you come to a fork. Keep to the right and pass through an old gate. A signpost announcing the Mystery Lake trail can be found adjacent to a nearby random campsite.

The trail immediately drops down to Drinnan Creek, which you must cross yet again. Ignore a track on your right that leads up the slope and go straight ahead as the trail follows the creek closely, crossing a meadow and then hugging the creekbed as it skirts beneath moss-covered slopes on the opposite bank. You cross another meadow before reentering the open forest. Your track then opens to a wide meadow, much of which is swampy. There is no option but to slog through the swamp to the other side where you quickly enter another meadow. This meadow, too, can be swampy but when we were here it had completely dried up despite being a wet year. The horse trail now enters the forest winding around wet spots and clambering over tree roots. Although your trail is still good it is obvious that you are entering a blow-down area. You have to cross Drinnan Creek again but it is now much smaller and its rocky bed makes an easy crossing. Immediately on the other side of the creek there is an intersection. Bear to the right and recross Drinnan Creek again. From here to Mystery Lake the horse trail has been largely obliterated by windfall. If in doubt hug the creek, making your way as best you can. You eventually rejoin the OHV track that you left earlier; this makes your passage a little easier but it is still a rough trail.

Your trail then crosses and follows a gravel wash. Until now you have had few glimpses of the mountains as you climbed. But a few hundred metres after joining the gravel wash the horse trail/ OHV track widens and opens to Mystery Lake and the surrounding mountains of the Front Ranges.

Why so few people seem to have visited Mystery Lake that year was a mystery to us. It's such a delightful spot. The kidney-shaped lake is surrounded on three sides by ridges and low mountains that, on a calm morning, are reflected in the lake. We overnighted at a horse camp located at the far end of the lake. Though there is a horse trail in the trees along the south side of the lake, the most direct and easiest route to the campsite is to walk along the lakeshore. There is no clear path

2.0 km	intersection
4.2 km	Drinnan Creek bridge
4.5 km	intersection
4.9 km	gravel pits
6.7 km	intersection
7.0 km	random campsite
7.2 km	intersection
7.8 km	intersection
8.1 km	Drinnan Creek, campsite, OHV track and trailhead

0.0 km	trailhead
0.3 km	cabin
0.5 km	random campsite
1.9 km	intersection
2.7 km	intersection
2.8 km	intersection
3.0 km	Drinnan Creek and gravel wash
3.1 km	OHV track
3.4 km	cutline
3.7 km	Drinnan Creek
4.2 km	Drinnan Creek
4.3 km	random campsite, gate, Mystery Lake trail, Drinnan Creek, cutline
4.4 km	2nd meadow
4.8 km	3rd meadow
5.0 km	stream crossing
5.0 km	4th meadow
5.6 km	start 5th meadow
6.0 km	end 5th meadow
6.1 km	begin braid
6.2 km	end braid

The east end of Mystery Lake. Photo Robin Chambers.

along the shoreline but less than a kilometre later, located 50 m from the water's edge, you find a well-established campsite. The presence of the lake means, of course, that water is not an issue. But if you do not trust the lake water, you can find a fast flowing creek behind the campsite. Simply follow a trail that leads straight through the campsite.

We took a day hike up to a ridge behind the campsite. From the top there is a wonderful 360° view. Take the trail that leads to the creek and continue along it as it begins to wind along the bottom of the ridge. Do not cross the creek but remain on the left side, scramble across the talus and begin a bushwhack up the fairly steep slope while continuing to move forward. Once on top, it's a glorious ridge walk to the Jasper Park boundary or back north along the ridge and down to he campsite.

To continue to Miette, find an intersection of rails at the campsite. One trail leads back to the reek. Another cuts diagonally through the ampsite heading toward the Jasper Park boundary. Yet a third trail continues to follow along the edge of the lake past the campsite to the westernmost oint of the lake. Here, the trail takes a 90° turn to e west. Of the two routes to Miette this one

7.6 km	Drinnan Creek and intersection
7.9 km	Drinnan Creek and bushwhack
8.5 km	OHV track
8.9 km	gravel wash
9.6 km	Mystery Lake
10.7 km	random campsite and intersections
10.9 km	Jasper Park boundary
14.4 km	intersection
16.8 km	Fiddle River ford
17.0 km	Fiddle River edge
17.1 km	intersection
19.4 km	intersection
21.5 km	Aquacentre

Crossing the Fiddle River. Photo Felicia Taylor.

seems to be the most heavily used although your horse trail passes through willows and stands of cow parsnip so thick that at times it is almost obscured. The beginning of your slow, easy descent toward the Fiddle River is marked by a cutline and a modest marker indicating the boundary of Jasper National Park. After swinging a little to the left for several kilometres the horse trail comes out onto a bench above the Fiddle River. The scene in front of you is fairly dramatic, the foaming river channelled between high canyon-like walls. A short distance later

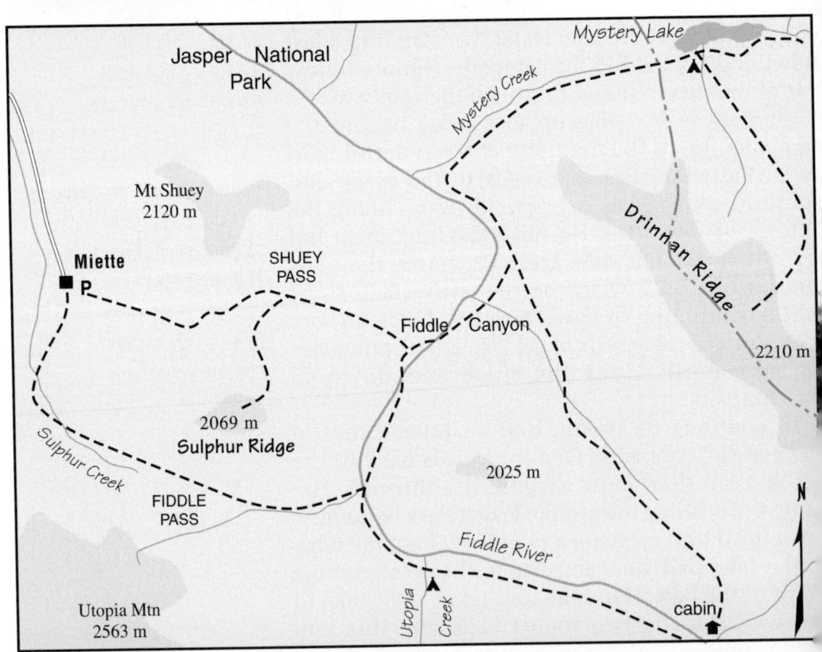

there is an intersection. If you continue straight ahead on a less used path you will end up at the Fiddle ranger cabin. The trail you want makes a 90° turn to the right and drops smartly to the river. At the river's edge it makes a sharp left turn to follow the river upstream. You have a somewhat tedious boulder hop along the river's edge for a kilometre or so before reaching the ford across the Fiddle.

Mountain rivers are not to be trusted. Rain—or meltwater—can raise the level of a river substantially in a very short time. Usually in late summer and autumn river levels are low, sometimes so low you can easily boulder hop or run across. However, this was not the case when we undertook this trip. Even though it had not rained for several days the weather had been warm, causing an early, light snowfall to melt. The result was a high river with a strong current. Also, part of the horse trail was under water, forcing us into deep pools to get around a cliff face. At least the water cooled us!

Pick up the horse trail that now begins to switchback up a steep pitch. At the top of the switchbacks you might want to rest a moment to take in the view up and down the Fiddle River valley before continuing. The trail enters the forest to climb steadily, if not as steeply. Finally, the trail flattens. The popular trail to Sulphur Ridge above Miette joins your trail on the left. Keep to the right along what is now a wide, well-used path as it drops quickly to the Aquacentre at Miette Hot Springs and your pick-up vehicle.

Mystery Lake

Mystery Lake was so-named during the 1920s by Alberta Forest Ranger Charlie Hughes because the lake appeared to have no outlet, hence the mystery of how water left the lake. The answer lies in an underground seepage to the east toward Drinnan Creek. Mystery Lake is very shallow and does not support any fish.

Mystery Lake.

Hot Springs

To relax in the warm, soothing waters at the Aquacentre at Miette is a marvellous way to cap your hike from Gregg River and Mystery Lake. The hot mineral waters erase sore feet and tired muscles. Their curative powers, of course, have long been known. But perhaps less understood by many of the centre's bathers is the geological nature of these, and other, hot springs.

Hot spring water begins as surface water. It seeps down along fractures and pores in what otherwise appears to be solid rock. As it trickles downward it is heated by the surrounding rock. The deeper the water travels, the hotter it becomes. Why? In the Canadian Rockies underground temperatures rise 1°C for every 33 m of depth, after travelling down perhaps as far as 3 km. The water is boiling hot and begins to rise to the surface. If it rises through a tortuous network of fractures and pores it will cool and stop rising. However, if it can rise more directly and, therefore, more quickly to the surface it will retain much of its heat. In certain locations in the Rockies the heated water finds such a direct route via fault planes that act as conduits to bring the hot water to the surface. At Miette, the super heated water rises along the Hot Springs Fault to discharge into the Sulphur Creek valley. The hot springs at Miette have the highest temperatures of all hot springs in Alberta, measuring at 53.9°C.

Many hot springs, including those at Miette, are mineral hot springs. As groundwater percolates downward, it heats and dissolves minerals from the surrounding rock. One mineral element that dissolves readily in hot water is sulphur, and in the Canadian Rockies sulphur-bearing minerals such as gypsum and pyrite are common. Miette Hot Springs, like others, emit a rotten egg smell. This is hydrogen sulphide, which has been transformed by bacterial action from the dissolved calcium sulphates and iron sulphides.

The Miette Hot Springs, again like other hot springs in the Canadian Rockies, are slightly radioactive. Decaying radioactive minerals lie deep in the earth's crust and so deep do the hot springs run that they come in contact with some of this radioactive material. But do not worry. The radioactivity is only slightly higher than normal groundwater and will not adversely affect your health.

Miette Hot Springs

Today's modern Aquacentre is the most recent development to corral the reputedly curative hot spring waters. It may seem hard to believe, but this small, remote valley and its hot springs were known as early as 1839 to Hudson's Bay Company fur traders and independent trappers. It was they who first dammed Sulphur Creek with boulders to create small bathing basins. Much later, in 1905, survey crews for the Grand Trunk Pacific Railway heard of the hot springs and struggled up the Fiddle River valley to enjoy a rare luxury—a hot bath. It was not an easy hike from Pocahontas. British travel writer, Frederick Talbot, wrote five years later, "It was a constant fight with brush, deadfall and rocks for every foot of the way. Riding was decidedly out of the question, and hiking was decidedly painful and laborious." Talbot's party found three pools, the higher two of which recorded temperatures of about 53° and 47°C respectively. "There was no very strongly developed odour, and the water was almost tasteless," reported Talbot. "These are so far the most important hot springs that have been found in Canada, possessing a greater degree of heat than those at Banff. The waters are rich in essential constituents, and there is little doubt but that 'taking the waters at Fiddle Creek [sic]' will develop into a craze within the next few years."

How right he was! The Canadian government was well aware of the popularity of hot springs such as those at Banff and, wishing to see a similar development for Jasper National Park, undertook its first modest development at the hot springs in 1913—a log shelter and a temporary bathhouse. It was a far cry from some of the more elaborate schemes that private entrepreneurs had dreamt. For example, the Grand Trunk Pacific toyed with the idea of building "Chateau Miette" at the mouth of the Fiddle River and a monorail from there into the valley, but as Chief Superintendent P.C. Barnard Harvey sighed on July 2, 1914, "The present oil boom seems to have struck them very badly and they can think nothing but oil, oil, oil." It was also the beginning of the First World War that quickly brought the collapse of both the Grand Trunk Pacific and Canadian Northern railways.

The lack of a road or even a good trail meant that few tourists made the difficult trek up the valley. However, coal miners from the Coal Branch, Pocahontas and Brule were made of tougher stuff and it was they who frequented the hot springs in the early years. In 1918, the government built a sweat house and a couple of change rooms at the hot springs but no latrines or garbage facilities. A park warden was unimpressed. He found the three pools to be unsightly and unsanitary. "A sweat house with an adjoining 10 x 12' tent, along with two shacks, one of which served as a men's dressing room, completed the inadequate facilities." The following year was one of tumult among the labouring classes in Canada and strikes were common. It was during one of these strikes that miners from Pocahontas camped at the hot springs and built the first log pool. Chinked with moss, mud and sacking the pool measured 7 x 7.3 m. Previously, the pools had been made of stone walls filled with sand.

By 1933 the unsanitary conditions at the hot springs were cause for embarrassment. "If these places cannot be maintained in a thoroughly clean, orderly and sanitary condition, then we must immediately close them." The following year the makeshift pool, change rooms and campsites were shut down in preparation for a major development at Miette. First, a road was blasted up the valley in 1935 and finally, in 1938, a campground and a large, modern bathhouse opened for business. The Miette Hot Springs Bungalows opened two years later. The postwar years saw a boom in tourism and by 1984 the bathhouse was too small to accommodate the numbers of tourists and a new facility, the present Aquacentre, was constructed on the site of the former campground.

The Miette Hot Springs, 1920s. Courtesy Glenbow Archives, NA 3934-14.

LUSCAR

After having been abandoned for several years, the townsite of Luscar was a scene of frenetic activity in the summer of 1963. Cameras rolled, the director called for "Action!" and a small cast of actors played out what, apparently, is one of the worst Canadian movies ever made. "Naked Flame," a 90-minute dramatic film about, in part, the Doukhobor breakaway sect the Sons of Freedom, was so bad that even the scenes of buxom young women running around naked as flames consumed Luscar's buildings could not rescue it. As one critic has noted, "You have to see it to believe it." Fading Hollywood star Dennis O'Keefe, perhaps, was fortunate not to live to see the release of his last film.

When the Luscar mine began production in the 1920s, no one would have believed that the town would ever be involved in what has become a cult movie. Instead, the townspeople knew that they were sitting on top of a rich coal seam, the Jewel Seam, that promised to make its owners rich and to give steady employment to hundreds of miners. By 1922, Luscar had a general store, a six-bed cottage hospital, a school, a beer parlour, a butcher shop and 25 or 30 homes built higgledy-piggledy throughout the valley. "Suburbs" with picturesque names such as Moonshine Hill, Aristocratic Hill, Giovinazzo Hill and Tin Town sprang up. The miners' homes were privately owned but their owners had to have the permission of the mine manager to proceed with the construction of their log or frame dwellings. Most homes had no insulation and were heated by wood and coal stoves. Indoor plumbing was a luxury restricted to the homes of the mine officials. Others had to carry water from Luscar Creek until an enterprising person supplied water from his horse-drawn water tank. Later, Roman Catholic and Anglican churches were built as were a cafe and a laundry.

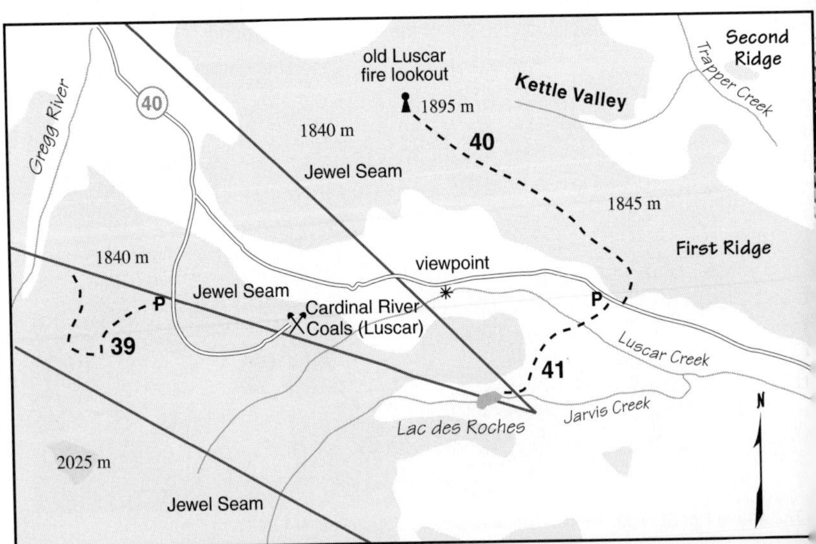

Luscar Collieries Ltd., ca. 1930. Courtesy Provincial Archives of Alberta, A10308.

Entertainment took many forms. Teas, school plays, dances and union meetings were held in the community hall built with materials supplied by the mine and the free labour of the miners. By the late 1930s an indoor arena was built where ice sports and the winter carnival were held. As with all Coal Branch communities, sports were very important to Luscarites. By 1925, the town had an outdoor skating rink, tennis courts and a football field. It was common knowledge that if you could kick a football, were a good stick handler or could play a musical instrument you had an edge when it came to finding employment in the mines. When Luscar's 20-piece Silver Band won top honours at the Edmonton exhibition in both 1928 and again in 1929, everyone rejoiced. Most of the cheering was held, though, for the Luscar Indians, the town's hockey team. In 1933 and 1934 the Indians won the Alberta Senior Hockey championship and again in 1936. Not to be outshone, the women formed their own hockey team in 1931 and won all their games that year.

When the mine whistle blew for the last time in 1956, some people dismantled their homes to rebuild elsewhere. Others simply walked away from a home that had meant so much for so many years. The valley reverted to the quiet it had known prior to the 1920s. It wasn't until 1970 when Cardinal River Coals opened its new strip mine that coal once again dominated this corner of the Coal Branch.

Luscar

Mine No.: #905

Owners/Operators: 1921-1936 Luscar Collieries Ltd.; 1936-1958 Luscar Coals Ltd.

Authorized Capital: $1,000,000 Luscar Collieries Ltd.; $650,000 Luscar Coals Ltd.

Coal: bituminous

Registered Trade Name: Luscar Coal

Market: steam

Mine Type: underground; strip pit

Total Extraction: 7,785,000 tonnes

Men Killed: 28

The first Luscar leases were staked in 1918 by John Gregg and R. W. Jones. The mine's development in 1921 was spearheaded by Col. Alexander Mitchell and Robert G. Drinnan. Mitchell, Drinnan and others owned the Mountain Park mine, but since that company was financially insecure, they decided to develop Luscar as a separate company.

Mitchell's son, Harold, visited Luscar in 1921. This son of a Scottish millionaire was soon caught up in the camaraderie of the mining camp: "Everyone was an optimist, for tremendous showings of coal had been found...Poles, Serbs, Ukrainians, Russians, French Canadians were at work, joined later by men of other European nations. Wages were high, and so were the spirits of the workmen. We ate at one table in the cook-house, off a wonderful collection of canned food, and after the evening meal we sat round exchanging experiences of other parts of the world."

Colonel Alexander Mitchell's death in 1934 led to a power struggle among the Mountain Park and Luscar directors that was not finally resolved until 1936 with his two sons, Harold and Alexander Jr., the victors. The company was reorganized as Luscar Coals.

The Luscar mine was plagued with methane gas. The gas was usually kept under control but accidents happened. In 1938, two miners died from suffocation. In 1943, two were injured by an explosion in the fan house after one of the miners chose to light up a cigarette. Then, on May 12, 1945, seven miners died as a result of an underground explosion. Two died instantly from the blast, the other five suffocated after being trapped behind a caved-in wall. The explosion was sparked by an overheated safety lamp carried by one miner who had gone toward a cordoned off area to retrieve some tools. Subsequent explosions and debris stopped rescue attempts and the mine was flooded to prevent any underground fires from spreading. Over the next year, the mine was slowly drained and the debris cleaned out. The last three bodies were not retrieved until almost a year later on May 3, 1946. The Luscar explosion was the worst mining disaster in Coal Branch history.

Stripping began in 1945 and by 1954 underground mining ceased. Fire in 1956 destroyed the briquette plant and later that year, owing to a lack of suitable coal orders, mining operations ceased. In 1958, the mine saw a glimpse of the future: it was briefly reopened and 1800 tonnes of coal were stripped and sent as a trial shipment to Japan.

Kaydee

Mine No.: #1392

Owners/Operators: 1928-1930 Gebo Coal Co. Ltd.; 1930-1932 Cardon Collieries Ltd.; 1932 Commercial Cartage Co.; 1932-1936 Alex Susnar & Associates; 1936-1945 K. D. Collieries Ltd.; 1946-1953 Gregg River Collieries Ltd.

Authorized Capital: $200,000 K. D. Collieries Ltd.; $250,000 Gregg River Collieries Ltd.

Coal: bituminous

Registered Trade Name: Kaydee Coal, Gregg River Coal

Market: steam

Mine Type: underground; strip pit

Total Extraction: 501,000 tonnes

Men Killed: 2

The first coal claim in the area was in 1907 near Sphinx Creek. Prospect work continued over the years with the first serious attempt to develop a mine beginning during the early 1920s. Luscar blocked this and a later attempt at development by denying running rights over its spur line from Leyland. The company had spent over $190,000 building the line and it did not wish to see any competing company use it. Luscar's legal arguments and obstruction tactics took the issue to the Supreme Court of Canada and the British Privy Council, but in the end it was obliged to allow the construction of an extension to its own spur line. The years of delay, however, combined with a deteriorating coal market, led Gebo Coal to sell its lease in 1930 to an American firm that had greater ambitions than just starting a new coal mine.

Cardon Collieries of New York tried to use the threat of opening a competing mine as a leverage tactic to take over Mountain Park and Luscar. Cardon went so far as to build a rail line from Luscar but could neither buy out the two mines nor force a merger. It abandoned both its efforts and its mine site. Cardon Collieries did not pay its contractor, Commercial Cartage of Calgary, for building the 6 km of track. To cover its loss, Commercial took over the mine for several months, stripping and shipping coal. A local group including Alex Susnar and Louis Stupar, took over the leases and sold them to K. D. Collieries of Saskatoon that, in 1939, sold out to an Edmonton-based group.

Kaydee was a difficult place to work a mine according to the District Mines Inspector, "This mine is a series of faults, the ground is so broken up it [the seam] is hard to follow. There are several places where the coal has pinched out and other places where it is pocketed, first on the right, then on the left." The bad ground combined with limited capital underlined what Kaydee was throughout its working life: a marginal venture wherein the miners contended with poor working conditions and irregular pay periods. Second World War subsidies kept the mine going but, by war's end, it was abandoned. It was reopened in 1947 by Gregg River Collieries, a subsidiary of the Cadomin Coal Company Ltd., which began open pit mining. It was closed in 1953.

39 GREGG RIVER HEADWATERS ACCESS TRAIL MAP PAGE 200

Offering hunters access into the headwaters of the Gregg River, this trail gives you, the hiker, a rare opportunity to experience first hand the reclamation work done at Cardinal River Coals (CRC).

This "trail" is not really a trail, it is a route marked out by directional stakes placed irregularly all the way from the trailhead to the edge of the reclamation area. At the trailhead you take a rough track that leads steeply up to the bottom of a notch between two contoured hillsides. The hillside on your left is vegetated with legumes and grasses, the one on your right is still mostly rock and gravel. The route follows the notch and can be rough in places but you quickly come to a mine haul road. Turn left for 50 m, cross the road and follow the directional stakes up through a notch between two hills. This climb is steeper than the first pitch but is clearly marked. At the top, where the trail flattens, there are good views of Luscar

Day hiking

Rating half day

Distance 4.2 km

Level of Difficulty short walk with some rough areas

Maximum Elevation 1840 m

Elevation Gain 180 m

Map 83 F/3 Cadomin

Access

Park your vehicle at the designated parking area along the Cardinal River Coals Road 1.4 km from the intersection with Highway #40. The road turnoff is 40 km south of the intersection with Highway #16 or 8 km north of the intersection with the Cardinal River Road.

0.0 km	trailhead
0.4 km	haul road
0.9 km	vehicle track
1.0 km	hot spot
1.1 km	intersection
1.6 km	picnic shelter
2.1 km	communication tower
4.2 km	trailhead

Returning to the trailhead through one of the notches.

Overlooking the headwaters of the Gregg River and part of the Gregg River mine site.

Mountain on your extreme left, Mount Sir Harold Mitchell and Mount Gregg, which overlooks the headwaters of the Gregg River.

Within a short distance you come to a vehicle track. Bear left onto the track and follow it all the way to the communication tower. Part way along the track you may be able to smell a mixture of sulphide gasses. The source of this unpleasant smell is found where a ditch crosses the roadway. Here, vents in the ground have opened emitting the gasses and the heat that generates them. Just beyond this "hot spot" you come to a crossroads. Bear to the right to continue along the roadway that the tour buses now take. The reclaimed basin stretches before you and to your right. In springtime, as many as 150 bighorn sheep and deer calve in this area; it must be quite the sight!

As you climb slowly along the road you can look down into a pit on your left. The rocky slopes of the pit are now home to marmots and you may hear their high-pitched whistle given as a warning to the rest of the colony. The roadway through the reclamation swings to the right to a picnic shelter. By the time you are here, the shelter may have been removed and the roadway reclaimed. But when we were here the picnic shelter, which was removed from Lac des Roches, provided a not particularly scenic place for the tourists to munch their complementary lunch provided by Cardinal River Coals.

From the picnic shelter your roadway snakes up toward the communication tower with good views of the mountains by the Gregg River headwaters. Beautiful open slopes to your left beckon the intrepid hiker or determined hunter.

The mine's communication tower overlooks the workings of CRC. To your immediate left is an untouched spruce forest. Directly below you is the worked coal seam. If you look carefully you can see a large culvert winding its way through the valley. This carries the waters of the Gregg River through the mine site to be discharged into the river near the Gregg River mine cleaning plant.

Return the way you came.

The Shot

On Nov. 13, 1999, Sherwin Scott levelled his .300 Jarret rifle, gently squeezed the trigger and fired the shot heard around the world. Scott was an American who had spent over two years and $1.1 million in license fees alone for the chance to take a trophy bighorn sheep. The animal he shot that day had the fourth-highest Boone & Crockett score for a bighorn sheep ever. That fact alone was cause for notice. Also noticed was the location and manner in which he shot that sheep. Scott was hunting beside the reclaimed lands of the Luscar mine site, which is prime sheep habitat and a no-hunting zone.

Since 1985, sheep numbers in the area have tripled to about 600 animals owing to the ongoing expansion of reclaimed mine lands at Luscar and Gregg River. Here the recontoured and open slopes are planted with legumes and grasses that in turn provide ideal winter habitat for the sheep. Wind reduces the snow cover and the open slopes give the sheep long vistas wherein they may spot predators. This growing sheep population and its dependence on the mine lands for winter forage were significant factors in the awarding in 1991 of the Order of the Bighorn to Luscar for its effort in wildlife conservation through reclamation.

One unforeseen side effect to this success was that, since the sheep were congregating in what was still an active mining area, they were becoming habituated to the presence of people. Once the mine reclamation program is complete the land will return to the province for management. If the province opens that area to hunters, the fear is that the sheep there will be too easy to kill. In response to this concern, options under debate include keeping the area off-limits to all hunters or opening it up to bow-hunters only.

These issues bring up another debate: What is sport hunting? If sport hunting means that man and animal are pitted against each other in a near equal balance that either can win or lose, then what Scott did is not sport hunting. After a trophy sheep was spotted within the mine lease, Scott with his rifle and his spotters with their walkie-talkies waited eight days for that animal to leave the property. Meanwhile, to make sure no rules were being broken, Fish and Wildlife officials watched the watchers. As one commentator noted, it was like waiting for a "big, well-fed, tame critter to walk out of the pen just so you could blast it."

The targeted ram never left the mine lease, but another sheep was seen coming toward it. Scott quickly studied it, made his decision and shot it. It fell within 200 m of the sanctuary.

"Wild" bighorn sheep at CRC's mine site.

40 LUSCAR FIRE LOOKOUT

MAP PAGE 200

Perched on mountain tops to give a commanding 360° view, fire lookouts are always interesting places to visit. In the case of the old lookout at Luscar, its straightforward access makes it a perfect hike for those in the Luscar vicinity.

From the Lac des Roches parking area turn right onto Highway #40 and walk 100 m to a rough track on your left. The old roadway to the fire lookout parallels the highway for a short distance before turning left to begin its long climb. After switching to the right, the roadway passes under a hydro power line. Only hikers use the trail now and at the height of summer it is overgrown with buttercups, Indian paintbrushes, vetches and white geranium.

It's a fairly steep climb for the first kilometre but flattens to enter a straightaway. Where the road bisects a small rivulet, views of the Front Ranges to the west open with Cardinal River Coals' (CRC) cleaning plant dominating the scene. The roadway dips and rises through a small saddle. By the time you reach a second power line right-of-way you can see straight ahead along the roadway as it rises toward the top of the hill. The last pitch is fairly

Day hiking
Rating half day
Distance 6.2 km
Level of Difficulty easy, steady climb
Maximum Elevation 1895 m
Elevation Gain 265 m
Map 83 F/3 Cadomin

Access

Park your vehicle at the Lac des Roches trailhead and parking area on the west side of Highway #40. The parking area turnoff is 44 km south of Highway #16 or 4 km north of the intersection with the Cardinal River Road.

0.0 km	trailhead
0.1 km	fire lookout roadway
0.3 km	power line right-of-way
1.0 km	rivulet
1.8 km	power line right-of-way
3.0 km	fire lookout location
3.1 km	viewpoint
6.2 km	trailhead

The view from the old Luscar fire tower showing, from left to right: Luscar Mountain, Mount Sir Harold Mitchell, Mount Mary-Jean and Mount Berry.

steep but mercifully short, ending with some scree at the very top. The panorama is well worth this short climb. To your right and straight ahead, there is the rolling carpet of the forested foothills broken here and there by cutblocks; to your left, the Cardinal River Coals' mine site at the base of Luscar Mountain. When the lookout was operational, the lookout personnel gazed down at the busy coal mining town of Luscar, but today, the town and old mine site have been obliterated by the modern open pit mine of CRC.

Return the way you came.

Luscar Fire Lookout

There have been two fire lookouts in the Luscar vicinity. The first, built in the 1920s, was perched on a knob above Berry's Creek immediately in the shadow of the mountains. It stood guard over the valley until the 1950s. Then, in 1953 in response to "The Fire Brief," the Alberta Fire Service was reorganized and expanded so it could better detect and control fires in Alberta's Green Zone, which covers approximately 65 per cent of the province. One of the Brief's 22 recommendations was to upgrade existing and build new fire lookouts. As a consequence, in 1956 the Luscar lookout site was moved to the Trapper Creek area. There were two buildings on site. There was a small residence and short tower tied down with gye wires. At first, the lookout was accessible only by a footpath but later that year a road was bulldozed up to the tower. And not a moment too soon. The summer of 1956 was hot and dry with severe electrical storms. Lightning strikes started an inferno that quickly threatened the town of Mercoal. Men from Mercoal, Luscar, the North West Pulp and Power Company in Hinton as well as forestry personnel were recruited to try to save the town. Meanwhile, the Luscar fire lookout reported 14 new fires in the vicinity of the Yellowhead Trail, Mercoal Creek and the McLeod River. With the raging fire less than 5 km from Mercoal, the wind changed. The town was saved.

Luscar fire tower, no date. Courtesy Alberta Environment, #19444.

The Luscar lookout continued to monitor the surrounding forests until 1978 when it was closed. The buildings were demolished and the roadway recontoured to the original topography. The reclaimed area was seeded with a mixture of creeping red fescue, white dutch clover, timothy, Canada bluegrass and alfalfa. To reduce the possibility of erosion on the steeper pitches, Forestry installed cross ditches.

41 LAC DES ROCHES

MAP PAGE 200

Cardinal River Coals Ltd. is justifiably proud of this showpiece of mine site reclamation at Luscar. An old mine pit, 50-B-6, was allowed to fill with water from Luscar and West Jarvis creeks to create a man-made lake. The lake, with its resloped and partially seeded dumps and backfills, is accessed via a pretty woodsy walk also designed and built by Cardinal River Coals Ltd.

The trailhead at the south end of the parking area is somewhat obscured by alder and other bushes so look for the green and black signs that mark the way. Once on the trail, it is very easy to follow for it has been well made and well marked with signage.

Day hiking

Rating half day

Distance 8 km

Level of Difficulty easy walk with some steep pitches

Maximum Elevation 1676 m

Elevation Gain 105 m

Map 83 F/3 Cadomin

Access

Park your vehicle at the Lac des Roches trailhead and parking area on the west side of Highway #40. The parking area turnoff is 44 km south of Highway #16 or 4 km north of the intersection with the Cardinal River Road.

0.0 km	trailhead
0.2 km	intersection
0.3 km	Luscar Creek and railway
0.9 km	intersection
1.0 km	intersection
2.0 km	viewpoint
2.3 km	Lac des Roches

West Jarvis Creek gushes from a culvert above to plunge into the lake below.

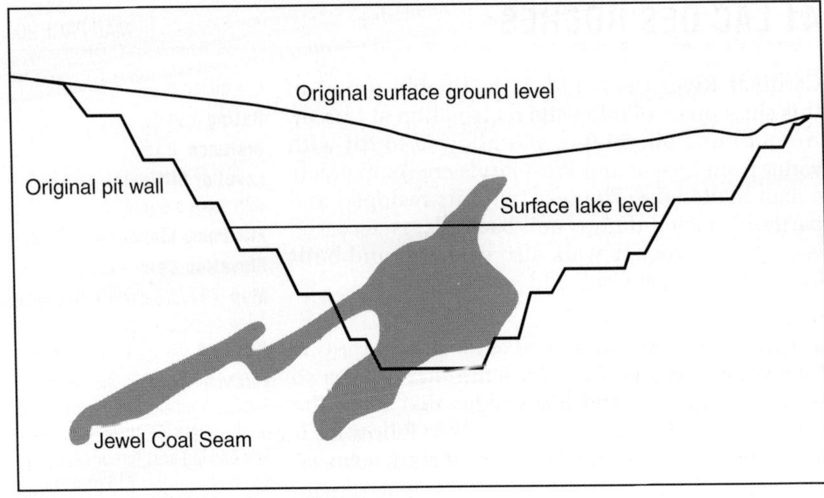

Cross-section of the east end of 50-B-6.

2.3 km	West Jarvis Creek
3.0 km	West Jarvis Creek
3.6 km	intersection
3.6 km	shelter
4.0 km	waterfall
8.0 km	trailhead

Note Owing to delays in the regulatory approval of the Cheviot Mine Project, Cardinal River Coals Ltd. was planning to rework this old mine pit. The lake was drained and additional exploration work done. With the announcement in late 2000 that the Luscar mine would be closing, it was decided not to re-mine the pit. It is now being refilled with water and will be reclaimed to its past glory with some fish habitat improvements. Public access to Lac des Roches will likely not be permitted until mid-2002. Check with Cardinal River Coals' main office along Highway #40 before starting out.

After 200 m your trail intersects with an old road. Bear right onto the road. As the road snakes down the slope you can first hear Luscar Creek below you on your left and, a short distance later, you can look down on the railway tracks that service the Luscar and Gregg River mines. Straight ahead you can catch glimpses of the Front Ranges and some of Luscar's mine reclamation. Near the bottom of the slope close to the railway tracks look for the green and black sign that leads you across the tracks at the correct place; if in doubt leave the road and cross the tracks just before the Luscar Creek culvert. Once on the other side of the tracks turn right and walk parallel to them until you see another route sign that leads up the ridge. Your trail swings south as it climbs. After a short, rather steep ascent your trail intersects with an old reclaimed roadway. Turn left onto the roadway and follow it for 100 m until you see the black and green signs that lead you back into the lodgepole pine forest along a walking path. This pleasant walk up through the forest ends at an intersection with another old roadway. Bear to the right along the old road. Within a short distance your trail re-enters the forest. Your trail flattens somewhat before it begins its descent toward Lac des Roches.

Unexpectedly, a lovely view of the Front Ranges and the Luscar mine site opens up. When we were here we could hear but not see the haul trucks across the valley; perhaps by the time you take this trail the trucks will be gone leaving the area quiet and undisturbed. At this point the trail descends quickly as it swings to the southwest through an old cutblock. Now, lodgepole pine, willows, grasses and wildflowers such as Indian paintbrush and harebells have reclaimed the slope. With the Front Ranges towering over the valley below you it is such a pretty walk that you almost miss your first view of Lac des Roches.

Snuggled among the slopes of the Front Ranges, Lac des Roches sparkles like a jewel in the sunlight. It is hard to believe that only a few years ago this lake was an active mine pit. Luscar has reclaimed and planted grasses in the slopes on the north and west ends of the lake, but has deliberately chosen to leave unreclaimed most of the benches on the south end. Although it sounds unbelievable, the physical diversity of this man-made landscape enhances its aesthetic appeal. Even from this viewpoint you can see a waterfall on the south side tumbling down into the lake.

The lake and waterfall draw you like a magnet down the steep slope. At the lake's edge the trail swings left along the lakeshore to where West Jarvis Creek discharges from the lake. Your creek crossing will be wet and cold but easy as the creek is quite shallow. On the other sido of the creek you find yourself at the end of an old mine road that now leads you part way up the south slope above Lac des Roches. If you are here in the spring or summer keep an eye out for the waterfowl that have claimed this lake as their breeding ground. The roadway passes beneath the rocky benches that have been left in their natural state. Below you to your right the slope has been reclaimed in a variety of grasses. Your roadway passes over a culvert that

The Tackle Box

Lac des Roches
Fish Management Area: #4

Because Lac des Roches is an old mine pit, it is very deep, as deep as 70 m! To establish a productive and self-sustaining fishery, Cardinal River Coals had to slope the adjacent dumps and groom safety benches to form a littoral zone where enough light could penetrate to support underwater vegetation and water insects that provide food for the fish. Once this was finished plant material from the east end of Mary Gregg Lake was transplanted to Lac des Roches' outflow. The coal company even placed large tires on some of the safety benches to provide cover for the fish. Cardinal River Coals was not allowed to stock the lake. A fishery could only be established once native fish migrate into the lake. To encourage this and to encourage spawning, a number of small log dams and pools were built immediately downstream of the lake and the channel bottom lined with one inch of washed gravel to allow optimum spawning. This system worked well in the original Lac des Roches and native Athabasca rainbow trout spawned there. In the new lake, the log dams will be replaced by more durable and natural rock weirs.

Species rainbow trout

Restrictions Use of bait fish and the collection of bait fish are prohibited. Trout limit is zero.

Season 16 June to 31 August

carries the waters of West Jarvis Creek from above. It is an odd sensation to hear water rushing down the cliffs on your left without being able to see any water. You can, though, see the stream on the right side of the road as it issues forth from the culvert. Do not attempt to gain access to the top of the waterfall here; the slope is steep and ends in a rocky cliff face. Instead, continue along the road to an intersection. Bear to the right as the road swings down and then up to a picnic shelter that Luscar has built at the northwest end of the lake. A couple of picnic tables are also located outside of the shelter making this a great place to munch on a snack.

From the picnic shelter another old roadway goes down to the unnamed waterfall. You will have noted earlier that the waterfall drops to the lake in two tiers. The roadway brings you to the bottom of the first tier. Do not attempt to catch a better view of the lower tier. West Jarvis Creek plunges over a sheer cliff. Instead, enjoy the scenery from the safety of the edge of the creek. Children of all ages have fun scrambling over the rocks near the bottom of the waterfall. Certainly the spray is refreshing on a hot day!

Return the way you came.

Lac des Roches

Previous name: Lake 50-B-6

Lac des Roches is an abandoned mine pit that has been converted by Cardinal River Coals into a lake with a viable sport fishery. The new lake received its name, which means Lake of the Rockies, in 1991. Native Athabasca rainbow trout entered the lake by way of Jarvis Creek and have since spawned there.

50-B-6 is the original strip pit designation. Mining began in 1982 and finished three years later. During that time over 15 million cubic metres of rock was removed to extract about 5400 tonnes of raw coal from what became a 120 m-deep hole. Flooding started in 1985, taking almost two years for water from Jarvis and Luscar creeks to fill the pit to its present level and outflow via Jarvis Creek. In 1999 it was decided to re-mine the pit and the lake was drained. With the announcement that the Luscar mine will close, it was decided not to re-mine the pit. Reclamation work and subsequent reflooding is not expected to be completed until mid-2002.

50-B-6 means that this was the sixth pit mined along the 50-B baseline. Exploration drilling was first conducted along this line in 1950 with "B" being the alphabetical designation for what was one of several baselines along which there was drilling that year.

Lac des Roches looking east from the picnic site. The man-made waterfall is just visible on the right.

42 FIRELINE TRAIL

MAP PAGE 216

When fire swept along the ridge above Mary Gregg Lake in the autumn of 1988 threatening to engulf the Mary Gregg Valley, firefighters bulldozed a swath from a logging road to the top of the ridge. Today this swath provides easy access to a satisfying walk along a ridge that offers nearly a 360° sweep.

From your trailhead walk or cycle up the abandoned logging road through an old cutblock. This area was logged and reforested a number of years ago but the trees are still too small to cast any shade on a hot summer's day. The lower part of the road is in good condition and you may be tempted to drive farther up the road to find another suitable parking area. Beware, though, that a little farther along the road becomes deeply rutted and is suitable only for four-wheel-drive vehicles.

Day hiking
Rating half day
Distance 8.8 km
Level of Difficulty steady climb with some rough footing
Maximum Elevation 1722 m
Elevation Gain 260 m
Map 83 F/3 Cadomin

Access

Park your vehicle at a logging road turnoff east off Highway #40. The turnoff is 31 km south of Highway #16 or 17 km north of the intersection with the Cardinal River Road.

0.0 km	trailhead
1.2 km	Throne Lake turnoff
1.9 km	end of cutblock
2.1 km	brule
3.1 km	viewpoint
4.2 km	top of ridge
7.2 km	Throne Lake turnoff
7.3 km	Throne Lake
7.4 km	throne
8.8 km	trailhead

Walking along the spine of the ridge through the brule.

For 1 km it's an easy ascent. Then the road dips briefly to cross a saddle between two hills. Although unmarked, this is the cutoff to Throne Lake. Continue along the old logging road. It deteriorates significantly now as it begins to climb steeply. If you are cycling, the loose rocks and deep ruts will make the going a challenge. At the end of the cutblock the logging road peters out but a broad swath through the trees indicates the route you are to follow. The swath is overgrown now with a thick understorey of grasses, wild roses and small shrubs, and here and there you must make your way around old piles of logs left when the bulldozers ploughed upslope to gain access to the ridge above you. Indeed, evidence of the forest fire quickly becomes clear as you enter the brule. It is a full kilometre through the blackened trees before you reach the top of the ridge.

One positive thing can be said about fires; they clear out view-obstructing trees, and the view looking south from the top of the ridge is quite impressive. The massive open pit workings of Cardinal River Coals are directly across from you and farther to the west across Highway #40 you can see the equally impressive Gregg River mine. When we were here the awesome sight was brought alive by the haul trucks that rumbled up and down Cardinal River Coals' main haulage road to the highway.

Follow the fireline trail as it cuts its way along the top of the ridge. It is an easy walk that is enhanced by a nearly 360° panorama; to your right is the Cardinal River Coals' Luscar mine and to your left is the Antler Creek valley. Beyond is a rolling carpet of forest, broken only by a series of cutblocks. And straight ahead your ridge walk stretches out before you. If you are here in late summer watch for wild raspberries, gooseberries and low bush cranberries along the way. The open hillside is likewise home to dainty blue harebells, red and orange Indian paintbrushes and the white heads of the yarrow plant.

Your trail leads slowly uphill. At the top look down to your right. You should be able to see Mary Gregg Lake although the density of the forest, unscathed here by the fire, makes it somewhat difficult. The fireline trail continues but as this is the highest point along the trail, turn around to return the way you came.

Once back on the old logging road, descend to the saddle connecting the two hills. If you want a quick side trip to Throne Lake look for a game trail that leads off to your right. Within 100 m you are at the lake. Throne Lake is not particularly picturesque, being little more than a slough. However, it is fun to hug the left bank of the lake to find the rock outcropping above that served as a "throne" to many a Coal Brancher here on a picnic.

Return to the old logging road. Turn right and follow it downhill to your vehicle.

The Gregg River Fire

The 1988 Gregg River fire was a 1300 ha blaze that, owing to high winds, took almost two weeks for firefighters to bring under control. It was first discovered November 30 on Gregg River mine property. Mine employees tried to contain the blaze with a bulldozer, but fanned by 150 km winds the flames jumped Highway #40 and spread to the northeast.

At its height, 175 men, 14 bulldozers, six water tankers, three water bombers and six helicopters were on the scene. One of the helicopters involved in fighting the blaze crashed, caught fire and burned beyond repair. None of the occupants were injured.

Inside the 1300 ha fire perimeter, only about 600 ha of timber actually burned. High winds caused the fire to jump, sometimes large distances, creating a patchwork of between 40 to 50 burned-out areas called brule. The burned trees were within Weldwood's forest management area and the lumber company filed a civil action against Gregg River claiming over $400,000 in timber losses alone.

Regardless of the damage claimed by man, forest fires are an integral part of the natural cycle to which many species have learned to adapt. Lodgepole pine are the most famous example. Their heat-resistant cones open quickly after a fire and sprout seedlings in the carbon-rich soil. Other fire adaptive species include the black-backed and three-toed woodpeckers. Both rely upon mature and burned-over conifer stands as prime habitat and are today regarded as uncommon throughout Alberta.

In November 1988, a fire at the Gregg River mine got out of control resulting in a $680,000 suit by Weldwood of Canada, which has the timber leases in the area, against the mine.

43 MARY GREGG LAKE

So popular was Mary Gregg Lake with fishermen and picnickers that Cardinal River Coals, the leaseholder of the property, built a trail into the lake after reclaiming the original access, an old roadway, in June 1988. The lake and its forested shoreline have been left untouched by the open pit mining immediately to the south.

Although the "Notice" sign warns that access into the lake is by foot only, irresponsible OHV owners have disregarded the sign. What would otherwise be a pleasant forest stroll into the lake has unfortunately been reduced to a tiresome walk. This is especially true if it has been raining recently as the OHVs have churned up the pathway, widening it in places and gouging deep

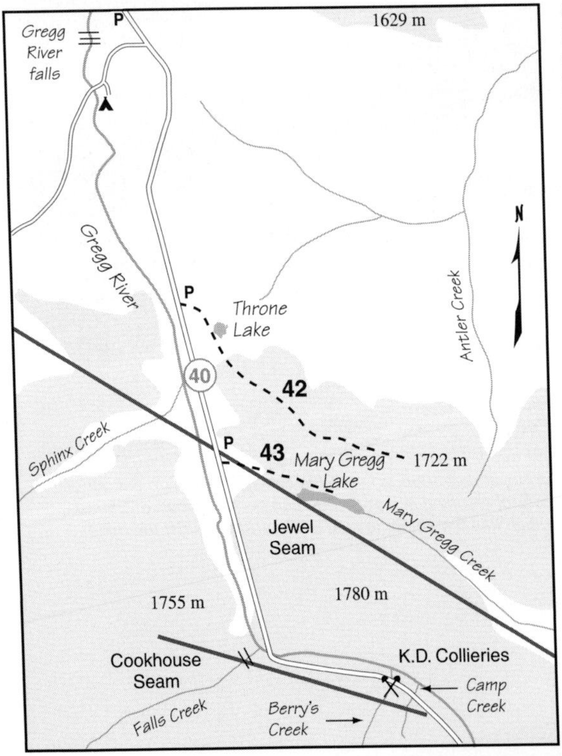

Day hiking

Rating half day

Distance 2.6 km

Level of Difficulty short walk along rough trail

Maximum Elevation 1539 m

Elevation Gain 30 m

Map 83 F/3 Cadomin

Access

Mary Gregg Lake lies in a narrow, deep valley off Highway #40, 33 km south of Highway #16 or 15 km north of the intersection with the Cardinal River Road. The turnoff to the lake is on the east side of the highway 100 m north of the Gregg River mine tunnel. Follow the turnoff for 200 m as it winds toward the mine site, then turn left at an intersection. The parking area for the lake is a scant 100 m from the intersection. Your trailhead is just to the right of the Cardinal River Coals' "Notice" sign.

0.0 km	trailhead
0.4 km	intersection
0.7 km	Mary Gregg Lake
1.3 km	bog
2.6 km	trailhead

The Tackle Box

Mary Gregg Lake
Fish Management Area: #4

Only 1 km in length, Mary Gregg Lake is a small, shallow lake. At an altitude of 1538 m Mary Gregg Lake is considered by Alberta Environment to be a "high mountain" lake. As such, its water temperature hovers between 11°C at the surface and 9°C at 10 m. Oxygen levels dip correspondingly. Likewise, lake stagnation owing to the lake's protection from strong winds has meant low oxygen levels at lower depths. This is critical for whitefish and trout that require relatively high oxygen concentrations.

Species eastern brook trout, stocked annually with rainbow trout

Competition winner brown trout, 1982 g, 1966

Restrictions Wall bull trout (Dolly Varden) must be released. Wall rainbow and cutthroat trout shorter than 17.5 cm must be released. Wall arctic grayling shorter than 30 cm in length must be released. Use of bait fish and the collection of bait fish are prohibited. Electric motors only.

Season 16 June to 31 August

ruts into it. But do not let this badly disturbed access discourage you for the lakeside itself remains unscathed and beautiful.

Half way to the lake you reach an intersection. Go straight ahead or to the right. A short distance later you arrive at Mary Gregg Lake. And what a pretty sight it is! Steeply forested slopes surround this 8.5 ha body of water. White spruce predominates on the south slopes while lodgepole pine is found almost exclusively on the north slopes of this kilometre-long lake. Protected from the prevailing westerlies by the surrounding high hills, the lake was subject to stagnation prior to 1984. Commencement of mining by Cardinal River Coals Ltd. immediately to the south necessitated the diversion of some of the lake's normal surface inflow. Cardinal River Coals compensated for this loss of inflow by pumping water from Gregg River into the lake. The lake's outlet to Mary Gregg Creek was also dammed, raising the water level another 0.6 m.

Over the years visitors have established several pleasant picnic spots along the lakeside. The first of these is at the extreme west end of the lake where you first caught sight of this popular fishing spot. From here you may be able to hear the haul trucks for the Cardinal River Coals' mine; their road is high above the south side of the lake, beyond the crest of the hills.

At this picnic area the trail forks. The steep trail to your left leads up the slope, promising a high route around the lake. But it ends abruptly at the top of the rise, so stay low and take the lakeshore path. The path crosses some steep slopes that may make you a bit nervous but within 200 m it flattens. Another 200 m or so brings you to a second informal picnic area. You can choose to fish from here or if you continue along the path you can proceed for another 100 m to a swampy point of land where the trail peters out.

Return the way you came.

Mary Gregg Lake

Mary Gregg Lake and creek are named after Mary Cardinal Gregg (1876-1915), wife of John Gregg. She married Gregg in 1904 and brought two daughters, Lucy and Gladys, from a previous marriage into the relationship. She and John Gregg had no children.

The marriage was a late example of a centuries-old fur trade practice called the country marriage. The Cardinals belonged to the Metis community then based in what is now Jasper National Park. In 1904 John Gregg was a partner in a fur trade business at Prairie Creek. By marrying Mary Cardinal, John Gregg confirmed his presence within this community where kinship and business were often interchangeable.

Not all country marriages ended happily. Mary's aunt, Suzanne Cardinal, married Hudson Bay Company fur trader Henry Moberly when he was stationed at Jasper House. When Moberly left Jasper House, he also left behind Suzanne and their children. By way of contrast, John Gregg kept faith with his wife and stepdaughters after he became a prospector, struck it rich with his Mountain Park coal claim and no longer needed his fur trade business.

John Gregg might have kept the faith one other way. It is 1920 and he is now alone. Mary Gregg and her two daughters are dead. Dominion Land Surveyor N. C. Stewart is asked about "Mary Gregg" lake, a name unfamiliar to his superiors in Ottawa: "I do not know the exact location of this lake, but it is in the NW quarter township 47, range 24, west of the Fifth meridian. It is named after a relative of an old prospector who lives near the lake. I obtained the name from the Forest Rangers." Stewart never gave the name of that old prospector who chose to live near Mary Gregg's lake.

Mary Gregg Lake.

WATSON CREEK RECREATION AREA

Watson Creek Recreation Area is one of two campgrounds in the Cadomin district. It is located north of Cadomin; the other recreation area is located south of Cadomin on Whitehorse Creek. Much larger than Whitehorse Creek Recreation Area, the campground at Watson Creek is often overlooked by vacationers with the delightful result that it is a quiet place to stay while exploring the Cadomin and Luscar areas.

The immediate environs around Cadomin and Luscar offer a variety of hiking trails ranging from one hour walks around town to full day hikes up some of the local ridges and mountain tops. You can visit an old fire tower site or arrange for a tour of Inland Cement. Whatever you decide to do, Watson Creek Recreation Area is an excellent staging area.

Location 60 km southeast of Hinton along Highway #40, or 33.5 km west of Coalspur along Highway #40, or 6.5 km north of Cadomin on Highway #40.
Facilities 38 unserviced campsites, pump, firewood for sale
Note no OHVs allowed

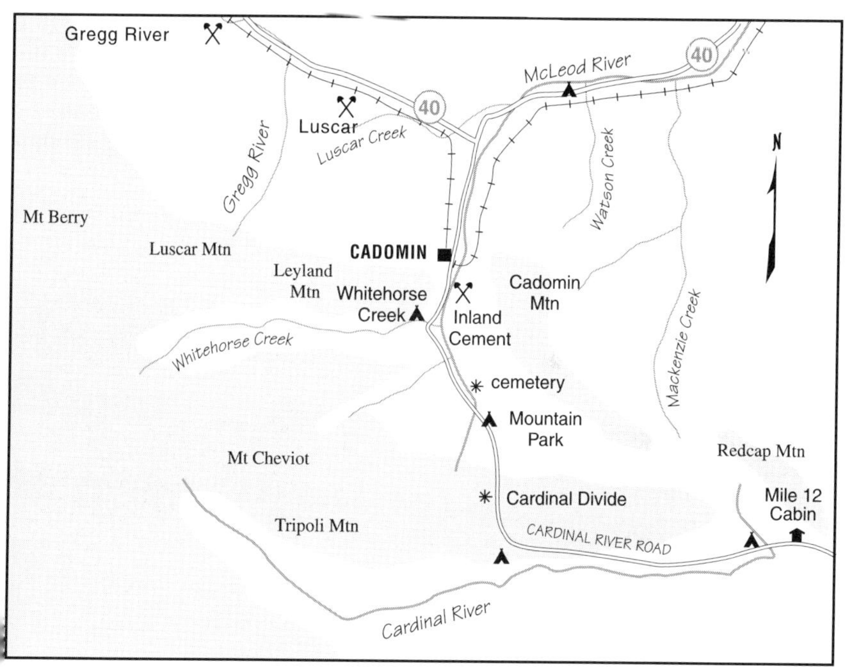

CADOMIN

Few of the old mining towns that gave life and meaning to the Coal Branch for so many years still exist. Along the West Branch, Luscar disappeared into the Cardinal River Coals' mine; Kaydee townsite met the same fate at the hands of Mannix's Gregg River mine. Mountain Park, although not obliterated, has only a few reminders of its heyday and most of these, too, will disappear if and when the Cheviot mine project goes ahead. Only Cadomin has survived. A mix of the old and the new, the town boasts a modest permanent population, but swells in numbers during summer when old time Coal Branchers return along with newcomers who have succumbed to the town's charm and easy accessibility to the mountains.

"The town is modern in every respect and there is a fine community spirit. There are three hotels and rooming houses, three churches and a large community hall where concerts and dances are held [where you can see] first class moving picture shows twice weekly," proclaimed the *Edson-Jasper Signal* in 1928. There was no doubt that Cadomin was the commercial hub of the West Branch. The town lacked nothing. In 1929 a recreation centre complete with a bowling alley, indoor curling rink, billiards and pool tables was built by the coal company. The construction of an outdoor skating rink was followed by a theatre. Yet, living conditions were crowded despite the rooms available at the hotels and the boarding house; some miners had to sleep in the basement of the boarding house, taking the beds vacated by workers on another shift. In time, this scenario changed and by 1950 Cadomin

Dairy. Photo Robert Scott.

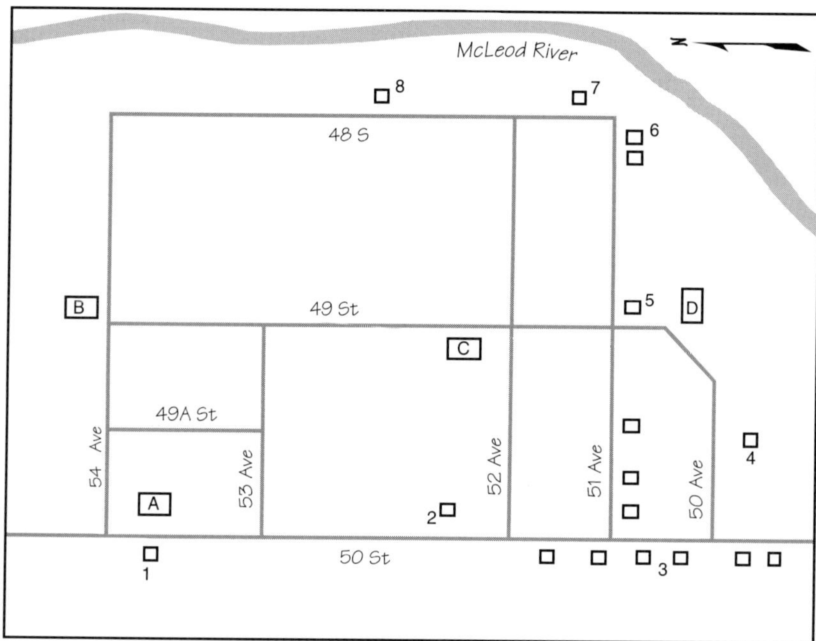

boasted a permanent population that supported, in addition to the above-mentioned enterprises, a dairy, a meat market, an automobile dealership, a bakery, a hardware store, a photographers's studio, a dry goods store, a gas station, a beauty parlour, and a brand new high school that attracted students from Luscar, Mountain Park and as far away as from Mercoal and Coalspur.

Over the years, Cadomin has faced its share of disasters. There were deaths in the mine; the infamous Cadomin wind occasionally tore roofs off houses; and then, there was the McLeod River. The river had flooded before, but the flood of 1950 was the worst. A heavy snowpack followed by hot weather and then rain unleashed a torrent of water that gathered in the headwaters of the McLeod and those of Whitehorse Creek to inundate the valley below. Rising four feet in a mere three hours, the river hurtled past the Cadomin Hotel picking it up and sweeping it downriver, smashing it to pieces against the railway bridge; three homes as well as the Riverside store in Leyland met a similar fate. All bridges between Cadomin and Mercoal were washed away by the wild river. The town recovered from the flood but the destructive forces of nature were a harbinger of worse to come. Cadomin couldn't ignore the future. When the first diesel train pulled into town, everyone knew that the end was near. Two years later, the mine closed, throwing the breadwinners of 2500 people out of work.

Unlike Mountain Park, the residents of Cadomin were not caught by surprise, neither were they forced to move. So, some simply remained in town. The mine demolished its buildings; others were moved out. Cadomin was reduced to a shadow of its former self. Then, in 1970, Cardinal River

Coals began open pit mining at the old townsite of Luscar. Cadomin took a new lease on life. Some miners moved into town. Electricity, which had been cut off when the underground mine closed, was restored. When the Mercantile general store burned in 1974, an entrepreneur, Millie Dunlop, purchased a Weldwood bunkhouse and moved it to Cadomin where she set up a store. The next owner, Gary Pearce, added a residence upstairs and a trailer on the west side to house a modern cafe and kitchen. Chuck and Marg Jacoby purchased the business in 1996. Over the past number of years, new residences have been built and old ones fixed up as old Coal Branchers and new residents come home.

A. Jacoby's Mountain Road General Store

Welcome to the place in the West Branch to "eat here and get gas," as the motto states on the front of the building. You cannot miss the store and gas bar when you drive through town. In summer, the deck at the front of the building is a riot of colour with petunias, temmari and lobelia spilling from hanging baskets and window boxes. The proprietress, a native of the west coast, even coaxes tender roses to grow. Inside, there is a general store and a cafe where you can tuck into miner-size burgers and omelettes served with homemade toast. Jacoby's is also the social hub of the community where the local populace gathers to visit over coffee. But more than this, the store serves as the memory of the West Branch. A cream separator, a sack from a Mercoal store, period advertisements, and photographs, lots of them, of Coal Branchers at work and at play keep the history of Cadomin and the other West Branch towns alive.

Jacoby's store is your starting point for the townsite walk.

Hours

Store: July-August 8:00 a.m.-8:00 p.m. Rest of the year 8:00 a.m.-6:00 p.m. except Thursday when 8:00 a.m.-3:00 p.m.

Hole in the Wall Cafe: 1 May-1 October 8:00 a.m.-3:00 p.m. every day.

1 October-30 April closed Sundays

B. The Cadomin Motel

The only accommodation in the West Branch. Kitchenettes, nightly or monthly.
Tel: 692-3663

C. Fire Hall

D. The Legion

The local watering hole. It is also the site for the annual barbecue—a real feast!—held in August. Everyone is welcome. Check at Jacoby's store or Whitehorse Creek campground for dates, time and cost.

These commemorative plaques can be found at the ball diamond.

Mining was hard work. A man could work up a thirst by the end of a long day and so it was customary for the miners to quench their thirst by stopping off at one of Cadomin's bars on the way home. Closest to the mine was the "Grey Beetle," otherwise known as "The Bucket of Blood" or "The Greasy Pig." Later, it was replaced by two other establishments, the Cadomin Hotel and the "Black Beetle," the latter so-named some say for the black tar paper exterior, or, claim others, for the black beetles that scurried across its floor!

1. The Eisler House

Its stucco exterior and cement foundation set this home apart from other historic homes in town.

2. Ball Diamond and Park

Each town had its sports teams and there was a friendly but fierce rivalry among the sporting teams of Luscar, Mountain Park and Cadomin. Cadomin had the Cadomin Miners, a baseball team that in 1932 nearly won the provincial baseball championship. Another local baseball team was the Cadomin Maroons. They, too, were serious contenders for the Alberta Senior Baseball Championship for a number of years. Their lineup included players who were known individually as "a steady moundman and also dangerous at plate" and "a good hitter and worthy manager of the hot corner" (third base).

Miners' homes.

The town also boasted a hockey team and a soccer team. For those who did not fancy contact sports, the town had four tennis courts. Along 50 Street you can find two memorials, one to the miners who toiled in the mines and another in appreciation of those who, over the years, have organized the Coal Branch reunions. The reunions, held every five years since 1985, are increasing in popularity; in 1995 some 3000 people attended the weekend fete.

3. Miners' Homes

The homes along 50 Street and up 51 Avenue are examples of the typical miners' homes, called "shacks." Constructed by the coal company in order to attract miners, these four-room, 28 x 28 foot log homes have dovetail corner joins and pyramidal roofs. On a number of the homes the sill logs have rotted resulting in the "sinking" of the homes.

4. RCMP Barracks

This green asphalt-sided log building was the RCMP barracks. There was, reputedly, little real crime in the Coal Branch. Fisticuffs among rowdy bar patrons were easily handled by the two-man detachment who threw the offenders into the "Crowbar Hotel" to cool off.

5. Cadomin Photo Studio

This photo studio dates to the end of the Second World War when William (Flash) Sherchuck established a successful portraiture business in Cadomin. When the mine closed in 1952, he switched to movie-making. One of his films, "Dawson City Joe," was shown in movie houses across Alberta and can be found at the National Archives of Canada.

Photo studio.

6., **7.**, **8.** Miners' Homes

These miners' homes are built on different plans than those of along 50 Street. Constructed of either lumber or logs, these homes date from a later period than the log homes along 50 Street.

9. Outhouse

Cadomin does not have a sewage system. Each home owner is responsible for installing and maintaining his own system, be it a septic field or the original, the pit toilet. This outhouse has been braced against the Cadomin winds that can howl down the alley.

The owner of this outhouse knows what he is doing!

Cadomin

Mine No.: #693

Owners/Operators: 1917 F. L. Hammond; 1917 Cadomin Collieries Ltd.; 1917-1952 Cadomin Coal Co. Ltd.

Authorized Capital: $45,000 Cadomin Collieries Ltd.; $2,000,000 Cadomin Coal Co. Ltd.

Coal: bituminous

Registered Trade Name: Cadomin Coal

Market: steam

Mine Type: underground; strip pit

Total Extraction: 9,999,000 tonnes

Men Killed: 32

The coal was discovered during the surveying of the railway to Mountain Park and staked in 1911 by Thomas McNab Burnett and James A. H. Church. These claims were controlled by Frederick L. Hammond (1874-1941) who offered to sell them to the Mountain Park Coal Company. Mountain Park refused to buy the claims, so in 1917 Hammond opened up a mine on the Burnett claim along the east bank of the McLeod River and became president of the Cadomin Coal Company.

Hammond had what came to be regarded as the best steam coal produced in Canada, but there was a problem. The coal had to be delivered to market over what was probably the worst section of railway in Alberta. Mountain Park had built the branch line from Coalspur and was responsible for its maintenance, which it did at minimal cost. With the extra traffic brought about by the opening of Cadomin, track conditions deteriorated to the point that it threatened Cadomin's ability to deliver its coal to market. This infuriated Hammond who, incidentally, was neither obliged to nor paid anything toward the upkeep of the railway line over which he moved his coal. "It is useless to avoid the fact that the Mountain Park Branch…is in abominable condition. Wrecks and derailments are the rule and not the exception," Hammond wrote. He warned that Cadomin would begin losing coal markets unless track conditions improved. Eventually Mountain Park received an increase from the federal government in its railway maintenance subsidy. Track conditions improved, markets were realized and Cadomin was soon on its way toward becoming the premier coal mine in the Coal Branch.

Fire in 1920 and 1923 forced the abandonment of the workings on the east side of the McLeod and a new entry was driven on the west side of the river. The mine was subject to high levels of methane gas and in 1929 a gas explosion killed two miners. In 1939 three miners died from suffocation and in 1942-43 four more miners died from the same cause.

Strip operations began in 1944 and four years later expanded to the recently purchased Gregg River mine. The two projects cost Cadomin by 1948 about $1,000,000. Faced with falling coal orders, both the Gregg River and Cadomin strip pits were closed in 1950. This set the stage for the 1950 mine disaster when water from the abandoned No. 1 east Cadomin strip pit broke into the underground workings and killed five miners.

By 1952 the Cadomin Coal Company had accumulated over $230,000 in losses mainly owing to a shrinking railway market for steam coal. That year the McLeod River flooded a section of the underground mine and washed-out roads, bridges and portions of the railway line. Citing the lack of working capital in the face of an uncertain coal market, the company closed the mine.

Coal Branchers

James Hutchison "Jack" McMillan (ca. 1888-1939)
Occupation: mining engineer, musician, poet

Money
I am the Law, the poor must heed my call
I have the power to damn, and starve you all
Bare your limbs, and feel this stinging rod
I am thy master—There is no God

Oh poor misguided fools. Lords of worldly power
Thy earthly forms will fall to dust and there will come the hour
When those whose bodies mark your scars so well
Will dwell for aye in peace, while you are damned in Hell
by J. H. McMillan

To say that Cadomin mine superintendent J. H. McMillan was high strung is to put it mildly; some of his less forgiving employees thought "Jekyll & Hyde" was a more appropriate basis upon which to evaluate the man. As in the above example of one of his poems, he did not hesitate to use the "stinging rod," then afterward consider the state of his immortal soul.

McMillan was born in Kilmarnock, Scotland, and immigrated to Canada in 1904 at the age of 16. He became a mining engineer and had been for six years in B.C. the provincial inspector of metalliferous mines before arriving in Cadomin as manager in 1922. Everyone soon felt the force of his near demonic energy as both mine and town were developed into what some regarded as Alberta's largest and best run mining camp. In terms of management style, he was a Scottish *laird*: authoritarian, at times ruthless, but imbued with a sense of social responsibility to the community under his charge.

He was the lord and master in all aspects, men followed his orders when they worked in the pit; they followed his orders in the community social events that he organized. McMillan was an extremely skilled violinist and formed the Cadomin Symphony Orchestra. He attracted musicians with the promise of higher than average salaries and soon this isolated mining community had not just the only symphony orchestra between Edmonton and Vancouver, but also one that matched them in ability. McMillan's passion for being and having the best was all encompassing: he composed music for his orchestra and wrote lyrics; he wrote and published poetry; he supported local sports teams and spearheaded the building of a state-of-the-art hockey arena and skating rink. His baseball team, the Cadomin Miners, reached the provincial finals in 1932.

McMillan did not keep his job, running Cadomin, for 13 years by being altruistic. The public goods that he provided the town were tightly measured against the increase in production and profit created by a well cared for work force. In 1932 there was scarlet fever in Cadomin and McMillan stood firm against an order by the provincial health inspector that sanitary conditions be improved: "...as long as the present depression obtains I feel that it is only right that we should not be asked to increase our capital expenditures or production costs,...it should be observed that to create expenditures at this time would simply mean cutting down on labour and the present is not a time for any company to indulge in such practices." The provincial government caught the hint, or threat if you will, and did not fully press the issue. McMillan, in turn, did order some improvements to the townsite.

McMillan's temper was legendary and a cause of great stress to man and beast. One day, his horse was more nervous than usual and McMillan could not mount him. Furious, he sent it back to the stable with the order that it be shot. The stable hand, by now well-schooled in the management of mad managers, hid the animal from McMillan pending confirmation of his order. Confirmation never came and the horse lived to face McMillan again.

Ill health forced McMillan to retire in 1935. He died four years later in Nanaimo, B.C.

44 CADOMIN TERRACE

MAP PAGE 232

This is the perfect walk for those staying in Cadomin or at the Whitehorse or Watson Creek recreation areas who wish an easy stroll while enjoying a lovely view overlooking the Cadomin townsite.

Cross the railway bridge over the McLeod River and walk toward the old Leyland railway station located just a little to your left. Behind the station is a slope with a well-worn path. Climb the slope. Your path soon takes a sharp 90° turn to the right and descends into a gully where you will have to cross a small stream. Climb out of the gully and up onto the terrace. Your path will braid now and then but for the best views keep to the right-hand braids. This is such a pretty walk, especially in early summer when the lugenwort, wild geranium, wild roses, forget-me-nots and a profusion of other wildflowers dot the hillside. On your right, the town of Cadomin is spread out below you, the McLeod River and the railway tracks being hidden beneath the slope. Your path swings in and out of poplar trees. You may notice that a number of the poplars have been scoured by wind; the Cadomin wind is infamous! Hop across a stream. From here the trail climbs a low slope and passes through poplar copses to emerge at an intersection of trails. Turn right; the trail straight ahead leads to Baldy Mountain. At the bottom of the slope cross First Creek and walk down the draw toward the railway tracks. Cross the tracks and pick up the OHV track on the other side. Turn right and follow the track that parallels the railway back to the McLeod River bridge.

Day hiking
Rating half day
Distance 1.8 km
Level of Difficulty easy walk with some short scrambles; optional stream crossing
Maximum Elevation 1526 m
Elevation Gain 20 m
Map 83 F/3 Cadomin

Access

Park your vehicle before the railway bridge that crosses the McLeod River near Leyland station. The turnoff to Leyland station is a gravel road that begins beside the railway crossing 600 m north of Jacoby's store in Cadomin along the Cardinal River Road. The trailhead is 300 m east along the road from the crossing.

0.0 km	trailhead and McLeod River
0.2 km	intersection
0.3 km	stream crossing
0.7 km	stream crossing
1.0 km	intersection
1.1 km	First Creek
1.2 km	intersection
1.3 km	McLeod River
1.5 km	intersection
1.8 km	trailhead

The Cadomin Wind

People always knew when it was coming. The signal would come from the top of Cheviot Mountain: the snow would start blowing and within the hour the wind would hit Cadomin.

The Cadomin wind had many names, many inappropriate for a family publication such as this. It would blow primarily between November and January and sometimes last a week. Rocks the size of eggs would be hurled through the air, railway cars would be thrown off the track and houses would either lose their roofs or be lifted off their foundations. The south-facing side of buildings would be pitted from the hurtling stones and outhouses not braced with poles would be blown away. The wind would seep through the cracks in window and door frames and make home interiors look as if they had been sprinkled with fine black pepper.

Valley of the Wind sign.

Cadomin residents, it was said, would need a month after leaving the Coal Branch to learn how to walk erect again, owing to their perpetual stooping against the wind. Despite the property damage, there is only one death directly attributed to the wind. On that occasion, a man heard the wind coming and was putting his chickens into the chicken coop. The wind struck the small building, tore it to pieces and blew the chickens into the surrounding boreal forest, never to be seen again. And the man? He was found dead with every bone in his limbs fractured.

A 1923 windstorm started the great Cadomin fire. It was December and men were clearing brush near the mine tipple when the wind came up and sent the brush fire out of control. Nearly all the buildings outside the actual townsite were burned as men fought in subzero Fahrenheit temperatures and wind gusts clocked at over 130 km/h to save the town and what remained of the mine buildings. Blasting powder from the powder magazine was dumped into the McLeod River to prevent a possible explosion while women and children were evacuated with food and bedding into the steam heated bathhouse. A crew of men armed with buckets of water stood guard outside the bathhouse to prevent it from catching fire.

Meanwhile, in the midst of all this mayhem, a child was being born. A woman had gone into labour and could not be evacuated. Steel rails were placed upon the roof of her Leyland home to keep the roof from blowing off, while outside, more men with buckets of water were continually putting out embers blown in from the surrounding fire. Inside, the town doctor delivered a healthy baby boy.

The wind's violence was owing to the unique local geography. The gap between Cadomin and Leyland mountains acts as the mouth of a funnel for the wind rushing down the valleys of the McLeod River and Whitehorse Creek. It collects then squeezes through the gap with increased force onto the town. Inland Cement has since widened the gap by cutting away the face of Cadomin Mountain. Has the widening lessened its force? As they say, "The answer is blowin' in the wind."

45 BALDY RIDGE

MAP PAGE 232

Looking up from the Cadomin townsite the white cross on top of Baldy Ridge piques your curiosity. Is it a grave marker? For whom was it raised and why? This pleasant half day hike will reveal all—and more. Once you have solved the mystery of the cross, another one lies at your feet!

Day hiking, horseback riding
Rating half day
Distance 8.4 km
Level of Difficulty steady ascent to windswept ridge
Maximum Elevation 1782 m
Elevation Gain 275 m
Map 83 F/3 Cadomin

Access

Park your vehicle before the railway bridge that crosses the McLeod River near Leyland station. The turnoff to Leyland station is a gravel road that begins beside the railway crossing 600 m north of Jacoby's store in Cadomin along the Cardinal River Road. The trailhead is 300 m east along the road from the crossing.

0.0 km	trailhead
0.0 km	McLeod River
0.2 km	intersection
0.6 km	intersection
0.7 km	First Creek
0.8 km	intersection
1.0 km	start braid
1.4 km	end braid and intersection
2.7 km	cross
2.8 km	cairn
4.2 km	cutline and intersection (1.5 km to Cadomin strip pit)
8.4 km	trailhead

From your vehicle cross the McLeod River railway bridge and swing right along the OHV track that parallels the railway tracks. One-half kilometre from your trailhead you will notice a stream, First Creek, in a draw on the other side of the tracks. Cross the tracks and walk up the draw until you are forced to cross First Creek. It is an easy crossing. Once on the other side of the creek follow a trail

The memorial cross to Claude Beaulieu.

that leads up the slope immediately to your left. The trail switches steeply up the hillside. As you climb, ignore a side trail on your left. At the top of the ridge you come upon an old roadway. Turn right onto the roadway. Pause and look back. It's a pleasant view of the McLeod River valley from here. You can see Cardinal River Coals' Luscar mine workings and Inland Cement's workings on Cadomin Mountain, and below you on your right you can hear the gurgle of First Creek.

Follow the roadway for 100 m to a fork in the trail. Continue straight ahead, ignoring the right-hand fork. Your path has now narrowed to a horse trail that almost immediately crosses a swampy area. If you have trouble discerning the trail here, swing a little to the right and pick up a distinct horse trail where it enters the open spruce forest. Numerous springs along the hillside can render the lower part of the trail quite spongy, especially if there has been a recent rain. Within a few hundred metres you arrive at an intersection with an old roadway. Continue straight ahead on the horse trail. As you climb, you join an old cutline for 100 m or so before your path veers to the right. You will rejoin the cutline closer to the top of Baldy Ridge. Another short walk up the trail carries you out of the forest and into thick alders that line both sides of your path. Soon, though, you find yourself on the open ridge of Baldy.

If you liked the view of the McLeod River valley from First Creek, you will like this view doubly for you have nearly a 360° panorama. You are now approximately 200 m higher than the river valley and Cadomin looks tiny from here. Behind the townsite are the Luscar mine workings and at your 1:00 o'clock you have a good view of Inland Cement's quarry. Rolling forested hills stretch as far as the eye can see on your left. And straight ahead just off

grand view follows you along the entire length of Baldy Ridge.

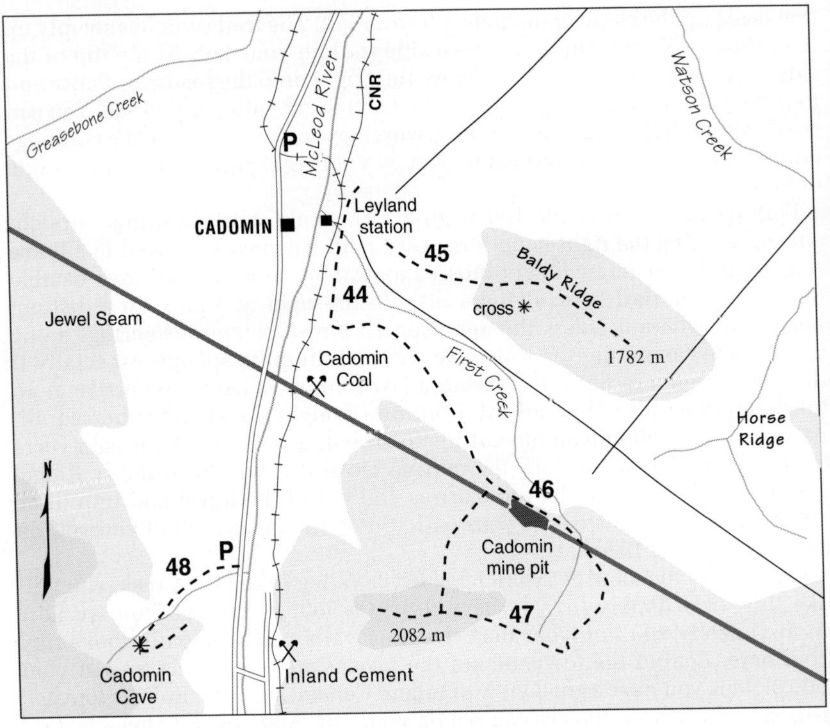

your path is the cross, perched on the edge of the slope. Walking around to the front of the cross you can read the inscription dedicated to Claude Beaulieu who, at the age of 29, froze to death after becoming disoriented when his skidoo ran out of gas not far from here.

The horse trail continues from here along the open ridge for more than a kilometre. A short distance from the cross you will find a rock cairn. It may be difficult to decide whether to take in the view or to watch carefully where you step. Baldy Ridge is well known locally as a fossil bed. Indeed, you can easily find marine fossils in the red sandstone scattered along the slope of the ridge, especially in the vicinity of the cross and cairn. As you continue along the horse trail you may also have to watch for the infamous Cadomin winds; we were nearly blown off the slope the day we were here! The distinct horse trail that you have been following ends at a T-junction with a cutline. Here you have a choice. If you turn right and follow the cutline you will end up at the Cadomin mine pit, joining that route at the 4.8 km point. Or you can return the way you came. The distance back to the trailhead is comparable.

Fossils

During the Lower Cretaceous period—from about 145 to 99 million years ago—a vast sea stretched from the Gulf of Mexico across the Great Plains and northward to the Arctic Ocean. Eroded sediments from the Shield to the east and the ancient mountains to the west settled so thickly on the sea floor that the sea eventually filled, creating a landscape of swamps and deltas. Beginning in the late or Upper Cretaceous, a collision of the Continental and Farallon plates caused the land to be uplifted resulting first in the draining of the sea and then in the formation of mountains. Further compression exerted from the west forced the land to buckle forming the Main and Front ranges and lastly, the foothills.

The late Cretaceous sea floor teemed with a wide variety of life. Mollusks, invertebrate animals such as ammonites, belemnoids, oysters and clams lived in the nutrient-rich warm waters. Today, throughout the Rockies, we can see evidence of this part of our past. In the Cadomin area you can find ammonite impressions, such as the one in the photo below, and a "battlefield" of belemnites. On Baldy Ridge we could not find evidence of ammonites and belemnoids, but found numerous clam fossils. If you are tempted to take home a specimen, remember that collecting fossils is not allowed within Whitehorse Wildland Park.

The impression of this ammonite is quite impressive. Photo Alfred Falk.

46 CADOMIN STRIP PIT

MAP PAGE 232

It's always interesting poking around old abandoned mine sites. This visit to the Cadomin strip pit is an activity that is enjoyed by hikers, cyclists, OHV riders and trail equestrians alike. The great views at the top are an added bonus.

Leaving your vehicle, cross the McLeod River railway bridge. Find the OHV track that swings to the right paralleling the railway tracks. One-half kilometre from your trailhead you will notice a stream, First Creek, in a draw on the other side of the tracks. Here, a trail coming down the draw can be seen. Ignore it and continue along the OHV track for approximately another 500 m to an intersection with an old mine road. Turn left onto the mine road and begin a slow climb up the hill. The mine road is in excellent shape, although if you are walking you may find the gravel road hard on the feet. En route you will pass an intersection with a trail that joins on the left. A kilometre later, at the bottom of a small hill, the mine road braids. Keep to the right and continue to climb to the mine site.

Day hiking, cycling, horseback riding

Rating half day

Distance 11.2 km

Level of Difficulty easy walk along old mine road

Maximum Elevation 1718 m

Elevation Gain 216 m

Map 83 F/3 Cadomin

Access

Park your vehicle before the railroad bridge that crosses the McLeod River near Leyland station. The turnoff to Leyland station is a gravel road that begins beside the railway crossing 600 m north of Jacoby's store in Cadomin along the Cardinal River Road. The trailhead is 300 m east along the road from the crossing.

The truck and shovel method of mining was employed at the Cadomin strip pit.

0.0 km	trailhead and McLeod River
0.6 km	intersection and First Creek
1.2 km	intersection mine road
1.5 km	intersection
2.7 km	start braid
3.3 km	intersection
3.4 km	end braid
3.8 km	intersection
4.1 km	strip pit pond
4.4 km	intersection
4.8 km	intersection
4.9 km	intersection
5.2 km	quadruple intersection
5.5 km	coal pit and seam
5.6 km	interior of pit
5.7 km	corresponds with 5.5 km
5.8 km	intersection
5.9 km	cutline
6.3 km	T-junction
6.4 km	intersection
6.7 km	viewpoint
7.0 km	intersection
7.4 km	intersection
7.6 km	viewpoint of strip pit
7.9 km	intersection
11.2 km	trailhead

Long slit-like trenches mark the location of a worked-out coal seam.

You are now entering a landscape that retains the scars of the open pit coal mine that operated here from 1944 to 1950. The mine road is now reduced to a four-wheel-drive track that snakes around the pits and through mounds of the rock overburden. OHV tracks lead off in all directions attesting to the popularity of the site with quad drivers. But the main track leads straight ahead. So, for now, ignore a track that joins from the right part way up the slope; you will loop back along this track on your return. The top of your braid joins your track within 100 m. Keep to the right climbing uphill to an intersection with another OHV track. Turn right and follow the track down into the pit. It is quite a view. A long slit in the earth's crust where men wrestled for the coal with dynamite and dump trucks stretches before you. Since the abandonment of the mine, water has filled the trench leaving a barren "lake" in the midst of this moon-like landscape. Water, though, is like a magnet and this might be a good place to stop for a snack or a drink, especially if it is a hot day.

Refreshed and your curiosity satisfied, retrace your route out of the pit. At the intersection with the main track turn right and continue your slow climb uphill skirting the trench on your right. Near the top end of the pit there is a series of OHV tracks. The first joins from the left; it leads over to Baldy Ridge. So keep to the right. Within 100 m there is another intersection that also goes to Baldy. Once again, bear right. You are now at the top end of the pit. Fifty metres below you is the water-filled trench. Looking straight ahead into the distance you can see the workings of the Luscar mine. To your left is Cadomin Mountain and to your right is Baldy Ridge.

Continue along the top of the pit. To begin your loop back to your trailhead, bear slightly to the right at a tangle of four quad tracks that appear on the far side of the open pit; if you turn left you climb Cadomin Mountain. Follow the track as it now drops along an old rock dump. Because you are on a small ridge you have good views straight ahead of the modern Luscar mine workings, of Baldy Mountain on your right and of Cadomin Mountain on your left. Your road leads down along an old slack pile to the entrance of yet another pit. A small "reflecting" pond in front of the gaping hole invites you to turn left and enter into the pit. Inside, you are awed by an impressive coal seam that hangs above you, encircling the pit. We hunted for fossils in the coal but could find none; perhaps you will have better luck.

Return to the road. Turn left to continue your descent. Very shortly you will arrive at an intersection. Bear to the right to go around a rock dump. The trail looks a bit dubious, but follow the horse tracks that lead you down through the coal slack to the bottom of the dump. Here, look to your right. The horse trail leaves the road and follows a cutline. The open forest of the cutline trail is a sharp contrast to the sterile unreclaimed mine site. You pass a clearing before the trail swings to the right to parallel the mine workings below. At a T-junction with the trail from Cadomin Mountain, turn right and continue downhill to another intersection.

Do you want to go to a viewpoint that overlooks the Luscar mine site, Cadomin and Inland Cement's quarry? Bear left at the intersection and follow the horse trail to an open meadow. It's a pleasant view that invites you to linger for a while before returning to the intersection; to continue down through the meadow will only lead you into trackless bush. At the intersection go left and descend to a strip pit. To the left you can see revegetation test plots. Through the pit past debris left over from the days when this part of the mountain throbbed with activity your track brings you to the intersection with the main mine road. Turn left. You are now on familiar territory as you drop all the way down the hill to the railway tracks. Swing to the right, cross the tracks and follow the OHV track to your trailhead.

The Cadomin Mine Disaster

It had been a long winter with heavy snow cover followed by an unusually late spring. The thaw began suddenly and after two extremely hot days, June 12 and 13, the snow was melting quickly and the McLeod River was rising. Then, on the morning of June 14, 1950, a rainstorm began that lasted all day. By evening, the already-flooding McLeod River had risen 1.2 m over three hours and was now smashing through Cadomin.

Cadomin mine manager A. J. Henderson, meanwhile, had other matters on his mind than the surrounding storm and flood. His carefully constructed drainage system was being overwhelmed. There were underground workings below the abandoned No. 1 strip pit and a ditch had been excavated along the pit side to carry away surface water. There had been a minor cave-in a week earlier and now, at the height of the storm, when he inspected the drainage ditch, he saw with horror that it was overflowing. Water was entering the underground mine through the cave at an estimated rate of 22,730 litres per minute. Henderson ordered bulldozer operators to repair the damaged ditch while he tried frantically to phone into the mine and order the 22 men working underground out. No one was answering the phone.

The moment the men underground "felt the air reverse" they knew they were in danger. Their fire boss didn't hesitate. He ordered them out of the mine. Soon they were struggling through water and debris as high as their waists as they fought their way to safety. Five of them did not make it.

Looking down into the cave after the disaster. Courtesy Provincial Archives of Alberta, 77-237/693ff.

Rescue operations started right away but there was no immediate hope of finding anyone alive. Between 40 to 60 men were employed in four six-hour shifts per day, seven days a week clearing away the mud. The work was slow and hazardous, as the sudden onrush of water had destroyed many of the mine supports and caused many large cave-ins. Every foot of mine cleared had to be retimbered and a ventilation system reestablished. Over 4000 tons of debris would be removed before the last body was taken out on August 5th.

Dead were Roy Carr, Radovin Kasonovich, Michael Kapuscinski, P. J. Morris and Steve Tomlinovich. The inquest reported that they died from "multiple crushing injuries produced by the application of a great rapidly moving force."

Natural Reclamation

When mining at the Cadomin strip pit ceased in 1952, there was no effort made to reclaim the approximately 140 ha of disturbed land. Starting in the 1970s this and other abandoned strips pit were studied to examine the geologic and micro-climatic conditions that were preventing natural revegetation from taking place.

The studies found that there is very little natural revegetation occurring owing to the extreme porosity of the spoil materials, lack of any topsoil and strong desiccating winter winds. While winds do transport seeds onto the sites, they are only dropped on the lee sides of boulders or mounds, or in depressions resulting in extremely azonal and sparse vegetation. Plants tend to occur as individual specimens in areas protected from abrasion by windblown snow and rock particles in winter and where there is adequate soil moisture.

While the spoil's porosity inhibits plant growth it also stabilizes the steep slopes. There is very little erosion caused by running water and what erosion that does occur is mainly owing to frost action on the sandstones and shales that make up much of the material. The water's speed as it percolates downward from the surface also results in minimal chemical reaction between water and spoil. Field reclamation trials show that topsoiling and fertilizing improve revegetation success. Native grasses seeded on the disturbed sites do not develop a ground cover as fast as cultivated grasses and legumes and if native grasses are desired it is necessary seed the faster growing cultivated species as companion crops.

When the spoil pile was created 50 years ago, the topsoil and its plant fibre were not saved. Rather they were dumped, then covered with an ever growing pile of broken rock. Today, Cardinal River Coals, as part of its reclamation process, stockpiles topsoil then later spreads it over the mine spoil—the opposite of what was done at Cadomin and other Coal Branch strip pits.

Vegetation test plots adjacent to the pit.

47 ARTHUR'S SEAT

MAP PAGE 232

Open ridge walks are among hikers' favourites. A beautiful alpine ridge along the spine of Arthur's Seat is your reward for a steep climb up the mountain's slope.

Leaving your vehicle, cross the McLeod River railway bridge. Find the OHV track that swings to the right paralleling the railway tracks. One-half kilometre from your trailhead you will notice a stream, First Creek, in a draw on the other side of the tracks. Here, a trail coming down the draw can be seen. Ignore it and continue along the OHV track for approximately another 500 m to an intersection with an old mine road. Turn left onto the mine road and begin a slow climb up the hill. The mine road is in excellent condition although if you are walking you may find the gravel road hard on the feet. En route, you will pass an intersection with a trail that joins on the left. A kilometre later, at the bottom of a small hill, the mine road braids. Keep to the right and continue to climb to the mine site.

Day hiking

Rating full day

Distance 13.3 km

Level of Difficulty easy walk and scramble to alpine area; risk of high winds

Maximum Elevation 2082 m

Elevation Gain 580 m

Map 83 F/3 Cadomin; 83 C/14 Mountain Park

Access

Park your vehicle before the railway bridge over the McLeod River near Leyland station. The turnoff to Leyland station is a gravel road that begins beside the railway crossing 600 m north of Jacoby's store in Cadomin along the Cardinal River Road. The trailhead is 300 m east along the road from the crossing.

0.0 km	trailhead
0.0 km	McLeod River
0.2 km	intersection
0.6 km	intersection
0.6 km	First Creek
1.2 km	intersection mine road
1.5 km	intersection
2.7 km	start braid
3.3 km	end braid
3.7 km	intersection
4.2 km	intersection
4.5 km	triple intersection
4.8 km	campsite/stream crossing
5.0 km	intersection
5.3 km	cutline
5.4 km	intersection

The view to the west from Arthur's Seat.

5.7 km end quad track
6.3 km first saddle
7.2 km second saddle
7.5 km summit
7.8 km second saddle
8.3 km gully
8.4 km ridge
8.8 km OHV track
9.3 km intersection
9.4 km intersection
9.5 km intersection
10.0 km intersection
10.6 km intersection (corresponds with 2.7 km)
13.3 km trailhead

Along the spine heading for the summit of Arthur's Seat.

The mine road is now reduced to a four-wheel-drive track that snakes around the pits and through mounds of rock overburden. OHV tracks lead off in all directions attesting to the popularity of the site with OHV drivers. But the main track leads straight ahead. Keep to the right climbing uphill to an intersection with another OHV track. Keep on the main mine road, or to the left, and continue your slow climb uphill skirting a water-filled mine pit on your right. Near the top end of the pit there is a series of OHV tracks. The first joins from the left; it leads over to Baldy Ridge. So keep to the right. Within 100 m there is another intersection that also goes to Baldy. Once again, bear right. You are now at the top end of the pit you have been paralleling. Looking toward the mine pit you can see the workings of the Luscar mine in the distance. To your left is Arthur's Seat, your destination, and to your right is Baldy Ridge.

Continue along the top of the pit. At a tangle of four quad tracks that appear on the far side of the open pit turn left. Cross a small stream. Here you will find a random campsite. Behind the campsite pick up the OHV track that leads up the slope through the open forest. At an intersection of trail keep to the right to remain on the OHV track. Cross a cutline. At another intersection your track makes a sharp 90° turn to the right. Soon you will emerge from the forest onto an open slope. Directly below are the old Cadomin mine pits and in the distance you can see the Luscar mine workings and reclamation. Turn around and begin climbing the slope to the top of Arthur's Seat. There is no track or trail leading up but one is not necessary. It's a short but steep climb through a beautiful alpine meadow liberally sprinkled with dots of yellow butter and eggs, potentilla and alpine poppies, of white heather, of blue alpine forget-me-knots, and of purple gentia and silky scorpionweed. Once on top you have nearly a 360° vista. Only your view to the southeast is blocked where Cadomin Mountain looms on your left. Turn west and follow this beautiful open ridge as it rises gently to the summit. En route, you will dip through two saddles. On your right, below you, is Cadomin; straight ahead is the hill where Cadomin Cave is located and looking down on your left you can see the confluence of the Whitehorse Creek and McLeod River. At the summit overlooking the McLeod River valley there is no cairn to mark your arrival.

There is a track that leads down and around. Ignore it; it dead-ends above Inland Cement's workings. To return to your trailhead retrace your steps to the nearest saddle and drop down the slope to a gully and over a small ridge. This course swings you to the lower end of the Cadomin mine pit. On the other side of the ridge you pick up an OHV track. Stay on it through three intersections, but at the fourth intersection bear to the left onto the main mine road. Follow it down the hill to the railway tracks. Cross the tracks and swing to the right onto the OHV track that will take you back to Leyland and your vehicle.

Alpine Poppy

Scientific name ~ *Papaver kluanensis*

It is always a happy occasion when hiking above the treeline to find alpine poppies, for although not rare they are also not common. But if you check amongst the rocks and crevices in higher altitudes you can find this relative of our garden variety. Four yellow petals enclose stamens and a star-shaped yellow stigma. Alpine poppies propagate by means of seeds that are allowed to scatter in the wind from small openings at the top of the seed capsule.

Cadomin/Mountain/Creek

Previous names: Leyland Mountain, Arthur's Seat, Mile 22

Cadomin takes its name from the Cadomin Coal Company Ltd., which started the local mine in 1917. Cadomin Coal was affiliated with Canadian Dominion Development Ltd., which since 1914 had its Canadian head office in the Cadomin Building in Winnipeg. Canadian Dominion was a Liverpool, England, based development company formed to channel British investment into western Canada. The word Cadomin is a contraction of Canadian Dominion and was not applied to the mining community until 1918 with the opening of the local post office that closed in 1989.

Cadomin Mountain was first named as such in 1922, but locals persisted in calling the peak Leyland Mountain, after the nearby train station. Their Cadomin Mountain was what they also called The Sleeping Lady, today's Leyland Mountain. On Sept. 1, 1859, the Earl of Southesk passed by and wrote, "The mountains now appeared close in front of us. One of them particularly struck me from its resemblance to Arthur's Seat, near Edinburgh; it was similar in shape, and apparently in formation, though on a greatly magnified scale." This similarity is being presently chipped away by Inland Cement. Near the future location of Cadomin, Southesk stopped for lunch and spent an hour reading Macbeth before moving on up the McLeod River.

Mile 22 is the distance count along the West Coal Branch railway from Coalspur.

Inland Cement's workings on Cadomin Mountain as seen from Leyland Mountain.

48 CADOMIN CAVE

MAP PAGE 232

Caves and their secret world have long fascinated us. The meandering, sometimes very narrow passageways that can open suddenly into cathedral-like galleries or end abruptly forcing you to slither your way back through silt and mud offer an adventure as exciting as any that you can hope to experience. Who cannot be awed by such a geological phenomenon? It is the promise of adventure and discovery that makes caves such popular destinations. The easy accessibility of Cadomin Cave gives everyone an opportunity to experience the strange world of the underground. But it is up to you whether or not you benefit from the experience and whether or not others will be able to enjoy their trip to the cave. Please leave the cave as you found it. Remember, too, that it is illegal to disturb the thousands of bats that hibernate in Cadomin Cave. Be a responsible visitor.

A well-groomed and well-marked path leads gently uphill from the parking lot through spruce forest to a T-junction with an old road. If you turn left onto the road you will descend back to the Cardinal River Road. So turn right and walk up the road as it follows the stream and valley on your left. Ignore a secondary path that joins on the right 200 m later. Beyond this point the old road withers to a pathway making this pretty climb easier on the feet. This is an easy walk that allows plenty of time to savour the scenery, which is dominated by the Sleeping Lady Mountain at the head of the valley. You soon cross a stream where an Alberta government sign warns that the bats that inhabit Cadomin Cave may carry rabies so cavers "Enter At Own Risk." There are two more stream crossings before you turn your back on the valley in which you have been walking.

Cadomin Cave has suffered grievously at the hands of irresponsible visitors. At the last stream crossing these people first make their presence known. Spray-painted graffiti on the rocks by the stream mar the idyllic surroundings and urge you to hustle past an informal campsite that is located at an intersection of secondary trails with the main trail. Remain on the main path as it

Day hiking

Rating full day

Distance 5.2 km

Level of Difficulty steady ascent with some steep scrambles

Maximum Elevation 1870 m

Elevation Gain 240 m

Map 83 F/3 Cadomin

Access

Park your vehicle at the parking lot marked "Alternate Parking Lot and Trailhead" located 2.5 km south of Jacoby's store in Cadomin along the Cardinal River Road. Your trailhead is just beyond the sign.

0.0 km	trailhead
0.6 km	T-junction
0.8 km	intersection
0.9 km	stream crossing
1.0 km	stream crossing
1.5 km	stream crossing
1.5 km	campsite
1.5 km	intersection
2.0 km	campsite
2.0 km	viewpoint
2.1 km	viewpoint
2.2 km	start braid
2.3 km	end braid
2.7 km	rock face
2.8 km	meadow
2.9 km	viewpoint
3.1 km	campsite
3.3 km	Cadomin Cave
3.5 km	gully bottom and braids
3.7 km	intersection
5.2 km	trailhead

Benches invite the hiker to sit a spell and enjoy the view of Leyland Mountain.

switches uphill. A view of Cadomin Mountain and the workings of Inland Cement lie straight ahead. The trail, now resembling an old roadbed, widens and flattens as it wends its way around a low shoulder of Leyland Mountain. Another random campsite on your right announces the first viewpoint, which lies straight ahead. Homemade benches offer a comfortable seat while you enjoy the view of Cadomin Mountain and the Inland Cement workings. If you turn around, you are rewarded with an equally satisfying vista of Leyland Mountain and the valley that you recently climbed. A second viewpoint, a mere 100 m farther up the path, offers a closer look at Cadomin Mountain and the McLeod River valley. In early summer this grassy knoll supports white forget-me-nots, avens, dainty yellow butter and eggs, and the low bush, kinnikinnick.

From here the trail climbs steeply, braiding across a windswept, sunbaked slope. This is only the beginning of a very steep climb so if you feel winded after 20 m or so you may want to turn around and return to the trailhead. The path snakes up and across the steep scree slope. If you need to catch your breath en route you can look for fossils in the limestone boulders and rocks, or stop to enjoy the unfolding vista below. The path leads you to a prominent rock face. Here, cold air escaping from the underground cave system holds promise for the rest of the hike. After enjoying the wonderful view down the McLeod River valley, traverse across the slope, climbing more slowly now up to a beautiful grassy knoll, yet another shoulder of Leyland Mountain. In early summer the meadow is sprinkled liberally with avens, alpine poppies and kinnikinnick. For a view both up and down the McLeod River valley turn left and climb to the end of the knoll. Be careful. The knoll ends in a cliff and it's a long way to the bottom of the valley. This might be a good place to enjoy a rest and a snack. Another lunch stop can be found by turning around and retracing your steps down the slope, this time all the way to the dwarfed spruce trees where you can find several fire pits. The fire pits are located adjacent to a game trail. Turn right onto the game trail and follow it as it drops from the meadow into the spruce trees below. Within 200 m you arrive at the mouth of Cadomin Cave.

Located 340 m above the valley floor the cave opening is impressively large, inviting all to enter whether they be properly trained and outfitted cavers or casual curiosity seekers. Its accessibility has been the cave's nemesis. Graffiti spray painted all along the entrance walls is only the first indication of the vandalism that has both spoiled and damaged the interior of the cave. At the entrance there is a plaque placed by the Alberta Speleological Society upon the completion of a major clean up of the cave in October, 1996, that

The entrance to Cadomin Cave.

The McLeod River valley lies more than 200 m below.

saw its members haul out garbage that ranged from candy wrappers to feces. Beautiful formations in the cave have long since been broken and chopped off, carried home by unthinking and uncaring visitors. Responsible spelunkers have three mottoes:

- take nothing but pictures
- kill nothing but time
- leave nothing but footprints

Do not disappoint those who follow by disregarding these simple but effective guidelines.

We recommend you explore the cave with an experienced guide. Not only will you learn about cave systems and the bats that hibernate in this cave but there is safety in numbers; Cadomin Cave is large enough and complex enough to get lost! Remember that the temperature inside the cave is only a few degrees above freezing and if you are not dressed properly you will soon become chilled. Check with your guide or the Alberta Speleological Society on other tips to help make your trip inside the cave a comfortable one.

Upon emerging from the cave you have two options. You can return the way you came or you can descend straight down the slope from the mouth of the cave. There are numerous braids but they all lead to a junction with the main path just above the third stream that you crossed on your way up to the cave. Turn left and descend the path to the trailhead and your vehicle.

Cadomin Cave

Cadomin Cave is the most accessible and, therefore, one of the best known caves in the Canadian Rockies. It was probably discovered in 1936 by Alex Jenkins, a local resident, who was out hunting. He had wounded a sheep on the upper meadow and when he followed it down the slope to dispatch it, he found a small opening. He and several other individuals returned with picks and shovels to enlarge the hole to permit entry, and informal exploration of the cave began.

It was only in 1959 that the first official survey of its underground chambers was carried out by a group that included R. S. Taylor of Alberta Lands and Forests, W. L. Bigg of the Civil Engineering Department at the University of Alberta and at least two others, Hugh Campbell and Jim Houston. Equipped with miner's lamps that they picked up in Mercoal, the cavers carried survey equipment up the mountainside and into the cave. Inside, they found formations such as stalagmites and stalactites; Taylor reported finding one stalagmite that was 30 x 46 cm. Today, the upper sections of the cave have all but been stripped of these formations by unthinking visitors. Taylor and Biggs mapped some 2000 m of passageways and named such prominent passages and rooms as the Mess Hall and the Main Gallery. Even though rumours persist that a Cadomin miner discovered a passageway twice as long as those discovered by the first survey, in fact only another 791 m have been subsequently mapped. Cadomin Cave has a known depth of 220 m. This is impressive but pales when compared to the 522 m depth of Arctomys Cave in British Columbia, the deepest known cave in Canada. Members of the Alberta Speleological Society are actively engaged in exploring new passageways that may connect with three known smaller caves in the immediate vicinity. There is only one entry known though a nearby air hole may connect with the cave. The entry has grown in size over the years. In 1959 there was still a reverse talus slope 16 m above the entrance that spilled back into the cave effectively concealing the mouth from all but a few vantage points. Since then cavers have clawed away at the entrance to create the present yawning opening.

Members of the first survey team to explore Cadomin Cave, June 1959. Courtesy Provincial Archives of Alberta, Public Affair Bureau Collection PA 2797/2.

Cadomin Cave was created in the typical manner of limestone caves. Groundwater becomes slightly acidic owing to the presence of carbon in the air. As the acidic groundwater seeped through fractures in the rock it slowly dissolved the limestone, creating over time the maze of passageways, some large, some small, seen today. Despite the fact that much of the mountainous regions of Alberta are composed of limestone, there have been relatively few caves discovered. Why? Geologists believe that either glacial erosion has scooped out the roofs of caves that left them vulnerable to infilling with sand and gravel during glacial retreat or frost shattering has possibly plugged passageways or left thick layers of gravel and rock over the cave entrances.

Little Brown Bat

Scientific name ~ *Myotis lucifugus*

The Little Brown Bat is probably the most common of the eight bat species found in Alberta. Medium sized, it sports a glossy coat that ranges in colour from a deep mahogany brown to a light, almost yellowish, brown. The bats average 95 mm in length, have a wingspan of 22-27 cm and weigh a mere 8-12 g. Bats are the only mammals that can fly.

The Little Brown Bat, like most bat species, remains in Alberta during the winter months hibernating in caves and old underground mine workings. Not all caves have the necessary prerequisites for a winter hibernaculum. Cadomin Cave, a known hibernaculum, offers the bats a fairly constant temperature of 10°C. This is very important. A cave that is too warm prevents the bats from entering a deep hibernation and to hibernate in colder temperatures is to risk freezing to death. Cadomin Cave also has a humidity of at least 78 per cent, an equally critical factor for the sleeping bats. High humidity helps prevent dehydration during hibernation.

Each year in late August the bats return, some arriving from as far away as 300 km. They swarm in the vicinity of the cave, possibly as a means of advertising the site to inexperienced juveniles. It is at this time that the Little Brown Bats mate, the females retaining live sperm in their reproductive tracts until spring when ovulation and fertilization occur. With the onset of colder temperatures and a decrease in their food supply (insects), the bats enter the cave not to reappear for six to eight months. By hooking the claws of their hind feet onto the cave roof or walls the bats hang upside down and go into a deep sleep. All bodily functions slow down and their body temperature drops, thus allowing the bats to expend very little energy. Every several weeks or so, the bats wake to drink from the moisture on the cave walls only to return to a deep sleep. It is crucial that the bats remain unmolested during their hibernation as frequent disturbances cause energy to be consumed, thereby depleting their bodies of stored fat. Too many arousals can result in the bats starving to death, especially the juveniles that enter hibernation weighing less than their adult counterparts. In spring, the pregnant females leave the hibernaculum to return to summer roosting sites where they establish maternity colonies of 300 to 600 bats; the males establish small separate colonies. The females give birth to one offspring in June or July. Three weeks later the young can fly. Bats are most active two hours after sunset and two hours before sunrise when they forage for their favourite foods—moths, beetles, mosquitoes and flies—by utilizing their sonar. They consume about half their weight in insects every night.

If picked up, bats will defend themselves by biting, not only an unpleasant experience but a potentially dangerous one as bats are suspected of carrying rabies. In the 1950s a massive outbreak of rabies in the province spread among wildlife such as red fox, coyotes, wolves, bears, weasel, mice and beaver to domestic animals, dogs, horses, sheep and cows. Literally thousands of animals had to be destroyed.

WHITEHORSE CREEK RECREATION AREA

Poised at the edge of the spectacular Front Ranges, Whitehorse Creek Recreation Area is very popular with hikers, rock scramblers, cyclists, fishermen and equestrians. At the east end of the recreation area there are six walk-in tent sites and 20 trailer sites. So popular is this area with equestrians that Alberta Environment has set aside the west end of the recreation area for horses and horse trailers. The village of Cadomin to the north is a convenient supply centre.

Whitehorse Creek Recreation Area is an excellent base from which you can explore the mountain valleys to the west and to the south. For those wishing for a day's outing to the west there are good trails into the new Whitehorse Wildland Provincial Park where you can access Farmer Valley, Drummond Creek, Harlequin Creek and the upper Whitehorse Creek falls, as well as some shorter trails closer to the campground. Overnight trips can be taken to Miette Hot Springs in Jasper National Park. Fourteen kilometres south of the recreation area are the abandoned townsite and cemetery of Mountain Park and the Cardinal Divide, both fascinating sites to visit for either the day or to use as a trailhead for longer excursions.

Location 6 km south of Cadomin on the Cardinal River Road
Facilities 26 unserviced campsites, 10 horse corrals, pit toilets, water pump, firewood
Note no OHVs allowed

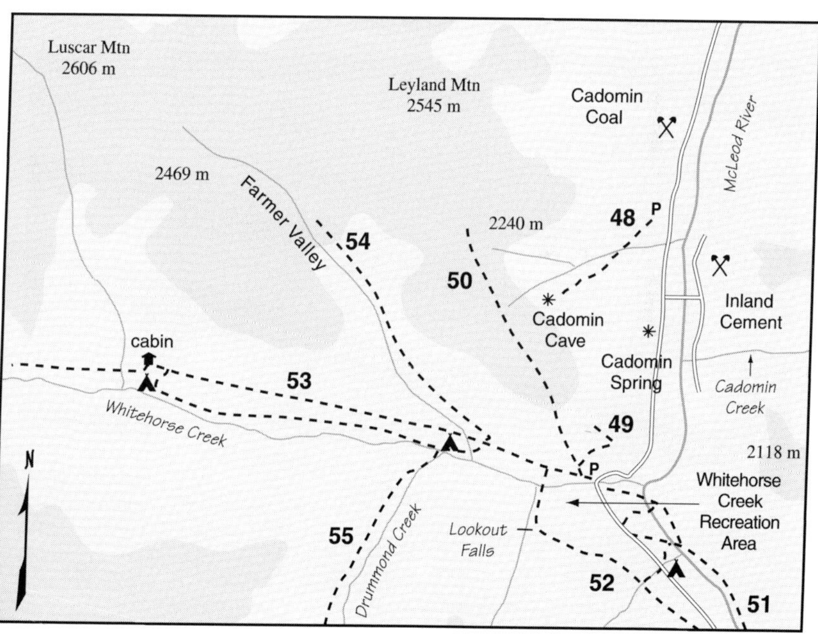

Whitehorse Wildland Park

Whitehorse Creek Recreation Area is one of the major accesses into Whitehorse Wildland Park. Formed in 1998 as a result of mounting public pressure, the 174 sq. km L-shaped park stretches from Jasper National Park to the east end of the Cardinal Divide. Its significant features include 277 plant species of which about 100 are either rare or disjunct. All 14 species of saxifrage found in Alberta north of Waterton Park are found here as is the provincially rare wooly lousewort. Disjunct species include skunkweed and silver rock cress. A nationally rare moss species, *Mielichhoferia macrocarpa,* is found in the park.

The park is prime habitat for grizzly bears and about 300 bighorn sheep. The Whitehorse Creek valley is breeding territory for about 50 nesting pairs of harlequin ducks while Cadomin Cave is one of only four known bat hibernacula in Alberta. Upper Prospect Creek is home to several rare butterfly species including the Dingy Arctic Fritillary. This species only flies on even numbered years. Since eggs are not laid every year, the population is sensitive to any disturbance, especially to its larval food plant, Arctic willow. Special geological features include rock glaciers, patterned ground caused by frost action and a karst system on Leyland Mountain.

Recreational uses include hiking, random camping, horseback riding, fishing, hunting and mountain bike riding. Portions of the park have been disturbed owing to past logging, mining and unrestricted OHV use. OHVs are now only allowed in restricted areas along Prospect Creek and to the top of Drummond Ridge. Continued OHV activity along Drummond Ridge, on Prospect Mountain and along the Cardinal Divide threatens the park's integrity.

Fiddle Pass is the significant wildlife corridor between Jasper and Whitehorse parks. Wildlife, including grizzly bears, also move between the park and Jasper by way of Cardinal Pass and the upper Cardinal River valley. For this reason, exclusion of these two areas from the Whitehorse Park remains a matter of some controversy.

Whitehorse Creek Recreation Area serves as an equestrian staging area as well as a trailhead for hikers and cyclists in Whitehorse Wildland Park.

49 WHITEHORSE CREEK CAMPGROUND TRAIL MAP PAGE 249

This easy walk from the Whitehorse Creek Recreation Area takes less than 30 minutes to ascend a low shoulder of Leyland Mountain where you gain a view up the McLeod River valley.

Just to the left of the campsite sign there is a shale pathway leading lazily up past the east end of the campground. At the top of a low terrace the path forks. Bear to the right; a left turn takes you to campsite #3. The shale path quickly gives way to a rough, rocky trail. Look to the right. You can see up the McLeod River valley toward Mountain Park. The rail line that hugs the east bank of the river once serviced the mining town of Mountain Park; now it services the new Cheviot mine project.

Where the path flattens it becomes an easy, needle-strewn pathway that winds its way through a small copse of pine trees. Then, the trail breaks out onto the open slope and switches up the hill. It's a steep little climb to the end of the trail, a flattened area overlooking the confluence of the Whitehorse Creek with the McLeod River. To your left is Cadomin Mountain, which is slowly being chewed away by Inland Cement.

Return the way you came.

Day hiking

Rating one half hour

Distance 1.2 km

Level of Difficulty steep ascent along abandoned cut

Maximum Elevation 1650 m

Elevation Gain 60 m

Map 83 C/14 Mountain Park

Access

Park your vehicle at the Whitehorse Creek Recreation Area 5.6 km south of Cadomin along the Cardinal River Road. The trailhead is at the recreation area campground sign-map.

0.0 km	trailhead
0.1 km	intersection
0.4 km	switch
0.6 km	viewpoint
1.2 km	trailhead

The short but fairly steep climb to the viewpoint is an excellent way to stretch your muscles first thing in the morning.

Mount Leyland Collieries Ltd.

In 1961, a newly incorporated company, Mount Leyland Collieries Ltd., proposed to start a mine near Leyland. Its president, "Count" van Oudenal, told shareholders that the company had a letter of intent from a "Japanese steel firm" to take over 250,000 tonnes of coal per year if a bulk test to be conducted by that firm confirmed the company's own test results.

This was good news to the Coal Branch, since for the past 10 years the area had seen one coal mine after another close down. This was also news to the provincial mines department and the Coal Operators' Association of Western Canada, who until the announcement had been unaware of any development work at Leyland or that there were any economical coal deposits underlying the leases in question.

Mount Leyland's coal lease was reported to contain over 90 million tonnes of coking coal in a 7 m-thick seam. According to the company's promotional documents, over $60,000 had already been spent by way of lease rentals, prospecting, development work, drilling tests, field charts, engineers' reports, etc., "...all of which may be seen upon request."

The Coal Operators' Association investigated Mount Leyland's claims but found no record of any drilling tests and no one who had seen an engineer's report. It contacted van Oudenal and asked for further information. Van Oudenal's reply was blunt and to the point,"It is not our policy to furnish information to organizations or interests with whom we have no direct dealings." Engineers' reports, he said, are confidential, "We do not share this information—we pay for it without contributions from others, and the temerity of your enquiry surprises me."

There would never be any development work and Mount Leyland Collieries mined no coal. The coal leases? Well, they were not as wonderful as initially advertised. As for that letter of intent from a "Japanese steel firm" brandished before so many potential investors, it contained a variety of escape clauses making it a meaningless document.

The Tackle Box

Whitehorse Creek
Fish Management Area: #4

A fast, clear mountain stream, Whitehorse Creek stretches more than 13 km from its headwaters adjacent to Jasper National Park to its confluence with the McLeod River. Its rocky bottom and deep rock pools make this creek a fine trout stream. Two small waterfalls located just above and below the recreation area present a barrier to only the smallest fish. A 10 m-high waterfall 10 km upstream from its mouth restricts migration farther upstream.

Species whitefish, rainbow trout, bull trout

Restrictions All bull trout (Dolly Varden) must be released. Use of bait fish and the collection of bait fish are prohibited. All rainbow trout shorter than 17.5 cm must be released.

Season 16 June to 31 August

50 LEYLAND MOUNTAIN

MAP PAGE 249

A steep climb up the mountainside carries you firstly to one rock cairn and then, as you walk along the ridge with its 360° vista, to three more cairns before ending above Farmer Valley.

Day hiking
Rating full day
Distance 6.0 km
Level of Difficulty steep ascent; fissures; easy ridge walk
Maximum Elevation 2240 m
Elevation Gain 650 m
Map 83 C/14 Mountain Park; 83 F/3 Cadomin

Access

Park your vehicle at the Whitehorse Creek Recreation Area 5.6 km south of Cadomin along the Cardinal River Road. Trailhead is the horse camp at the west end of the recreation area.

0.0 km	trailhead
1.8 km	1st cairn
2.1 km	2nd cairn
2.6 km	3rd cairn
3.0 km	4th cairn
6.0 km	trailhead

You begin this climb immediately behind sites #19 and #20 at the Whitehorse Creek Recreation Area. There is a path that leads you to the base of the hill where you will find a very steep path leading up through the gravel. Make no mistake; this is a steep climb and the pitch you see in front of you continues all the way to the top. At the top of the first 40 m pitch swing a little to the left staying above a ravine and continue climbing. A faint trail behind a large boulder continues to lead up through the pines and up another steep open slope. There is no trail, per se, but you can find game trails that help your climb. Frequent rests along the way give you the opportunity to enjoy the unfolding vista behind you of the McLeod River and Whitehorse Creek valleys.

Finally, you break out of the pines and onto an open slope of kinnikinnick, potentilla, gentian and white camas. But the pitch does not relent and it

dramatic scene as you draw near the first cairn.

Deep fissures crisscross the lower end of Leyland Mountain.

continues to be a steep climb. At a gully keep to the right. This will bring you under a small cliff. As you approach the top, deep fissures appear in the limestone. Pick your way around and through them. At a point above one such fissure there is the first of the rock cairns. From here you can see—and hear—the trucks and drilling at Inland Cement. If you wish, you can stop here, in the fissure and out of the wind, to enjoy a well-deserved rest. However, there are other cairns farther along the ridge to the west. It's an easy 1.2 km walk along the spine of the ridge to the highest point and the last of the four cairns on The Sleeping Lady. The true 2545 m-high summit to your north–west is over 2 km away. To the west and far below is the silver ribbon of Whitehorse Creek. Following the creek with your eyes you can see the "Gap" and the head of the valley. Below, you can see an old quarry site tucked near the head of Farmer Valley.

You can return the way you came, or you can begin your descent from the last cairn. If you do so, remember to swing constantly to the left as you drop down the mountainside. Once you reach treeline it will be a bushwhack all the way down to the Whitehorse Creek trail.

Leyland Station/Flats/Mountain/Creek

Previous names: The Sleeping Lady/Beauty, Cadomin Mountain, Greasebone Flats/ Creek, Mile 21

Leyland Mountain and surrounding features take their name from the Leyland railway station that in turn is named after Christopher John Leyland (1849-1926), who spearheaded the development of the Mountain Park coal mine. Leyland was his British titled name. His family name was Naylor.

In 1910 Leyland sent N. M. Thornton to investigate the John Gregg and R. W. Jones coal claims in the area. Thornton's assessment was positive and, with an associate, Leyland bought the leases and formed the Mountain Park Coal Company Ltd. Leyland visited Mountain Park in 1913 bringing with him Lieutenant-Colonel Alexander Mitchell who had invested in the venture. Leyland's presidency of Mountain Park was a difficult one. The company did not achieve its initial expectations and he lost an estimated $250,000 as a result of its restructuring. Leyland resigned from the board in 1922 owing to ill health.

The original Leyland Mountain is today's Cadomin Mountain. Locals applied the name Cadomin to today's Leyland Mountain, though a more popular name was The Sleeping Lady or Beauty. This is descriptive of the mountain's north-south profile. The word "leyland" comes from the Old English *læge land* meaning "estate with untilled ground." This is an appropriate description of the station's location on the Leyland Flats that into the 1920s was called the Greasebone Flats. Greasebone is the original name for Luscar Creek and was first recorded in 1912. Alberta Forestry's ranger cabin on the flats was named Greasebone Cabin and as the name Luscar Creek entered popular use, a tiny tributary running past the cabin became known as Greasebone Creek. This tributary is now called Leyland Creek.

Mile 21 is the distance count to the station along the West Coal Branch railway from Coalspur.

The Sleeping Lady from the Cadomin Terrace.

51 MCLEOD RIVER CANYON

MAP PAGE 249

What a perfect short hike for those staying at the Whitehorse Creek Recreation Area! Foaming waterfalls, an historic rail line complete with trestles and a dramatic gorge are the highlights of this trail.

Day hiking
Rating half day
Distance 2.4 km
Level of Difficulty steep scrambles; cliff edges
Maximum Elevation 1640 m
Elevation Gain 50 m
Map 83 C/14 Mountain Park

Access

Park your vehicle at the Whitehorse Creek Recreation Area 5.6 km south of Cadomin along the Cardinal River Road. The trailhead is the road entry into the recreation area.

0.0 km	trailhead
0.1 km	Whitehorse Creek bridge
0.1 km	intersection and informal campsite
0.2 km	intersection
0.3 km	T-junction

From the Whitehorse Creek campground, turn right and walk south along the Cardinal River Road to cross the bridge over the McLeod River. Immediately to your left is a rough road leading to an informal campsite area. Follow the road down and as far as the McLeod River. Once at the river, find a footpath that leads to the right.

Your path now climbs the riverbank. Within 100 m you come to a T-junction. Turn left and follow the path as it winds its way through willow bushes. The path climbs steeply, but once on top you can hear the roar of the waterfall. Your path now snakes its way along the top of what is the McLeod River canyon. Be careful to stay on the path and not to tempt fate by leaning over the edge in an effort to get a look at the falls. Soon enough you reach a viewpoint overlooking the lower waterfall. No one can resist a close-up view of a waterfall. Twenty

This punchbowl waterfall is just upstream of your ford across the river.

0.5 km	first falls
0.5 km	intersection to top of first falls
0.6 km	viewpoint second falls
0.6 km	intersection into canyon
0.7 km	viewpoint in canyon
0.8 km	intersection
0.9 km	Cardinal River Road
1.0 km	intersection
1.3 km	intersection
1.4 km	railway right-of-way
1.4 km	trestle
1.8 km	trestle
1.8 km	intersection; begin braid
1.9 km	end braid
2.1 km	McLeod River
2.1 km	intersection
2.4 km	trailhead

Prospect Creek Option

1.4 km	railway right-of-way
2.0 km	trestle
2.2 km	begin braid
2.3 km	end braid
2.5 km	trestle
2.8 km	Prospect Creek

Looking upstream to one of the waterfalls on the McLeod River.

metres past the viewpoint, where the trail forks, take the left-hand fork to the top of the falls. Then return to the junction. Turn left and continue along the path as it climbs up the canyon. Along the way there are several viewpoints of the canyon with its sculpted walls.

A second waterfall soon comes into view. Above the falls on the other side of the McLeod River you can see the Mountain Park railway line and straight ahead is the flat ridge of the Cardinal Divide. Once again the trail forks. To access a great view of the canyon, take the left-hand fork and climb down the embankment to a rocky ledge along the river's edge. Then return to the fork. Turn left and climb steeply to the Cardinal River Road. Once at the road turn left and walk up the road for approximately 100 m. Watch for a horse trail leading into the lodgepole pine on the left side of the road. Follow the horse trail to a junction with another horse trail. Take the left-hand fork that drops you sharply down the embankment to the old Mountain Park railway line.

Here you have a choice. To loop back to the Whitehorse Creek Recreation Area along the canyon turn left along the rail line. Shortly, you must cross a long, curved trestle perched high above the McLeod River. Even though the trestle is still sturdy, showing few signs of decay, be careful, and do not try to

Many of the trestles over the McLeod River are still in good condition despite their age.

peer over the edge. Across the trestle with the river now on your left continue along the trail. At a major rock cut, you can hear the McLeod River roaring through a deep canyon on your left. For a look at the upper waterfall, cross another short trestle and watch for faded orange tape in a poplar tree to your right. This marks an intersection with a horse trail that you can find left of the railway right-of-way. A short distance down along the horse trail you come to a promontory overlooking the narrowest part of the canyon. It is also here that there are two white crosses, one on either side of the canyon. On August 13, 1996, Thomas Kratchmer and Liam Patrick Shea died when their car left the Cardinal River Road and crashed down the hillside into the canyon. Bushwhack down the hillside bearing to the right so you can pick up the horse trail. Follow it to the top of the lower waterfall where you have another good view of the gorge. From here, a rough hiking trail drops you to the river's edge. Deep pools have formed at the base of the lower waterfall but you can ford the river if you keep upstream of a line of rocks across the river. Once across pick up the horse trail as it climbs steeply and then drops to an intersection. Turn right and follow the trail back to a rough gravel road that leads up to the Cardinal River Road and the bridge of Whitehorse Creek. The recreation area is just on the other side of the bridge.

Prospect Creek Option

At the junction of the horse trail and the railway right-of-way turn right along the track. A short trot along the horse trail that follows the old rail line brings you to a spot above cascades in the river where you must leave the railway line. A mud slide has swept the line down the hillside leaving the rails and ties lying precariously downslope. It's easy enough, though, to swing a little to the right and bushwhack through the shrubbery to circumvent the slide. Within 400 m you come to a short trestle that is still solid despite its age and lack of maintenance over the years. Cross over and, almost immediately, you come to another trestle that is now washed out. Your horse trail continues along the edge of the river's embankment until it rejoins the railway line at the far end of the old trestle. You have been climbing out of the McLeod River canyon and by the time you cross your third trestle you are among willows and alders that cover the valley floor. A short distance later you arrive at Prospect Creek. Retrace your steps down the rail line to the junction of the horse trail leading up the embankment to the Cardinal River Road. You have a choice: you can climb the embankment, gain the Cardinal River Road, turning right to go downhill to Whitehorse Creek Recreation Area, or you can ignore the intersection with the horse trail and continue along the railbed. If you choose the latter route, follow the directions above to return to the recreation area.

The Mountain Park Branch

The 50 km-long Mountain Park branch of the Coal Branch railway was originally a colliery railway built by the Mountain Park Coal Company Ltd., owners and developers of the mine and town at Mountain Park. Construction began in January, 1912, and finished in July, 1913, at a total cost of $1,185,000. Unfortunately for Mountain Park, the railway line soon proved to be a burden it could barely afford with the result that maintenance costs were kept at a bare minimum.

The problem was initially caused by an engineering mistake. The original line in 1912 was routed too close to the McLeod River. Flash flooding that year took out some of the finished grade and that portion of the line had to be rebuilt by the contractors, Phelan and Shirley. Such washouts would be repeated each year as the line continued to be rebuilt as cheaply as possible with track being laid on the river flats in many places. The 1915 washout was particularly severe forcing Mountain Park to close its mine for two months while about $90,000 was spent repairing the track.

Alberta Trade Commissioner Howard Stutchbury was especially unimpressed when he travelled up this branch in 1921: "Ties are rotting under the track, and I found it possible in places to pull out spikes by hand. I am informed that wrecks are the order and not the exception, and one railway official advised me that the cost of the wrecks to the CNR totalled upward of $10,000 per month."

Stutchbury stated it would be futile for the Mines Branch to begin promoting the higher grade West Branch coals in the Pacific market until the track was first put into better shape. The situation was further worsened by the shipping of heavy steel gondola cars over track laid with light sixty pound steel and the increased traffic volume brought on by the opening of the Cadomin mine. Cadomin, incidentally, was neither obliged to nor did it contribute directly to any of the maintenance costs for the railway line, though Mountain Park's budget was partly based upon revenue collected from every ton of coal shipped on its line by Cadomin. This, apparently, was not enough to cover the branch's true maintenance costs if it were brought up to standard, so despite complaints from Cadomin and hand wringing from the Mines Branch, track conditions remained dismal.

It would not be until 1927 that Mountain Park freed itself from its by now totally unwanted obligations. The Canadian National Railway (CNR) agreed to lease the line for $15,000 per year and assume all taxes and maintenance costs. It would later buy the line for $500,000. The CNR would improve track conditions and the aggravations of travel along the Mountain Park branch line quickly became history.

52 LOOKOUT FALLS

MAP PAGE 249

Many trips out of the Whitehorse Creek Recreation Area are lengthy. In contrast, everyone can enjoy this short trip along a well-used horse trail to a pretty waterfall.

Day hiking, horseback riding
Rating half day
Distance 3.7 km
Level of Difficulty easy walk; Whitehorse Creek crossing
Maximum Elevation 1730 m
Elevation Gain 140 m
Map 83 C/14 Mountain Park

Access

Park your vehicle at the Whitehorse Creek Recreation Area 5.6 km south of Cadomin along the Cardinal River Road. The trailhead is the road entry into the recreation area.

0.0 km	trailhead
0.1 km	Whitehorse Creek bridge
1.0 km	random campsite; intersection
1.2 km	intersection
1.3 km	stream crossing
1.4 km	stream crossing

Turn right onto the Cardinal River Road, walk across the bridge over the Whitehorse Creek and hike up the road. Although a bit of a trudge, you will leave the hard-packed road a kilometre later for the softness of the forest floor opposite a random campsite that you can see on your left. The horse trail winds up through willows and dwarf birch and twice crosses a tiny rivulet. At an intersection with another trail, keeping to the right will bring you out onto a wide meadow. Tantalizing peeks of the mountains in the far distance urge you along as your trail skirts the meadow on the left. The horse trail then swings to the right and into the open forest where it climbs slowly past a marsh, crests and then begins its slow descent down the backside of the hill. Good views of the outliers of the Front Ranges open up where the trail re-enters willow slopes. A quick braid in the trail and the trail swings into the lodgepole pine. From here you can

An easy horse trail carries you through a wide subalpine valley.

1.4 km	intersection
2.3 km	pond
2.4 km	braid
2.6 km	intersection; viewpoint Lookout Falls
2.8 km	braid; viewpoint Lookout Falls
3.0 km	intersection
3.3 km	Whitehorse Creek
3.7 km	Whitehorse Creek Recreation Area

Lookout Falls.

detect the roar of the waterfall. A short, pleasant walk through the woods brings you suddenly to a promontory overlooking a lovely waterfall, its 15 m drop plunging over moss-lined rocks. From this vantage point, you can see the Whitehorse Creek valley with the trail leading to Farmer Valley and the main trail heading westward to the Gap. To have a look at the falls from the other side of the small creek, find the horse trails that lead down and across the creek. Once across you climb the embankment where there is an intersection of horse trails. Bear to the right. It's only a few metres to the edge of the cliff overlooking the falls.

Backtrack to the promontory and pick up the horse trail as it leads away from the waterfall to climb a hillside. It then drops quickly to a fork. A better view of the waterfall and the cascades below it can be had by taking the left-hand fork. After returning to the main trail, turn left to continue your descent. At the bottom of the pitch there is another intersection with a horse trail. Continue straight ahead. The trail now enters the willow flats as it leads to a ford across Whitehorse Creek. Once across the creek you will want to turn right to return to the recreation area.

Grizzly Bear

Scientific name ~ *Ursus arctos*

The much respected king of the mountains, the grizzly bear, is alive and well in Whitehorse Wildland Park and, indeed, throughout the foothills and Front Ranges adjacent to Jasper National Park.

The grizzly has long been recognized as an umbrella species, a bellwether on the status of the environment and its ability to sustain healthy populations of wildlife. Scientists have known that grizzlies generally prefer large, undisturbed areas away from the presence of humans. They also knew that grizzlies are vulnerable to stress and changes in the habitat of their home ranges. It was suspected that these criteria combined with the grizzly's low reproductive rate were adversely affected by increasing human industrial activity such as oil and gas exploration, forestry and coal mining—all major players in the Coal Branch. What was unknown were the details: how many grizzlies are there in the area east of Jasper National Park? How large are their ranges? What types of habitat are included in their ranges? To what extent do their ranges overlap with current or planned industrial activity? And lastly, but most importantly, to what degree do the cumulative effects of our invasion into their habitat—roads, clearcuts, mines—affect the behaviour of the grizzly?

These questions may well have remained unanswered if it had not been for the controversy that arose over the proposed Cheviot mine project. The mine site is located close to Cardinal, Fiddle and Ruby passes, known corridors for wildlife moving in and out of Jasper National Park. It also borders important alpine regions of the Coal Branch such as the Cardinal River Divide and the headwaters of the Cardinal River and Prospect and Whitehorse creeks. To answer some questions and to make recommendations on how best to manage land use so that a healthy grizzly bear population is maintained, a five-year study, the Foothills Model Forest Grizzly Bear Research Program, was launched in April 1999. Supported by more than 40 partners including Weldwood of Canada, Parks Canada, Alberta Environment and the Canadian Forest Service, the study encompasses the Alberta Yellowhead ecosystem, a large area including Jasper National Park, Willmore Wilderness Park and the foothill regions east to the Brazeau and Pembina rivers and northward to Fox Creek and Whitecourt. A Regional Carnivore Management Group (RCMG) was established not only to assess current grizzly populations and habitat conditions but to identify opportunities for habitat maintenance and improvement, to establish goals for parameters on development and to recommend a monitoring programme and criteria for measuring progress.

Within the group is a research forum that is taxed with the responsibility to provide scientific advice and to design and deliver research to support that advice. Led by biologist Gord Stenhouse, the team began by radio collaring 19 grizzlies in the area immediately adjacent to Jasper National Park. Through satellite tracking, they have been able to plot the movement of the bears, thereby establishing their ranges, den sites, habitat use and the bears' response to humans and other bears. While they are attaching the collars to the bears, the team takes blood, tooth and hair samples. Hair samples are also gathered from bears not radio collared by snagging samples from barbed wire surrounding a bait site. The samples are then sent to DNA labs where the animal's genetic fingerprint can be determined; this will help establish population trends.

The RCMG refers to each bear's range as a Bear Management Unit (BMU). Fifteen have been plotted on a map. What is interesting—and most important to visitors in the West Branch—is that six of these BMUs overlap in the Whitehorse and Prospect Creek valleys. Beware! These valleys are prime grizzly habitat! Exercise caution. You are in bear country.

53 WHITEHORSE CREEK GORGE

MAP PAGE 249

Waterfalls, gorges and a trapper's cabin are only some of the points of interest along this easy, delightful trip perfectly suited for the whole family.

From the west end of the campground and horse corrals walk up the old roadway. Whitehorse Creek is on your left. Within a short distance, a made-to-order photo opportunity presents itself as the Whitehorse foams over rock ledges, forming cataracts. People are always attracted to waterfalls and this is a popular spot for strollers from the campground. Within one half kilometre you will come to a quick series of forks in the road. Bear left at the first fork; if you go to the right you end up in Farmer Valley. A mere 50 m later there is yet

Day hiking, horseback riding, cycling

Rating half day

Distance 10.4 km

Level of Difficulty steady walk some steep pitches

Maximum Elevation 1710 m

Elevation Gain 120 m

Map 83 C/14 Mountain Park

Access

Park your vehicle at the Whitehorse Creek Recreation Area 5.6 km south of Cadomin along the Cardinal River Road. The trailhead is at the west end of the recreation area.

0.0 km	trailhead
0.3 km	waterfall
0.8 km	quadruple intersection
0.9 km	campsite
1.0 km	waterfall
1.5 km	intersection
1.6 km	beginning gorge
2.0 km	end gorge
2.8 km	begin braid
3.2 km	end braid
3.3 km	stream
4.1 km	beaver pond
5.1 km	campsite and intersection
5.2 km	intersection
5.5 km	cabin and T-junction
6.0 km	intersection
7.3 km	stream
8.8 km	begin braid
9.0 km	end braid
9.2 km	begin braid
9.5 km	stream
9.6 km	end braid; intersection
10.4 km	trailhead

In autumn the hillsides on the opposite side of Whitehorse Creek are very colourful.

Babala's cabin.

another fork. Take the horse trail that leads to the left and follow it past an old, now disused, horse camp. The trail bends to the right to follow Whitehorse Creek. Little cascades in the Whitehorse add interest to this pretty walk. The horse trail braids and it doesn't matter which one you take. Your trail climbs a little while you continue to hug the creek side.

As the trail climbs a slope it forks. Keep to the right; bearing left takes you across Whitehorse Creek to Drummond Creek. The trail climbs along the ridge to the beginning of a pretty gorge where the Whitehorse cuts through the shales and sandstones that comprise the ridge that you are on. For the next 500 m the trail follows the lip of the gorge overlooking Whitehorse Creek and the Drummond Creek valley. Ahead, you can see the dramatic silhouette of the Gap.

The gorge ends abruptly and from here the trail descends into willow flats. Keep right at a braid in the trail; going left leads into a swamp. Cross a sulphur spring and then a stream. Continuing along through dwarf birch, green aspen and willow bushes, the trail skirts a beaver dam and lodge close to Whitehorse Creek. The trail ends at a horse camp with logs and hitching posts that beg you to stop for a snack and a rest while enjoying an excellent view of the Gap.

The main Whitehorse Creek trail is adjacent to the horse camp. Turn left onto this wide trail and follow it for 100 m to an intersection with a much narrower horse trail that joins from the right. Turn onto the horse trail as it winds through the forest. Suddenly, a mere 100 m beyond the intersection, the forest falls away to reveal a log cabin in the middle of a small meadow. Quite distinctly on the door and the window are painted the numbers "1728." This number signifies the trap line registration number of the owner of the cabin. This cabin, then, is still in active use and is private property. By exploring around the site you can easily find the cellar of an older cabin just beyond the cabin currently in use.

Past the old cellar your trail ends at a T-junction. To loop back to the Whitehorse Creek Recreation Area campsite, turn right and climb along a wide track that then descends gently through open forest for 500 m where it joins the Whitehorse Creek trail. Turn left onto the trail. A wide slash tha offers tantalizing peeks at the mountains to your right, the Whitehorse Cree trail descends through pine forest. There are two braids en route to you trailhead. The left-hand forks are the main trail but are rougher underfoo than the right-hand braids that we recommend. The second braid ends jus above the Farmer Valley trail that joins on your left. Ignore this trail an continue along the main trail as it descends the Whitehorse for another 80 m to your trailhead.

Whitehorse Creek

Previous name: West Branch McLeod River

"Whitehorse" originates as the Whitehorse Canyon on the McLeod River immediately south of its confluence with Whitehorse Creek. This canyon name appears on a 1912 blueprint showing the proposed route of the railway to Mountain Park and probably refers to the lower waterfall in the canyon that came to be called the Whitehorse Falls.

Up to the 1930s, the stretch of the McLeod was called by local residents Whitehorse Creek. Since the Geographic Board of Canada chose to call this the McLeod, the name Whitehorse was transferred to its present location. Seventy years later there is still some confusion caused by this transfer as both the canyon and falls along the McLeod as well as the chutes along Whitehorse Creek are called "Whitehorse" by various local residents.

In 1911 Dominion Land Surveyor John Francis named the Whitehorse (the present stream) the West Branch of the McLeod River. This was confusing because prior to his entry, the phrase West Branch McLeod River referred to what is today called the Gregg River. To clarify matters, Francis called the West Branch McLeod River (the Gregg River) the West Fork McLeod River and as a final inspired entry named another stream the West Branch of the West Fork McLeod River. Today we call it Drinnan Creek.

Be this as it may, Francis knew where he was going.

The original Whitehorse Canyon on the McLeod River.

54 FARMER VALLEY

MAP PAGE 249

This trip is certain to be popular with those staying at the Whitehorse Creek Recreation Area campground. While the distance to the head of the valley is only a few kilometres, the beauty of the valley and the elevation gain beg for you to linger, making this a full day tour.

Access into Farmer Valley is either by foot, mountain bike or horseback. Adjacent to the horse corrals located at the west end of the campground is a sign announcing that no motorized vehicles are allowed beyond this point. There is no water along the trail so be sure to fill your water bottle before leaving the campground.

Day hiking, horseback riding, cycling

Rating full day

Distance 8.4 km

Level of Difficulty steep ascent along abandoned road

Maximum Elevation 2055 m

Elevation Gain 465 m

Map 83 C/14 Mountain Park; 83 F/3 Cadomin

Access

Park your vehicle at the Whitehorse Creek Recreation Area 5.6 km south of Cadomin along the Cardinal River Road. The trailhead is at the west end of the recreation area.

0.0 km	trailhead
0.3 km	waterfall
0.8 km	intersection
0.8 km	begin braid
1.8 km	end braid
2.0 km	gate
2.3 km	begin gravel wash
2.7 km	end gravel wash
2.8 km	gravel wash
3.0 km	begin braid
3.2 km	gravel pit
3.2 km	intersection
3.3 km	end braid
3.4 km	gravel wash
3.5 km	end road; campsite; abandoned cabin
4.0 km	bottom of pitch
4.2 km	top of pitch
8.4 km	trailhead

Wildlife making a home in the abandoned rock crusher.

Looking toward Farmer Valley.

From the west end of the campground and horse corrals walk up the old roadway. Whitehorse Creek is on your left. Within a short distance, a made-to-order photo opportunity presents itself as the Whitehorse foams over a couple of cataracts. People are always attracted to waterfalls and this is a popular spot for strollers from the campground. Soon you will come to a fork in the road. Bear to the right to go up the Farmer Valley; the left fork continues to Fiddle Pass and Miette Hot Springs. Fifty metres later at a bend in the old road there is an intersection with a bridle path on the right. Here you have a choice. You can remain on the road or take the horse trail; the horse trail rejoins the road a full kilometre later. Both lead sharply up the shoulder of the mountain. The road offers a more direct route but is rocky and offers little shade on a hot day while the horse trail wends its way up through cool lodgepole pine forest.

Shortly beyond where the bridle path rejoins the road, your trail levels out and vistas of the head of Farmer Valley come into view. Huge boulders the size of cars indicate that at some time in the remote past a portion of the mountain on your right sliced away sending rock and debris into this part of the valley. Adjacent to a big rock by the side of the trail is an old gate that at one time blocked passage to motorized vehicles going up the valley. Today, though, the rusted gate remains permanently open. Just beyond the gate you will notice on your left what appear to be three yellow posts. A closer examination reveals that these are supports for a canopied roof of a caterpillar that has been deliberately buried in the rubble of the dry streambed! It is through this dry streambed that your trail now meanders several times.

You now come to a braid in the roadway. Bearing to the right will soon bring you to an old quarry site. The first thing you notice as you round a corner in the road is a derelict dump truck that rises abruptly above you. Scattered about the site are a bright orange rock crusher and other debris. You can spend some time here poking among the rubble of this short-lived operation. Everything seems to have been simply abandoned to the elements by the operators of the quarry.

From the rock crusher follow the road as it swings to the left and down the hill. At the bottom of the hill there is an intersection with the top end of the braid. Turn right. At a gravel wash go straight ahead or to the right to remain on the trail. The road ends at the site of an old cabin, perhaps the living quarters for those working the quarry. The wind-flattened frame building lies just to the right of the road while an old stove that has been removed from the building has been relocated to flat ground just above. Someone has constructed two makeshift chairs out of lumber from the building and placed them close to the stove.

From here a horse trail swings sharply to the left and climbs briskly up toward the head of the valley. What a superb view! From a viewpoint at the top of the pitch you can look up into the cirque beneath Mount Leyland. A nameless but nonetheless interesting mountain with its alternating beds of hard limestone and dolomite and softer shales and sandstones is just to the left. Green meadows on the ridges to the left invite the intrepid hiker to explore.

Return the way you came.

Rockslides

As you walk up the trail into Farmer Valley you pass by a number of large boulders that look very like the ones at the Whitehorse Creek Recreation Area campsite. These boulders are the result of rockslides from the karst landscape that makes up Leyland Mountain.

A karst landscape forms when limestone is dissolved by water into sinkholes, caves and underground drainage. The west side of Leyland Mountain is tilted to an approximately 30° angle and is made up of several rock layers permeable to water. Water seeps in between the layers and in winter expands as it turns to ice therefore slowly prying the layers apart. In the spring meltwater acts as a lubricant to any rock masses that have become unstable during winter and gravity does the rest: rocks come tumbling down resulting in interesting scenery along the Farmer Valley trail and an ill-considered location for a campsite at Whitehorse Creek.

An old rockslide on the way up Farmer Valley.

55 DRUMMOND CREEK

MAP PAGE 270

In our opinion, the trip along a good horse trail up Drummond Creek is one of the prettiest that anyone could wish. But Drummond Creek offers much more than just its alpine beauty. Ancient fossils and rock glaciers make this a fascinating trek for everyone interested in the rocks beneath their feet.

Day hiking, horseback riding

Rating full day

Distance 18.2 km

Level of Difficulty three initial stream crossings; steady walk

Maximum Elevation 2040 m

Elevation Gain 450 m

Map 83 C/14 Mountain Park

Access

Park your vehicle at the Whitehorse Creek Recreation Area 5.6 km south of Cadomin along the Cardinal River Road. The trailhead is at the west end of the recreation area.

0.0 km	trailhead
0.8 km	quadruple intersection
0.9 km	campsite
1.5 km	intersection
1.6 km	campsite
1.7 km	Whitehorse Creek; intersection
1.9 km	Drummond Creek; intersection
2.1 km	intersection
2.2 km	intersection; Drummond Creek
2.3 km	braid
3.1 km	stream crossing
4.1 km	stream crossing
5.0 km	viewpoint waterfall
5.9 km	stream crossing
7.4 km	stream crossing
8.3 km	intersection
8.5 km	intersection; stream crossing
9.1 km	viewpoint rock glacier
18.2 km	trailhead

From the west end of the campground and horse corrals walk up the Whitehorse Creek trail. Within the first kilometre you come to a quick series of forks in the road. Bear left at the first fork; if you go to the right you end up in Farmer Valley. A mere 50 m later there is yet another fork. Bear left and follow the horse trail past an old, now disused, horse camp. The trail bends to the right to follow

The Drummond Creek valley.

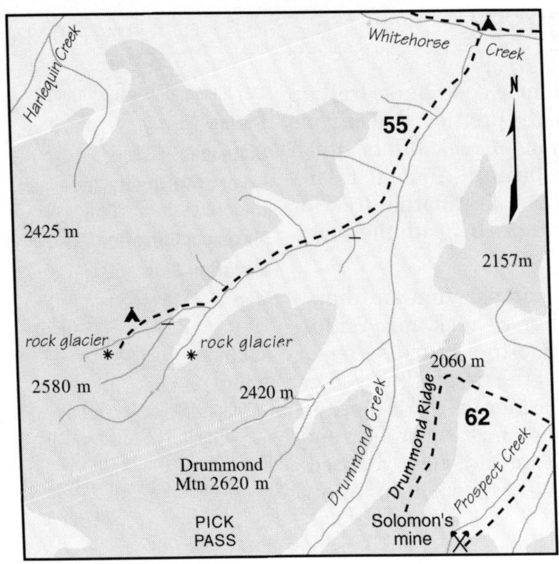

Whitehorse Creek with its cascades. Your trail climbs a little above Whitehorse Creek offering pleasant views up the valley. At a fork bear left and drop down toward another informal campsite. Continuing past the campsite brings you to a ford across Whitehorse Creek. Upon climbing out of the creekbed there is an intersection with faint tracks on your left and your right. Continue straight ahead and follow the horse trail down to Drummond Creek, which you now need to ford. After crossing the stream there is another intersection. Bear to the right. Your trail winds past a rock face where you may be able to detect the pungent odour of pack rats that inhabit the crevices at the base. Almost immediately there is an intersection. Keep to the right. In less than 100 m you come to another intersection with a trail on your left. Swing to the right to your second ford across Drummond Creek.

It's somewhat of a long climb up along the horse trail through the forest and then up a meadow before you arrive at a viewpoint overlooking the Drummond Creek valley. A short, steep descent is followed by an easier gradient as the trail drops to first one stream and then a second one. Once out of the creekbed, the horse trail hugs the hillside. It's a very open walk that offers plenty of views of the Drummond Creek valley. In autumn, the poplar trees across the valley create vivid splashes of gold against the hillside. Ahead, you can easily see the alpine meadows of upper Drummond Creek as well as Prospect Mountain, which rears its stately crown at the head of the valley. At one point you can hear the sound of water and if you look sharply across the valley you can see a small waterfall plunging into the creek below.

As you progress up the valley you leave the open forest and enter a meadow of willow and dwarf birch that stretches to the scree slopes ahead. Hop across a stream. A slow, steady uphill climb brings you to a viewpoint overlooking the junction of two branches of Drummond Creek. It's obvious that your horse trail will continue along the north branch, but look across the valley to just above where the two forks meet. A small rock glacier can be seen near the base of the mountainside. It's too far away to explore, so continue along the horse trail as it crosses a small rivulet. As you continue up the valley through a meadow of willows, krummholz spruce and huckleberries you are drawn forward by the sight of a large rock glacier tumbling from the base of the scree slope. Ignore an intersection with a trail on your right; it leads to an informal campsite most likely used by hunters in the autumn. Shortly beyond, your trail ends at a small stream where Arctic cotton grass grows in abundance. Skip across the stream swinging to the left to stay out of the willows. The footing is soft and spongy as you climb a prominent knob. On top you are presented with a magnificent view of a large rock glacier. Although now vegetated, its outlines are clearly defined so there is no mistaking this geological feature. If you wish, drop down to its toe and climb up onto this formation for a view down the valley before returning the way you came.

Rock Glaciers

The rock glacier at the head of Drummond Creek is a common geomorphological feature in the Canadian Rockies. Found at or above treeline at the base of cliffs, rock glaciers have been reported in mountainous regions around the world, from Antarctica to the Swiss Alps.

Rock glaciers are visually similar to ice glaciers, particularly their lobe-like or tongue-shaped mass; you can easily see the glacier-like shape of the Drummond Creek rock glacier. But, in fact, rock glaciers have little or no ice and are almost entirely composed of coarse rubble, silt and clay. Some are comparatively small but others have a width of more than 3 km and a height of 50 m. In looking over to the Drummond Creek rock glacier you can also see typical concentric lobes or wrinkles within its margins. These lobes imply that the rock glacier flowed slowly downslope.

Rock glaciers could originate in several different ways. Some began as ice-cored moraines; others are rockslides in which ice has cemented the talus with fine-grained silts and clays. The presence of ice is a probable indicator that a rock glacier is active; that is, it continues today to flow downslope. Scientists have identified a number of active rock glaciers in the southern part of Jasper National Park and throughout Banff National Park. By a variety of ways—measuring, examining a series of photographs taken over several decades and studying tree rings—they have found that some of our rock glaciers flow at a rate between 30 and 60 cm a year. Other rock glaciers are no longer creeping downslope. These are either inactive or fossil rock glaciers. Inactive rock glaciers are no longer moving although they still contain some ice. In fossil rock glaciers, their ice, necessary for flow, has melted with the result that they no longer are moving. Owing to the loss of ice, they are not as thick as active rock glaciers.

The Drummond Creek rock glacier is unusual in that it is well vegetated. Its boulders and talus, composed mostly of shale, has weathered to a fine soil that now supports an alpine flora. Its finely-textured soil and resultant vegetation would indicate that this is a fossil rock glacier.

The Drummond Creek rock glacier. Photo Alfred Falk.

56 HARLEQUIN CREEK

MAP PAGE 276

Named in 1922 for the harlequin duck that frequents this stream, Harlequin Creek is a long day trip from the Whitehorse Creek Recreation Area campground. Despite this and the roughness of the horse trail, the beauty of this wide alpine meadow at the creek's headwaters makes it all worthwhile.

From the west end of the campground walk up the wide horse trail as it skirts Whitehorse Creek on your left. Five hundred metres later you arrive at a quick series of forks in the trail. Bear left at the first fork. A mere 50 m later there is yet another fork. Go straight ahead. Your trail braids as it begins an easy but steady climb up through open pine forest along the Whitehorse Creek valley. Just beyond where the braid rejoins you find yourself at the bottom of a low pitch where your trail once again braids. Ignore an intersection with a trail on your right and continue along what is a pleasant trail through the forest to a clearing on your left where, before the creation of the Whitehorse Wildland Park, there

Backpacking, day hiking, horseback riding

Rating two days

Distance 26.2 km

Level of Difficulty rough horse trail

Maximum Elevation 2060 m

Elevation Gain 470 m

Map 83 C/14 Mountain Park; 83 C/13 Medicine Lake

Access

Park your vehicle at the Whitehorse Creek Recreation Area 5.6 km south of Cadomin along the Cardinal River Road. The trailhead is at the west end of the recreation area.

0.0 km	trailhead
0.8 km	triple intersection and braid
1.2 km	end braid
1.4 km	begin braid
1.6 km	end braid
4.4 km	intersection
4.7 km	campsite and intersection
4.8 km	intersection
4.9 km	gravel wash
5.0 km	begin braid
5.1 km	end braid
6.6 km	intersection
6.7 km	stream crossing; Craig's Camp

In the hollows near the waterfall, purple asters spread like a carpet; in other protected sites, purple monkshood made a striking contrast to the dwarf willows.

Harlequin Creek above the waterfall at the head of the valley.

was an informal campsite. An intersection with a trail on your right marks the place where your trail leaves the forest for the open vistas offered along the creek. Just beyond here your trail crosses a gravel wash, braiding as it climbs out of the gravel wash. At the top of the creek terrace, the horse trail crosses an open meadow dotted with willows, pines and dwarf birch. One kilometre later there is a Y in the trail. The somewhat narrower path on the left, a horse trail, leads to Harlequin Creek.

The horse trail leads down through willows, crosses a small stream and opens onto a grassy meadow that was Craig's lumber camp. Today this is a favourite camping site for hikers and, in the autumn, for hunters. Someone has even built a picnic table and constructed hitching posts so, if no one has camped here, this might be a good spot to rest before continuing to Harlequin Creek. Locating the continuation of the trail must have confused someone for just beyond the campsite the trail has been marked with blue tape. The trail crosses a gravelly stream imaginatively named Sawmill Creek and arrives at a fork. Turn left and continue to a T-junction where once again you want to go left. At yet a third fork bear left again to go down into a willow meadow. You can easily

6.7 km	intersection
6.8 km	stream crossing; intersection
6.9 km	intersection
7.0 km	begin braid
7.1 km	end braid
7.2 km	begin braid
7.3 km	end braid; Whitehorse Creek
8.4 km	random campsite
9.2 km	"Pinky died trying"
9.4 km	Harlequin Creek crossings
10.6 km	gravel wash
11.8 km	stream crossing
12.2 km	random campsite
12.3 km	enter subalpine meadow
12.6 km	Harlequin Creek
13.0 km	tarn
13.6 km	horse trail
13.7 km	falls viewpoint
13.8 km	random campsite
26.2 km	trailhead

Approaching Harlequin Mountain.

hear the pleasant sound of a small cataract on Sawmill Creek on your left. Just past a small rivulet there is another fork. Once again keep to the left. You will quickly come to a gravel wash. Walk up the wash as far as the confluence of Whitehorse and Harlequin creeks. Continue to a ford just above the confluence and cross Whitehorse Creek.

Once across the Whitehorse, the horse trail becomes much rougher as it follows Harlequin Creek on your left. Keep a sharp lookout for the shy and reclusive harlequin duck; the creek's numerous cataracts and chutes make it a favourite breeding ground for this diving duck. We were fortunate to see several in the tumbling waters of Harlequin Creek close to the confluence with Whitehorse Creek. As you wind through the forested banks of the creek you pass a small random campsite on your right. A short but steep pitch followed by a quick walk brings you alongside the creek for a short distance only to swing away for a second short pitch. Part way up this pitch look for a sign nailed to a tree on your right that reads "Pinky died trying." Pinky apparently was a pack horse that suffered a fatal heart attack while trying to climb this rough slope. Now you come to several quick crossings of Harlequin Creek until, once again, the stream is on your left. Trail conditions remain rough as you face a steady climb. At a fork, keep to the right. Cross a gravel wash. At the top end of a braid you begin a longer pitch until finally, where you catch your first views of the head of the valley, the trail flattens and improves. Pass a random campsite on your left that, in high summer, sits in a field of purple asters. Shortly afterward the trail breaks out of the trees entirely and you find yourself looking over a beautiful alpine valley with the headwaters of Harlequin Creek tumbling down from a tarn.

You could easily spend a full day exploring this meadow and enjoying the alpine flowers that include forget-me-nots, avens, gentians, alpine harebells and heather. En route to the tarn at the base of the rocky slope you may find yourself being watched by curious marmots; they show little fear of humans. After exploring the edges of the tarn we turned around and walked down the meadow following the creek to where it drops a surprising 10 m over a rocky ledge. Looking up to the ridge we spied four elk browsing on the hillside.

To return to Whitehorse Creek Recreation Area, move upstream swinging a little to the right until you find the horse trail that brought you to this beautiful valley.

Harlequin Duck

Scientific name: *Histrionicus histrionicus*
Status: not at risk (Pacific population)

There are two harlequin duck populations in Canada, one on the Pacific coast and one on the Atlantic coast. The status of the Atlantic coast population is listed as endangered with only about 1500 individuals remaining. The Pacific population, with an estimated population of one million, is not at risk. Alberta is the easternmost limit of the Pacific population and the number of breeding pairs in the province appears to be stable, largely owing to the fact that much of their breeding territory lies within national and provincial parks. However, because of the harlequin duck's restricted breeding areas and long-term decline in numbers, it has been placed on Alberta's Yellow list as a species to monitor for further decline.

The males are distinguished by their bold colouration of slate blue along their backs, reddish-brown flanks and white areas along their back, neck and head. The females are an unremarkable brown, but like their male counterparts, have white areas on the cheeks, forehead and the ear area between the eye and the back of the head.

These small diving ducks arrive in Alberta from the Pacific coast in early May preferring to breed along fast-flowing mountain streams where they eat molluscs, crustaceans and water insects. Shortly after incubation begins in June, the males return to the west coast. The females and their young leave for the coast in mid-September. A few, though, have been reported to overwinter in northeastern Alberta and in the Calgary area.

Harlequin ducks are long-lived (15-20 years), experience very low rates of population turnover and return to the same geographic areas year after year. They are also very sensitive to human disturbance. These factors make them good indicators of environmental quality. They have, therefore, become the subject of numerous studies and some environmental conflict; in Jasper National Park, for example, whitewater rafting along the Maligne River is restricted to protect the local breeding population. In the Coal Branch, there are an estimated minimum of 20 breeding pairs along the upper McLeod and Cardinal River systems. Of the two, the McLeod is the more important breeding area. The proposed Cheviot mine may impact their numbers by removing some creek sections from their habitat. The local duck population continues to be studied and mitigation measures are proposed should the Cheviot mine go ahead.

57 UPPER WHITEHORSE FALLS

A favourite trip with hikers, cyclists and equestrians, the upper Whitehorse delivers not just one but two pretty waterfalls.

From the west end of the campground walk up the wide horse trail as it skirts Whitehorse Creek on your left. Five hundred metres later you arrive at a quick series of forks in the trail. Bear left at the first fork. A mere 50 m later there is yet another fork. Go straight ahead. Your trail braids as it begins an easy but steady climb up through open pine forest along the Whitehorse Creek valley. Just beyond where the braid rejoins you find yourself at the bottom of a low pitch where your trail once again braids. Ignore an intersection with a trail on your right and continue along what is a pleasant trail through the forest to a clearing on your left where, before the creation of the Whitehorse Wildland Park, there was an informal campsite. An intersection with a trail on your right marks the place where your trail leaves the forest for the open vistas offered along the creekbed. Just beyond here your trail crosses a gravel wash, braiding as it climbs out of the creekbed. At the

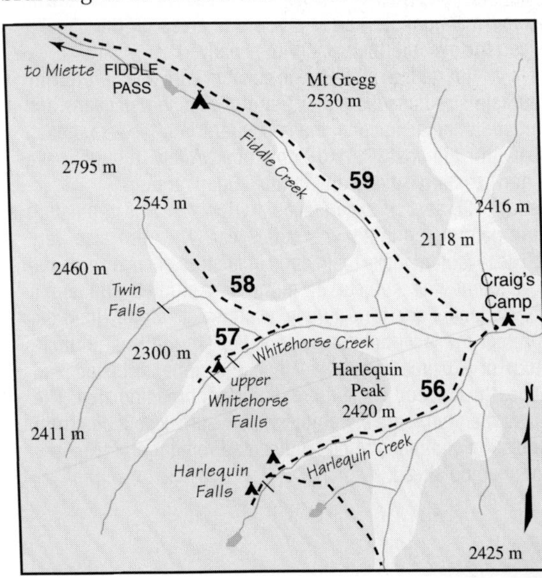

Day hiking, horseback riding

Rating full day

Distance 24.6 km

Level of Difficulty rocky and muddy sections along OHV track

Maximum Elevation 1870 m

Elevation Gain 280 m

Map 83 C/14 Mountain Park; 83 C/13 Medicine Lake

Access

Park your vehicle at the Whitehorse Creek Recreation Area 5.6 km south of Cadomin along the Cardinal River Road. The trailhead is at the west end of the recreation area.

0.0 km	trailhead
0.8 km	triple intersection; braid
1.2 km	end braid
1.4 km	begin braid
1.6 km	end braid
4.4 km	intersection
4.7 km	campsite; intersection
4.8 km	intersection
4.9 km	gravel wash
5.0 km	begin braid
5.1 km	end braid
6.6 km	intersection Craig's Camp
6.9 km	random campsite; stream crossing
7.0 km	intersection
7.1 km	intersection
7.5 km	Fiddle Pass intersection; braids

8.8 km	stream crossing
11.1 km	begin braid
11.2 km	end braid; stream crossing
11.3 km	intersection
11.4 km	stream crossing
11.5 km	lower falls
11.7 km	Whitehorse Creek
12.1 km	random campsite
12.3 km	upper falls
24.6 km	trailhead

At the upper waterfall.

top of the creek terrace, the horse trail crosses an open meadow dotted with willows, pines and dwarf birch. A kilometre later there is a Y in the trail. The somewhat narrower trail on the left leads to Harlequin Creek, so keep to the right. Now you descend to a small stream that presents no difficulty in crossing. Within 100 m the upper Harlequin Creek trail joins on the left. Keep straight ahead to climb sharply through an open spruce forest as far as another Y in the trail. On a tree to the left of the trail there are a couple of signs. One indicates that the left fork leads to the Whitehorse Falls. Another sign, erected by the Department of Environmental Protection, gives the distances to both the upper and lower falls. So bear left; the right-hand fork leads to Fiddle Pass and Miette Hot Springs.

The rather rough horse trail climbs for 200 m before swinging downhill. Undulating up and then down, the trail nevertheless climbs slowly up the valley. At a braid, keep left for a gentler pitch. Cross a stream. At 1.5 km past the Y, views of "the Gap" open promising spectacular scenery along your way. Here the Whitehorse Valley has narrowed and you find yourself surrounded by towering headwalls. From time to time we heard rocks falling off the cliff on our left across the valley and could see numerous weeps on its face. Straight ahead equally impressive rock faces dominate your view. Cross a small gravel wash and continue your climb through spruce forest. Another feature of note along your way is a rockslide that tumbled from the headwalls above you on your right. It nearly comes all the way down to the trail. If you have time you might want to scramble up to take in the view.

At a fork, bear to the right. Climb a pitch where, at the top, there is a great view of the "Gap." Shortly, the trail dips sharply to a small stream. As soon as you cross the stream there is a major intersection. To go to the right is to go to Poachers' Path. So turn onto the left-hand fork and go downhill. Round a bend and there, on your left across and down the ravine, is the lower Whitehorse Falls. They are far too pretty to simply continue on to the upper falls without a better look. Several paths lead down the steep slope to the creek bottom where you can spend some time relaxing at the base of the falls.

Back on the trail you must first cross Whitehorse Creek, a mere rivulet at this point, and then recross it again at an informal campsite on your right. From here it is only 500 m along a straightaway to the upper falls. A fire pit, a comfortable log practically within reach of the cascade's spray, makes a wonderful place to enjoy a snack before returning the way you came.

Relaxing at the lower of the two waterfalls.

Along Whitehorse Creek looking toward the "Gap." Photo John Farley.

Craig's Road

As you follow the trail up the Whitehorse Creek valley, you will notice it is covered in places with coal ash. Coal ash, since it compacts and is porous, is ideal material for cheaply paving a road or trail. This upgraded road is a reminder that for 14 years, between 1925 and 1939, there was logging along the Whitehorse.

Richard "Dick" Allan Craig was young, ambitious and wanted to enter the lumber business. His first problem was landing his first contract, which after some effort he did in 1925 from Cadomin mine manager James H. MacMillan. Now he had a second problem: getting the timber out of the Whitehorse Creek valley. Working by himself, with only a pick, shovel and dynamite, he proceeded to build a road. When he reached the chutes, just west of the Whitehorse Creek Recreational Area, he hired two helpers and blasted a right-of-way past the barrier.

Craig began hauling out timber by sleigh that winter and next summer pushed his road farther up the valley to what is today called Craig's Camp across from the mouth of Harlequin Creek. For the next 13 years this would be the base of his operations as he supplied mine timbers to the Cadomin mine and lumber to the community. He purchased Cadomin's first truck, a four-wheel-drive, with which he not only hauled timber and mine props, but coal ash from the power plant to spread on his and other roads nearby. On Sundays that truck carried a much different load: Cadomin residents out on a picnic or a berry picking excursion.

In 1939 Craig transferred his operation to the Tri-Creeks area and built a new camp and mill near Hell's Gate. From here he built a new road following Wampus Creek to the McLeod River. He stayed for 17 years until 1956 when, with the Cadomin mine closed and timber leases being distributed to large companies rather than small independent operators as himself, Craig closed his Coal Branch operation. By then he was cutting around 2.5 million board feet of lumber a winter and employed around 60 men. He had come a long way down the road since that first day in 1925 when he went walking out of Cadomin by himself, with a pick, a shovel and some dynamite.

58 POACHERS' PATH

MAP PAGE 276

Poachers have long used the upper Whitehorse Valley and Fiddle Pass to illegally hunt game in Jasper National Park. This rather long backpacking trip takes you to a great viewpoint where you can look toward one of the routes frequented by the poachers.

Leaving the campground, walk up the horse trail as it skirts Whitehorse Creek on your left. Five hundred metres later you arrive at a quick series of forks in the trail. Bear left at the first fork. A mere 50 m later there is yet another fork. Go straight ahead. Your trail braids, then, just beyond where the braid rejoins you find yourself at the bottom of a low pitch where your trail once again braids. Ignore the next two intersections with trails that join on your right. Just beyond the second intersection your trail crosses a gravel wash, braiding as it climbs out of the creekbed. At the top of the creek terrace, the horse trail crosses an open meadow. A kilometre later there is a Y in the trail. The somewhat narrower trail on the left leads to Craig's Camp and Harlequin Creek, so keep to the

Backpacking, day hiking, horseback riding

Rating two days

Distance 27.0 km

Level of Difficulty rocky and muddy sections along OHV track; muddy pitch

Maximum Elevation 2090 m

Elevation Gain 500 m

Map 83 C/14 Mountain Park; 83 C/13 Medicine Lake

Access

Park your vehicle at the Whitehorse Creek Recreation Area 5.6 km south of Cadomin along the Cardinal River Road. The trailhead is at the west end of the recreation area.

0.0 km	trailhead
0.8 km	triple intersection; braid
1.2 km	end braid
1.4 km	begin braid

Looking across the upper Whitehorse Creek valley toward the hanging valley slung between "CN" and "CP."

right. Now you descend to a small stream that presents no difficulty in crossing. Within 100 m the upper Harlequin Creek trail joins on your left. Keep straight ahead to climb sharply as far as another Y in the trail. This is a major intersection. To bear right is to go to Fiddle Pass and Miette Hot Springs. So take the left-hand fork where, on a tree, there are a couple of signs indicating the way to the upper Whitehorse Falls.

The rather rough horse trail swings up and then down, nevertheless climbing slowly up the Whitehorse Creek valley. At a braid, keep left for a gentler pitch. Cross a stream. At 1.5 km past the Y, views of "the Gap" open as a harbinger of the spectacular scenery you will see at the end of the trail. Cross a small gravel wash and continue your climb through spruce forest past a rockslide on your right. At a fork, bear to the right. Climb a pitch where, at the top, there is another great view of "the Gap." Shortly, the trail dips sharply to a small stream. As soon as you cross the stream there is a major intersection. Going left takes you to the upper Whitehorse Falls. The right fork leads you up toward Poachers' Path.

The wide trail that you have been following since leaving the Whitehorse Creek Recreation Area peters out within 100 m and the much narrower horse trail begins. The trail climbs sharply immediately upon leaving the intersection. After wending its way up through Engelmann spruce forest for a couple of kilometres, Poachers' Path breaks out of the forest.

1.6 km	end braid
4.4 km	intersection
4.7 km	campsite; intersection
4.8 km	intersection
4.9 km	gravel wash
5.0 km	begin braid
5.1 km	end braid
6.6 km	intersection Craig's Camp
6.9 km	random campsite; stream crossing
7.0 km	intersection
7.1 km	intersection
7.5 km	Fiddle Pass intersection; braids
8.8 km	stream crossing
11.1 km	begin braid
11.2 km	end braid; stream crossing
11.3 km	intersection
11.4 km	end OHV track
13.4 km	random campsite
13.5 km	viewpoint
27.0 km	trailhead

Hanging Valleys

At the end of Poachers' Path you can look down on twin waterfalls of Whitehorse Creek. Their spectacular 80 m-high fall plunges from the lip of a hanging valley that you can clearly see snuggled between "CN" and "CP." The Whitehorse Creek valley above the falls ends abruptly at the precipice, leaving the upper valley "hanging," hence the term hanging valley.

Hanging valleys are a product of the ice ages when glaciers flowed down the main valleys with "tributary" or side glaciers flowing from valleys higher up. These side glaciers eventually joined the main glacier. Since the main glaciers were thicker than the tributary glaciers, they were able to gouge deeper and wider valleys than glaciers in the side valleys. The melting of the ice sheets exposed a much altered landscape. What were once winding, V-shaped valleys were now straighter and wider, sporting the classic U-shape. Meltwaters from the tributary glaciers in the valleys above continued to follow the earlier drainage resulting in spectacular waterfalls cascading from a higher or "hanging" valley.

A knoll above beckons you up through an alpine meadow to a viewpoint. It's quite a sight. Across the Whitehorse Creek valley are two massive limestone headwalls named by a local resident "CN" and "CP" because they reminded him of railway locomotives. In between, the Whitehorse Creek drops precipitously in twin waterfalls from a hanging valley above. From here, the waterfalls look tiny but in reality they have a drop of approximately 80 m! Unfortunately, only a rough bushwhack can take you down to the base of the waterfalls. We were satisfied with taking in the rest of the view. To the right your alpine meadow slopes down toward two passes. These lead up to the boundary of Jasper National Park and the valley of Poacher's Creek with its infamous reputation beyond.

Return the way you came.

The Ram's Head

You can see the photograph on the wall at Jacoby's Cafe in Cadomin. There she is, lovely Ethel Hawkins, posing beside a dead ram. She is holding her Winchester rifle and smiling broadly. The animal was shot in 1923 in the Ruby Lake area. Its horns were measured and both found to be about 40 inches long. This was a trophy animal and therein lies the mystery.

Trophy that it was, it seems that it was never registered while members of the hunting party would not say who shot it. Considering the photograph, the circumstantial evidence points to Hawkins. Why the secrecy, no one knows. The most likely explanation seems to be that no one in the party had a sheep license.

Regardless, it was mounted and remained on display for almost 20 years at the Coalspur Hotel dining room. Following a change in hotel ownership the head was taken off the wall and thrown into the garbage.

Ethel Hawkins and her trophy sheep. Photo Charles Jacoby.

59 CADOMIN TO MIETTE

MAP PAGE 276

Although jostling two vehicles between Cadomin and Miette is time consuming, you have the satisfaction of knowing you will be following in the footsteps—or horse steps—of many Cadomin miners who first cut this trail over the Fiddle Pass to the soothing, healing waters of Miette Hot Springs.

From the west end of the campground and horse corrals walk up the wide horse trail. A series of pretty cascades in Whitehorse Creek diverts your attention a few hundred metres beyond the trailhead. One-half kilometre later you arrive at a quick series of forks in the trail. Bear left at the first fork; swinging to the right will take you to Farmer Valley. A mere 50 m later there is yet another fork. Go straight ahead. Your trail braids as it begins an easy but steady climb up through open pine forest along the Whitehorse Creek valley. Small rivulets and springs alongside the trail can make the trail spongy and soft in spots, especially if the season has been wet, but present no real problem. Just beyond where the braid rejoins you find yourself at the bottom of a low pitch where your trail once again braids. An easy climb brings you to the top of

Backpack, horseback riding

Rating two or three days

Distance 37.5 km

Level of Difficulty steady walk, some steep pitches

Maximum Elevation 2118 m

Elevation Gain 528 m

Map 83 C/14 Mountain Park; 83 F/3 Cadomin; 83 F/4 Miette

Access

Park your vehicle at the Whitehorse Creek Recreation Area 5.6 km south of Cadomin along the Cardinal River Road. The trailhead is at the west end of the recreation area.

Note #1 This hike requires two vehicles.

Note #2 A Wilderness Pass is required for all overnight stays in the backcountry of Jasper National Park. Wilderness passes are available at the Jasper

Crossing Fiddle Pass into Jasper National Park.

the braid. A pleasant trip up the wide, good trail is broken by an intersection with a trail on your right. Ignore it and continue to a semi-clearing on your left where, before the creation of the Whitehorse Wildland Park, there was an informal campsite. An intersection with a trail on your right marks the place where your trail leaves the forest for the open vistas offered along the creekbed. When we were here the hillsides on the opposite side of the valley were turning autumn red and gold making for a pretty picture.

The trail crosses the wash area and then braids as it climbs out of the creekbed. From here, the horse trail crosses through an open meadow dotted with willows, pines and dwarf birch. Your pleasant forest walk is broken a kilometre later at a Y in the trail. The somewhat narrower trail on the left leads to Harlequin Creek, so keep to the right. Now you descend to a small stream that presents no difficulty in crossing. Within 100 m the upper Harlequin Creek trail joins on the left. Keep straight ahead to climb sharply through an open spruce forest as far as another Y in the trail. Here, there are signs indicating the left fork leads to the Whitehorse Falls and the right fork, the one you are to take, leads to Miette Hot Springs. Shortly after the Whitehorse Falls intersection, the Miette trail passes through a wet section that has been partially corduroyed followed by a trail joining on the left. Once again, remain on the main horse trail. From this junction the Miette trail begins its serious ascent climbing through the cool forest to Fiddle Pass, or as others call it, Whitehorse Pass. Where the trail flattens vistas open toward the Whitehorse Creek valley below on your left. Once past a rockslide to the right of the trail there is another long pitch to climb before you break out onto a flat and open meadow that offers views on your left. Your trail braids and rejoins just before skirting a scree slope on the right. A couple of small stream crossings bring you to a random campsite to the left of the trail. When we were here the Whitehorse Wildland Park had just been created and this campsite was hikers' first opportunity to pitch camp before crossing Fiddle Pass into Jasper National Park. From here, it is only 100 m or so to the lower end of the pass. Marmots inhabiting a scree slope on your right may whistle a warning as you pass by.

Information Centre located at 500 Connaught Drive, Jasper. Reservations may be required.

0.0 km	trailhead
0.8 km	triple intersection and braid
1.2 km	end braid
1.4 km	begin braid
1.6 km	end braid
4.4 km	intersection
4.7 km	campsite and intersection
4.8 km	intersection
4.9 km	gravel wash
5.0 km	begin braid
5.1 km	end braid
6.6 km	intersection Craig's Camp
6.9 km	random campsite; stream crossing
7.0 km	intersection
7.1 km	intersection
7.5 km	Fiddle Pass intersection; braids
9.0 km	stream
11.3 km	stream
11.6 km	campsite
12.8 km	stream
13.4 km	Fiddle Pass
13.9 km	stream crossing
14.7 km	stream crossing
15.4 km	intersection
16.9 km	intersection
17.5 km	Whitehorse campsite
17.6 km	stream crossing
18.3 km	Fiddle River
19.4 km	gully
21.3 km	begin braid
21.4 km	end braid
22.6 km	gravel wash
23.2 km	intersection
24.4 km	Fiddle River
24.7 km	Slide Creek campsite
24.8 km	Slide Creek
26.3 km	stream crossing

The boundary marker for Jasper National Park at the apex of Fiddle Pass.

What a glorious pass! Alpine meadows, interspersed with coppices of dwarf birch and willow and krummholz Engelmann spruce run to the base of the surrounding peaks and ridges and over the low saddle straight ahead that marks the apex of Fiddle Pass. The beauty of the pass is enhanced further by the presence of a small tarn situated, almost unbelievably, in the middle of this park-like setting. Surely, Fiddle Pass must be one of the prettiest in the Front Ranges! The open ridges that surround the pass are a hiker's delight; you can easily spend a day here exploring both the meadows and the ridges. Remember, though, that like all alpine meadows, Fiddle Pass is appreciated equally by the bruin. By early autumn part of the meadows resemble a well-cultivated garden where grizzlies dig for roots and grubs. An unnamed creek, a ributary of Whitehorse Creek, drains the lake hrough a small gully and drops down through the pruce-lined ravine that paralleled the route you ave followed to this point.

At the far end of the lake you begin your climb oward the top of the saddle, crossing en route a mall stream that feeds into the lake below. At the op of Fiddle Pass there is the boundary marker for asper National Park. On either side of the pass

27.9 km begin braid
28.3 km end braid
31.6 km intersection
31.7 km Utopia Creek
32.7 km intersection
35.6 km stream
35.9 km stream
36.7 km Sulphur Creek
37.2 km stream and intersection
37.3 km boardwalk
37.5 km Aquacentre

Camping at Fiddle Pass.

scree slopes sweep down the hillsides to meet alpine meadow. So low is the pass that you realize the meadow merely continues over the saddle and into the park extending the entire way down to the treeline. Ahead you can see the Fiddle River valley that you will follow almost the entire way to Miette Hot Springs. Dropping down from the saddle you cross a small stream gurgling out of the hills on your right. It is quickly joined by another stream that plunges from the peaks on your left. Their confluence marks the headwaters of the Fiddle River.

Your horse trail continues down through the meadow into head-height willows and past thickets of krummholz spruce. Cross the Fiddle River that is still less than a metre wide. Having left the alpine behind, the horse trail drops into spruce forest where, 2 km from the apex of the pass, it forks. Keep to the right; bearing left will force you into a 3 km walk to the warden's cabin. You now begin a sharp drop down the valley. Ignore a trail that joins from the left; it returns uphill to the warden's cabin. Within a couple of kilometres you arrive at the Whitehorse campsite. Situated alongside the Fiddle River in a tight ravine, the Whitehorse campsite is the first of three backcountry campsites between Fiddle Pass and Miette. One moulded green plastic biffy, three campsites and two picnic tables can be a welcome sight at the end of a long day! From the campsite the horse trail crosses the Fiddle River, the first of a number of river crossings that you will make before arriving at Miette. Lining the river's edge are blueberries, crow berries and bog cranberries. Another river crossing and your trail plunges into the forest. The trail can be uneven along the entire park stretch as the horses have exposed tree roots and numerous rocks. Next, cross a stony gully and climb a low rise where the trail has braided. You are now walking on flat, i rocky, ground as you cross another gravel wash that once hosted a horse camp but that now has been eaten away by the Fiddle River. Access to the new horse camp is only a few hundred metres farther along the trail where another trail joins from the left. Crossing the Fiddle River once again almost brings you into Slide Creek campsite, the second of the trio of backcountry campsites provided by the park. Hikers out of Miette often overnight at Slide before day hiking up to Fiddle Pass the next day. There is no water in the immediate vicinity of the Slide campsite, but Slide Creek is only about 100 m or so down the trail. A sturdy log bridge has been thrown over the narrower of two braids of the stream leaving you to deal with the wider of the two braids as best you can. From here the trail climbs up and through an extensive, ancient rockslide, now fairly well vegetated. The end of your exploration of the slide is marked where the horse trail crosses a small gully and stream. Once again you are following the Fiddle River, sometimes on the flats alongside the river, at other times in the forest where the trail climbs above the river. Ahead you can see the cleft through which your trail goes and, on your right, a long rocky ridge that parallels the Fiddle. Approximately 7 km after leaving Slide you arrive at a marked intersection. To turn left is to climb a short distance to the Utopia campsite. For those hiking from Cadomin to Miette, Utopia is a popular overnight location before completing their trek. Utopia Creek, located a short distance down the trail, presents no obstacle especially during low water season.

An obstacle that you cannot avoid is a steep pitch 1 km beyond Utopia. Up to this point it has been an easy, pretty walk. At the junction of two trails the one straight ahead leads to Mystery Lake; keep left to go to Miette Hot Springs. Here you begin a no-nonsense climb up through the spruce forest. It can be a tiring trudge especially if you have walked from the Whitehorse campsite that same day. At the top of the pitch the trail flattens considerably but nevertheless continues its relentless uphill route through the forest. Finally, the trail levels and breaks out of the forest to skirt a scree slope on your right. Then it's back into the cool forest as you begin your descent to Miette. At this point the trail widens, evidence of its popularity with day walkers out of Miette. A small stream has to be dealt with, but the trail is so wide here that you can easily avoid getting your feet wet. One last switch down the hillside brings you to a bridge over Sulphur Creek. The last kilometre takes you quickly by an intersection to the horse camp, along a boardwalk, followed by the ruins of the old hot springs pool and, from there, up a macadamized walk to the parking lot and the Aquacentre where your second vehicle should be waiting.

Fiddle River/Range

Previous names: Riviere au Violon (river by the violin), Fiddle Back Mountains, the Fiddlebacks
Cree name: Kitocikan Sipiy

Fiddle River is a translation of the French name for the stream: Riviere au Violon. It is one of a number of area place names whose history goes back to the early 19th century and the local French-speaking fur trade community. In 1865 James Hector of the Palliser Expedition recorded the present variations of the names: Fiddle Range and Fiddle River.

Hudson's Bay Company fur trader Henry Moberly wrote that when the wind struck the nearby mountains from a certain direction, one would hear the sound of a fiddle. According to Moberly, fiddle is a translation of the original Cree name: kitocikan. A kitocikan is a musical instrument and the music presumably came from either the wind whistling in the nearby canyon or through standing dead trees left behind by a forest fire. The French name Riviere au Violon implies that the stream was named after the nearby musical mountain.

Travel writers Frederick Talbot and B. W. Mitchell called the range the Fiddle Back Mountains and the Fiddlebacks respectively. A ridge near the mouth of the Fiddle looks like the outline of a violin tipped onto its side.

Along the Fiddle River.

Anne Hudyma's Walk

Eight year-old Helena Hudyma did a wonderful thing: she saved a five year-old child, Marguerite Moldowan, from drowning in the McLeod River. Helena's heroism did not go unnoticed and Cadomin mine superintendent J. H. McMillan decided to reward the young girl with a wristwatch at the upcoming village picnic.

This presented a problem, however, to Helena's parents, John and Anne, who only received the news of the scheduled presentation two days before the picnic. They were at Miette where John was recuperating from a mine accident by bathing in the hot springs. It had taken them three days on foot and by train to make the trip from Cadomin to Miette and they would never make it back in time to witness the presentation, unless....

It is 1929 and there is only a horse trail from Pocahontas to Miette. Going to Miette to recover from an injury was a common practice among the Coal Branch miners and it would take them two days making the train connections to leave the Coal Branch and reach Pocahontas, from where they would walk on the third day to Miette. Miette was a very rustic place then with several outdoor log lined pools for bathing and a choice among several log cabins or permanent tents for accommodation. Anne and John had chosen one of the tents where they slept on a simple log bed laid out with evergreen boughs. They had brought their own blankets and pillows.

When they heard the news about their daughter, John and Anne wanted to attend the reward ceremony and decided they could make it back on time if they walked the 38 km-long horse trail along the Fiddle River from Miette back to Cadomin. They left in the morning and didn't arrive in Cadomin until past midnight. Apart from sighting a moose with a calf and several bears, the trip was uneventful, but the scenery dazzled Anne, especially at Whitehorse Pass: "We went up that hill and there was one higher than that. We went up the higher one than that and 'Oh beautiful!' A lake just like glass and just covered with ducks."

Anne's walk amazed superintendent McMillan who told her that she was probably the first "white woman" to walk the distance from Miette to Cadomin. Despite her effort, she missed the watch presentation to her daughter Helena. Anne had done the trip without the luxury of hiking boots and was forced to stay home recovering from a severe case of blisters. "But you know, I'm never sorry that I did go [from Miette to Cadomin]."

PROSPECT CREEK RANDOM CAMPSITE

At the Prospect Creek random campsite.

There is no recreation area with formal campgrounds at Prospect Creek. Rather, the area on both sides of and immediately adjacent to the Cardinal River Road has long been used as a random campsite. You, then, have a choice of staying at the Whitehorse Creek Recreation Area 2.5 km north, at Mountain Park Recreation Area 6.3 km south along the Cardinal River Road, or random camping at Prospect Creek where there are no amenities including washrooms or drinking water.

Prospect Creek/Mountain

Previous names: Solomon Creek, Matthews Creek, Tie Creek, Deadhorse/Horse Creek, Camp Creek, Green Timber Creek

Prospect Creek takes its name from the coal prospects located along it. A prospect is the name given to any mine workings whose value has not yet been made manifest. This creek's name goes back to at least 1922.

Solomon Creek refers to Regina contractor Fred Solomon who owned and operated Solomon Collieries at the head of the stream. Solomon bought his coal lease in 1931 from Donald Cameron "Cam" Matthews of Mountain Park. Matthews also ran a lumber camp in the area, hence Matthews Creek.

Tie Creek is another local name that goes back to at least 1922. Tie Creek is a common name and usually refers to the past presence of a "tie camp" where railway ties were cut. Its other meaning is based upon survey methodology. When staking a claim in an area not legally surveyed, the claim boundaries would be described or "tied" in relation to a physical feature not liable to change. A common choice was the fork of a stream.

Deadhorse or Horse Creek is the east branch along which Matthews wintered his string of horses. Deadhorse recalls an incident where two men had been hired to stay the winter and look after the animals. The men ran out of food supplies, so therefore ate at least one of the horses. Camp Creek is the centre branch and refers to the King Coals mining camp once located beside it. Green Timber Creek, a descriptive name, is the west branch.

Prospect Mountain was named after the creek.

Prospect Creek

Mine No.: #1363; 1631

Owners/Operators: 1930-1931 Val D'Or Collieries Ltd.; 1931-1933 Solomon Collieries Ltd. #1363/A; 1933-1934 Pyramid Mountain Collieries Ltd. #1363/A; 1936-1938 Mount Cheviot Coal Co. Ltd. #1363/B; 1945-1946 King Coals Ltd. #1631; 1946 Arctic Coals Ltd. #1631

Authorized Capital: $20,000 Mount Cheviot Coal Co. Ltd.; $500,000 Arctic Coals Ltd.

Coal: bituminous

Registered Trade Name: King Coal

Market: steam

Mine Type: underground; strip pit

Total Extraction: 1,100 tonnes

Men Killed: 0

All of these mines were little more than prospects. Their main problems were faulted seams and dirty coal. The mines struck the same seam but in two locations: along the main branch of Prospect Creek at the base of Prospect Mountain and along Prospect Creek's east branch, also known as Horse Creek, at the base of Cheviot Mountain.

The first mine was begun in 1931 by Fred Solomon, a Regina contractor who bought the lease in 1930 from Donald Cameron "Cam" Matthews of Mountain Park. Solomon opened up a strip pit then sold it for $50,000 to Pyramid Mountain Collieries headed by James G. Pickard, a Saskatoon contractor. Under the terms, Pickard would operate the mine and pay for it on a royalty basis. Pickard gave up the operation by 1934. These operations were on the main branch of Prospect Creek.

Mount Cheviot Coal, headed by Mike Vitaly, opened an underground mine on Horse Creek in 1936. Vitaly drove a level, struck a fault and ceased operations by 1937. The separate locations of the Vitaly and Solomon mines confused the Mines Branch that allocated initially the same mine number to both operations. In 1937 the Mines Branch ordered a legal survey of the area, then afterward redesignated the two sites as "A" and "B."

The most serious attempt to open up a mine was in 1945 by King Coals headed by Harold H. Croxton of Edmonton. Croxton reopened the Vitaly mine on Horse Creek and drove his entry about 40 m before striking a fault. The coal produced was hauled from the mine site 6 km by truck to the mouth of Prospect Creek and loaded into railway cars through a chute located beside the railway siding. Croxton sold out to Arctic Coals and went on to start a more successful mine at Coalspur.

Arctic Coals reopened the strip operation at the head of Prospect Creek and abandoned the mine within a year.

60 CHEVIOT MOUNTAIN

Your artery-cleansing climb over loose, unstable scree is rewarded on top with a glorious 360° panorama and the knowledge that you, too, have completed this Coal Branch rite of passage.

This is a long day hike so an early start is recommended even though you can, if you wish, cycle from the trailhead to the base of Cheviot Mountain. The weather around Cheviot Mountain is changeable so only attempt your climb if the morning dawns clear and cloudless; the chances are, even then, that before you return to the trailhead you will have experienced a change in the weather. We had the unpleasant experience of being caught in a thunderstorm on the mountain on our descent. While of short duration, the storm nevertheless caused us some uncomfortable moments.

From the random campsite at Prospect Creek find the horse trail on the right bank of the stream and follow it upstream as it enters a pretty, narrow valley. Cross a small tributary of Prospect Creek

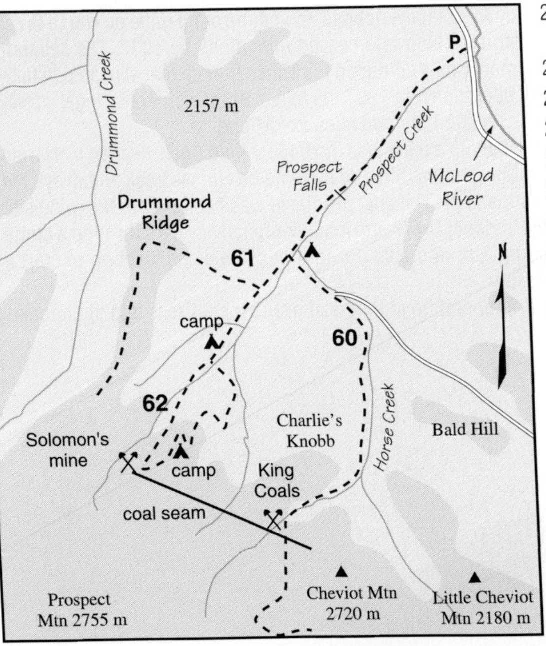

Day hiking, cycling

Rating full day

Distance 15.6 km

Level of Difficulty steep ascent on loose rock

Maximum Elevation 2720 m

Elevation Gain 1060 m

Map 83 C/14 Mountain Park

Access

Park your vehicle at the Prospect Creek random campsite. The campsite lies along the west side of the Cardinal River Road 8.1 km south of Cadomin.

0.0 km	trailhead
0.6 km	stream crossing
1.2 km	Prospect Creek
1.6 km	falls
1.7 km	Prospect Creek
1.8 km	Prospect Creek
1.9 km	stream crossing
2.1 km	intersection; Prospect Creek; random campsite
2.2 km	Horse Creek
2.4 km	intersection
2.9 km	intersection
3.1 km	intersection
3.6 km	intersection
4.1 km	OHV track
5.3 km	Horse Creek canyon viewpoint
5.4 km	King Coal mine camp
5.8 km	Horse Creek
7.4 km	saddle
7.8 km	Cheviot Mountain
15.6 km	trailhead

Horse Creek, at the base of Cheviot Mountain, is your last place to fill your water bottle before beginning your climb.

We completed a Coal Branch rite of passage.

A few timbers are all that remain of first, Mount Cheviot Coal, which opened in 1936, and later, King Coals, which opened in 1945. Both operations were short lived owing to the faulting of the seam.

and continue up a very narrow ravine. From the top of the ravine it's a short distance to a ford across Prospect Creek. As you approach a chute or small waterfall in Prospect Creek you have your first peek at Cheviot Mountain. Just above the chute you must ford the creek again so that once again the creek is on your left as you continue to climb slowly up the valley. Almost immediately you arrive at an intersection with a horse trail on your right and a small stream that you must cross. Continue straight ahead along the main track and within a couple hundred metres you reach the confluence of Horse Creek and an intersection with another horse trail. Bear left onto this trail and ford Prospect Creek over to a random campsite located on the left bank of Horse Creek. Follow the gravel wash past an informal campsite on your left. Within 50 m you must cross Horse Creek. This crossing is followed by two more quick fords. Walk up the track as it climbs to a Y junction. Bear right; to take the left-hand fork takes you into Mountain Park.

A myriad of intersections with old logging roads and OHV tracks confronts and, possibly, confounds you beyond this point, so follow the directions below carefully. At the first intersection keep to the left to remain on your hard-packed old road and proceed for 500 m to another intersection with a track on your left. Keep to the right, and right again at yet another intersectior that occurs within a couple hundred metres. Another 500 m brings you to ar intersection with a road that joins from the left. Keep to the right again However, at an intersection with an OHV track that joins from the right, bea to the left. You are climbing steadily along a hard-packed, good dirt road tha winds its way up through spruce and pine forest. Straight in front of you i Cheviot Mountain, beckoning. The road swings to the right, now approachin the northeast slope of your quest. Below you is a small canyon cut by Hors Creek. Across the creek is the lower shoulder of the mountain. From thi vantage point you cannot see the summit, only the alpine meadow on its lowest shoulder and the scree of the first pitch. Finally the roadway flattens. As you continue to skirt Cheviot Mountain from across the creek you pass an old log building on your right, now quite dilapidated, that speaks to the ever-constant search for a producing coal field. Its large logs, saddle notched at the corners, indicate that this was once a substantial building. Now, colourful Indian paintbrush, and those grizzly favourites, cow parsnip and hedysarum, grow inside its walls. The road continues to sinew its way down and around, crests and then swings down to Horse Creek where it ends abruptly.

In front of you is the lowest shoulder of Cheviot Mountain. Throughout your climb you have been passing through a pine and spruce forest. Now, at Horse Creek, you suddenly leave the forest and cross into the alpine. Before scrambling up the shoulder fill your water bottle from the creek. There is no water on the mountain itself and on a hot day the sun's rays bouncing off the scree combined with your exertions can dehydrate you quickly. Two litres of water will not be too much.

There is no marked route up the mountain. There is also no easy route to the top, the degree of slope remaining fairly constant throughout your climb. If you like rock work, turn right and walk upstream until you come opposite a set of cliffs, cross the stream and begin your climb. Once on top of the cliffs the most direct route is straight ahead toward a saddle, thereby skirting the steeper slopes on your left. We chose to climb straight up from the creek that avoided the cliffs but carried us over three main pitches. The first pitch lifts you sharply up through a beautiful alpine meadow liberally sprinkled with hedysarum, monkshood, alpine forget-me-nots, moss campion, rock jasmine and white dryads. As you climb, the alpine flora becomes thinner and thinner until you leave the meadow entirely and climb onto the scree. Above you, directly in front, is a rocky outcrop. Once on top of this second pitch it is a steeper and longer challenge to the top of the third pitch. We chose to negotiate our way beneath and to the right of this second outcrop to work our way over to the saddle. Once on the saddle we turned left and had an easy walk on firm rock to the summit.

En route to the top you, no doubt, have had plenty of opportunity to admire the unfolding scene below you. Once on top you have a complete 360° sweep that takes in the Cardinal Divide and the Nikanassin Range to the east and the mountains of Jasper National Park to the west. It's a glorious vista. A large cairn lures you to the mountaintop. Poke around the walls of the cairn and locate a large jar hidden in the walls. Inside the jar is a piece of paper where you can write down your name and the date of your climb. At some point someone will retrieve the jar and, hopefully, will add your name to the list of successful climbers at Jacoby's store in Cadomin.

Return the way you came.

Cheviot Mountain/Creek

The cairn at the top of the mountain is a good place to enjoy a rest and eat a snack before descending.

Cheviot Mountain (2720 m) was named by Norman Muschamp "Robert" Thornton (1876-1919), a British mining engineer who, in 1910, first evaluated the coal claims at what later became Mountain Park. The mountain reminded Thornton of the Cheviot Hills in northern England, though on a much larger scale. Thornton would have pronounced the "Che" in Cheviot the same as in "cheat." Coal Branchers have since softened the "Che" to the same as in "Chevrolet."

While not the highest mountain in the area, Cheviot's location and singular shape make it stand out among the surrounding peaks. Its earliest probable reference is by the Earl of Southesk who on September 1, 1859, camped near Mountain Park "...in a deep glen that intersected our course, a grand rocky peak could be seen crowning the end of the ravine we had chosen for our halting place."

Cheviot's first recorded ascent was in 1920 and since then has become a rite of passage among Coal Branchers who leave their names written on a piece of paper stored in a jar deposited in a cairn at the top. This tradition probably dates back to the original 1920 ascent. A list of those who have climbed Cheviot is posted at Jacoby's store in Cadomin.

Cheviot is subject to quick dramatic changes in weather that acted as a signal to residents in Mountain Park and Cadomin: in the winter, snow blowing off the top meant that a chinook or "Cadomin wind" was coming.

Cheviot Creek is named after the mountain.

Cheviot Mountain as seen from Mountain Park.

61 DRUMMOND RIDGE

MAP PAGE 292

The establishment of the Whitehorse Wildland Park will protect the fragile alpine of this beautiful ridge from OHVs that used to switch up the slope.

From the random campsite at Prospect Creek find the horse trail on the right bank of the stream and follow it upstream as it enters a pretty, narrow valley. In the distance are the mountains that lie inside the Whitehorse Wildland Park. Skip across a small tributary of Prospect Creek and continue up your trail as it winds through a very narrow ravine. From the top of the ravine it's a short distance to a ford across Prospect Creek. Here you can clearly see Prospect Mountain straight ahead. You can see Cheviot Mountain for the first time as you approach a chute or small waterfall in Prospect

Day hiking
Rating full day
Distance 11.6 km
Level of Difficulty steep ascent along OHV track
Maximum Elevation 2150 m
Elevation Gain 490 m
Map 83 C/14 Mountain Park

Access

Park your vehicle at the Prospect Creek random campsite. The campsite lies along the west side of the Cardinal River Road 8.1 km south of Cadomin.

0.0 km	trailhead
0.6 km	stream crossing
1.2 km	Prospect Creek
1.6 km	falls
1.7 km	Prospect Creek
1.8 km	Prospect Creek
1.9 km	stream crossing
2.1 km	intersection; Prospect Creek; random campsite
2.8 km	intersection
2.9 km	intersection
3.0 km	intersection
3.5 km	cutline
3.6 km	begin braid
4.1 km	end braid
4.1 km	begin braid
4.3 km	end braid
4.3 km	begin braid
4.5 km	end braid
4.6 km	Drummond Ridge
5.8 km	lower slope Prospect Mountain
11.6 km	trailhead

At the Whitehorse Wildland Park boundary on top of Drummond Ridge.

Creek. In several thousand years, the creek may have scoured out a small canyon at this point. For now, though, you have to be satisfied with a pretty chute. Just above the chute you must ford the creek again so that once again the creek is on your left as you continue to climb slowly up the valley. Almost immediately you arrive at an intersection with a horse trail on your right and a small stream that you must cross. Continue straight ahead along the main track and within a couple hundred metres you reach the confluence of Horse Creek and an intersection with another horse trail. Ignore this intersection and continue to the right along the main track that soon swings away from Prospect Creek and follows Centre Creek.

While you have had tantalizing views of the alpine since starting out it is only when your track breaks out onto a meadow thick with dwarf willow and birch that you can see the head of the valley that you have been following. Directly in front of you is Prospect Mountain with its beautiful alpine meadows that sweep down from the scree. At your 11 o'clock is the flat-topped Cheviot Mountain and to your right is Drummond Ridge. What was once pristine alpine has long since been overrun by motorized vehicles that have created a network of tracks throughout the headwaters. The first of these trails can be found on your right; ignore it. Shortly, though, you come to an intersection of several trails. Continue straight ahead. Just before a ford across Centre Creek there is a wide, major track on your right that climbs Drummond Ridge.

Bear right onto this track. It's a steep switchback up the slope. The OHV had ignored the switchbacks and opted to go straight up the slope of the ridge. A combination of the steepness of the slope and the prolonged use of the shortcut have caused heavy erosion on many sections of the shortcut. Now, though, with the advent of the new park the OHVs have been limited to the valley floor. You cross into the park when you have nearly reached the top of the ridge. If you are walking you may want to stop from time to time as you climb to marvel at the scenery that unfolds below and behind you. The long ridge in the background is the Cardinal Divide. The little peak just to the left of the divide is Mount Harris. Directly below you can easily see the myriad of tracks and trails that crisscross the Prospect Creek valley. Too, as you climb, the vegetation changes as you leave the subalpine and the treeline, and enter the alpine.

The view from the top of the ridge is wonderful, to say the least. A complete 360° panorama lies beneath and around you. To your left an old OHV track cuts through the fragile alpine toward the slope of Prospect Mountain. Straight ahead is the Drummond Creek valley and to your right the ridge stretches to the east. The ridge top is a botanist's delight and most of the plants found on the Cardinal Divide can be found here as well—alpine forget-me-not, mountain fleabane and moss campion.

Return the way you came.

62 SOLOMON'S MINE

MAP PAGE 292

Solomon's mine has to be one of the smallest and more isolated mines in the Coal Branch. Perched atop a windswept knob on a shoulder of Prospect Mountain, this operation at least had a magnificent view of the Prospect Creek valley. The old mining camp can be found below.

From the random campsite at Prospect Creek find the horse trail on the right bank of the stream and follow it upstream. Skip across a small tributary of Prospect Creek and continue up the horse trail as it winds through a very narrow ravine. From the top of the ravine it's a short distance to a ford across Prospect Creek. Here you can clearly see Prospect Mountain, your destination, straight ahead. Just above a chute in Prospect Creek you must ford the creek again so that once again the creek is on your left as you continue to climb slowly up the valley. Almost immediately you arrive at an intersection with a horse trail on your right and a small stream that you must cross. Continue straight ahead along the main track and within a couple hundred metres you reach the confluence of Horse Creek and an intersection with another horse trail. Ignore this intersection and continue along the main track that soon swings away from Prospect Creek and follows Centre Creek.

Day hiking

Rating full day

Distance 11.5 km

Level of Difficulty steep ascent along OHV track; risk of high winds

Maximum Elevation 2100 m

Elevation Gain 440 m

Map 83 C/14 Mountain Park

Access

Park your vehicle at the Prospect Creek random campsite. The campsite lies along the west side of the Cardinal River Road 8.1 km south of Cadomin.

0.0 km	trailhead
0.6 km	stream crossing
1.2 km	Prospect Creek
1.6 km	falls
1.7 km	Prospect Creek
1.8 km	Prospect Creek
1.9 km	stream crossing
2.1 km	intersection; Prospect Creek; random campsite

Approaching the 1946 strip mine.

At the strip mine site.

While you have had tantalizing views of the alpine since starting out, it is only when your track enters a meadow thick with dwarf willow and birch that you can see the head of the valley that you have been following. Directly in front of you is Prospect Mountain with its beautiful alpine meadows that sweep down from the scree. At your 11 o'clock is the flat-topped Cheviot Mountain and to your right is Drummond Ridge. Unfortunately, prior to the establishment of Whitehorse Wildland Park, this once pristine alpine was overrun by motorized vehicles that have created a network of tracks throughout the headwaters. The first of these trails can be found on your right; ignore it. Shortly, though, you come to an intersection of several trails. Continue straight ahead. Just before a ford across Centre Creek there is a wide, major track on your right that climbs Drummond Ridge. Ignore it and continue straight ahead along what is now a good gravel mine road and cross Centre Creek. Farther up the roadway there are two quick intersections with old roads on your left. Ignore these and continue to a major intersection where you will want to keep to the right to head toward the alpine. At the fourth intersection swing to the left and cross a stream; to go to the right will dead-end

2.8 km	intersection
2.9 km	intersection
3.0 km	intersection Drummond Ridge; stream crossing
3.1 km	intersection
3.4 km	intersection
3.5 km	intersection; stream crossing
3.8 km	begin braid
3.9 km	end braid
4.6 km	road; intersections
5.0 km	strip pit; OHV track
5.2 km	base strip pit
5.5 km	intersections [corresponds to 4.6 km]
6.0 km	intersection
6.1 km	mine camp
6.2 km	return intersection
6.3 km	mine camp
6.4 km	return intersection
7.2 km	intersection
7.8 km	intersection
8.1 km	stream crossing; intersection
11.5 km	trailhead

within a kilometre. From the stream crossing it's a steep climb, braiding up a cutline. Along the way you can find cable lying on the road, evidence of earlier industrial activity in this valley. At the top of the braid you begin to leave the subalpine and climb sharply into the alpine toward a knob on the shoulder of Prospect Mountain. The spruce trees are dwarfed and finally disappear from the slope altogether. Straight ahead Prospect Mountain sports snow lingering in its gullies, even at the height of summer.

Just below the knob there is a major intersection of tracks. Go right at the first intersection. At the next quick intersection the track braids. We chose a track on the left that led us upward less sharply than the continuation of the cutline straight ahead. We thoroughly enjoyed the glorious view of the alpine meadows of Prospect Mountain that fell away on our left. Despite years of OHV traffic in the area, only a few tracks lead across the fragile alpine, and now that motorized vehicles are banned from the park, these scars will have the opportunity to heal. The last pull to the top of the knob takes your wind away, quite literally; the winds can howl down from Prospect Mountain with nearly gale-force. Finally, just past a curve that skirts a promontory, you arrive at the strip mine.

Here a major coal seam lies just beneath the surface. Once the operators cleared the few metres of overburden a wide but fractured seam was exposed. As you cross the mine site, you are literally walking on the coal seam. Despite the fierce wind we encountered on top of the knob, we lingered a little, poking about looking for further evidence of this doomed operation while at the same time drinking in the views of Prospect Mountain.

To locate the mining camp and a "gopher hole" underground mine we backtracked to the promontory and followed the coal slack down the slope to another mine road that

Solomon's mining camp.

returned us to the intersection of tracks beneath the knob. We ignored the cutline, choosing instead to keep on the roadway as it swung to the right. This was the road used by the mining companies that tried their luck here. Within 500 m we found an intersection on our right with another roadway. Tucked in between the road and the lea of the hillside we found evidence of the mining camp—numerous flattened buildings and oil drums. On our return to the main mine road we saw below us on our right more building ruins. Twenty metres down the mine road brought us to another intersection on our right that led us to the underground operation. Little remains of this futile attempt to eke a living out of this difficult seam; only a few large timber buildings, now completely flattened, remain. But it stirs the imagination to think what it must have been like to live and work in this remote spot.

Back on the mine road we switched down the mountainside with Cheviot Mountain commanding our views. We ignored all intersections with an old logging road until we arrived at the T-junction with the main Prospect Creek trail. Turning to the right took us back down the valley to our vehicle.

The Poppies

Scientific name: *Papaver Nudicaule*
Other name: Icelandic poppy

Growing a flower garden in the Coal Branch is a challenge owing to the thin soil and threat of early or late frosts. In the 1940s, Annie Antonenko of Mountain Park took up the challenge leaving behind as her testament the orange and yellow Icelandic poppies that can be seen growing in Cadomin and Mountain Park.

Annie first began growing her poppies in her Mountain Park garden, which she had labouriously created by bringing in dirt, a bucket at a time. The flowers grew well in the brisk subalpine environment, but for Annie it wasn't enough. She had visited Southesk Lake, in Jasper National Park, and was filled with the vision of bordering that lake with her poppies. So, each summer for two years she would go by pack horse to that lake where she scattered the poppy seeds collected from her garden. By her hand, and that of others, the poppies also spread to Cadomin and soon established themselves there as well.

Annie left Mountain Park in 1947, but her poppies have prospered. They can be seen growing wild in the Cadomin area and along Whitehorse Creek and Prospect Creek. They can also be seen at Southesk Lake where one biologist insists upon digging them out. Why? Icelandic poppies are a non-native plant and do not belong in a national park.

Icelandic poppy. Photo Akemi Matsubuchi.

MOUNTAIN PARK RECREATION AREA

The Mountain Park Recreation Area serves as a staging area for OHV users and dirt bikers.

Framed by Cheviot Mountain to the west and the Cardinal Divide to the south, the townsite of Mountain Park was once famous as the highest post office in the British Commonwealth. Spread across a wide valley of the upper McLeod River, Mountain Park is located at an elevation of nearly 1800 m. Today it is a deserted ghost town. Only piles of coal slack, a few cement foundations and a cemetery remind visitors that this once was a town of 1000 souls.

In summer, though, Mountain Park comes alive with numerous visitors and campers who, whether on foot, by OHV, bicycle or dirt bike, take advantage of the numerous logging and mining roads to explore this beautiful alpine valley. After having fallen into disrepair for a number of years in anticipation of the Cheviot Mine project, the recreation area has been refurbished owing to the stalling of the mine development.

Location 14.4 km south of Cadomin along the Cardinal River Road
Facilities 12 campsites, pit toilets, loading/unloading ramp
Note no water pump

MOUNTAIN PARK

Perhaps because there are enough vestiges left of this once thriving town, Mountain Park evokes strong sentiments. For those who grew up here as well as for those who lived elsewhere in the West Branch, Mountain Park symbolizes a way of life that old Coal Branchers look back on with fond memories.

One might think that rose-tinted glasses have coloured these memories. Mountain Park was, after all, a company town. The mine owned most of the buildings including the Cheviot Hotel, the bakery and the theatre, formed the local government and ensured that water was delivered to the 100-odd homes. The size and location of a home spoke of its inhabitants' status in the mine. Three "big" homes complete with indoor plumbing were occupied by the mine manager, the office manager and the master mechanic. Robert Thornton, the mine manager, christened his home that was perched on a hill overlooking Thornton Creek valley Dove's Cottage in honour of his wife. The pit bosses and fire bosses lived in slightly smaller homes but were nevertheless a cut above the miners' homes. Strung out along either the "long" or "short" row, the miners' white with black-trim homes were of two sizes. A 28 x 28 foot four-room bungalow with a pyramidal roof rented for $9.00 a month; a six-room two storey rented for $10.00 a month. To supplement the tinned goods sold through the Mercantile, the company store, most tried valiantly to grow root crops in small garden plots. If there was plenty of work in the mines, the families could pay their bills; if not, they negotiated extensions with the Mercantile. Private entrepreneurs were few. One man, though, Soren Madsen, not only owned The Summit, a largely male hang-out, but manufactured socks that he then sold to GWG!

Despite the hardships and uncertainties of living and working at the highest coal mine in Canada, life was comparatively good and justifies the affection the ex-residents have nurtured. During the lean years of the Depression when so many rode the rails and filled soup kitchens, the Coal Branch mines including that at Mountain Park continued to employ their

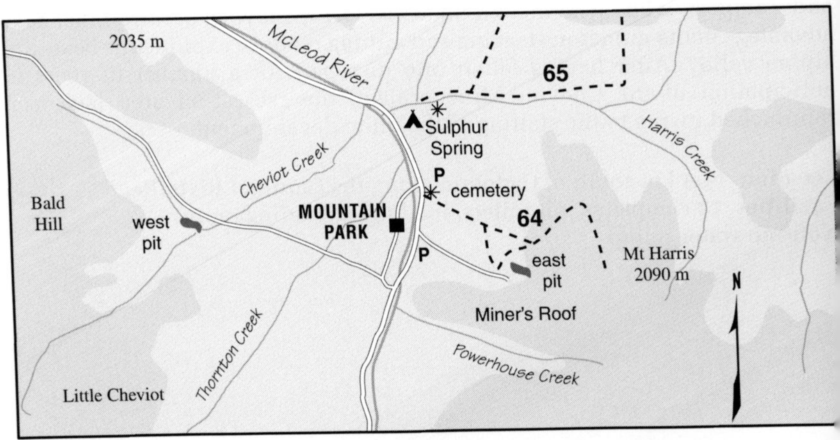

Mountain Park, ca. 1943. Courtesy Edson and District Public Library, 76/2/24.

workforce. Isolation fostered a strong community spirit. Movies were shown twice weekly and once a month on a Saturday night you could always count on a dance that would draw people from Cadomin and Luscar and continue into the wee hours. For many there were poker games; for others there was the library where you could find books in Italian or German, or a friendly game of gin rummy. In the winter, sports such as hockey—both men and women teams!—and curling attracted large crowds; in summer, sports days, tennis and baseball likewise brought together people from the West Branch.

The Mercantile was the social centre where shoppers would meet to exchange local gossip. The train station, on the other hand, was the nerve centre of the community. The "Blue Flea" chugged into town every Monday, Wednesday and Friday bringing fresh foodstuffs and visitors. On Tuesday and Thursdays it left town laden with coal and other freight. Its last appearance in town was June 20th, 1950, the day the mine closed. The next day, the McLeod River washed out the railbed. There was no sense in repairing the line.

Mountain Park

Mine No.: #282

Owners/Operators: 1911-1923 Mountain Park Coal Co. Ltd.; 1923-1936 Mountain Park Collieries Ltd.; 1936-1950 Mountain Park Coals Ltd.

Authorized Capital: $1,500,000 Mountain Park Coal Co. Ltd.; $1,042,000 Mountain Park Collieries Ltd.

Coal: bituminous

Registered Trade Name: Mountain Park Coal

Market: steam

Mine Type: underground; strip pit

Total Extraction: 6,387,000 tonnes

Men Killed: 33

The first coal claims were staked in 1909 by John Gregg and a year later by R. W. Jones. Jones was the divisional engineer for the Grand Trunk Pacific (GTP) railway being built at that time. The GTP, however, was more interested in the coal claims at Lovett so eventually Jones and Gregg turned to a British syndicate headed by Christopher Leyland for the capital to start a mine.

The man who "built" Mountain Park was Norman Muschamp "Robert" Thornton (1876-1919), a British mining engineer. Leyland had sent Thornton to evaluate the claims in 1910 and based upon his recommendation opened the mine in 1911. Thornton became the mine manager. Mountain Park's early years were difficult ones for Thornton. The mine suffered from escalating development costs, natural disasters and labour unrest. The colliery railway built by Mountain Park from Coalspur and that it was responsible for maintaining was a financial drain, especially after the opening of the Cadomin mine in 1917. The competing coal mine increased the traffic volume on the line yet contributed nothing toward its upkeep. Thornton was also in perpetual conflict with Charles Bremner, the managing director. Matters eventually came to a head and Thornton resigned in 1918, then committed suicide eight months later. He was buried in Edmonton.

The ongoing problems brought in Alexander Mitchell, the man credited with "saving" Mountain Park. Mitchell had been a shareholder since 1911 and later a director but had not taken an active part in company affairs. This changed in 1920. He visited the mine, evaluated the situation and began to initiate changes. He negotiated with the federal government an increase in the colliery railway maintenance subsidy and recapitalized the mine. Via a corporate raid on Cadomin he brought in a new management team to run Mountain Park: Robert Drinnan became managing director of mining operations and Andrew Scott became mine manager. Bremner was forced to resign.

In 1926, 15 years after the mine first opened, Mountain Park shareholders received their first dividend. They continued to receive modest dividends over the next 10 years, then in 1938 company officials made, what turned out in retrospect, a bad decision. Mountain Park needed a new cleaning plant. Rather than close the mine, they chose to replace the tipple at a cost of $375,000. Over the next decade, labour shortages and low coal prices plagued the operation. The mine was old and wet and the long underground workings were becoming increasingly more expensive to maintain. Strip operations began in 1947 but the company continued to lose money. In 1949 the operating loss reached $161,000 and the underground workings were closed.

Strip operations continued for another year but the coal's high ash content and dampness made it difficult to sell to the Canadian National Railway. At one point there were 15 railway cars of rejected coal standing in the yard at Mountain Park. The mine closed in 1950.

63 MOUNTAIN PARK TOWNSITE

The threat of the destruction of the old Mountain Park townsite by the Cheviot Mine Project in the late 1990s spurred a number of ex-residents to sign the locations of the town's main buildings. This easy tour around the old townsite is a fascinating trip back in time, and a realization that nothing in life is permanent.

Day hiking, cycling
Rating two hours
Distance 1.2 km
Level of Difficulty easy walk
Maximum Elevation 1830 m
Elevation Gain 60 m
Map 83 C/14 Mountain Park

Access

Park your vehicle at the Mountain Park Recreation Area. The recreation area is 14.4 km south of Cadomin along the Cardinal River Road.

0.0 km	trailhead
0.1 km	intersection
0.1 km	McLeod River
0.6 km	Mountain Park
1.2 km	trailhead

This self-guiding tour begins by returning to the Cardinal River Road and turning right for 600 m to the old train station sign, the railway spur that you can still see and the Mountain Park cemetery. Piles of coal slack aside, the Mountain Park cemetery is the only tangible reminder of the existence of the town. So take a few minutes to wander about the old graveyard that, at 1800 m, is still the highest cemetery in Canada. Although the first burial here dates to 1913, registration of burials began two years later. At the turn of the 21st century, more than 160 people have "gone home" to the Mountain Park cemetery. Today the cemetery is protected by the Alberta Forest Service through the stewardship of the cemetery, the Mountain Park Environmental Protection and Heritage Association.

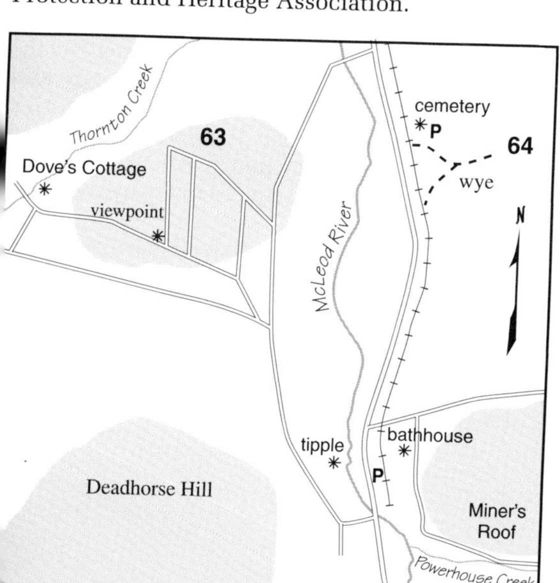

Signs throughout the townsite mark the location of the various buildings that once stood in the highest town in the British Commonwealth.

In the summer of 1997, a restoration project saw some 85 ex-residents and their families clear the willows around the marked grave sites in the Mountain Park cemetery.

Returning to the road turn right and go as far as an intersection with an old roadway on your left. Cross the trickle that is the McLeod River and make your way up the hillside to an intersection with an old street on your right. Turn onto the street and begin your climb through the business section of Mountain Park. "Tree" signs mark the location of the hotel, the stores, churches and other buildings. Walk up and down the streets where miners' cottages once lined the roadways. Work your way to the viewpoint at the top of the hill. If you look west you can see Thornton Creek valley. At the base of the hill by Thornton Creek was Dove's Cottage, the home of mine manager Robert Thornton. The cottage was an exact replica of the one he had in the old country. After his death it became the town's schoolhouse. Immediately below along a roadway was what was known as the short and long rows of houses.

Walk down the hill. At a T-junction at the bottom of the hill turn right and follow the roadway back to the Cardinal River Road. Turn left to return to the recreation area. It sits at the base of Miner's Roof, the hill where the coal company first drove its entries. Immediately above the toilets you can find the foundation of the bathhouse where the miners changed into their work clothes at the beginning of their shift and where they cleaned up after they came off shift. The remains of the tipple are across the road.

The Cheviot Project

The Cheviot Project is an approximately $250 million proposal by Cardinal River Coals to establish an open pit mine in the Mountain Park area. The mine would also include a coal processing plant and associated infrastructure including roads and a railway. The permit area is a 23 km-long and about 3.5 km-wide strip extending west from Redcap Creek to within 3 km of the Jasper National Park boundary. The mine was expected to employ about 400 miners and associated staff and produce 3.2 million tonnes of coal annually. An increasingly competitive international coal market forced Cardinal Coals in 2000 to delay the project indefinitely.

The mine plan called for about half the leasehold to be disturbed with over two dozen pits being dug over the 20-year lifespan of the mine. The spoil from each new pit would be used to backfill an older completed pit. The extraction of coal has resulted in not enough material to refill all the pits, so 10 lakes would also be created as a part of the overall reclamation plan.

The project raised both federal and provincial regulatory issues and a joint review panel was established in 1993 to review the project application and hear concerns. The project's size, its location in sensitive alpine and subalpine terrain, and intensity of other land uses in the area brought together a rainbow of consultants and environmental groups each arguing their interest in the cumulative effects the project might have. The review lasted over five years and brought forward a range of issues including: social, environmental and economic impacts of the project itself; conduct by certain environmental groups; and the review process itself.

The Joint Review Panel originally approved the Cheviot Project in 1997 ruling that it was economically viable and would have positive social and economic benefits to Hinton and the surrounding areas. Mitigation measures regarding fish and grizzly bear habitat, harlequin duck nesting areas and other wildlife, the panel ruled, would have to be implemented. To protect certain plants and animals, areas along upper Prospect Creek were taken out of the mine permit area and a 1 km-wide buffer zone imposed between the Cardinal Divide and the mine.

The public debate regarding Cheviot included a continuum of scientific precision, honest opinion, emotional reaction and deliberate misinformation. For the record, the mine lease area is not a "pristine wilderness." It is a landscape disturbed by past lumber, mining and prospecting activity and current unrestricted OHV use. Positive side effects of the debate have included the creation of the Whitehorse Wildland Park, restrictions on OHV activity, financial support for a series of environmental studies and a more critical evaluation of land reclamation practices.

The review process was criticized for failing to deliver anticipated improvements in environmental and resource management. It was long, costly and interspersed with legal challenges. The problem appeared to be the vacuum in which both proponents and opponents operated. There was neither the necessary baseline information nor a policy and planning framework to which both sides could relate. The lack of baseline information was highlighted by the duplication in environmental studies as proponents and opponents each gathered their own, at times, conflicting data. The lack of a proper and enforced policy and planning framework resulted in competing groups each trying to gain advantage over the other by "writing the rules" in their favour.

64 MOUNT HARRIS

MAP PAGE 304

The elevation gain in the distance between the trailhead and the summit of Mount Harris makes this a good hike for those camping at Mountain Park. When you realize you are repeating the historic route taken by runners during the town's Labour Day races, you cannot but help appreciate their stamina!

From the "train station" information booth walk toward the wooden steps at the foot of the cemetery and cross the first set of railway tracks. Turn right onto the railway tracks and follow them as they wind through the willows and spruce trees. At the termination of the old railbed you need to find a game trail through the willows on your right that will lead you to an old roadway. Turn up the roadway to a T-junction where you want to bear to the left. Within metres there is another intersection with a roadway on your right. Keep straight ahead. At an old logged area your roadway switches to the right where you have great views of Cheviot Mountain. Climb to another T-junction. Turn right, ignoring an intersection on your left. Below you on your right you can see a modern building; you will investigate the test plots adjacent to the building on your return trip. For now continue through the intersection by turning left and climbing sharply.

Day hiking

Rating half day

Distance 5.3 km

Level of Difficulty short bushwhack; many intersections; steep climb

Maximum Elevation 2090 m

Elevation Gain 310 m

Map 83 C/14 Mountain Park

Access

Park your vehicle at the Mountain Park cemetery parking area. The cemetery is 14.4 km south of Cadomin or 600 m north of the Mountain Park Recreation Area along the Cardinal River Road.

0.0 km	trailhead
0.0 km	cemetery
0.1 km	wye
0.4 km	old roadway
0.6 km	T-junction
0.9 km	intersection
1.2 km	T-junction
1.4 km	multiple intersection
1.7 km	intersection
2.0 km	begin braid
2.3 km	end braid
2.6 km	summit of Mount Harris
3.8 km	intersection [corresponds with 1.4 km]
4.1 km	OHV track and mine pit
4.3 km	intersection and test plots
4.3 km	intersection
4.4 km	intersection [corresponds with 0.9 km]
5.3 km	trailhead

At the top of Mount Harris.

The rounded profile of the hills of the Nikanassin Range above Mackenzie Creek valley.

En route to the top of the rise there are numerous intersections, all ending within 50 m. Ignore them to continue along the main road. At the top of the rise there is another intersection. Turn right. Directly in front of you is Mount Harris, your destination. Within 20 m there is yet another intersection. Keep left and go down a short slope to a six-way intersection. Here, take the intersection at your 11 o'clock and climb sharply passing an intersection on your right as you reach the top of the pitch. Mount Harris with its old logging roads crisscrossing its flank is directly in front of you. Your road now levels as it swings to the left skirting along the bottom of the last pitch. Then it's a steep pull to the top of the back shoulder of the hill. From here you can see the peak of Mount Harris at your 11 o'clock. Trot across the flat shoulder to the base of a steep, braided pitch.

On top, it's only a quick walk over to the rock cairn and a recently installed granite marker announcing that this hill is named for Lloyd Henry Harris 1882-1954. The 360° vista is worth the puff. Behind you is the long sweep of the Cardinal Divide with Mount Mackenzie, Mount Lindsay and Tripoli Ridge. To your 11 o'clock is Red Cap Range and the Mackenzie Creek valley. Below, at your 3 o'clock is Miner's Roof crisscrossed with logging roads. Cheviot Mountain with Little Cheviot, Prospect Mountain and Mount Drummond rise behind. Looking down the Cardinal River Road toward Cadomin you can see Mount Leyland, Mount Luscar, Cadomin Mountain and White Mountain, a shoulder of Cadomin Mountain.

Return the way you came as far as the six-way intersection. Go straight ahead. Within 300 m you come to an open pit where, in the dying years of the Mountain Park mine, attempts were made to employ new technologies to strip mine. An OHV track leads around the pit and then swings down to the trailer. If you wish to see a revegetation test area bear right at an intersection and climb up the slack pile to where Cardinal River Coals is testing various grasses.

To drop to your trailhead, return to the intersection and bear right. Continue along the road as it swings past test pits. Ignore an intersection and continue to the second intersection. Take the roadway at your 11 o'clock. You are now back on familiar territory so retrace your steps back to the "train station" adjacent to the Cardinal River Road.

The Mount Harris Run

The Mount Harris Run was the highlight of the annual Labour Day picnic and sports day at Mountain Park. Run at an altitude of about 2000 m, the approximately 3.5 km-long race was an endurance test for the runners and a source of great excitement and betting for the spectators who came from as far away as Edson.

Race records are sketchy with the 1930 race being the best documented. That year, watched by a crowd of about 1000 onlookers, nine men crossed the traffic bridge across from the cemetery and began to find their own route to the top of Mount Harris before returning. Two officials were posted at the summit to verify that the racers actually reached the top. Only three of the nine finished the race with N. Cinnamon taking the $50 first prize with a time of 25 minutes. The runs could be exceptionally competitive. One year, Gordon Graham lost the lead and the race when he stopped briefly for a drink of water.

The closure of the mine in 1950 meant the cessation of what was by now an annual event. Then, on August 1, 1999, the first reenactment of the race was held as part of the celebrations of the Coal Branch Reunion. The raw weather did not hinder the 14 men and women who ran and walked up Mount Harris and returned. The winner matched the time set by Cinnamon in 1930.

The Mount Harris annual race. Photo Charles Jacoby.

65 CADOMIN MOUNTAIN

MAP PAGE 314

A long but beautiful climb along an old OHV track leads you to the cairns at the top of Cadomin Mountain and a glorious 360° view of the Front Ranges.

Day hiking

Rating full day

Distance 16.3 km

Level of Difficulty long approach in alpine area; eroded OHV trails

Maximum Elevation 2401 m

Elevation Gain 650 m

Map 83 C/14 Mountain Park

Access

Park your vehicle at the Harris Creek random campsite. The campsite entrance is on the east side of the Cardinal River Road 100 m past a bridge over the McLeod River 13.4 km south of Cadomin.

0.0 km	trailhead
0.1 km	Harris Creek
0.2 km	intersection
0.6 km	intersection
0.7 km	stream crossing
0.8 km	intersection
1.0 km	intersection
1.6 km	OHV track ends; gravel road
1.8 km	intersection
1.9 km	stream crossing; intersection
2.1 km	intersection
2.8 km	intersection and cutline
2.9 km	cutline
3.1 km	begin braid
3.2 km	end braid
4.2 km	Forest Land Use zone boundary
5.4 km	intersection

From your trailhead follow the four-wheel-drive track across Harris Creek and up the hill. At the top of the slope there is an intersection of tracks. The track on the left looks promising but actually leads you in a loop back to the main track, so keep to the right. You are now slowly climbing up the Harris Creek valley, a long, beautiful subalpine valley dotted with dwarf willow and birch. The valley is also a tangle of OHV tracks and old roads so follow the directions for the next 2.6 km carefully. At a Y-junction again keep to the right and shortly thereafter cross a small stream. The track on your left is your return route. From this point the track swings a little to the left and away from Harris Creek. Continue up this lovely broad valley keeping to the right at the next two intersections. Just beyond where your track swings sharply to the left there is another intersection. Bear to the right off the OHV track and onto a gravel road. It dips down to cross a small, unnamed creek. If the day promises to be warm or if you had not filled your water bottle at the trailhead, do so now. This is your last chance for water. Ignore a track on your right just past the stream and remain on the gravel road as it continues to climb slowly. There are several intersections with grassy tracks along the way but continue along the gravel road as far as a cutline. Turn left onto the cutline and the OHV track that follows it.

Before gaining the forested slope you must cross a swampy area that, mercifully, is short. Then, you begin a stiff climb up the first pitch. En route you will pass another cutline that leads off diagonally to your right. The OHV track along the cutline levels for a short distance before climbing the second pitch. Cutlines do not make allowances for steep grades and are cut in straight lines up slopes, across bogs and through forests. We found this cutline up the slope to be badly eroded owing to the OHV traffic. The second pitch is fairly steep

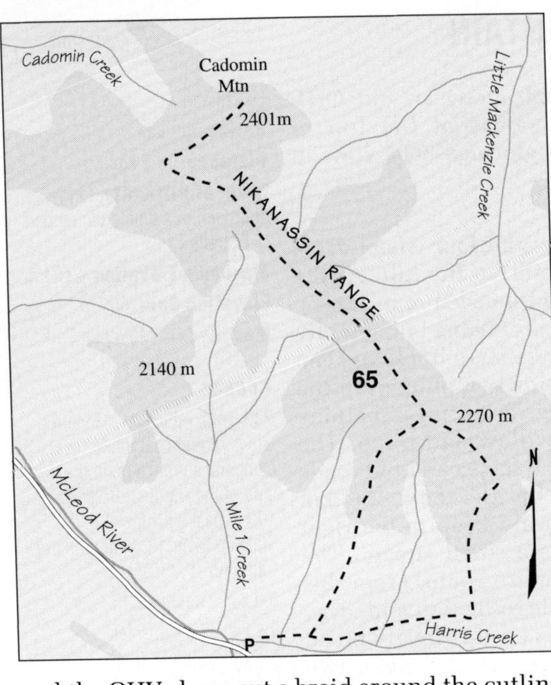

5.6 km unnamed peak; intersection
5.9 km first dip
7.6 km second dip
9.8 km Cadomin Mountain
12.0 km second dip
12.4 km OHV track
13.4 km begin braid
13.5 km end braid
14.2 km Forest Land Use zone boundary; cutline
15.3 km stream crossing; begin braid
15.4 km end braid; stream crossing
15.7 km intersection [corresponds with 0.6 km]
16.3 km trailhead

and the OHVs have cut a braid around the cutline, causing further erosion of the slope. OHVs are now prohibited from this route between 25 June and 15 October each year. While still below the treeline you cross the Forest Land Use zone boundary. Then you break out of the trees and onto a beautiful wide alpine meadow.

It's a long, steady climb along the OHV track that cuts up the slope past a couple a rock outcrops to the top of the ridge. Here there is a T-junction of tracks. The track to the right ends within a few metres, so turn left. You are now along a ridge that features steep cliffs on your right and the alpine meadow you climbed on your left. The view is nearly 360°. Looking to your left you can see up and down the Harris Creek valley. Beyond, the long slope of the Cardinal Divide and the peaks of Tripoli Ridge dominate your sightline. We chose to stop here after our climb to rest and to enjoy the scenery. Continuing, the OHV track reaches a rocky outcrop where it swings 90° to the right. Ahead of you is a long expanse of alpine meadow that dips down and then climbs toward the white limestone summit of Cadomin Mountain. This is one of the largest, most stunning alpine meadows that we discovered in the Coal Branch. As we followed the OHV track down this windswept slope we had plenty of opportunity to identify such hardy alpine flowers as the pink mounded moss campion, the yellow common stonecrop, the vibrantly blue alpine forget-me-not and the purple inflated oxytrope. At the bottom of the slope the track swings slightly to the left climbing slowly along the edge of a ridge with the meadow on your left and a rocky cliff face below you on your right. The track dips through a wet area that sports lusher vegetation then climbs a shoulder of the mountain. The summit is now on your right bu

Cadomin Mountain.

you do not approach the mountain top directly. Rather, the track leads you up along the shoulder past the apex of the mountain. Then, it makes a sharp 90° turn toward the limestone peak. It's a short but fairly steep climb to the top of the first limestone ridge. On a sunny day you might want to wear sunglasses; the glare from the sun's rays bouncing off the white rock can be quite intense. On top of the ridge, pick up the OHV track that leads you across to a saddle that connects the shoulder you are on to the summit of Cadomin Mountain.

If the number of cairns at the top of easily accessible mountains is any indication of the popularity of such a route, Cadomin Mountain must be quite a popular destination for three large stone cairns mark the summit of the mountain. Take a few moments to enjoy the view before retracing your steps off the summit. Once you have descended from the limestone pitch, pick up the OHV track that leads you back down along the ridge and up the long slope. When you have almost reached the top look for another OHV track on your right. Swing onto it as it cuts across the hilltop. We thoroughly enjoyed the view as we dropped along the top of the ridge. Below is the Harris Creek valley with its myriad of trails cut by the old Mountain Park mine, forestry and OHVs. Beyond is the Cardinal Divide and, looking to the peak on the horizon at your 12 o'clock, Mount Mackenzie. Swinging your eyes from left to right you see Armchair or Tusk just to the left of Cardinal Pass and The Brother or Windy Mountain to the right of the pass. Located at your 2 o'clock is Tripoli Ridge with its three peaks and farther to your right you find the distinctive flat-topped Cheviot Mountain.

Your trail braids briefly before rejoining. You continue to drop along the track as far as the treeline where the OHV track swings to the right to skirt a rock face. This begins your rather steep descent to the valley floor. Some of the worst erosion we saw in the Coal Branch was on this first pitch with some of the gullies being thigh deep. Another pitch and you are down and off the hill. The subalpine of the Harris Creek valley is as beautiful as the high alpine of Cadomin Mountain except where it has been chewed up by OHVs. At the base of the hill you must cross a boggy patch. Unfortunately, the OHVs have cut a 40 m swath through the soft earth leaving an eyesore.

At the next two intersections keep to the right. Splash across a small stream. At a Y-junction keep to the right to regain the main track. From here your return route down to the trailhead is clear.

Coal Branchers

Donaldson Bogart Dowling (1858-1925)
Occupation: geologist

D. B. Dowling was a member of the Geological Survey of Canada (GSC) and was the most prominent among a group of early geologists who documented the Coal Branch coal deposits. As early as 1872 the presence of coal along the eastern front of the Rocky Mountains was well known. George Grant, during his "ocean to ocean" journey, was told by his packer Beaupre that there was abundant coal along the rivers west of Edmonton. Two years later, GSC director Alfred Selwyn wrote: "There can be no question that in the region west of Edmonton, bound by the Athabasca [sic] River and on the south by the Red Deer River, there exists a vast coal field covering an area of no less than 25,000 square miles…."

In 1898 GSC geologist James McEvoy crossed the Coal Branch from the south to north and identified coal seams along a tributary of the Cardinal River and along the McLeod. By the time Dowling visited the Coal Branch in 1909, he was entering an area that was being actively prospected. He reported on a number of claims, including the Thomas Russel claim at the head of Mackenzie Creek and what appears to be British Collieries beside Chimney Creek. Dowling also visited the Pacific Pass and Yellowhead Pass leases at Lovett and Coalspur respectively.

Dowling identified the West Branch coal as an extension from the Bighorn coal basin that he had discovered in 1906. The line of mineable coal from the North Saskatchewan River to the Cardinal Divide, he reported, was not more than 2 km in width but nearly 125 km long. The deposits were excellent steam and coking coals and their commercial development awaited only the construction of railways and roads, he said. The East Branch coal, Dowling wrote, was of lower quality than on the West Branch, but still yielded domestic and a fair grade of steam coal. He noted the presence of two coal seams one above the other, but did not give their names. These would be the Silkstone and Mynheer seams. Dowling listened to anecdotal reports of the seams thickening in places to over 10 m but did not believe them. The truth was more spectacular. It would later be found that at Sterco and Coal Valley the Mynheer seam would thicken, owing to folding, to over 50 m.

During his 1909 visit Dowling named the Nikanassin Range, of which Cadomin Mountain is a part. Nikanassin is Cree meaning front range (*nikan*: "in front," "first"; *assin*: "rocks"), a descriptive name as it lies before the Rocky Mountains. Dowling's knowledge of Cree was typical of a GSC man at the time. He had joined the survey in 1885 and worked for it until his death during its glory years. At the turn of the century, geologists such as Dowling explored what was then a scientifically unknown northern interior of North America. They reported not only the geology, but the geography, flora, fauna, commercial possibilities and anthropology of a new country bursting out in commercial and national expansion. To be a GSC man meant not only being an outstanding scientist in a diverse range of disciplines, but also an outstanding and tough woodsman.

Dowling sometimes starved while doing his field research as in 1907 when he accompanied Martin Nordegg to the Blackstone River. The plan was to continue following the coal measures to the northwest, but a lack of food supplies and a very wet season forced them to abandon this idea. Instead they turned west to dryer ground in the mountains, crossed Southesk Pass, descended the Rocky River and reached John Gregg's trading post at Prairie Creek near Hinton. Gregg was away guiding Raymond Brutinel to Lovett, so unsupplied, Dowling and Nordegg returned the way they came, subsisting as best they could by catching fish and squirrels. The privations and aborted trip worked out well for Dowling. Two years later he would visit and report upon the coal found at Lovett by Brutinel.

66 CARDINAL DIVIDE EAST

MAP PAGE 326

The Cardinal Divide offers you a rare opportunity to enjoy the sensitive ecosystem of the high alpine with very little effort on your part. A stupendous view from the crest of the divide is an added bonus.

From the parking area, cross the Cardinal River Road and find the demarcated trail that leads across the alpine meadow and winds up the slope to the top of the divide. Stay on the old OHV track. OHVs were banned from the Divide in 1994 but prior to that much damage was done. Do you know that it will take the fragile ecosystem 40 to 50 years to recover from years of misuse by off-highway vehicles?

The track climbs slowly but steadily until you are finally at the top of the Divide. In most cases, to reach high alpine, there is a long access and considerable elevation gain to endure. Your relatively short walk has brought you to an ecoregion normally enjoyed by only a few people. What a glorious view! Looking northwest you can see the old townsite of Mountain Park, destined to be the headquarters of the Cheviot mine project. Directly below you lies a beautiful valley that takes your eye past Mackenzie Creek east toward Red

Day hiking

Rating half day

Distance 9.6 km

Level of Difficulty a short, steep climb followed by an easy walk

Maximum Elevation 2220 m

Elevation Gain 190 m

Map 83 C/14 Mountain Park

Access

Park your vehicle at the Cardinal Divide parking area 20 km south of Cadomin along the Cardinal River Road.

0.0 km	trailhead
1.5 km	crest of ridge
3.7 km	ridge high point; cairn and survey reflector
4.6 km	survey marker
4.7 km	survey marker
4.8 km	survey reflector
9.6 km	trailhead

Walking westward along the top of Cardinal Divide.

Looking toward Cardinal Pass from the Cardinal Divide.

Cap Creek, all backdropped by the forested hills of the Nikanassin Range. Turn around to view your ascent. The Front Ranges of the Rocky Mountains form a seemingly impenetrable wall in front of you. This isn't so, of course. Cast your eye from right to left. Tripoli Mountain lies slightly to the right of the parking lot that you can easily see below. Tripoli Mountain forms the right flank of a valley that leads to Cardinal Pass and Jasper National Park; Mount Mackenzie forms the left flank. Mount Russell is the next peak followed by that of Ruby Mountain. With such a stupendous view it may not be surprising to learn that a number of Coal Branchers have chosen to have their ashes buried or scattered on the Divide. Since no permanent markers are allowed, there is no record of the number of people who have chosen this as their final resting place.

For many, the climb to the top of the Divide satisfies and they return to the parking lot the way they came. We found the Divide too beautiful for such a short visit and we recommend a longer walk. A hiking path stretches along the top of the Divide in both directions. For a longer hike to the apex of the Divide turn right. Before you is the beautiful sweep of the Divide. Your path leads slowly uphill over sandstones and past hardy alpine flowers and shrubs. At the crest of the Divide you come upon a survey reflector.

Once here you realize you are only part way along the Divide. The open ridge stretches in front of you for another kilometre, so keep walking eastward. You will notice that the vegetation is lusher on this side of the Divide's crest; heather and mosses hug the hollows and the trail softens as a variety of plant colonies take root among the stones and rocks. Your trail takes you slowly downhill toward a federal topographical survey marker that neatly lines up with a township cutline to your right. A yellow survey reflector located 100 m farther east makes a convenient point at which you can turn around and return to your vehicle the way you came.

The Brazeau Coal Lands

The Brazeau coal lands were about 20,000 acres of coal claims along the Cardinal River valley that included two blocks held by the Canadian Northern Railway (CNR). The main block was at the head of Mackenzie Creek while the other was at the confluence of the Cardinal and Brazeau rivers. They were staked in 1906 by Thomas Russell, a prospector under contract to the CNR.

The CNR had hired Russell to prospect for steam coal owing to a coal war with the Canadian Pacific Railway (CPR). At the time, the Crowsnest Pass was western Canada's primary source of steam coal. The mines were served by the CPR, which regarded the area as its own domain. Matters came to a head by 1906 when the CPR locked the CNR from purchasing Crowsnest coal by refusing to release CPR cars to ship the coal. When the CNR offered its own cars, the CPR refused to handle them on its own line. What this meant for the CNR was that it had to bring in steam coal from as far away as Pennsylvania to run its trains. The CNR, therefore, had to secure its own western source of steam coal if it were to become truly competitive with the CPR.

The coal lands were the first significant discover of steam coal near the projected routes of the Grand Trunk and CN transcontinental railway lines. The area became the scene of intense survey activity in anticipation of their development and three different railway charters would be issued to reach them, but no track would ever be laid. A joint Canadian-American operation, British Collieries along Chimney Creek, went only as far as surveying the right-of-way from Lovett to its mine. With the 1913 depression this project was shelved and the mine closed.

Geologist D. B. Dowling visited the Mackenzie Creek block in 1909 and identified the coal as belonging to the Kootenay formation and established its position in the Nikanassin coal basin. Next year, American mining engineer Charles Hower examined the area and reported the coal to be a high grade bituminous fuel. Despite the quality, he did not encourage any major development. "The field affords no very good plant site and from point of development offers no great advantages for a large operation. The grade of the valleys are very steep making access by railroads difficult."

In 1909 the CNR properties in the Brazeau coal lands were amalgamated with the coal holdings of the German Development Company led by Martin Nordegg. The resulting holding company, called Brazeau Collieries, was a partnership wherein German Development would develop a coal mine while the CNR would build a railway to that mine. They would eventually settle upon opening up Nordegg, but the Brazeau coal lands did retain their interest for a while. The CNR went so far as to survey and clear a railway right-of-way from Wolf Creek south to the confluence of the Brazeau and Cardinal rivers where the second block was located. That was as far as any development went. The right-of-way would only be used as a pack and freighting trail by Pacific Pass Coal, which was developing its coal mine at Lovett. Upon the arrival of the Coal Branch railway to Lovett, this trail would be abandoned.

The promise of the Brazeau coal lands, however, would eventually initiate another discovery. In 1910, John Gregg and R. W. Jones staked the western extension of the coal seams at the Mackenzie Creek block. This adjoining area would be quickly developed and the problems of steep railway access overcome. What was built came to be known as the highest coal mining community in Canada: Mountain Park.

67 TRIPOLI RIDGE

MAP PAGE 326

To enjoy the beauty of an alpine meadow usually entails a strenuous day hike or even a backpack expedition. This short, delightful walk allows every visitor to the Cardinal Divide the special opportunity to experience the remarkable variety of alpine flora, to say nothing of a magnificent vista of the Front Ranges.

Day hiking
Rating two hours
Distance 6.0 km
Level of Difficulty short walk through an alpine meadow
Maximum Elevation 2100 m
Elevation Gain 70 m
Map 83 C/14 Mountain Park

Access

Park your vehicle at the Cardinal Divide parking area 20 km south of Cadomin along the Cardinal River Road.

0.0 km	trailhead
3.0 km	end of trail
6.0 km	trailhead

Looking west from the Divide parking lot just beyond the interpretive signs, you cannot help but notice an old OHV track that cuts across the top of the meadow from the parking lot toward the foot of Tripoli Ridge. This track is your trail. Prior to 1994 when OHVs were banned from the delicate alpine of the Cardinal River Divide, this was a favourite jaunt for off-highway vehicles. Now, as the botanical communities struggle to stage a comeback on this windswept ridge, the only visitors allowed are hikers. And what a wonderful treat it is for those who have a couple of hours to explore the meadow! Come in early summer and you will walk among a floral carpet that can only astound you. Let your eyes feast on the vista around you. To the north lies the McLeod River valley with the flat-topped Cheviot Mountain looking down. To its left is Mount Mackenzie, then Tripoli Mountain. Straight in front of you is Tripoli Ridge. The enticing-looking pass to the left of Tripoli Ridge is Cardinal Pass, formerly known as Rocky Pass. And finally as you look back over your shoulder you catch the sweep of the Cardinal River valley and the Grave Flats Road.

The OHV track braids several times as it dips then begins a slow ascent to the foot of Tripoli Ridge. Willows have established a foothold in the ravines where they are more protected from the winds that often scour the Divide. The track climbs along the foot of the mountain until it finally peters out. From here you can look down on your trail below and up to the Divide on the other side of the parking lot. Most people do not venture beyond this point but simply turn around and return the way they came.

Tripoli Ridge

Previous names: Katherine, Snowdon, Alice, The Three Sisters, The Brother, Windy Ridge, Missel

Tripoli Ridge is the local unofficial name for the mountain range on the west end of the Cardinal Divide. This local name was already well established when the highest point (2620 m) was officially named Tripoli Mountain in 1922. Tripoli Ridge was so-named by the Italian mining community that first began to arrive at Mountain Park in 1912. There are two origin stories that may be connected. Tripoli means "three towns" and is a euphemism for the three peaks along the ridge. Tripoli is also a city in Libya and in 1913, the focus of an Italian victory over the Ottoman Empire that ruled the area at the time.

In 1910 mining engineer Norman Muschamp "Robert" Thornton drew a geophysical map of the area and named the three peaks, from north to south, Mounts Katherine, Snowdon and Alice. His wife's name was Katherine Alice. Snowdon was a mountain he reportedly climbed in Wales. The three peaks are also known unofficially as The Three Sisters with the ridge toward Rocky Pass being The Brother. Another unofficial name for The Brother is Windy Ridge; an obvious reference to the winds that often sweep across the Divide. A tiny unobtrusive bump between The Brother and The Three Sisters is called Missel.

Tripoli Ridge from the Cardinal Divide.

Alberta Native Plant Council

The demarcated trail that you noticed on your way up the Divide was done under the stewardship of the Alpine Club of Canada and the Alberta Native Plant Council. As stewards of the Cardinal Divide, these organizations are deeply concerned over the damage done to this fragile alpine area by the OHVs that once were allowed free access onto the Divide. After OHVs were banned from the natural area in 1994, the Alberta Native Plant Council had the opportunity to work toward the rehabilitation of the damaged areas. The demarcated trail is one of their efforts to protect the plants and the whole ecology of the Divide. Other efforts include an annual field trip to the Divide to collect seeds, plant in the damaged areas alongside the trail and to continue with a native plant study of the Divide. You will often see council botanists on the trail, at the parking lot or at the top of the Divide monitoring the results of their work.

These activities reflect the council's three general objectives: to promote knowledge of Alberta's native plants; to conserve our native plant species and their habitats; and to preserve this diverse resource for the enjoyment of present and future generations. To fulfill this mandate, the Alberta Native Plant Council disseminates information about native flora through displays such as those that are at the Divide's parking area, and lectures. They conduct field trips and courses. Its membership also looks at Alberta's rare plants, monitoring populations, setting priority lists for rare plants and developing a rare plant data bank. The Alberta Native Plant Council also aims to protect our rare floral species and their habitats by lobbying government on the most pressing issues, gaining stewardship of natural areas such as the Cardinal Divide and monitoring how habitats are affected by development.

Interested? Contact the Alberta Native Plant Council at Box 52099, Garneau Postal Outlet, Edmonton, AB T6G 2T5

Botanizing on the Cardinal Divide.

68 CARDINAL PASS

MAP PAGE 326

For those who wish more of a challenge in visiting the alpine than that offered at the Divide itself, this short hike is for you. A quick easy walk carries you to the top of Cardinal Pass and to a beautiful view into Jasper National Park.

Day hiking

Rating half day

Distance 11.7 km

Level of Difficulty several stream crossings and pitches to subalpine pass

Maximum Elevation 1970 m

Elevation Gain 140 m

Map 83 C/14 Mountain Park

Access

Park your vehicle at the Upper Cardinal Headwaters access trail parking area along the Cardinal River Road 1.6 km south of the Cardinal Divide. The Divide is 20 km south of Cadomin along the Cardinal River Road.

0.0 km	trailhead
0.8 km	stream crossing
1.8 km	intersection
3.2 km	Tin Roof Lakes
3.6 km	intersection
3.8 km	random campsite
4.0 km	Cardinal River
4.5 km	gravel wash
4.6 km	Cardinal River
4.7 km	Cardinal River
5.8 km	Rocky Pass
8.0 km	intersection [corresponds with 3.6 km]
8.1 km	Tin Roof cabin ruin
8.5 km	begin braid
8.6 km	Upper Cardinal Headwaters access trail
9.9 km	intersection [corresponds with 1.8 km]
11.7 km	trailhead

From your trailhead you can easily see the four-wheel-drive track leading to the headwaters of the upper Cardinal River. In fact, 100 m beyond the trailhead, Alberta Environment has erected a Cardinal River Headwaters access trail sign. This is one of the few trails in the Coal Branch that has been designated specifically for OHVs, dirt bikes, four-wheel-drive vehicles and snowmobiles and is under the stewardship of the Alberta Off Highway Vehicle Association.

The turnoff for Cardinal Pass is located 1.8 km past the trailhead, after having made a small stream crossing on the main trail. The trail to Cardinal Pass forks left off the Upper Cardinal trail, quickly entering a meadow and passing by the three Tin Roof Lakes. At the top end of the third lake there is an intersection with a trail on your right. You will take this trail on your return trip, but for now bear left into Engelmann spruce forest. Within 200 m there is a random campsite on your left and just

Looking down at the Cardinal River valley en route to Cardinal Pass.

At Cardinal Pass looking into Jasper National Park.

beyond you come to a steep embankment overlooking the Cardinal River. A good horse trail switches down to the river that you must ford. Once across, bear right and follow the track to a second ford, and then shortly beyond, a third ford. The trail now swings away from the river to begin a short but steep pitch up along a rocky streambed. At the top of the pitch the trail passes through a small fenny area where orchids, gentians and Arctic cotton grass grow. Another short and less steep pitch through dwarf spruce and willow brings you to a broad expanse of alpine meadow that is Cardinal Pass. The ascent on the south end is more gradual so you look down onto a wide alpine meadow interspersed with spruce trees. Mountains surround you. The Tusk is on your left; on the right is Mount Windy of Tripoli Ridge; straight ahead is snowcapped Mount Balinhard in Jasper National Park. Mount Mackenzie can be seen left of the Tusk.

After enjoying a walk through the meadows, return down the trail, cross the Cardinal and reclimb the embankment. Very shortly you will come to the intersection noted on your way up. Keep left. Within metres you come to the remains of Tin Roof cabin. Now a jumble of tin and saddle-notched logs, this cabin was probably a cache cabin for forestry rangers. It is located by the uppermost of the three Tin Roof Lakes where residents of Mountain Park once held skating parties.

Your trail quickly brings you back to the main Upper Cardinal Headwaters access trail. Turn right, cross a bridge and return to your trailhead.

Cardinal Pass

Previous names: Rocky Pass, Tin Roof

Tin Roof is the local unofficial name for the area at the foot of Cardinal Pass centred around a series of small ponds called the Tin Roof Lakes. Tin Roof took its name from a nearby cabin, now in ruins, covered by...you guessed it, a tin roof. This was a forestry tool cache cabin built around 1920 and named the Rocky Pass cabin, after nearby Rocky Pass. Forestry abandoned the cabin by 1929.

Rocky Pass was then, and still is, the popular and unofficial name for Cardinal Pass. The pass received its unofficial name because it is the access to the Rocky River. Though a long and well-established local name, Rocky Pass was officially named Cardinal Pass to prevent duplication with another pass with the same name. Cardinal takes its name from the nearby Cardinal River and Jacques Cardinal.

Tin Roof and the pass were popular recreation areas for Mountain Park residents. They came in summer on horseback rides and in winter ice skated on the lakes. Looking up toward the pass from Tin Roof, they called the mountain immediately to the south Armchair Mountain. At the pass, the view and descriptive name of that same mountain changed to Tusk.

The first recorded visitor to the area was the Earl of Southesk who camped and feasted beside one of the lakes September 2-3, 1859. Southesk was on an extended hunting trip at the time and that day had spotted several bighorn sheep near Tripoli Ridge and a mountain goat near Mount Mackenzie, but was unable to make a kill. One of his guides shot a marmot and that evening, Southesk, who was a *gourmand*, got down to business: "...eating that most delicious meat, which tastes like very delicate mutton, with the fat of a suckling-pig."

He left the next day via Rocky Pass, but not before, over breakfast, marvelling at the scenery and marmot leftovers, "The camp is surrounded with magnificent rocky heights; I leave it with sorrow. Would that it were the beginning of summer instead of the end! Had a hind-leg of siffleur [marmot] for breakfast, and find it the best part. In shape and distribution of fat it is a miniature haunch of venison; it is possible to eat the whole at a meal."

The remains of Tin Roof cabin.

69 UPPER CARDINAL HEADWATERS ACCESS TRAIL

Day hiking, cycling

Rating full day

Distance 27.6 km

Level of Difficulty rocky trail into alpine valley

Maximum Elevation 2160 m

Elevation Gain 330 m

Map 83 C/14 Mountain Park

Access

Park your vehicle at the Upper Cardinal headwaters access trail parking area along the Cardinal River Road 1.6 km south of the Cardinal Divide. The Divide is 20 km south of Cadomin along the Cardinal River Road.

0.0 km	trailhead
0.8 km	stream crossing
1.8 km	intersection
3.2 km	intersection
3.9 km	stream crossing
4.0 km	bridge
4.3 km	begin braid
4.5 km	end braid
4.8 km	intersection

Under the stewardship of the Alberta Off Highway Vehicle Association, the Upper Cardinal Headwaters access trail is one of the few trails that has been put aside specifically for the use of OHVs, snowmobiles, dirt bikes and four-wheel-drive vehicles. The impact on the environment has been predictable. Although a straight run from the trailhead into what is essentially a box valley, heavy OHV use has left the roadway boulder-strewn and pot-marked with mud holes. Where the mud holes are too much for even the OHVs, their owners have simply moved to either side resulting in an ever-widening trail. To their credit, the association has attempted in one or two places to corduroy and bridge the worst mud holes. Fortunately, once the alpine is reached, the OHV owners have, by and large, remained on the trail so that others can enjoy this fragile and beautiful valley.

Within metres of the access trail sign you cross a stream. From here it is a straight and relatively flat run for 6 km along an old cutline through Engelmann spruce forest. Ignore an intersection with a trail on your left; it leads to Cardinal Pass. Two quick stream crossings, the second of which has been planked by the OHV Association, brings you to the bottom of a braid. The fork in better condition is on the left. Three hundred metres past

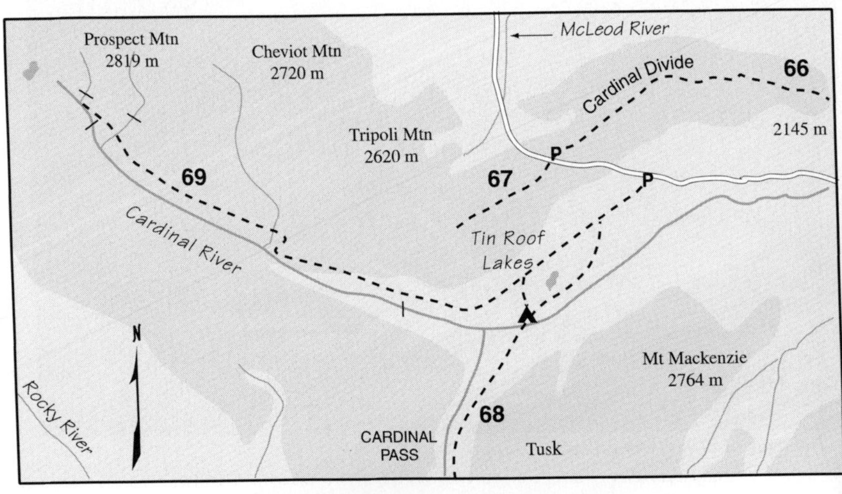

the top of the braid there is an intersection with a trail on your left; it, too, leads to Cardinal Pass. Within 500 m, part way up a ridge, listen for the sounds of a waterfall. For a view, find the horse trail on your left that, 50 m later, ends at a cliff. Here, overlooking a gorge in the upper Cardinal, you can see a series of waterfalls. The porous limestone has allowed water to flow through the rock to disgorge through numerous holes in the rock face. This was such a pretty spot we stopped here for a quick snack before returning to the main trail to continue up the rough, rocky roadway. A kilometre later you cross a gravel wash.

You leave the old cutline where the roadway enters a willow meadow. It's a good track that leads you through the wide valley toward the peaks straight ahead. By the time you leave the meadow to return into Engelmann spruce forest you are surrounded by mountains. But don't take your eyes off the roadway; it becomes quite rough especially when you reach a gravel wash. Fortunately, it only lasts a short distance and at the top of the gravel wash you finally leave the forest for the beauty of the alpine meadows of the upper Cardinal River.

As you pass a Forest Land Use zone sign, you can see the sharp triangular peak of an unnamed

5.3 km	viewpoint upper Cardinal Falls
6.2 km	gravel wash
6.7 km	begin braid; enter meadow
6.9 km	end braid
7.6 km	leave meadow
8.1 km	enter gravel wash
8.3 km	leave gravel wash
8.5 km	Forest Land Use zone boundary
9.5 km	begin braid
10.0 km	viewpoint canyon
10.3 km	end braid; stream crossings
10.9 km	begin braid
11.0 km	stream crossing; end braid
12.1 km	stream crossings
13.5 km	stream crossing
13.7 km	waterfall
13.8 km	gravel wash
27.6 km	trailhead

You can meet many different users along this trail.

Progression of erosion, 1983, 1996 and 2000. Photos Allison Dinwoody.

mountain straight ahead and, slightly to the right, Prospect Mountain. On your left is Blackwall Mountain Range, so called for the colour of the rock. This solid wall of rock extends all the way up the valley. As you proceed up this 6 km-long valley, the views just get prettier and prettier. Moss campion, dwarf willow and birch, heather, dryads, potentilla and hedysarum are only some of the plants that carpet the valley floor. In the distance, you can see the OHV track leading over the alpine and into the hills at the end of the valley. The distance is deceptive; it's farther than it looks. In a copse of dwarf spruce and birch the OHV track braids. We chose to go straight ahead. It soon veered sharply to the right to go around the top end of a deep gully. Where the braid rejoined at the top of the gully there is also an easy stream crossing. At another braid we once again continued straight ahead. As you wend your way up the valley along the OHV track you will have several small stream crossings. As you reach a high point near the end of the trail you can see a tarn below you to your left tucked beneath Blackwall Mountain. A waterfall cascades from the headwalls on your right. The OHV track continues down to the base of a series of small hills. From here a horse/hiking trail leads up through the rocky hills toward another tarn. If you have plenty of time, enjoy the valley's beauty before returning to the trailhead the way you came.

The Problem With OHVs

Within the past two decades, off-highway vehicles (OHVs) have become extremely popular forms of outdoor recreation. Through their use, large numbers of people have gained ready access to wilderness areas normally out of reach. OHVs include snowmobiles, all terrain and sport utility vehicles and trail bikes. The literature on snowmobiles appears to show little long-term ecological damage, but the effect of the other three types of OHVs has been devastating.

The main problem lies in the routes favoured by OHV users—cutlines. Cutlines, often called seismic lines, are a by-product of seismic surveying. In a seismic survey, a straight line is cut through the forest along which a line of receivers, called geophones or "jugs," are laid out. Dynamite charges are placed in shallow holes along the cutline, then detonated. The geophones record the wave pattern of the shock waves caused by the explosion, resulting in a cross-sectional view of the underground rock formations where oil and gas may be found.

Since cutlines are cut straight ignoring hills and muskegs, OHVs, especially when they climb steep slopes, quickly cut through the surface layer of vegetation exposing the soil underneath to erosion. Along some popular OHV routes, hillside gullies more than a metre deep, and getting deeper, have formed. In muskeg, churned fields of mud grow steadily wider as OHVs leave the trail searching for firmer surface to traverse. At stream crossings, the continued traffic muddies the water and damages fish habitat and spawning areas.

The worst long-term damage caused by unrestricted OHV use is in the ecologically sensitive alpine and subalpine zones where it may take centuries for the plant disturbance caused by their traffic, if no longer disturbed, to heal itself. The Cardinal Divide has been closed to OHV traffic since 1994, yet the effects from their past presence is easily seen. To the northwest, Folding Mountain has OHV traffic resulting in the same type of damage. Reclamation efforts, such as at Mary Gregg Lake, have been ruined and there is fear that they might do the same on the reclaimed mine lands at Luscar and Gregg River.

It only takes a small number of machines to cause a disproportionate amount of disturbance. One rough estimate calculates that either 200 hikers or 150 horses are needed to replicate the same amount of disturbance caused by one wheeled OHV. Most OHV users are responsible individuals who recognize that recreation should not include damage to public lands. Such groups of OHV enthusiasts now work to mitigate their machines' effect: routes across muskeg have been corduroyed, bridges thrown across streams and gullies, mud holes filled in with gravel or coal slack and they stay away from ecologically sensitive areas.

OHV-initiated gully on Cadomin Mountain.

Further Reading

In researching the various topics covered by this book, we compiled a bibliography of more than 400 titles. Obviously, we could not include them all here. Consulted primary documents found at the Provincial Archives of Alberta, Glenbow Archives, University of Alberta, Edson Public Library, Yellowhead Museum, National Archives of Canada, newspapers, government reports and published works not easily obtained have not been listed here. Below is a list of readings that should be readily available at public libraries and bookstores for those whose interest in the history, geology and/or the flora and fauna of the Coal Branch has been piqued by this book.

Environmental Studies

Cardinal River Coals Ltd. "Cheviot Mine Project Application" 10 Vols.

History

Bercuson, David Jay (ed.). *Alberta's Coal Industry 1919.* Historical Society of Alberta Vol. 2. Edmonton: Alberta Records Publication Board and the Historical Society of Alberta, 1978.

Chiesa, Nino and Bob Smilanich. "Mountain Park: Forever Home: Memories from the Thirties."

Davies, Bill. "Lists of the Men Who Worked at Mountain Park: An Historical Record Book 1."

———. "Lists of the People of Mountain Park: An Historical Record Book 2."

den Otter, Andy A. "A Social History of the Alberta Coal Branch." M.A., University of Alberta, 1967.

———. "Railways and Coal: The Alberta Coal Branch." *The Albertan Geographer* No. 5 1968-69.

———. "Social Life of a Mining Community: the Coal Branch." *Alberta Historical Review* 17 (4) Autumn, 1969.

Gariepy, Rick and Monty Reid. "A Story of the Coal Branch." Provincial Archives of Alberta 971.233.St.76a.

Hawkins, A. H. "Surveys of Parts of the Twelfth and Thirteenth Base Lines West of the Fifth Meridian." *Sessional Papers* Vol. 16, Session 1910.

Holmgren, Eric and Patricia M. *Over 2000 Place Names of Alberta.* Expanded Third Edition. Saskatoon: Western Producer Prairie Books, 1976.

Hughes, Vern. *My Life On the Alberta Coal Branch.* Kamloops: Vern Hughes, 1995.

Huth, Robert. *Horses to Helicopters: Stories of the Alberta Forest Service.* [Edmonton]: n.p., 1980.

Jackson, Joyce. "Luscar Come Back." n.p., 1978.

Karamitsanis, Aphrodite. *Place Names of Alberta: Mountains, Mountain*

Parks and Foothills. Volume I. Calgary: Alberta Culture and Multiculturalism and Friends of Geographical Names of Alberta Society and University of Calgary Press, 1991.

Lake, David. "The Historical Geography of the Coal Branch." M.A. thesis, University of Alberta, 1967.

Legris, Maurice. "Saint of the Coal Branch." *Alberta History* 37 (1) Winter, 1989.

Maydonik, N. Allen (comp.). *The Luscar Story*. Edmonton: Luscar Ltd., 1985.

Mitchell, Sir Harold P. *In My Stride*. London: W. & R. Chambers Ltd., 1951.

Ross, Toni. *Oh! The Coal Branch*. Edmonton: n.p., 1974.

Salzsauler, Mary Lee and Joan Talbot Wegert. "Mountain Park Memories."

Southesk, The Earl of. *Saskatchewan and the Rocky Mountains: A Diary and Narrative of Travel, Sport, and Adventure, during a Journey through the Hudson's Bay Company's Territories, in 1859 and 1860*. Edinburgh: Edmonston and Douglas, 1875.

Thomson, Don W. *Men and Meridians: The History of Surveying and Mapping in Canada*. Vol. 2 1867-1917. Ottawa: Queen's Printer, 1967.

Geology

Allan, John. *Second Annual Report on the Mineral Resources of Alberta 1920*. Edmonton: King's Printer, 1921.

Allan, John and Ralph L. Rutherford. *Geology Along the Blackstone, Brazeau and Pembina Rivers in the Foothills Belt, Alberta*. Edmonton: King's Printer, 1924.

Campbell, J. D. *Coal Mines and Coal Leases, Alberta Rocky Mountains and Foothills Research Council of Alberta Report 66-5*. Edmonton: Queen's Printer, 1967.

Dowling, D. B. "Rocky Mountain Coal Areas between the Bow and Yellowhead Passes." *Sessional Paper No. 26, Summary Report of the Geological Survey Department of Canada, 1906*.

———. "Explorations in the Rocky Mountains." *Sessional Paper No. 26, Summary Report of the Department of Mines, Geological Survey, 1907*.

———. "Coal Fields South of the Grand Trunk Pacific Railway, in the Foothills of the Rocky Mountains, Alberta." *Sessional Paper No. 26, Summary Report of the Geological Survey Branch of the Department of Mines, 1909*.

Gadd, Ben. *Handbook of the Canadian Rockies: Geology, plants, animals, history and recreation from Waterton/Glacier to the Yukon*. Jasper: Corax Press, 1986.

Luscar Sterco (1977) Ltd. "Mynheer 'A' Mining History, January, 1982."

McEvoy, James. "Report on the Geology and Natural Resources of the Country traversed by the Yellow Head Pass Route." *Geological Survey of Canada Annual Report* Vol. XI, 1898.

McKay, B. R. "Stratigraphy and Structure of Bituminous Coalfields in the Vicinity of Jasper Park, Alberta." *The Canadian Mining and Metallurgical Bulletin* No. 222, October 1930, pp. 1306-1342.

Mussieux, Ron and Marilyn Nelson. *A Traveller's Guide to Geological Wonders in Alberta*. Edmonton: The Provincial Museum of Alberta, 1998.

Rutherford, Ralph. *Geology of the Foothills Belt between McLeod and Athabaska Rivers, Alberta*. Edmonton: King's Printer, 1925.

————. *Geology of the Area between Athabaska and Embarras Rivers Alberta*. Edmonton: King's Printer, 1926.

Whittaker, W. C. "Strip Pit Mining in Coalspur Area, Alberta." *The Transactions of the Canadian Institute of Mining and Metallurgy and of the Mining Society of Nova Scotia*. XXXVIII, 1935, pp. 358-368.

Williams, G. D. (ed.). "Guidebook: Eighth Annual Field Trip to Cadomin, Alberta, August, 1966." Edmonton Geological Society.

Flora and Fauna

Kershaw, Linda. *Edible & Medicinal Plants of the Rockies*. Edmonton: Lone Pine Publishing, 2000.

Packer, John G. and Cheryl E. Bradley. *A Checklist of the Rare Vascular Plants in Alberta*. Provincial Museum of Alberta Natural History Occasional Paper No. 5, 1984.

Scotter, George W., Tom Ulrich and Edgar Jones. *Birds of the Canadian Rockies*. Saskatoon: Western Producer Prairie Books, 1990.

Scotter, George W. and Halle Flygare. *Wildflowers of the Canadian Rockies*. Edmonton: Hurtig Publishers, 1986.

Van Zyll de Jong, C. G. *Handbook of Canadian Mammals*. Ottawa: National Museum of Natural Sciences and the National Museum of Canada, 1985.

Willard, Terry. *Edible and Medicinal Plants of the Rocky Mountains and Neighbouring Territories*. Calgary: Wild Rose College of Natural Healing, Ltd., 1992.

Index

ABOUT THE AUTHORS

Dan Kyba is the owner of Kyba & Associates, a market research firm based in Edmonton. He loves the outdoors and has hiked in Baffin Island, Greenland, Great Britain, the Himalayas, New Zealand, Papua New Guinea and the Canadian Rockies. He coauthored *The David Thompson Highway: A Hiking Guide.*

Author **Jane Ross** is trained as an historian and has worked in the heritage resources field for 25 years. She has written several social studies textbooks and historical monographs. Jane has hiked in Baffin Island, Greenland, New Zealand and the Canadian Rockies. She coauthored *Hiking the Historic Crowsnest Pass* and *The David Thompson Highway: A Hiking Guide.*